Cleansing the Cosmos

Cleansing the Cosmos

A Biblical Model for Conceptualizing and Counteracting Evil

E. Janet Warren

PICKWICK *Publications* · Eugene, Oregon

CLEANSING THE COSMOS
A Biblical Model for Conceptualizing and Counteracting Evil

Copyright © 2012 E. Janet Warren. All rights reserved. Except for brief quotations in critical publications or reviews, no part of this book may be reproduced in any manner without prior written permission from the publisher. Write: Permissions, Wipf and Stock Publishers, 199 W. 8th Ave., Suite 3, Eugene, OR 97401.

Pickwick Publications
An Imprint of Wipf and Stock Publishers
199 W. 8th Ave., Suite 3
Eugene, OR 97401

www.wipfandstock.com

ISBN 13: 978-1-62032-403-5

Cataloguing-in-Publication data:

Warren, E. Janet.

Cleansing the cosmos : a biblical model for conceptualizing and counteracting evil / E. Janet Warren.

x + 326 pp. ; 23 cm. Includes bibliographical references and indexes.

ISBN 13: 978-1-62032-403-5

1. Spiritual warfare. 2. God and evil—Religious aspects—Christianity. 3. Metaphor—Religious aspects—Christianity. 4. Good and evil. I. Title.

BS680.G6 W324 2012

Unless otherwise indicated, Bible quotations are from the New Revised Standard Version, copyright 1989, by the division of Christian Education of the National Council of the Churches of Christ in the United States of America. Used by permission. All rights reserved.

Note: Portions of Chapters 1, 2, and 3 have been published as "Chaos and Chaos-Complexity: Understanding Evil Forces with Insight from Contemporary Science and Linguistics," in *Perspectives on Science and Christian Faith* 63/4 (Dec 2011), 255–66; and as "Spiritual Warfare: A Dead Metaphor?" in *Journal of Pentecostal Theology* 21 (2012), 1–20.

Contents

Figures

Acknowledgments

THIS BOOK IS AN adaptation of my PhD thesis through the University of Birmingham, UK. I am indebted to my supervisors, Mark Cartledge and Andrew Davies: Mark for pointing me towards metaphor theory and challenging me on theological issues; Andrew for his biblical knowledge, attention to detail, and advice regarding clarity. Their critique and patience with the process has been tremendously helpful. I am also thankful to Mark Boda for encouraging my boundaries idea, suggesting research into priestly theology, and for feedback on chapters 4 and 5. Thanks to Ronald Simkins for granting permission to use his diagrams in Figures 4.2 and 4.3. Fellow students at the University of Birmingham Research Seminars have helped develop my ideas; I especially appreciated dialogue with Graham Smith. Thanks also to Roy Matheson for his continuing encouragement, to Scott Moreau for his comments on chapter 1, to Andrew Gabriel for his advice regarding publication, to Aloma Jonker for her feedback, and to Paul Niesiobędzki for his help with diagrams and proofreading. Finally, many thanks to the team at Pickwick for bringing this project to fruition.

Abbreviations

General

ANE	Ancient Near East(ern)
BCE	Before Common Era
CE	Common Era
Esp.	Especially
NT	New Testament
OT	Old Testament
Sup.	Supplement(s)
Vol.	Volume

References

AB	Anchor Bible Commentary
BDAG	Walter Bauer, Frederick W. Danker, W. F. Arndt, and F. W. Gingrich. *A Greek-English Lexicon of the New Testament and Other Early Christian Literature,* 3rd edition. Chicago: University of Chicago, 2000.
CBQ	Catholic Biblical Quarterly
DCH	*The Dictionary of Classical Hebrew.* 8 vols. Edited by David J. A. Clines. Sheffield: Sheffield Press, 1993.
DDD	*Dictionary of Deities and Demons in the Bible.* Edited by K. van der Toorn, Bob Becking, and Pieter van der Horst. Leiden: Brill, 1995.
DSS	Dead Sea Scrolls
EPCC	*Encyclopedia of Pentecostal and Charismatic Christianity.* Edited by Stanley M. Burgess. New York: Routledge, 2006.

IBC	Interpretation Bible Commentary
LXX	Septuagint
NIV	New International Version
NRSV	New Revised Standard Version
NSBT	New Studies in Biblical Theology
JBL	*Journal of Biblical Literature*
JETS	*Journal of the Evangelical Theological Society*
JSNT	*Journal for the Study of the New Testament*
JSOT	*Journal for the Study of the Old Testament*
NIC	New International Commentary on the New Testament
PC	Pentecostal Commentary
RB	*Revue Biblique*
SBL	Society of Biblical Literature
SJLA	*Studies in Judaism in Late Antiquity*
ZAW	*Zeitschrift für die Alttestamentliche Wissenschaft*

Holy Spirit, making life alive,
Moving in all things, root of all creative being,
Cleansing the cosmos of every impurity,
Effacing guilt, anointing wounds,
You are lustrous and praiseworthy life,
You awaken and re-awaken everything that is.

HILDEGARDE OF BINGEN
HYMN TO THE HOLY SPIRIT

1

INTRODUCTION: "SPIRITUAL WARFARE"?

Since then, God has fought an open battle against [the devil] … this is how things will remain until the conflict with Satan is fought to the very end.[1]

FOR THE PAST TEN years, in my capacity as a Family Physician, I have counseled a remarkable woman who is a survivor of satanic ritual abuse. From approximately age two to twenty, she was subject to the most heinous abuse imaginable at the hands of her parents, foster parents, siblings, and other cult members. She survived by splitting into many parts, so that each could handle one aspect of her nightmarish reality (Dissociative Identity Disorder). She also reports being afflicted by multiple evil spirits that continually torment her and sometimes "take over" her body, distorting her face and voice, and exhibiting super-human strength. Nothing in my medical training, church experience, or early theological studies had prepared me to deal with this particular affliction. Although I was helped by a mentor and gained some practical insights from popular writings on demonology and deliverance, I was dissatisfied with the available literature on the subject. Most of what I read was anecdotal, with limited or questionable exegesis, and based on dubious theology.[2] It was phrased almost exclusively in terms of "spiritual

---

1. Hildegarde of Bingen, *Divine Works*, 1.4.14.

2. Psychiatrist M. Scott Peck makes a similar observation during his first encounter with demonization (*People of the Lie*, 183). Of course, once I began my doctoral work, I found the literature to be broader than I had first perceived.

warfare"; language that translates poorly into counseling. Conversely, I found most academic literature to be largely disbelieving of demonization. Moreover, I perceived a gap between clinical practice and theology. This study represents an attempt to fill the void and offer an alternate framework for conceptualizing and counteracting evil.

Demonology and deliverance are important topics for many reasons. First, counselors can benefit from an awareness of potential demonic influence on people. In Western culture, an association between mental illness and demonization has been noted.[3] Second, an understanding of demonology is important for those involved in cross-cultural mission (e.g., those who follow traditional African religion believe evil spirits are highly involved in everyday life, therefore knowledge of biblical demonology is essential for Christians working in such settings).[4] In many cultures, healing and deliverance are intertwined and both are associated with conversion to Christianity.[5] Indeed, given the growth of Christianity in the global South, demonology is not an optional topic in Christian theology. Third, the age of scientific rationalism and materialism is over or at least declining. Therefore, the disregard for spiritual reality characteristic of this view (e.g., Rudolph Bultmann's famous claim that "it is impossible to use electric lights and the wireless and to avail ourselves of modern medical and surgical discoveries, and at the same time to believe in the New Testament world of spirits and miracle"[6]) is losing validity. Science is now recognizing that the nature of reality is not deterministic and linear, but often unpredictable, dynamic, and chaotic (discussed further in chapter 3). Most phenomena in life are irreducibly complex, and scientists increasingly recognize that much in the universe remains unknown. Materialism and reductionism are now considered inadequate representations of reality. Furthermore, scientific evidence is accumulating for the existence of paranormal phenomena (e.g., the psi effect, near-death experiences, apparitions), with a concomitant belief in a spiritual

3. Peck, *People of the Lie*; Shuster, *Power, Pathology*; Bufford, *Counseling and Demonic*; Friesen, *Mystery of MPD*.

4. Ferdinando, "Spiritual Realm," 21–41. The same is true for Buddhism and Native American religions; M. Kraft, *Spiritual Power*.

5. A recent cross-cultural study provides numerous examples; Brown, *Global Pentecostal Healing*.

6. Bultmann, "New Testament and Mythology," 5. Walter Wink makes a similar claim: "it is as impossible for most of us to believe in the real existence of demonic or angelic powers as it is to believe in dragons, or elves, or a flat world"; *Naming the Powers*, 4.

dimension of reality.[7] Contemporary Western society, likely influenced more by the New Age movement than scientific evidence, has seen a renewed interest in the occult and descriptions of demonic experiences.[8] Finally, demonology is an important topic in theology simply because of its presence in the Bible.

However, it is a difficult topic to study and describe for several reasons. First, the spirit world is inaccessible to the usual senses, making objective study nearly impossible. Second, the Bible does not provide a single, cohesive demonology; biblical references to the devil and demons are scattered and often obscure; the language is frequently metaphorical and mythopoetic (discussed further in chapters 2 and 3, and unsurprising given the inherent difficulties in describing supersensible realities). Third, much study of evil has been done through the lens of philosophy, which seldom deals with the spiritual dimension of evil.[9] Finally, culture and history continue to influence views on demonology. While some Christians labor under the legacy of rationalism, others embrace deliverance enthusiastically. Literature, art, and folklore also affect popular beliefs.[10] This study attempts to address some of these difficulties by re-examining the biblical portrayal of evil forces, and developing an alternative model for conceptualizing and counteracting them. Secondary goals are to investigate the ontology of evil plus the role of the Holy Spirit in counteracting evil. In this introductory chapter, I review the "spiritual warfare" literature, both popular and academic, and its critiques, then discuss reasons why an alternate model is needed, and outline the plan for the remainder of the book.

"Spiritual Warfare": A Brief History

The term "spiritual warfare" has mostly been applied in contemporary Christianity, although the concept has been used throughout the history of Christianity. Popular and academic literature on the subject are not

7. E.g., Radin, *The Conscious Universe*. See also summaries in Shuster, *Power, Pathology*, 15–89, and Yong, *Spirit of Creation*, 184–96.

8. E.g., Kyle, "Occult Roars Back," 91–97.

9. Exceptions include Boyd (discussed below), Hart, *Doors of the Sea*, and N. T. Wright, *Evil*.

10. E.g., Russell, *Mephistopheles*, 168–296. Movies dealing with magic, spirits, and exorcism are perennial favorites. Among Charismatic Christians, Frank Peretti's novels have been popular; these portray almost a one-to-one ratio of humans to spiritual beings; e.g., *This Present Darkness*.

easily distinguished from each other, but for the sake of clarity, in this section I provide a brief review of demonology from the beginnings of the church until the early twentieth century, followed by a synopsis of popular contemporary "spiritual warfare" literature and then reviews of the contributions of Gregory Boyd and other scholars. This overview provides background for this research project. Many of these works will be referred to throughout the study and are critiqued below.

Historical Review

Belief in "spiritual warfare" was common in the early church. The church fathers believed that intermediary beings exist between God and humans, and frequently discussed the battle between good and evil spirits and how Christians can deal with attacks from the devil. Demons were considered responsible for false religion, disease, and natural disasters, and were believed to participate in magic, divination, and astrology. A semi-dualistic worldview was common; people were indwelt by either God's Spirit or evil spirits.[11] The early church frequently practiced exorcisms and the desert fathers are well known for their descriptions of demonic attack.[12] Later on Augustine affirmed the reality of a spiritual world and associated demons with Roman gods. He described them as having enhanced abilities (e.g., foreknowledge), although insisted that they only appear to have power.[13] Similarly, Gregory the Great viewed the world as a battleground in which the devil continually incited people to sin.[14] In the popular culture of the Middle Ages, the devil and demons were believed to be able to transform themselves and enter into every aspect of life, causing illness and stealing children. Witchcraft and magic were widely practiced—it was thought magicians derived their power from demons.[15] The devil was frequently

11. Ignatius (c. 107 CE) described the devil as "assaulting" Christians; *Epistle to the Magnesians* 1; Russell, *Satan*; Daunton-Fear, *Healing*. Both Tertullian (*Apology*, 22) and Origen (*Against Celsus*, 1.31, 8.31) believed natural evils, like floods or earthquakes, to be the work of demonic forces. Barnabas described the way of light and the way of darkness; *Epistle*, 16, 18–20; this view of the "two ways" was common in antiquity. Justin Martyr believed Christians participate in the cosmic conflict between God and Satan; 2 *Apology*, 5.

12. Eusebius, *Church History*, 6.43, 8.6. Evagrius (c. 375 CE) believed demons attack through mind and body; *Practical Advice*, 5, 43–45, 59.

13. Augustine, *City of God*, 9.7–23, 11.11, 21.6.

14. Russell, *Lucifer*, 100–103.

15. Russell, *Lucifer*, 62–91; Keck, *Angels*, 173. Superstition abounded: people

depicted in folk stories, art, and theatre.[16] Descriptions varied, but he was often associated with animals or deformed humans.[17]

The recovery in the twelfth century of the *Celestial Hierarchy* of Pseudo-Dionysius wherein he postulated three hierarchies (first: seraphim, cherubim, thrones; second: dominions, virtues, powers; third: principalities, archangels, and angels) had a tremendous influence on medieval theologians.[18] Bonaventure and Aquinas elaborated extensively on his ideas, viewing the last triad as being most involved in human affairs. Bonaventure believed a soul could be tempted by demons even before birth,[19] and Aquinas developed an elaborate, albeit imaginative, demonology, exploring questions like whether demons have bodies or can know the future.[20] Medieval mystics also wrote extensively about demonology and demonic encounters.[21] Exorcism ran rampant during the Middle Ages but by the end of this era there were attempts to harness this practice through rational guidelines. In the early fifteenth century, Gerson wrote extensive guidelines for discernment of spirits and the Roman Rite of 1614 cautioned against assuming someone was demonized.[22] As a result of the Reformation, Protestants moved the focus away from witchcraft and demonology, and onto God, emphasizing *human* responsibility for sin. Their insistence on *sola scriptura* initially renewed interest in biblical demonology, but eventually their emphasis on absolute divine sovereignty

---

believed laughter defeated the devil and said "bless you" when someone sneezed to counteract the potential backlash from myriad demons in the surrounding air.

16. Dante's *Divine Comedy* being a well-known example; Russell, *Lucifer,* 62–158, 208–44, 274–301.

17. The influence of Greek and Roman mythology is apparent, e.g., many descriptions of the devil are remarkably similar to the Greek gods Pan and Dionysius; Russell, *Lucifer,* 67–69.

18. Pseudo-Dionysius was probably a Syrian monk; he wrote around 500 CE; Russell, *Lucifer,* 29–36.

19. Keck, *Angels,* 54–70, 161–62.

20. Aquinas, *On Evil,* Question 16, Articles 1–12. He stated: "the Catholic faith declares that demons are able to do harm by their operations"; *Comment on Job.* i (quoted in Levack, *New Perspectives,* 27).

21. Hildegarde of Bingen believed evil spirits deceive humans by inciting to idolatry, and advised fighting the devil with Scriptures; *Scivias,* 1.1.22; *Rewards of Life,* 1.12, 62, 63; Catherine of Siena considered the devil a persecutor of God's servants, but believed humans can choose to follow the way of light and truth or the way of darkness and falsehood; prayer, humility, patience, and suffering can overcome the devil; *The Dialogue,* 4, 11, 22, 27, 65, 116, 131, 159.

22. Sluhovsky, *Believe Not Every Spirit,* 175–78, 202.

led to a minimization of the devil's power.[23] Nevertheless, Luther described many encounters with the devil and wrote on the need for Christians to guard against attacks from the enemy, since the world was "with devils filled."[24] Despite the Reformation and subsequent rise of scientific rationalism, interest in demonology did not disappear. A seventeenth-century Puritan spiritual manual was titled *Christian Warfare*; in the late nineteenth century, Lutheran Johann Blumhardt described his encounters with a demonized girl, and, in the early twentieth century, Jessie Penn-Lewis wrote an account of the 1904 Welsh revival, *War on the Saints*, describing the numerous demons who seek to attack Christians.[25] However, interest in deliverance came to the fore in the twentieth century.

Contemporary Popular Literature

James M. Collins has recently provided an excellent overview of the "spiritual warfare" movement in twentieth-century Western Christianity. He classifies this movement into charismatic deliverance, evangelical fundamentalism, and enthusiastic sacramental deliverance.[26] The first type emerged from Pentecostalism. At the Azusa Street revival, deliverance was performed in conjunction with healing and reflected a somewhat dualistic worldview. William Branham and Oral Roberts were early figures who regularly practiced deliverance; they taught for instance that demons gain access through a person's eyes.[27] Later, the so-called Fort Lauderdale Five

23. Clark, "Protestant Demonology," 179–215; Russell, *Mephistopheles*, 30.

24. Luther, *A Might Fortress is Our God,* public domain. Luther apparently experienced the devil as a serpent and a pig, emitting strange noises and smells; Russell, *Mephistopheles,* 34–44.

25. Downame, *Christian Warfare*; Blumhardt, *Blumhardt's Battle,* cited in N. G. Wright, *Dark Side,* 106–9; Penn-Lewis, *War on the Saints.*

26. Collins, *Exorcism*; Nigel Scotland classifies deliverance practitioners into expansives (e.g., the Hammonds, Subritzky, Wagner), moderates (e.g., Arnold, Green, Wimber), and progressive charismatics (e.g., Smail, Walker, Wright). He believes the expansive view prevails and is driven by consumerism (e.g., street marches and battle songs). Scotland is critical of this movement, noting that "Jesus did not believe in a demon-infested universe"; "Charismatic Devil," 84–105. Journalist M. Cuneo divides the movement into charismatic, evangelical, and Roman Catholic exorcism and suggests that the rise of exorcism is partly due to changing social climate and media influence; *American Exorcism.* Briefer reviews from charismatic/evangelical perspectives can be found in Walker, "Devil You Think You Know," 86–105 and C. Kraft, "Contemporary Trends," 177–202.

27. Collins, *Exorcism,* 20–25, 29–34. Roberts claimed to detect demons using his right hand.

(Derek Prince, Don Basham, Ernest Baxter, Bob Mumford, and Charles Simpson) turned to group deliverance as a way to manage the demand and developed somewhat idiosyncratic theories and practices, such as the need to cough in case a demon was lodged in the throat. Roman Catholic Charismatic, Francis MacNutt, was influenced by Prince and was in turn influential. Frank and Ida Mae Hammond were popular deliverance practitioners who claimed everyone needs deliverance, and that demons are the cause of illnesses such as schizophrenia.[28] In the "third wave" of the Charismatic movement, John Wimber and Peter Wagner were prominent deliverance practitioners. Wagner coined the term "strategic-level-spiritual-warfare" to describe encounters with territorial spirits that ruled over nations. Fellow missiologist Charles Kraft is another noted late-century "spiritual warfare" practitioner.[29]

In terms of evangelical fundamental deliverance, Kurt Koch was an early proponent with an interest in occult bondage. Theologian Merrill Unger had a somewhat moderate view of demonization, but he thought all believers were plagued to some degree; Mark Bubeck encouraged aggressive "spiritual warfare"; and Neil Anderson was more judicious in emphasizing "truth encounters" rather than "power encounters" and encouraging prayer rather than deliverance.[30] Key figures in the Catholic charismatic deliverance movement were Malachi Martin and Gabriel Amorth. Differences between charismatic and evangelical deliverance include the use of elements such as water, oil, and salt, use of the term "exorcism" instead of "deliverance," and the belief that demons can only be detected during the course of the exorcism ritual. Collins notes that towards the end of the twentieth century there was a convergence of charismatic and evangelical deliverance ministries, perhaps as a result of the "third wave," and evidenced in the writing of Ed Murphy, a "charismatic-evangelical."[31] Others agree that there now appears to be a blurring of charismatic/Pentecostal/evangelical boundaries with respect to "spiritual warfare."[32] Collins concludes that by the 1990s, the "rough edges" of the "spiritual warfare" movement had worn away and the resulting view more

28. Collins, *Exorcism*, 44–67.

29. Ibid., 100–103. Kraft, *Christianity with Power*; Kraft, *Dark Angels*; Kraft, *Powerless Christianity*. Wagner, *Confronting the Powers*; Wagner, *Engaging the Enemy*. Other advocates of "territorial spirits" include Dawson, *Taking our Cities*; Otis, *Twilight Labyrinth*; and Jacobs, *Gates of the Enemy*.

30. Collins, *Exorcism*, 126–34, 193.

31. Ibid., 151–73, 190.

32. See Kraft, "Contemporary Trends," 187.

moderate. His thesis is that deliverance grows in the context of Christian enthusiasm and itinerancy: "Enthusiastic faddism is driven to a great extent by the practical implications of itinerancy."[33] He believes this enthusiasm "burned out."

Whether the "heyday" of public deliverance ministries is over or not, the topic remains important for counseling and mission. In fact, most literature arose from these two fields. Some of the beliefs and practices of "spiritual warfare" advocates are worth detailing. The theological views of Charles Kraft are perhaps representative: There is a kingdom headed by Satan and populated by a large number of demonic associates; these beings are out to disrupt God's work as much as possible; they are especially concerned to hurt God's favorite creatures—humans—the only ones God made in his image; Satan and his followers can work only within the rules God has laid down for them. Satan is a high-ranking angel, like an archangel; demons are "ground-level" troops that take their orders from those further up in the hierarchy; and the Pauline powers are cosmic-level principalities that have authority over places, social organizations, and sinful behaviors.[34] It is common practice to ascribe personhood to demons. Anderson outlines the "personality" of demons: they "can exist outside or inside humans," "they are able to travel at will," "they are able to communicate," "each one has a separate identity," "they are able to evaluate and make decisions," "they are able to combine forces."[35] Many authors suggest different demonic categories such as spirits of the occult, spirits of sin, spirits of trauma, and ancestral spirits, noting that they often cluster.[36]

33. Collins, *Exorcism*, 1, 105, 108, 197.

34. Kraft, *Dark Angels*, 18–19, 99. Viewing demons as organized hierarchically is common: Unger refers to Satan's "highly organized empire of roving spirits" and divides this into a Satanic order of the earth (ruling over humankind) and of air (ruling over fallen spirits); *Biblical Demonology*, 52, 72; Bubeck states demons are "structured, organized and disciplined" with Satan as "commander-in-chief"; *The Adversary*, 71–73; Murphy claims that Satan "ruled in the heavenlies over a vast kingdom of evil spirits. He ruled almost unhindered on earth, his spirits having free access both to heaven and earth"; *Handbook*, 299.

35. Based on Luke 11:24–26; Anderson, *Bondage Breaker*, 102–5. Unger similarly claims that demons can adopt human form, "possess personality, are everywhere presented as intelligent and voluntary agents," and possess superhuman knowledge and strength; *Biblical Demonology*, 64–67.

36. E.g., MacNutt, *Deliverance*, 88–93. John and Mark Sandford describe "seductive spirits," "mental demons," "power-grabbing spirits," "demons of greed," "Jezebel spirits," "death wish demons," and "controlling spirits"; *Deliverance and Inner Healing*, 241–74; Scanlan and Cirner name spirits of anger, fear, insecurity, depression, and bitterness, and believe spirits can cluster; *Deliverance from Evil Spirits*, 84, 96–97.

Some even describe the appearance of demons. Wagner relates a story of his wife waking one night in fear and seeing a "shadowy form, about nine feet tall, with luminous green eyes and teeth."[37] Others suggest the classic appearance of "beast-like with horns and a forked tail."[38]

In terms of demonization and reasons for it, there is a wide spectrum of views—some believe demonization is rare,[39] others claim that everyone is demonized to a degree.[40] Although Roman Catholics use the term "possession," admitting it is rare,[41] the term "demonization" is generally preferred by charismatics/evangelicals because it better reflects the biblical term.[42] Many deliverance practitioners associate demonization with sin and/or occult involvement. Kraft thinks that demons can only affect people when there is a pre-existing weakness, sin, or "entry-point."[43] Murphy describes four primary areas of sin that can lead to demonization: illicit sexual practices, anger/rage, guilt/shame, and occult involvement.[44] Some contemporary deliverance practitioners note that evil spirits affect people to differing degrees. MacNutt, for instance, distinguishes between external (temptation, emotional oppression) and internal (demonization) influence.[45] Many authors claim that demons can also enter someone through curses and generational sin, and some believe inanimate objects and places can be afflicted by demons.[46] This is especially applied to the

---

D. Brewer describes various demons often having Greek names, which tend to cluster in groups of six; "Jesus and the Psychiatrists," 133–48.

37. Wagner, *Warfare Prayer*, 81.

38. Friesen, *Mystery of MPD*, 241. Peck describes a snake-like appearance of a demonized person; *Glimpses* 173–74.

39. E.g., Walker, "Devil You Think You Know," 89 (from a 1972 statement by the Bishop of Exeter).

40. E.g., Hammond, *Pigs in the Parlour*, 12.

41. MacNutt, *Deliverance*, 67.

42. *Daimonizomai*; BDAG 209–10. Shuster believes the language of possession (rather than demonization) carries power implications; she suggests oppression or infestation instead; *Power, Pathology*, 189.

43. Kraft, *Dark Angels*, 100–111, 120–21, 139–56; see also Unger, *Biblical Demonology*, 27; Scanlan and Cirner, *Deliverance*, 84, 96–97. Shuster's approach is more nuanced; she believes sin may result in "emptiness" which demonic beings can then fill; *Power, Pathology*, 178–79.

44. Murphy, *Handbook*, 433.

45. MacNutt, *Deliverance*, 69–72. Friesen describes three levels of demonic influence: flirtation, invitation, and union with Satan; *Mystery of MPD*, 26–30.

46. E.g., Murphy, *Handbook*, 437–45; Kraft, *Dark Angels*, 74–76; Kraft, *Confronting Powerless Christianity*, 20–25, 168–69; Sandford and Sandford, *Deliverance and Inner Healing*, 205–40.

concept of "territorial spirits" (high-level demons holding sway over cities and other regions) popularized by Wagner and followed by Kraft and others.

There are varying views with respect to discerning demons. In his interviews with Charismatics, journalist Michael Cuneo reports that discernment is described variously as visualization of demons, smelling demons, testing air currents with fingers, or a mystical perception.[47] Many contemporary deliverance practitioners provide "diagnostic" lists. Bubeck, for example, includes a compulsive desire to curse God, a revulsion against the Bible, compulsive suicidal or murderous thoughts, feelings of bitterness and hatred, compulsive temptations and desires, terrifying feelings, violent rage, and sensations like dizziness or choking.[48] By contrast, Shuster points out the lack of "checklists" in the Bible, noting the overlap between demonization and psychopathology, the various ways the devil can afflict someone, the multifarious manifestations of the demonic, and the lack of correspondence between the degree of demonization and ease of exorcism.[49] Anderson defines discernment as "the divinely enabled ability to distinguish a good spirit from a bad spirit," although there is debate as to whether discernment is primarily natural or supernatural.[50] Many point out the value of experience and divine insights (a "word from the Lord") in facilitating discernment.[51]

---

47. Cuneo, *American Exorcism*, 118.

48. Bubeck, *Adversary*, 144–45. Psychologist M. Kelsey suggests indications of demonic influence include beliefs that are contrary to Scripture and Christian tradition, actions that are divisive or power seeking, and attitudes that are hateful, egotistic, despondent, or resistant to growth; *Discernment*, 79–85. Amorth notes the presence of symptoms such as superhuman strength, resistance to medication, headaches, stomachaches; and the person's reaction to religious symbols; *Exorcist Tells*, 69–71. MacNutt suggests asking the afflicted person, who is usually very aware of the presence of demons, and noting physical manifestations; *Deliverance*, 76–86. Psychiatrist G. May suggests a common sense approach: evil spirits are associated with distress, willfulness, animosity, or confusion, in contrast to the peace, humility, and love of good spirits; *Will and Spirit*, 289.

49. Shuster suggests being alert to the possibility of demonization if a patient has multiple diagnoses and medication is ineffective; *Power, Pathology*, 183–92.

50. Anderson, *Bondage Breaker*, 166. Scanlan and Cirner believe discernment is primarily a result of revelation by the Holy Spirit and cannot be learned; *Deliverance*, 83, 95; by contrast, MacNutt states that observing symptoms is the primary method he uses; *Deliverance*, 77; C. Kraft thinks discernment involves both natural and supernatural components, noting that the first is more common; *Dark Angels*, 181–83.

51. This is a common practice among contemplatives, e.g., Teresa of Avila notes that only one with long experience in contemplation can discern evil spirits. She offers

Finally, some comments on deliverance techniques. The necessity of dialoguing with demons in order to know their name, personality, or rank is debated.[52] Kraft provides guidelines for deliverance including the importance of prayer, counseling, and ministering in teams. He advises asking demons their name and place in the hierarchy before commanding them to leave in the name of Christ.[53] MacNutt suggests a liturgy: "In the name of Jesus Christ," "I command you" spirit of (name or function of demon) to depart "without doing harm to (name of afflicted person) or anyone else in this house or in her family, and without making any noise or disturbance" "and I command you to go straight to Jesus Christ to dispose of you as He will. Furthermore I command you never again to return."[54] Anderson, who emphasizes truth encounters and discourages dialogue with demons, suggests that people who are influenced by evil forces should focus on healing through Christ, renouncing sins and requesting forgiveness when appropriate.[55] Although there is much that is questionable in popular "spiritual warfare" literature (see below), the anecdotal and experiential evidence reported by many of these authors should not be discounted and perhaps needs to be integrated into a sound theological model.[56]

---

suggestions for discernment based on feelings: the divine spirit produces consolation, calm, clarity, assurance, and virtue; evil spirits cause disquiet, agitation, turbulence, and restlessness; *The Interior Castle*, 6.3–18; Sluhovsky, *Believe Not Every Spirit*, 210–14. L. Payne suggests praying for ability to discern the demonic; *Christian Soul*, 188–90.

52. Most Roman Catholics dialogue extensively with demons to gain information. E.g., Amorth, *Exorcist*, 93; Peck, *Glimpses*. Others who suggest dialogue with demons include Friesen, *Mystery of MPD*, 263–64, and C. Kraft, *Dark Angels*, 181–98. MacNutt advises identifying the demons by asking the afflicted person or those gifted in discernment, and seldom by addressing the demons themselves; *Deliverance*, 75–86, 157–64; Anderson discourages dialoguing with demons and advocates ignoring them; *Bondage Breaker*, 109.

53. Kraft, *Dark Angels*, 181–98. Friesen similarly suggests "eight steps of exorcism": establish readiness for deliverance, bind the spirits, get the spirit's name, how it gained entry, its function, send it out in the name of Jesus, find out if there are other spirits, and seal the ministry with prayer; *Mystery of MPD*, 263–64.

54. MacNutt, *Deliverance*, 173–74.

55. Anderson, *Bondage Breaker*, 185–212. Powlison (*Power Encounters*) and Moreau (*Essentials of Spiritual Warfare*) suggest similar approaches. Payne emphasizes practicing the presence of God (for both therapist and client) and seeking the truth of the Spirit as a way to overcome evil; *Christian Soul*; *Healing Presence*.

56. As P. Wiebe remarks, experiential evidence has all too often been considered subordinate to experimental evidence; "Philosophical Perspective," 156–80.

Contemporary Academic Literature

In this next section, I examine "spiritual warfare" literature that has been written from a more academic perspective, beginning with Boyd's work, and followed by other contributions.

BOYD'S "GOD AT WAR"

A notable recent theological treatment of "spiritual warfare" is the comprehensive two-volume work on evil by Gregory A. Boyd, *God at War* and *Satan and the Problem of Evil*. Boyd is a self-confessed evangelical who has Pentecostal roots, and is known as an advocate of open theism.[57] He contributes to the open theism movement by incorporating biblical theology, in particular the existence and influence of evil spirits: There is a "very real world in between in which reside conscious, free beings who . . . possess power to influence others," the biblical belief is that the world is "virtually infested with demons" and "the number of these demons (is) indefinitely large." Boyd aims to construct a "contemporary compelling theodicy that understands evil within a warfare worldview."[58] Both volumes of his work are set in opposition to (his interpretation of) the Augustinian view of divine providence—that all evil is a result of God's mysterious purposes.

In his first volume, subtitled "The Bible and Spiritual Conflict," Boyd develops a biblical theology of "spiritual warfare." Part 1 examines the OT worldview. Chapter 1 sets up his argument with a vivid example of a child tortured during WWII; he notes that evil is *particular*, not abstract. The next two chapters mostly comprise the cosmic-conflict accounts of creation (e.g., God "locking up the sea" and defeating Canaanite sea monsters). He believes the OT view is that the world has been "seized by hostile, evil, cosmic forces," and that "creation itself has fallen into a state of war." He argues for the autonomy of evil forces and attributes the origin of evil to the angelic fall.[59] Chapter 4 examines the "other gods" over whom Yahweh is supreme, and chapter 5 looks at the role of Satan in the OT. Part 2 deals with the NT warfare worldview. Boyd discusses the kingdom

---

57. Boyd, *Oneness Pentecostals*; Boyd, *God of the Possible*; Boyd, *Is God to Blame?* For an introduction to open theism, see Pinnock et al., *Openness of God*.

58. Boyd, *God at War*, 24, 194, 199. He states that demons and the powers exist in a hierarchy (271).

59. Ibid., 19, 85, 99, 176.

of God in chapter 6, believing it to be a warfare concept: "Almost everything that Jesus and the early church were about is decisively colored by the central conviction that the world is caught in the crossfire of a cosmic battle between the Lord and his angelic army and Satan and his demonic army," and that "warfare itself shares center stage" with the supremacy of God. Chapter 7 examines the miracles, healings, and exorcisms of Jesus, which should all be interpreted as "acts of war." Chapter 8 looks at the teachings of Christ, and chapter 9 the atonement, following the *Christus Victor* model. Boyd stresses the cosmic significance of Christ's death and resurrection: It "is rooted in something more fundamental and broad that God was aiming at: to defeat once and for all his cosmic archenemy, Satan, along with the other evil powers under his dominion, and thereby to establish Christ as the legitimate ruler of the cosmos, and human beings as his legitimate viceroys upon the earth." In chapter 10 Boyd examines Acts and the epistles, which show that the Christian life is one of warfare. He concludes that our understanding of evil depends on our perspective: "Do we start with a view of God as being at war with evil or with a view of God as controlling evil? Do we start with a view of the world as a hostage to an evil cosmic force or with a view of the world as one in which God's will is perfectly carried out? Do we start with a view of evil as a hostile alien intrusion into God's cosmos or with a view of evil as always and everywhere fulfilling God's sovereign, always beneficent, purposes?"[60]

Boyd's second volume, subtitled "Constructing a Trinitarian Warfare Theodicy," is a philosophical/theological discussion of evil. In it, he proposes and defends six theses: love must be freely chosen, freedom implies/requires risk, risk entails moral responsibility, moral responsibility is proportionate to the potential to influence others, the power to influence is irrevocable, and the power to influence is finite. Boyd further notes that the mystery of evil is "*not about God's character or plan* . . . it is rather a mystery about *the complexity of creation*. Relocating the mystery of evil is . . . one of the most distinct features of the Trinitarian warfare theodicy."[61] Boyd clarifies his idea of free will: "God sets the parameters in which all free activity must take place . . . but within these parameters he allows free agents room to make their own decisions." A warfare worldview highlights the power and urgency of prayer. He argues against the concept of "natural" evil, believing that God does not ordain it and attributing it instead to

---

60. Ibid., 172, 240, 291.
61. Boyd, *Satan*, 215–16; italics original; see also 149.

the work of evil forces. "Evil permeates *the structure of the stage itself,* for the one given authority over the structure (Satan) has become corrupt."[62]

Boyd's work is noteworthy for his incorporation of demons into a philosophical framework of evil and his attribution of much evil to these beings. Unlike much of the popular literature, *God at War* includes discussion of texts within the entire Bible. Boyd is also helpful in his suggestion that to understand evil we should focus on the complexities of creation, not the mysteries of God (as philosophical approaches tend to do).[63] However, his work has its problems. Much of the critique of Boyd's two volumes has centered on his open theism perspective. Ron Highfield, for example, believes Boyd "defines evil wrongly," from a human rather than a divine perspective, minimizing the notion of sin.[64] Boyd implies that God is not involved in evil events. Highfield does not think Satan has the explanatory power that Boyd suggests. Boyd's methodology has similarly been critiqued. D. A. Carson claims that he sets up an "absolute antithesis" against the Augustinian view, which is in fact more nuanced and multifaceted. He argues against Boyd's views on free will and omniscience, and accuses him of being selective in the passages he chooses. Carson summarizes: "Boyd's stance is exegetically unconvincing, theologically troubling, historically selective, philosophically naive, and frequently methodologically unfair."[65] Although this critique is harsh, I agree that Boyd's work contains some methodological and exegetical concerns, which will be addressed throughout this book. Boyd's overuse of warfare language will be critiqued below.

Other Academic Literature

Aside from Boyd's work, most academic treatments of "spiritual warfare" have been done from a NT perspective, with some historical reviews, multidisciplinary collections of essays, and psychological perspectives. Exorcism in the Gospels has been studied by Graham Twelftree, Richard Bell, and Eric Sorensen, among others, but they minimally if at all incorporate ministry issues. Stephen Noll and Sidney Page have both written helpful biblical theologies of evil spirits.[66] From a Pauline perspective,

62. Boyd, *Satan*, 115, 226, 298, 301.

63. Ibid., 215–16.

64. Highfield, "Problem with Evil," 165–80. He reviews both volumes.

65. Carson, "God, the Bible," 258; he reviews *God at War*.

66. Noll is fairly neutral; *Angels of Light*; Page is critical of "spiritual warfare" literature, and is very conservative; *Powers of Evil*.

Clinton Arnold has written on "spiritual warfare," albeit from a semi-lay perspective. He points out three reasons to explore demonology: "awareness of the opponent is helpful," "it wakes us up to the reality of supernatural powerful opposition," and "it prompts us to depend on God." Arnold describes the devil as an "intelligent, powerful spirit-being . . . not an abstraction."[67] He believes demons can influence Christians through temptation, false teaching, feelings of guilt, doubt, and fear, and physical attack and persecution, and advocates considering avenues or grounds for demonic influence in ministering to a demonized person. In terms of discernment, he is conservative, noting that most symptoms of demonic influence can be explained by psychological phenomena: "Unless the person manifests some sort of supernatural power or abilities such as levitation or superhuman strength, it is difficult to diagnose the presence of a spirit merely by a set of symptoms." Spiritual discernment is critical but empirical verification challenging. Arnold offers a biblical framework for dealing with the demonic: first, draw near to God, and then resist evil through considering avenues for demonic influence such as sin, and only if needed deal directly with the evil spirit.[68]

Historian J. B. Russell has provided a well-researched resource in his four volumes on the history of the concept of the devil.[69] "Spiritual warfare" has been discussed in relationship to anthropology by Paul Hiebert, Charles Kraft, and Marguerite Kraft. Hiebert has drawn attention to differences between Western (which often ignore the spiritual dimension) and non-Western (which view spirits as involved in all aspects of life) worldviews and the "flaw of the excluded middle" (the West tends to ignore the layer of angels and demons that exist in the "middle" between heaven and earth).[70] C. Kraft has written on worldview issues and spiritual power; and M. Kraft has examined "spiritual warfare" in the Navajo, Thai, and Kwame peoples, suggesting that Westerners need to understand the importance that spiritual power has to non-Westerners.[71] From an interdisciplinary

---

67. Arnold, *3 Crucial Questions*, 35, 69, 97–100, 115–29.

68. Ibid., 115–29.

69. Russell, *The Devil; Satan; Lucifer* and *Mephistopheles*. He has also written a summary: *The Prince of Darkness*. Russell affirms the reality of the devil but notes the importance of historical and cultural contexts. Other historical treatments of demonology include Stanford, *The Devil* and Ellis, *Raising the Devil*.

70. Hiebert, "Excluded Middle," 35–47; Hiebert, "Spiritual Warfare and Worldviews," 114–24; Hiebert, "Anthropology, Missions," 13–23.

71. C. Kraft, *Christianity with Power*; M. Kraft, *Understanding Spiritual Power*; see also Tippet, *Introduction to Missiology*, 310–22.

perspective, a few collections of essays are worth mentioning. John Warwick Montgomery compiled case studies and papers dealing with demonization from a meeting of the American Christian Medical Society. Scott Moreau's volume emerged from the Lausanne Committee for World Evangelism (LCWE) and includes commentaries on contemporary "spiritual warfare," as well as theology, counseling, and cross-cultural mission.[72] Anthony Lane's collection contains a similar broad perspective, Peter and Beverly Smith Riddell's book includes essays on demonology from diverse religious traditions, and Kay and Parry's recent multidisciplinary volume provides a useful current perspective on deliverance.

"Spiritual warfare" has also been discussed within a psychological framework. Pauline scholar Walter Wink, for example, builds on the work of psychologist Carl Jung, who views evil as necessary, the interior shadow side of humanity.[73] This approach is helpful for its emphasis on human responsibility, but tends to demythologize evil, following an outmoded rationalistic worldview, and discounting demonization and deliverance. In contrast, psychiatrist Scott Peck believes Satan is real because he has "met it," and that evil can exist both inside and outside humans. He suggests a diagnosis of "evil" for certain people, and has detailed his experiences with exorcism.[74] Psychiatrist Gerald May and psychologist Marguerite Shuster both employ sophisticated psychologies that include awareness of potential influence from evil spirits.

From a theological perspective, Karl Barth includes some discussion of the demonic, and Edwin Lewis has written about the devil in opposition to God. More recently, the work of Nigel Wright has been well received. Uniquely, he attempts to integrate biblical evidence, theologies of evil (including those of Barth, Wink, and Jürgen Moltmann), and experiential reports in the "spiritual warfare" literature. Somewhat confusingly, he adopts a "non-ontological realist" view of the devil and demons. The devil has ontological ground but no ontological status. Evil is inherently deceptive, masquerades as organized and personal, but is by nature chaotic.

---

72. Moreau et al, *Deliver Us from Evil.*

73. Wink's trilogy, *Naming the Powers, Unmasking the Powers, Engaging the Powers,* is well regarded.

74. Peck, *People of the Lie,* 43, 183. Evil is discerned through feelings of revulsion (65–66). He views evil as a form of narcissistic personality disorder (67, 128–29) and believes psychotherapy is only possible after exorcism (198). He follows a Roman Catholic model and suggests multiple models, including medical and theological, are needed for understanding evil (38–39).

Evil is parasitical but not passive, akin to antimatter.[75] Wright affirms the possibility of demonization and the need for deliverance but advises caution. He points out that humans are psychologically, socially, psychically, and spiritually complex, and calls for the church to be loving, listening, prayerful, discerning, and authoritative.[76] Amos Yong develops a similarly negative ontology of evil spirits from a Pentecostal perspective.[77] He uses the triadic metaphysics of C. S. Peirce, Wink's view of evil as interior, and the scientific theory of emergence to describe the nature and origin of evil spirits. Although Yong is creative, his ideas are speculative. The above scholars contribute to our understanding of demonology and deliverance and will be engaged throughout this study. However, they often only provide one perspective; an ideal approach would incorporate the entire Bible, plus theology and ministry.

"Spiritual Warfare": Critiques

The "spiritual warfare" movement and its accompanying literature have been much critiqued, mostly from the perspectives of evangelical missiology, theology, and anthropology. Concerns are largely directed towards radicals who see a demon under every proverbial bush. Most critiques endorse the need for additional academic work on the subject. One aspect that has received little criticism is the underlying warfare model that is assumed. In this section, I survey previous critiques of popular and academic "spiritual warfare" literature with respect to theology, method, and warfare language, and suggest further critiques.

Theology and Method

Critics of "spiritual warfare" usually attempt to steer a middle course. British Anglican charismatics Michael Harper and Michael Green both cautiously affirm but marginalize deliverance ministries.[78] Wright

75. Wright, *Dark Side*, 72–74, 79–81. This is a revised edition; it was previously published in the UK as *The Fair Face of Evil* and in the U.S. as *The Satan Syndrome*. See update and summary in Wright, "Deliverance and Exorcism," 203–21.

76. Wright, *Dark Side*, 119–30, 182–90.

77. His ideas are presented first in dialogue with Wink (*Discerning the Spirit(s)*, 97–148), continued in *Beyond the Impasse*, 129–61, and more fully developed in *Spirit of Creation*, esp. 173–228.

78. Harper, *Spiritual Warfare*; Green, *Satan's Downfall*; see also Collins, *Exorcism*, 71–74.

encourages restraint, especially in light of reports of violent or fatal exorcisms, and David Powlison questions the common assumptions of popular "spiritual warfare" literature.[79] There have been many article-length critiques of "spiritual warfare," suggesting caution and pointing to the need for further academic study.[80] As Robert Guelich notes, what was originally a biblical metaphor (warfare) has now become an extensive movement.[81] Andrew G. Walker coined the term "paranoid universe" to describe a worldview that divides the world into two kingdoms: God's and Satan's. Because of this dualism, certain groups are sometimes seen as demonized. He is concerned about the dangers of "literalizing" parable and metaphor.[82] Walker believes it is "wise to make modest claims about the origins of devils, the workings of the demonic world, and the methodology of exorcisms when the Bible remains virtually silent on these matters," and notes that the Bible uses mythological language to describe the devil.[83]

Missiologists Priest et al. critique the "spiritual warfare" movement at length, especially the teachings of Kraft, Wimber, and Murphy. They accuse these theorists of misreading animism, and promoting a magical worldview, not a biblical one. Specifically, they question the validity of teaching regarding vulnerability to the demonic through physical objects, curses, genealogical transmission, and geographical location. The effect

79. Wright, *Dark Side*, 26–27; Powlison, *Power Encounters*. Powlison accuses those involved in an "ekballistic mode of ministry" of ignoring moral evil and buying into "occult theology" for example (66–74, 127). He also separates situational (e.g., evil spirits, illness, storms) and moral (sin) evil.

80. C. Breuninger highlights the need for a biblically based theology of "spiritual warfare" and suggests we need to go beyond blindness, fixation, and stardom; "Where Angels Fear," 37–43. J. Theron is more supportive of deliverance ministries, noting that most did not begin out of a morbid fascination with the demonic but as a result of experience. He believes demythologizing approaches are no longer acceptable, and calls for more academic study, clarification of terminology, and increased dialogue between academics and ministry; "Critical Overview," 79–92.

81. Guelich, "Spiritual Warfare," 34.

82. Walker, "Devil You Think You Know," 88–100. Collins rebuts Walker's idea of a paranoid universe, arguing that deliverance ministries are always the fruit of enthusiasm, and that people are usually unaware of worldviews; *Exorcism*, 106. Theron argues that Charismatic Theologies are too diverse for Walker's critique to apply; "Critical Overview."

83. Walker, "Devil You Think You Know," 99. Elsewhere he notes that humans can choose either to follow God or the Devil, that the world is enemy occupied territory, and that evil is both personal and systemic; he describes the devil as a non-person whose behavior is irrational; *Enemy Territory* 15, 16, 34, 35, 49, 58, 245.

of this teaching on social relationships, spiritual security, and missionary methods is of great concern. They also question methodology: anecdotal evidence (we should not "accept accounts of event as the epistemological basis for constructing new doctrines about unseen realities"), questionable biblical interpretation, appeals to pragmatism, and the construction of new doctrines based on personal "words of knowledge."[84] Kraft counters these critiques with the claim that both the Bible and experience are important in demonology.[85] Admittedly, Priest et al. are harsh in their criticism, but their concerns need to be seriously considered.

René Holvast focuses his critique on the concepts of territorial spirits and spiritual mapping (deciding which "spirits" rule in which areas) in America and Argentina. He provides an excellent review of the history of spiritual mapping including its critiques and social/anthropological contexts. Spiritual mapping was a product marketed to American evangelicals as a tool for missionary work, promoting a dualistic worldview that required a response. Holvast believes its short, tempestuous career was a result of harsh critiques, limited cross-cultural applicability, insufficient theological and anthropological underpinnings, reliance on questionable anecdotal reports, and ultimate failure to locate evil geographically. He claims that the movement is over and was merely a "blind alley in Evangelicalism."[86] Unlike Holvast, I am not convinced the movement is over, even though the public aspects of it may have waned.

Collins, discussed above, is critical of many aspects of deliverance ministry. He describes much of it as unconvincing and inconsistent, with idiosyncratic theology, and often a "parade of outlandish demonic encounters."[87] He calls the Hammonds' work "dangerous nonsense," believes Unger's assertion that demons have names (English ones at that!) to have a "flimsy biblical basis," and questions the credibility of Amorth's large number of exorcisms. Interestingly, he thinks Peck's hope for collaboration between exorcism and mental health care failed because "exorcism and deliverance live in the context of religious enthusiasm; deprived of this clement environment they cannot last for long."[88] Collins

---

84. Priest et al., "Missiological Syncretism," 39. They also criticize the views of T. Warner, E. Murphy, G. Otis, J. Dawson, and C. Jacobs.

85. Kraft, *Powerless Christianity*, 18, 65–68, 101–2.

86. Holvast, *Spiritual Mapping*, 281–307. Similar critiques have been made by Chuck Lowe (*Territorial Spirits*), and Scott Moreau (*Gaining Perspective*).

87. Collins, *Exorcism*, 48, 90, 92, 136.

88. Collins, *Exorcism*, 69, 132, 173, 170 respectively.

seems to overstate his case here—I would argue that religious enthusiasm is not the only factor in deliverance. Many non-enthusiasts (myself included) quietly practice deliverance.

The above critiques provide a valuable corrective to many of the bold claims of "spiritual warfare" advocates. I agree with the critics that many authors writing on demonology ignore biblical ambiguities, although, perhaps because of the inconsistencies in the biblical text, they attempt to "fill in the gaps." They often come to confident conclusions and are not always clear whether these are biblically or anecdotally based. However, critics are usually reactive rather than proactive and seldom offer alternative approaches. Neither do they address the challenge of anecdotal evidence. There is seldom solid integration of biblical exegesis, theology, and ministry. Martin Parsons is correct in saying that our hermeneutics need to consider the entire Bible, the worldwide church, and practical ministry experience.[89] An alternative model may enable new perspectives on biblical evidence and its applicability to experience.

Warfare Language

Although many aspects of "spiritual warfare" have been critiqued, seldom is its underlying warfare language questioned. Discussion about evil spirits in contemporary Christianity is almost exclusively phrased in terms of "spiritual warfare." Numerous popular and some academic books include the term in their title. Warfare language has been used throughout the history of Christianity but the term "spiritual warfare" became established in the context of charismatic renewal, popularized in 1970 as in the title of Harper's book. The idiom has been used by charismatics,[90] evangelicals,[91] and Calvinists;[92] has been applied to missiology,[93] counseling,[94] and women;[95] and has endured for four decades.

---

89. Parsons, "Binding the Strong Man," 107–9.

90. E.g., Wagner, *Confronting the Powers*; Jacobs, *Possessing the Gates*.

91. E.g., Kraft, *Dark Angels*, Anderson and Warner. *Beginner's Guide.*

92. Bolt, "Satan is Alive and Well," 497–506.

93. E.g., Jabbour, *The Unseen Reality* (he worked in Egypt) and Engelsviken, "Spiritual Conflict," 116–25 (he worked in Ethiopia). Even missiology texts sometimes include a section on "spiritual warfare," e.g., Ott et al., *Theology of Mission*, 238–61.

94. E.g., Adams, *The War Within*; Johnson, *Spiritual Warfare for the Wounded.*

95. Sherrer and Galrock, *Woman's Guide to Spiritual Warfare."*

Warfare language is so prevalent that a few examples from the popular literature will suffice. The Hammonds proclaim that "spiritual warfare" involves the weapons of the blood of Jesus and the word of God; George Mallone advises Christians to choose weapons wisely, prepare for battle, wear appropriate armor, and have a battle plan; and Murphy refers to Satan's vast army of "co-devils" and asserts repeatedly that "we are at war."[96] The language of power came to prominence perhaps with the "third wave" and Wimber who emphasized power evangelism, including encounters between the spiritual powers.[97] Although most of these authors take the term "spiritual warfare" for granted, occasionally alternative language is used. Kraft, for example, in addition to warfare language, compares demons to rats that are attached to garbage (sin, occult-ties, or wounding in a person's life).[98] Interestingly, Wagner states that he would prefer not to use warfare language (he suggests football imagery instead) but he is "not free to do this" as the Bible describes our spiritual fight as warfare, a struggle between life and death.[99] Somewhat similarly, Dudley Woodberry, in his introduction to a section on "spiritual power," admits he chose this title in preference to words that were too militant or too anemic.[100] A few authors use warfare language minimally, such as Anderson, who takes a truth-oriented approach, and MacNutt, who focuses on healing.

Boyd's work contains frequent warfare language: "God wages war" against "hostile, evil, cosmic forces," "Christ has now secured the overthrow of the evil cosmic army." He claims that the kingdom of God, and therefore the kingdom of Satan, is a military concept. Jesus' "healings, exorcisms and especially his resurrection, were definite acts of war that accomplished and demonstrated his victory over Satan."[101] Indeed "the

---

96. Hammonds, *Pigs in the Parlour*, 33; Mallone, *Arming for Spiritual Warfare*, 21–38; Murphy, *Handbook*, 270.

97. E.g., Wimber, *Power Evangelism*. He states "any system or force that must be overcome for the gospel to be believed is a cause for a power encounter" (16). Ott et al believe the Bible is "clear that spiritual power is the foundational prerequisite for mission"; *Theology of Mission*, 238.

98. Kraft, *Dark Angels*, 43, 125.

99. In his introduction to his essay collection on territorial spirits; Wagner, *Engaging the Enemy*, 4. Similarly J. C. L. Gibson thinks warfare metaphors, although problematic, are too frequent to be dropped from biblical/theological language; *Language and Imagery*, 12.

100. Woodberry, "Introduction," 87–89.

101. Boyd, *God at War*, 19, 185, 213.

whole of the Christian life is an act of warring against the enemy," and we are to throw "all we have into guerrilla warfare against the occupying army."[102] Boyd believes "the New Testament and early church always thought of evil in the context of spiritual warfare." He asserts that the "possibility of love among contingent creatures . . . entails the possibility of its antithesis, namely, war."[103]

Arnold also discusses the topic using a warfare framework with subheadings such as "kingdoms in conflict" and "arming for spiritual warfare."[104] Even those who critique the movement are uncritical of the language. Hiebert expresses concern regarding the overuse of power in "spiritual warfare" but nonetheless uses military metaphors himself.[105] Walker and Wright, otherwise conservative, both use warfare language, and Carson, who harshly criticizes Boyd, does not object to warfare terminology.[106] Mennonites Gerald Ediger and Randy Friesen are likewise critical of the movement, but not the term "spiritual warfare."[107] Bolt and Theron, in their critiques, do not oppose warfare language but place "spiritual warfare" in quotation marks.[108] There are some academic works on evil spirits in which warfare language is missing or minimal, such as Lane's compilation of essays and Noll's biblical theology. Interestingly, the *EPCC* lacks an entry on "spiritual warfare," although the term is used in other articles.[109] Overall, the term "spiritual warfare," with its concomitant imagery, has been uncritically adopted in popular and academic circles.

However, there are numerous concerns with warfare imagery, some of which have been mentioned. I categorize these as biblical, theological,

102. Boyd, *God at War*, 217, 281.

103. Ibid., 16, 56. However, war is not necessarily an antithesis of love; consider indifference or hate.

104. Arnold, *3 Crucial Questions*, 19, 44.

105. Hiebert, "Spiritual Warfare and Worldviews," 203–15.

106. Walker claims "to be a Christian is to be at war with the Devil," describes the divine biblical drama as the "great battle" and states that Christians are soldiers called to fight behind enemy lines; *Enemy Territory* 13, 21, 58. Wright's concluding chapter is titled "God's Holy War"; *Dark Side*, 80–91, 173–77, although he does mention the risks associated with warfare language (166–68), emphasizing the "power of love" over the "love of power." Carson agrees we "are indeed in a warfare situation"; "God, the Bible," 266.

107. Ediger, "Strategic-Level Spiritual Warfare," 125–41; Friesen, "Equipping Principles," 142–52.

108. Suggesting less than complete acceptance; Bolt, "Satan is Alive and Well"; Theron, "Critical Overview."

109. E.g., Henderson, "Deliverance," 123–26.

and psychosocial. Biblical concerns mostly involve issues of exegesis, especially with regard to linguistics. Much of the popular literature, and some scholarly literature, builds a whole theology based on one biblical passage, Ephesians 6:10–20, which contains military metaphors.[110] This results in an imbalance, an elevation of warfare imagery, and potential neglect of other metaphors, which in turn may give a distorted perspective. On the scholarly level, NT scholars, specifically Pauline scholars, have done much of the work on evil spirits. Although there is certainly a role for exegetical work on specific passages, it is helpful to consider demonology from a broader perspective in a framework encompassing both OT and NT perspectives (as Boyd does). The use and misuse of metaphor is also concerning. To my knowledge, none of the "spiritual warfare" literature to date includes interaction with metaphor theory. Some express concern about warfare metaphors but do not employ metaphor theory.[111] Finally, the necessity of warfare interpretations of certain biblical passages can be questioned (discussed throughout this book). Warfare imagery is not the only language available to demonology. Indeed, using multiple metaphors can enhance our understanding of this unseen reality.

There has been little academic work done on evil spirits and deliverance by systematic theologians. Because of this lack, "spiritual warfare" is sometimes associated with those on the "fringe" of Christianity, with the subject consequently being dismissed entirely. Yet the plethora of popular books on "spiritual warfare" indicates a hunger for information; the lack of healthy food available from the academy has led consumers to gorge on fast food.[112] Perhaps because of the language, the topic is seldom integrated into ecclesiology or Christian life and ethics. Another theological concern is that "spiritual warfare" literature is largely theocentric: there is a focus on God as the "divine warrior" with a relative neglect of the roles of Christ and the Holy Spirit. Warfare imagery may also result in an overly dualistic worldview. Although most popular writers emphasize the

---

110. E.g., Bubeck claims Ephesians is "the Christian's handbook on spiritual warfare against the devil and his kingdom"; *The Adversary*, 70; Murphy devotes an entire chapter to this passage; *Handbook*, 402–15. Other commonly cited texts include Rom 13:12, 2 Cor 10:3, 4, and Col 2:15.

111. E.g., Guelich and Walker, as mentioned above. Metaphor theory will be discussed in the following chapter.

112. Breuninger makes a similar point: "evangelicalism, having been shaped by the secularizing effects of Western rationalism, has ironically, helped create a craving for an experiential spirituality that an evangelical hermeneutic is often unable to satisfy"; "Where Angels Fear," 42.

supremacy of Christ over demons, and scholars are careful to state that they do not endorse metaphysical dualism,[113] warfare imagery lends itself to a view of a battle between two equal and opposite forces, which can lead to Walker's "paranoid universe" (a "spiritual warfare" model can be depicted as in Figure 1.1).

Figure 1.1: A "Spiritual Warfare" Model

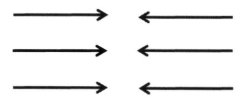

The dualism of warfare imagery has implications regarding the sovereignty of God and the ontology of evil spirits. If God is pitted against a "formidable foe,"[114] he must need to expend much effort in the battle. If Christians are called to wage war, the enemy is assumed to be considerable. Yet God expels evil from his good creation with merely a word (Pss 18:15; 104:7; 106:9; Matt 17:18; Mark 1:25; 9:24). And many scholars who affirm the reality of evil spirits nevertheless minimize their ontology.

An obvious psychosocial concern with warfare imagery is its association with violence. Even though the warfare is "spiritual," it may still evoke the fear, anger, and hatred associated with war. Kraft notes that deliverance-based approaches to evil spirits (compared with truth-oriented or healing approaches) focus on simply *blasting out* the demons, which often results in violence.[115] Hiebert points out that the "cosmic battle between God and Satan" is "not one of power"; "might does not make right, nor does the battle make the victor legitimate."[116] He suggests the parables of the wayward son (emphasizing human responsibility) and the rebellious stewards (emphasizing legitimacy and authority) provide a better perspective on

---

113. Boyd notes that biblical dualism is provisional and transitory; powers that exist "with some measure of autonomy over against God . . . never pose a threat of overthrowing" him; *God at War,* 228, 230, 284.

114. Ibid., 94.

115. Kraft, "Contemporary Trends," 191.

116. Hiebert, "Spiritual Warfare and Worldviews," 119; see also, Hiebert, *Anthropological Reflections,* 203–15.

the biblical view of "spiritual warfare." Hiebert acknowledges the reality of demons but insists the cross and the establishment of the kingdom of God are more important to Christianity than spiritual battles. The LCWE, along with critiques regarding the methodology and theology of "spiritual warfare" literature, expressed concerns that a preoccupation with the demonic "can lead to avoiding personal responsibility for our actions" and that "warfare language can lead to adversarial attitudes," which is problematic when dialoguing with people of other faiths who can interpret such language as violent and political.[117] Moreau, part of that committee, describes some societal myths and images that have been appropriated by the "spiritual warfare" movement. In "the joy is in the fight" model, as in action movies, more attention is given to the deliverance process than to the spiritual life of the person. Similarly, "spiritual warfare" literature tends to endorse a "full speed ahead" approach. For some authors, it seems that "it is easier (and more fun) to expel a demon than to walk through the realities of broken, shattered lives built on the foundations of relational dysfunctionality." The myth of the "North American hero," who always defeats the enemy using violence, when applied to deliverance, may externalize the enemy, allowing for an avoidance of responsibility for sin. Some authors assume that "good violence may be used to overcome evil violence"; "the trap we may fall into is loving power rather than using the power of love." Moreau suggests that "the core metaphor for spiritual conflict should not be that of conflict but that of God's rule and our resulting ethos of shalom built on the foundation of kingdom ethics."[118] Harriet Crabtree similarly points out that, since beliefs shape behavior, "spiritual warfare" can foster violent attitudes and carries a danger of militaristic thinking. This metaphor is also problematic if it is seen as guaranteeing victory, success, and power; it can "distort what it has been evoked to illuminate."[119] She notes that most feminists reject any form of warfare imagery, while some authors believe Christian life *is* war—not a metaphor, but a literal fact.

Another social concern of military imagery is its limited applicability to counseling and pastoral situations. Warfare is primarily a masculine

117. LCWE, "Spiritual Warfare." A missionary conference in 2000 also expressed concern over the use of military metaphors; "Biblical Language."

118. Moreau, "Survey," 121–23. He does not develop this image.

119. Crabtree, *Christian Life*, 87–97, 113–17. She also notes the metaphor of warfare can operate at many levels; Christian life viewed as participating in actual warfare or simply as a shadow of heavenly battles. Other metaphors of the Christian life include discipleship and stewardship.

metaphor, which many women and children may have difficulty relating to, especially if they have experienced violence. But, without appropriate language, counselors may not consider the demonic as a potential contributor to personal difficulties. Warfare imagery can be counterproductive in counseling, especially when dealing with anger issues. The fear associated with "spiritual warfare" can lead to paranoia and consequent violence. As noted above, it is easy for a metaphor to move beyond its intent. Since we already live in a society plagued by violence, it is unhelpful to perpetuate such imagery. A "spiritual warfare" model can also lead to an "us versus them" mentality and decreased responsibility for our own weaknesses and sin. The black-and-white thinking characteristic of "spiritual warfare" ignores the shades of grey in humans who are psychologically and spiritually complex, and who live in a similarly complex world.

With a few exceptions that have not been developed, "spiritual warfare" is the only model for demonology and deliverance available to contemporary Christianity. This fact alone suggests the need for an alternative model. Given the above concerns regarding warfare language, perhaps another model could offer an improvement upon the present one.

The Need for an Alternative Model

The literature on "spiritual warfare" and its critiques confirm my earlier assertion that demonology and deliverance are important topics in contemporary Christianity. This work is a partial response to the cries of critics for further academic work on the subject. There is a need for an integrated approach that is thoroughly biblical and soundly theological, yet resonates with experience. The problems with much of the "spiritual warfare" literature may be partly due to the difficulties inherent in the topic. Many authors expand upon biblical knowledge by appealing to experience. Moreover, their views are likely limited by their commitment to warfare language. Their teachings are also perhaps influenced by their worldview. Typically, the questions asked determine the answers received.[120] Despite the waning of rationalism, many "spiritual warfare" authors appear to approach the topic through rationalistic, modernistic lenses.[121] Consequently, they suggest hierarchies, ascribe personal-

120. Apparently, Einstein recommended 55 minutes to determine the proper question, and 5 minutes to solve it.

121. Powlison claims "both the disenchanted world of modern rationalism and the charmed world of pre-modern spiritism are wrong"; *Power Encounters*, 25.

ity to demons, and detail steps for deliverance. By contrast, postmodern approaches tend towards demythologization, which is not helpful for the missionary in societies that view evil spirits as involved in daily affairs, or for the counselor dealing with a person who claims to be afflicted by demons. Those who attempt a moderate approach do not fully develop their views or suggest alternative models. There are no comprehensive models that utilize non-warfare language. These observations about the current state of academic demonology point to the need for an alternative approach.

Criticisms of "spiritual warfare" literature include concerns regarding methodology (exegesis, hermeneutics, neglect of OT texts, neglect of metaphor theory), theology (magical and paranoid worldviews, imbalanced, overly dualistic), plus warfare language (association with violence, dualistic, avoidance of personal responsibility, limited applicability to counseling). Although Boyd's work represents an advance in the field, because it is more comprehensive, it still has weaknesses, notably his overuse of warfare imagery. Further issues include the questions of whether there are non-warfare images of evil in the Bible, and better theological underpinnings for counseling and mission than those offered by a warfare model. I concur with Theron and others that more academic study, clarification of terminology, and reconciliation between theology and ministry is needed. This study attempts to address these questions through an investigation of non-warfare biblical metaphors for evil. The aim is to provide a broad perspective that can inform Christian ministry. It is time to remove our warfare spectacles and investigate alternative language.

Objectives and Outline of Book

The aim of this project is to develop a biblically-based model for conceptualizing evil. Not only will this provide an alternative to the "spiritual warfare" model but, through the investigation of alternate metaphors for evil and the subsequent development of a new model, it is hoped this investigation will increase our understanding of evil and how to counteract it. In particular, it may provide further insight into the ontology of evil, and suggest metaphors that are appropriate to counseling. Progress may be made in reconciling biblical studies and theology, philosophy and theology, and psychology and theology. Different metaphors can open conceptual space. Since counseling is language based, since we are discussing unseen reality, and since most of the biblical texts pertaining to demonology are arguably metaphorical, figurative language as a primary methodology is a logical choice. Metaphor theory and models, which are closely related, will be reviewed and discussed in chapter 2, along with some discussion regarding the nature of truth and reality. Spatial metaphors in particular, which are universal, provide a useful tool for developing a model. In order to develop an alternate model, biblical metaphors for evil are examined and the disciplines of anthropology (common in "spiritual warfare" literature and relevant to missiology), theology (including theodicy and ontology), and science (especially chaos-complexity theory) are delved for insights into the definition and understanding of evil. This forms the content of chapter 3.

Chapters 4 through 7 form the basis for the model. A thematic approach is used including the categories of sacred space (and the evil forces that threaten it) and sacred actions (including divine and human responsibility). Evil is examined in its spatial opposition to God, goodness, and holiness. Metaphors of cleansing and boundary-setting are discussed in contrast to warfare metaphors, and the role of the Holy Spirit with respect to expelling evil is considered. Chapter 4 investigates the theme of creation in the OT and a preliminary model is developed. Israel's cult is an area that has not been explored for insights into demonology. The structure and function of the cult, including sin, impurity, and ritual, is examined in chapter 5 and the model developed further, using the idea of graded holiness. Chapter 6 discusses Christ, the depiction of demons and deliverance in the Gospels, the atonement, and the eschatological separation of evil. The church is examined in chapter 7, including Satan, the powers, and sin, the concept of the indwelling Spirit, discernment and guidelines for the church in deliverance ministry. Finally, the conclusion provides a summary in the context of the "new creation." The relevance of this study to pneumatology and demonology is discussed and some potential applications of this model are examined, especially with respect to missiology and counseling. Finally, possible limitations of this study are evaluated with suggestions for future research.

Although I write from a charismatic-evangelical perspective, this is not a primary focus here; my desire is to inform Christian theology in general. This study is not intended as a counseling/deliverance or missiology manual but has implications for ministry. I hope to contribute to the literature on evil and demonology through a fresh approach to the topic, while building on and integrating previous scholarship.

2

METHOD, METAPHOR,
MODEL, AND MEANING

O weak person ... because you are timid about speaking ...
and unskilled about writing those things, speak and write those things ...
according to the extent that you see and hear those things
in the heavens above in the marvelousness of God.[1]

LANGUAGE IS UNIVERSAL AND ubiquitous, delicious and delightful, marvelous and multidimensional, passionate and powerful. Yet language is to be respected. There is remarkable responsibility required of both reader and writer. Nowhere is this more critical than when engaging sacred texts or discussing divine reality. Even a cursory reading of biblical texts reveals a language rich with imagery, metaphor, symbol, and myth. It behooves us therefore to examine the type of language used by ancient writers in order to discover and uncover divine truth from the Bible's diversity and fertility.

This chapter develops the methodology that guides the remainder of the study. Biblical linguistics investigates the type of language used as well as the form of language—words, sentences, and extended texts. It questions possible meanings and correspondence with reality.[2] Semantics is an aspect of linguistics, concerned with meaning (authorial, textual, and perceived). Historical- or form-critical methods, which have predominated

---

1. Hildegarde of Bingen, *Scivias*, introduction.
2. For an overview, see Cotterell and Turner, *Linguistics and Biblical Interpretation.*

biblical studies until recently, operate at the micro-level, whereas linguistic methods use holistic, thematic, "big-picture" approaches. Terminology can be confusing; therefore, I begin with an overview of figurative language, then address the application of metaphor theory to theology, elaborate on the relationship between metaphor, truth, history, and reality, and discuss the relationship between metaphor theory and "spiritual warfare." The conclusion will clarify the methodology used in this study.

Types of Figurative Language

The Bible describes God as a shepherd and a fortress, the devil as a roaring lion, and humanity as a branch and a bride. Stories of both beginning and end incorporate multiple vivid images. Jesus spoke in parables and Paul used analogies. In fact, it could be argued that the Bible contains more figurative than literal language. Biblical authors did not make the same distinctions between literal and figurative language that Western culture does. They piled metaphors on top of each other, clearly aware of their descriptive value, and implied multiple meanings. Myth, symbol, and history were intertwined as reflections of divine truth.[3] Given the plethora of figurative language in the Bible, it is surprising that much of Western theology has focused on abstractions and doctrine. During the Enlightenment period, figurative language was distrusted, deemed inferior to scientific rationalism, empiricism, and literalism. This perhaps explains the origin of the clichés "*just* a myth" or "*merely* a metaphor."[4] Empiricists and positivists viewed figurative language as deceptive, undermining correct reasoning. Metaphor in particular was further downgraded by philosophers of modernity who believed it to be damaging to truth and incompatible with serious study. They made a sharp distinction between logic (encompassing truth, knowledge, and progress) and imagination (deemed false and superstitious).[5] Biblical scholars during the late eighteenth and early nineteenth centuries contended that "revelation be subordinated to reason . . . the result being that the supernatural was largely eliminated from their theology."[6] Studying the imaginative aspects

3. Ryken et al.'s *Dictionary of Biblical Imagery,* more than 1,000 pages, attests to the prevalence of figurative language in the Bible.

4. See Avis, *Creative Imagination,* 14–22, for a discussion of the "fate of the imagination in modernity."

5. E.g., Locke and Hobbes; Stiver, *Philosophy of Religious Language,* 114.

6. Scobie, "History of Biblical Theology," 13.

of the Bible is a relatively recent phenomenon, although defining types of figurative language is complex.[7] Figurative language and imagery is a broad term encompassing all nonliteral language, the latter also associated with pictures. In this section, I discuss symbol, metaphor, and model, as well as other terms that are peripheral to this study but important to define in relationship to metaphor. The distinction between literal and figurative language is discussed later.

Symbols

A symbol is an image that represents something; it can be non-linguistic, has no conventional function and points to reality beyond itself. Symbols, such as the cross, are ubiquitous and well known in Christianity. They often refer to cosmic, transcendent realities and therefore are relevant to this study. Symbols can be defined generally as "images, words, or behaviors that have multiple levels of meaning." They are polysemic (having multiple meanings) and multivalent (having many appeals) but typically have their origins in universal experiences of life (e.g., light, dark, water, death). Symbols are dynamic, shaped by multiple sources, and can be considered developed metaphors that suggest realities.[8] French philosopher Paul Ricoeur has a high regard for symbol, viewing it as cognitive and pointing to reality, or stimulating reflection on reality. In his work on the symbolism of evil, he famously claims, "the symbol gives rise to thought."[9] He believes symbols are more closely bound to their referents (frequently of a cosmic nature, like sun and trees) than metaphors, which are free to create new meaning.[10] Peter Macky defines a symbol as "one (usually common) reality that stands for, or represents, and gives analogical insight into, more mysterious realities." He thinks every metaphor incorporates a

---

7. As Crabtree notes, theologians are often "sloppy" in their use of terms; *Christian Life*, 7. For discussions of figurative language in theology, see Soskice, *Metaphor and Religious Language*, 54–66; Macky, *Centrality of Metaphors*, 49–55; and Caird, *Imagery of the Bible*, 131–43.

8. Womack, *Symbols and Meaning*, 1–12, 48; Grelot, *Language of Symbolism*, 18.

9. Ricoeur, *Symbolism of Evil*, 347–48. Ricoeur is truly interdisciplinary, having written for four decades on theology, phenomenology, existentialism, psychoanalysis and structuralism.

10. Ricoeur, *Interpretation Theory*, 61. Theologian Sally McFague concurs that with symbols, the similarity is assumed, whereas metaphors are surprising; *Metaphorical Theology*, 17.

symbol and that symbols are related to models in terms of representing reality.[11]

Metaphors

Two broad theories of metaphor can be described, although different authors use different terms for them.[12] In this section, I discuss the classical view, followed by the interaction view, and then consider conceptual metaphors and semantic fields.

THE CLASSICAL VIEW

Aristotle provided the classic definition of metaphor (Greek etymology "carry with"): "the application of an alien name by transference."[13] The implications of this designation are threefold: meaning lies in words rather than larger linguistic units; metaphors are deviants, nonliteral; they rely on a known similarity. Consequently, the meaning of figurative language can only be understood if it is translated or reduced to literal language. This idea, the classical, comparison, or substitution view, dominated literary studies for centuries and remains common today. Metaphor is seen as mere ornamentation, comparison, or substitution for a more accurate, literal word. This definition, albeit applicable to some metaphors, is particularly problematic with regard to biblical texts—metaphors used to describe divine reality are not easily translated into literal language (e.g., Jesus as "the light of the world," "the breath of God," or being "born-again"). Scholarship of the last four decades has convincingly argued that metaphors are much more than imagination and ornamentation, but there is no consensus regarding a precise definition.[14] Metaphor theory has been

11. Macky, *Centrality of Metaphors,* 54. Avis similarly believes symbols mediate the transcendent and are a constitutive part of myths; *Creative Imagination,* 8, 11. Furthermore, "the truth is contained in symbols." Soskice views symbols almost synonymously with models; *Metaphor and Religious Language,* 55.

12. E.g., Avis uses the terms "classic" (corresponding to the ornamental or substitution views) and "romantic" (corresponding to interaction or incremental views); *Creative Imagination,* 93; Soskice uses "substitution" and "incremental," and adds a third category, "emotive," for metaphors that do not add meaning but evoke emotion; Soskice, *Metaphor and Religious Language,* 31.

13. Aristotle, *Poetics,* 3. XXI; in 400 BCE.

14. Soskice estimates that more than 125 definitions have been proposed; *Metaphor and Religious Language,* 15.

influential in philosophy, linguistics, psychology, politics, science, and of course, religion. And neuroscientists have discovered that humans process with the right hemisphere of their brain (primarily imaginative) as well as the left (primarily analytical). With respect to philosophy, generally the twentieth century marked a turn from metaphysics to language and consequently metaphor has taken center stage.

THE INTERACTION VIEW

The renewed respect for metaphor is usually accredited to Max Black in his 1962 publication, *Models and Metaphors*. However, he acknowledges reliance on I. A. Richards's neglected work, *The Philosophy of Rhetoric*. Richards claims that "when we use a metaphor we have two thoughts of different things active together and supported by a single word, or phrase, whose meaning is a resultant of their interaction." He thinks that the human mind works naturally by connecting concepts. Thus the cognitive value of metaphor was first recognized. Richards notes that the two ideas "co-operate in an inclusive meaning." Metaphor occurs at the level of the sentence and is irreplaceable; it is pervasive and impacts reality.[15] Richards believes we exercise control over our world through the command of metaphor.

Black agrees that metaphors usually comprise a system of words as opposed to a single word. New meaning can derive from the interaction between two ideas; there is dual-directionality. He notes that literal use of words is restricted by syntactical rules, whereas metaphors allow more freedom of expression. Sometimes a metaphor "plugs the gap in the literal vocabulary" (catachresis) and a metaphor often creates a similarity rather than implying an existing one, thus extending meaning. Metaphors can be seen as filters, or organizational maps, through which we view the subject. Interactive metaphors are not replaceable and their interpretation may vary with culture and context.[16] In a later work, Black assigns a high

---

15. "The exchange between the meanings of words which we study in explicit verbal metaphors, are super-imposed upon a perceived world which is itself a product of earlier or unwitting metaphor"; Richards, *Philosophy of Rhetoric*, 93, 108, 119, 125, 135.

16. Black summarizes: A metaphorical statement has two distinct subjects—a "principle" subject and a "subsidiary" one; these subjects are often best regarded as "systems of things," rather than "things"; the metaphor works by applying to the principle subject a system of "associated implications" characteristic of the subsidiary subject; *Models and Metaphors*, 33, 40, 44.

cognitive function to metaphors. He describes three types: extinct (no longer recognizable as metaphor), dormant (not recognizable as metaphor but easily explained), and active (easily discerned as metaphor).[17] Black's work has been highly influential. He opened the way for a new view of metaphor and there have subsequently been multiple studies on metaphor.[18]

Ricoeur follows Black's interaction theory in advocating a strong cognitive function of language and multiplicity of meaning. He prefers the term "metaphorical statement" and notes that metaphor is fundamental to language, a vehicle of truth, involving movement from one concept to another. Ricoeur believes meaning is derived by looking beyond words: "Metaphor is a semantic event that takes place at the point where several semantic fields intersect"; "its place in language is between words and sentences."[19] He thinks that metaphor reduces deviation (against Aristotle) by limiting the possible meanings of words through association with others. Metaphor involves the notion of resemblance but not simple substitution; it bears information. Ricoeur uses the term "semantic impertinence," claiming a "semantic shock" results in new meaning, a "semantic innovation."[20] He describes the original function of metaphor: "The rhetorical process by which discourse unleashes the power that certain fictions have to redescribe reality," metaphor thus has "ontological vehemence."[21]

Theologian Janet Soskice follows the interaction theory and adds valuable clarifications. She agrees that metaphor involves an association of terms, however, unlike Black, notes that not all metaphors contain two distinct subjects (e.g., a "writhing script"). In particular she opposes the idea that all metaphors are dual-directional.[22] Soskice believes metaphor only has one meaning, that intended by the speaker. "Either we understand

17. Black, "More about Metaphors," 19–43.

18. Although he has been criticized for being imprecise and ambiguous. Soskice and Macky think his idea that both subjects can be changed does not fit with his idea of the metaphor as a filter, which presumably could not be changed; Soskice, *Metaphor and Religious Language*, 42–47; Macky, *Centrality of Metaphors*, 45. For a bibliography on metaphor, see van Noppen, *Metaphor*, and van Noppen and Holls, *Metaphor II*.

19. Ricoeur, *Rule of Metaphor*, 7, 65, 76–78, 80, 98, 133.

20. Ibid., 95, 152, 247.

21. Ricoeur believe both metaphor and metaphysics allude to a reality beyond the obvious; ibid., 7, 22, 245, 257–313.

22. She suggests returning to Richard's view of "interanimation" in that metaphor has only one subject. "It is only be seeing that a metaphor has one true subject which tenor and vehicle conjointly depict and illumine that a full, interactive, or interanimative theory is possible"; Soskice, *Metaphor and Religious Language*, 20, 47.

[a] passage as a metaphor or we do not understand it." Metaphors function in the background, like a river, providing a frame for literal language; all speech requires metaphor. Her definition is simple: "Metaphor is that figure of speech whereby we speak about one thing in terms which are seen to be suggestive of another."[23] Soskice notes that metaphor incorporates semantic as well as syntactic dimensions, semantic being the smallest unit of a metaphor; metaphors are fully cognitive. Therefore metaphors, unlike literal terms, do not appear in dictionaries. Unlike Ricoeur, who states that metaphor "redescribes" reality, Soskice believes metaphor often discloses something anew. Metaphors are not descriptively exhaustive, but can offer partial depictions of reality.[24]

CONCEPTUAL METAPHORS

Following from the interaction theory is the conceptual view of metaphor developed by linguist George Lakoff and philosopher Mark Johnson. In the aptly titled, *Metaphors We Live By*, they argue that metaphors are much more than words but permeate everyday thought and action. Conceptual metaphors are systematic and based on conceptual correspondence between two ideas, not simply similarities. For instance, the metaphor "life is a journey" incorporates other metaphors like babies "arriving" and the dead "departing." In another example, "time is money" ("living on borrowed time," "that flat tire cost me an hour"), they explain how one idea can incorporate a "coherent system of metaphorical expressions." Lakoff and Johnson believe conceptual metaphors allow us to organize experiences and conversations into a multidimensional structured whole. Each metaphor provides a partial picture; together they provide a coherent understanding of a whole concept. Conceptual metaphors usually have internal consistency and coherency; many metaphors can structure one concept.[25] Metaphors contribute to categorization and generally correlate with experience. Lakoff and Johnson note that container and spatialization metaphors are universal, rooted in common physical and

23. Soskice, *Metaphor and Religious Language*, 15, 51, 85.

24. Ibid., 44, 56, 68, 89, 133.

25. Lakoff and Johnson, *Metaphors We Live By*, 5, 9, 81, 89, 97. Unlike Soskice who claims metaphors are only linguistic, they believe metaphors are neurological phenomena and note in their afterward that the conceptual theory of metaphor is supported by recent developments in neural theory which connect the development of cognitive associations with neural pathway formation. These develop in childhood and are universal (254–56).

cultural experience. Territoriality is a basic human instinct; our bodies, houses, land, and even nature (a "clearing in the woods") are containers.[26] Metaphors can also enhance meaning. Lakoff and Johnson believe metaphors *create* similarity, rather than describing existing similarity. Abstract ideas particularly are largely expressed metaphorically. A metaphor highlights some features while suppressing others. Thus the "life is a journey" metaphor minimizes a journey's destination aspects and provides a new understanding of life. Lakoff and Johnson discount the notion of objective truth, believing it to be relative to our conceptual systems. There is seldom clear correspondence between metaphors and literal truth; metaphors are mostly irreducible and nontranslatable, and truth dependent on categorization systems. They claim experientially-based metaphorical systems offer a middle-way between absolute objectivity and subjectivity.[27] This view of language as part of thought processes (cognitive semantics), and metaphor as a factor in our categorization of our world has been enormously influential and has opened channels between linguistics and other disciplines.[28]

Sallie McFague follows the conceptual view of metaphor and introduces the term "metaphorical theology." She defines metaphor as "an assertion or judgment of similarity and difference between two thoughts in permanent tension with one another, which redescribes reality in an open-ended way but has structural as well as affective power."[29] Metaphor is related to concepts ("abstract notions" which rely on conventional meaning) and models, but McFague insists there should be no hierarchy

26. Ibid., 17–30. Especially relevant to this study.

27. Ibid., 140–42, 159–61; unfortunately they do not define "literal." Furthermore, "we understand our world through our interactions with it" (194).

28. Despite the success of their work, Lakoff and Johnson lament that twenty-three years later fallacies still persist: metaphors being seen as words, based on similarities, not concepts, and that all concepts are literal (ibid., 244). They have been criticized for having a radical view of metaphor in seeing all language as essentially metaphorical and ascribing it too much power. They do not consider contextual limitations on metaphor, such as situation, authorial intent, or rhetoric; e.g., Macky, *Centrality of Metaphor*, 138–42.

29. McFague, *Metaphorical Theology*, 42. Her aim is to provide contemporary Christians with alternative (nonmasculine) images of God. She has been criticized for viewing all biblical language and theology as metaphorical. Macky claims that McFague is too radical in her assertion that all thought is metaphorical; *Centrality of Metaphor*, 138–42. D. Bromell notes she is unclear regarding the relationship between the mystery of reality, metaphorical language, and abstract metaphysical thought; "Review, 'Metaphorical Theology,'" 485–503.

among them. She also points out the dangers of having only one metaphor: it can be overused, the original referent forgotten and the metaphorical tension lost. The terms become part of ordinary language, known as a dead, extinct, or conventional metaphor (e.g., the "legs" of a table, a "field" of research).[30] Macky defines metaphor as "that figurative way of speaking . . . in which one reality . . . is depicted in terms that are more commonly associated with a different reality." He suggests combining views to assist in interpretation, especially of spiritual reality. Metaphors are like having multiple snapshots of a scene. Typically, metaphor works because we know one realm better than the other one.[31]

Related to conceptual metaphors is the notion of semantic domains. In this idea, associated meanings of words cluster to form a field of meaning. "In metaphor, two otherwise unrelated conceptual domains are brought into contact in a manner specified through the use of the linguistic notion of a semantic field."[32] Metaphors can move across different fields of meaning. Semantic domains assist with language categorization and organization, and semantic frames provide a structured background to comprehend word or sentence meaning.[33] To summarize, contemporary metaphor theory claims that metaphors have semantic power. They are cognitive and conceptual, can provide new meaning, and aid in our organization of concepts. Metaphors function to describe reality in a manner not possible with literal language. The idea of semantic domains elucidates and extends conceptual metaphor theory. Multiple metaphors used to describe one concept relate to each other within one field of meaning and

---

30. McFague, *Metaphorical Theology*, 38–41. Religious language is prone to this occurrence because of its repetition of terms biblically and historically. McFague describes three stages of metaphor use: novel and surprising, living and insightful, commonplace and dead. Macky similarly thinks it is essential to distinguish between retired metaphors and hidden metaphors, which can sabotage thinking because the reader believes the term to be literal. Furthermore, theological language is prone to this error; *Centrality of Metaphor*, 153.

31. Macky, *Centrality of Metaphor*, 49, 114.

32. Kittay and Lehrer, "Semantic Fields," 31, 59; see also Kittay, *Metaphor*.

33. In later works, Lakoff expands the idea of conceptual metaphor to incorporate semantic domain and metaphorical mapping. Understanding involves correlating aspects of one field with those of another; Lakoff, *Women, Fire*; Lakoff and Turner, *More than Cool Reason*. Another recent idea is "conceptual blending," proposed by Fauconnier and Turner in *The Way We Think*. This is seen as an overarching frame with which we organize thoughts. New meaning is derived from blending already known ideas with new ones. Metaphor is seen as a subset of conceptual blending and is more stable than blends that represent emergent thinking. Fauconnier and Turner claim that conceptual blending is both physiological and cultural.

there is coherence between different metaphors. This leads to a discussion of models.

Models

Black equates models and metaphors. The former, especially when applied in science, always imply an interaction between two ideas. He describes various types of models, the theoretical (which attempts to describe unseen reality or explain observed phenomena) being the most relevant.[34] The model is taken from a familiar realm and applied to an unfamiliar one; one is used as a lens through which to see the other. Both model and metaphor require "analogical transfer of vocabulary"; a model is like a "sustained and systematic metaphor."[35] Scientist-theologian Ian Barbour defines model as "an imaginative tool for ordering experience."[36] Models should be intelligible as a unit and allow for extension of a theory. They function to understand reality and often make ontological claims or offer a partial view of reality. Like metaphors and symbols, models are analogical and open-ended but have a broader scope. Barbour notes that in contemporary science many phenomena require more than one model, often complementary; the classic example being light as both particle and wave.[37]

McFague, like Black, views models as dominant metaphors; "organizing networks of images," "comprehensive ways of envisioning reality," "sustained and systematic metaphors," and "comprehensive metaphors

34. E.g., Bohr's model of the atom; Black, *Models and Metaphors*, 219–39. The other types include scale (like a model train), analogue (usually involving a change of medium, like electrical circuits in computers), and mathematical (a simpler, more abstract form of the original but offering no explanation).

35. Black, *Models and Metaphors*, 236, 238.

36. Barbour, *Myths, Models*, 6; or a "symbolic representation of selected aspects of the behavior of a complex system for particular purposes"; see also Barbour, *Religion and Science*. He agrees that theoretical models are most applicable to religion. These are "postulated by analogy with familiar mechanisms or processes and used to construct a theory to correlate a set of observations"; *Myths, Models*, 30. Theologian John Goldingay has a somewhat similar definition: "a model is an image or construct that helps us grasp aspects of these realities by providing us with something we can understand that has points of comparison with the object we wish to understand, thus helping us get our mind round its nature"; *Models for Scripture*, 7.

37. Barbour, *Myths, Models*, 27, 75–77. He lists similarities between scientific and religious models: both are analogical, help explain observations, offer partial views of reality and recognize that experience is interpreted.

with organizing, structural potential."[38] Models consider relationships between different aspects of reality and offer an indirect but genuine reflection of reality. One concept may require multiple models and there should be no hierarchy among them.[39] Soskice believes metaphors and models are related; both refer to one thing in terms of another: "An object or state of affairs is a model when it is viewed in terms of its resemblance, real or hypothetical, to some other object or state of affairs." In fact, metaphors usually rely on an underlying model, both forming part of an associated network of meaning (semantic domain). Metaphors function to activate models, which extend the metaphor and advance understanding.[40] Vincent Brümmer, in developing his "model of love," prefers the term "key model," which is like a "root metaphor." He helpfully suggests four criteria for developing a comprehensive theological key model: consonance with tradition, comprehensive coherence, adequacy for life, and personal authenticity.[41] Hence the term model can be used synonymously with extended metaphor, dominant metaphor, systematized metaphor, and perhaps, metaphorical framework. The term model is preferable as it is simpler and less confusing and makes no claim to be the only way to understand a concept.

Simile, Analogy, Myth, Worldview, and Cosmology

Models and metaphors can be further understood through a brief review of other types of figurative language, which are peripheral to this study but bear some relationship to metaphors and models. A simile is often defined as a metaphor that makes the comparison explicit by adding "like." It is usually simpler and carries less semantic weight than metaphor, but there are many types of similes, some functioning more like metaphors.[42] A confusing term is analogy which also involves comparisons, but is perhaps

38. McFague, *Metaphorical Theology*, 25, 67, 103, 193.

39. Since models only offer indirect, partial views of reality, more than one is required; ibid., 74. Goldingay concurs it is unwise to seek an overarching model; theology requires a multiplicity of models; *Models for Scripture*, 16.

40. If a metaphor proposes a model, Soskice suggests the appellation "conceptual metaphor" or "theory-constitutive metaphor"; Soskice *Metaphors and Religious Language*, 50–53, 73, 102.

41. Brümmer, *Model of Love*, 20, 24. This is similar to the classic Wesleyan quadrangle of Scripture, tradition, reason, and experience.

42. Soskice thinks it is helpful to distinguish between a simple, or illustrative simile, and a modeling simile, which is like a metaphor; *Metaphor and Religious Language*, 18–19.

more specific and deliberate than metaphor. Soskice notes that analogy only extends existing language, rather than offering new perspectives as metaphor can do.[43] Allegory, present since the early days of biblical interpretation, is often seen as a story told in figurative language that could be easily translated into literal language.[44] Theory is a term usually related to science, which involves proposing a hypothesis to explain certain observable phenomena.[45] Theories are less flexible than metaphors. Paradigm is somewhat similar to theories and models.[46]

At a broader level is myth, which is not quite figurative but overlaps and interacts with metaphors. Myth is frequently misunderstood and regarded as primitive, being equated with untruth; a misconception that likely originated with modernity's mistrust of anything not literal.[47] Myths can be described as stories that function to provide order or explanation to societal difficulties, and are often considered alongside ritual.[48] Barbour views myths as stories about cosmic order, which serve to order experience and are usually acted out in rituals. They have social, psychological, and structural functions; myth, metaphor, and model are interrelated.[49]

43. Ibid., 64. Macky defines analogy as "a relationship between two realities in which there are significant similarities and noticeable differences"; *Centrality of Metaphor*, 56.

44. Bunyan's *Pilgrim's Progress* is a classic example; Caird, *Imagery of the Bible*, 161–71. It usually has quite specific applications but can be ambiguous. As figurative language, it often contains metaphors; the primary difference being that many metaphors are irreducible and nontranslatable. Parables can be understood as allegories.

45. In the early days of biblical interpretation, it was used similarly to allegory, or related to the deeper meaning of a text; Grant, *Interpretation of the Bible*, 66. Barbour thinks a good theory should be simple, coherent, and consistent with experimental observations; *Myths, Models*, 92–95.

46. Thomas Kuhn, who brought attention to paradigms and paradigm shifts in science, suggests paradigms are similar to theories and accepted models; they usually develop in community; *Structure of Scientific Revolutions*, 17, 23, 47.

47. Modernity, associated with the Scientific Revolution, had a high regard for observable and measurable "truth." A classic example is Bultmann (*Primitive Christianity*), who viewed myth in opposition to science, hence to be dismissed. Bultmann's method has generally been discredited.

48. Segal, *Myth*. Lévi-Strauss defines myth as "a logical model capable of overcoming a contradiction"; *Structural Anthropology*, 1, 229. The "myth and ritual" school, pioneered by anthropologist Robertson Smith, examines rituals in order to discover the underlying creed or myth; *Religions of the Semites*; Segal *Myth and Ritual Theory*.

49. Barbour, *Myths, Models*, 5, 20–23. Maurice Wiles believes myths should not be evaluated as "true or false" like scientific theories, but that more than one interpretation is possible; they contain "some ontological truth corresponding to the central characteristics of the structure of the myth"; "Myth in Theology," 148–66.

In biblical studies, myth can be considered a technical term for a story whose primary purpose is theological, not historical. As Brevard Childs says, myth "concerns itself with showing how an action of a deity, conceived of as occurring in the primeval age, determines a phase of contemporary world order. Existing world order is maintained through the actualization of the myth in the cult."[50] However, myth has multiple confusing associations. G. B. Caird believes myth functions to provide an interpretive framework for life, but that myth is surrounded by a "fog of misunderstanding" caused by its pejorative use.[51] Barbour advises avoiding the term since people find it difficult to take its cognitive function seriously and usually believe myth to be untrue.[52] A better approach is probably to use myth only with its classic/biblical understanding.

Worldview is another term frequently used and seldom elucidated. David Naugle defines it as "a network of narrative signs that offers an interpretation of reality and establishes an overarching framework for life."[53] The term worldview is broad and can be ambiguous. A related term is cosmology, which has two general definitions (Greek etymology, "to make rational sense of the world"): the scientific/technical view that investigates the evolution and structure of universe, and the pre-modern/mythic/biblical view that attempts to locate the human drama within the universe.[54] Biblical cosmology incorporates metaphor, is relevant to creation theology, and is often used with respect to the spirit world. A final broad term is biblical theology, the methodology Boyd uses in *God at War*,

---

50. Childs, *Myth and Reality*, 29.

51. Caird, *Imagery of the Bible*, 160. He also notes the inter-relationship between myth, model, and metaphor and views myth as a specialized type of metaphor. In the Bible he believes myth and eschatology are used as metaphorical systems, and were sometimes used to interpret history (219–20).

52. Barbour, *Myths, Models*, 179.

53. Naugle, *Worldview*, 291. Walsh and Middleton identify four basic questions, the answers to which determine a worldview: Who am I? Where am I? What's wrong? What is the remedy? They note that worldviews need to be comprehensive, internally coherent, and match our faith experience; *Transforming Vision*, 36–39. N. T. Wright believes worldviews are profoundly theological. They "provide the *stories* through which human beings view reality"; *NTPG*, 123.

54. The latter is more applicable to this study. Tshishiku offers a helpful, if longwinded, definition: "a general framework for the intellectual and spiritual organization and integration of the world in its totality, within which human beings locate themselves in relation to other beings and set up a system for interpreting their lives, with particular reference to their origin, present development and final destiny"; "Eschatology and Cosmology," 27.

but which evades precise definition.[55] It is described as a bridge discipline between the Bible and doctrine, and is becoming widely accepted. Biblical theology is generally canonical in form and often thematic in structure with an emphasis on continuity. The similarities between worldview, cosmology, and biblical theology are apparent, although the last is perhaps more intentional.

Summary

Biblical examples can be used to summarize the various types of figurative language. "God is love" is a nonfigurative abstract statement; light is a standard symbol for Christ, truth, and goodness; the devil described "like a roaring lion" is a simile; "I am the bread of life" is a simple metaphor; "put on the whole armor of God" is a metaphorical system or model; the "dragon in the sea" is a myth (relating to ANE myths). From the preceding discussion, it can be seen that models, or systemic metaphors, offer an intermediary approach between similes (too small and limited) and worldviews (too broad and potentially ambiguous). They allow for intentionality and precision while maintaining a thematic and broad perspective. Not surprisingly, figurative language has been employed in theology.

Figurative Language and Theology

In the Bible, metaphors and symbols are often used to represent transcendent realities. Most academic work has focused on the use of figurative language in speaking about God: Caird believes almost all language about God is metaphorical,[56] Pierre Grelot points out that symbolic language is essential to theology because God is inaccessible to the senses,[57] and Robert Neville asserts that theology is "best understood as symbolic engagement."[58] Many scholars agree that figurative language is important. For instance, Gene Davenport expresses concern that contemporary Christian culture has lost a sense of transcendence, with a resultant

55. For a review of biblical theology see Scobie, "History of Biblical Theology."

56. Caird, *Imagery of the Bible* 16. Gibson claims the ancient Hebrews accepted that all descriptions of God were metaphorical; *Language and Imagery*, 26.

57. Grelot, *Language of Symbolism*, 15, 18. Symbols evoke aspects of reality, which the spirit intuits and reconstructs.

58. Neville, *Scope of Truth and Theology*, 1. Furthermore, "religious and theological symbols are the building blocks of religious life and its intellectual theology" (43).

trivialization of metaphors and excessive biblical literalism: there is a danger of lost meaning by both rejection and reduction of symbols;[59] Margaret Barker even avows, "if we lose touch with biblical imagery, we lose the real meaning of the Bible."[60] Figurative language used in relation to supersensible reality represents a special case. As discussed, most metaphors involve an interaction between two concepts. However, transcendent reality is unknown. Therefore, the interaction is imbalanced—the weight is on the image that is known. This section examines the views of various scholars with regard to how symbols, metaphors, and models can be used to elucidate the mysterious realities depicted in the Bible. Although most discussions focus on divine reality, the same principles can be applied to demonic reality.[61]

Symbols and Myths

Symbols represent concepts that are often too complicated for literal language, therefore are ideally suited for biblical depiction of supersensible realities (e.g., light and dark). They can have diverse meanings (e.g., water can symbolize chaos/evil or cleansing). Avis asserts that theological endeavors, or any attempts to describe ultimate reality, require symbol (his preferred term), metaphor, and myth.[62] Symbolism has been discussed by OT scholars, especially with reference to the foundational narratives of Israel.[63] Philip Jenson examines the temple with respect

59. Davenport, *Into the Darkness*, 33–34. The NT "perceived symbols as the means by which Truth is conveyed" and there was no distinction between symbol and referent.

60. "Explanation of the images and pictures in which the ideas of the Bible are expressed" is needed; Barker, *On Earth*, 2. Similarly M. Coloe thinks failing to recognize a symbol can lead to misunderstanding; *God Dwells*, 6.

61. Noll, in his discussion of angels and demons, claims: "Myth and metaphor are real ways of describing beings who are hidden from us above the firmament of heaven"; *Angels of Light*, 204. Wa Gatumu also suggests the use of metaphors for discussion of the demonic; "Deliverance and Exorcism," 222–42.

62. Avis, *Creative Imagination*, 144. He believes the Bible is primarily nonliteral, addressed to our imaginative, not analytical faculties (3), and that it is a "literalistic fallacy" that metaphors can be translated into literal terms (100–102). Grelot notes the symbolism of good and evil in the Bible: this imagery "evokes two domains that are radically inaccessible to human experience, or at least to clear definition of the realities they contain"; *Language of Symbolism*, 21.

63. Jon Levenson, in his discussion of temple symbolism, states biblical history is in "service of transcendental truth." Israel's identity was formed through the cosmic symbolism of creation. "Mythic symbols are invulnerable to obsolescence (and) are more 'real' than the flux and change of history"; *Sinai and Zion*, 17, 40–41, 103.

to holiness: "Metaphor, symbol and analogy allow us to understand the lesser known (the Holy God) in terms of the materially constructed (the Holy Tabernacle)."[64] Symbolism in the NT has likewise been addressed. Craig Koester defines a symbol as "an image, an action, or a person that is understood to have transcendent significance"; it spans "the chasm between what is 'from above' and what is 'from below' without collapsing the distinction."[65] He notes that dark/light imagery is fundamental to human experience and can be described as archetypal. There has also been much written about temple symbolism in the Gospels (discussed in chapter 6).

With respect to myth, Mircea Eliade (discussed in chapter 3) pioneered study on myth in diverse religions. He claims "myth narrates a sacred history" as it provides an opening to the superhuman world, the "plane of absolute realities."[66] Avis similarly believes myth functions to make sacred reality accessible: "Myths, which are archetypal stories studded with numinous symbols, embody a sacral narrative of human identity in the face of divine reality."[67] In biblical studies, myths have typically been discussed when comparing the people of God with their neighbors; for example, Ronald Simkins describes Israel's stories of beginning and end as mythological, incorporating ANE creation myths.[68]

Metaphors

Biblical metaphors include ornamental, comparative, retired/dead, hidden, familiar, standard, and novel metaphors.[69] Recall that metaphors

---

64. Jenson, "Holiness," 93–121. He further believes that "metaphor, not mysticism, is the way forward."

65. However, an element of mystery remains; Koester, *Symbolism*, 4, 29, 141. He believes there is a continuum between symbols and metaphors, the latter being more abstract (5–7). Symbols frame daily life and function to describe transcendent reality. Texts are often simultaneously symbolic and historical. Because of the multivalent nature of symbols, interpretation is complex and dependent on context (16–26).

66. Eliade, *Myth and Reality*, 5, 139.

67. Avis, *Creative Imagination*, 11. "Realities beyond our ken must be depicted in symbol and myth or else not at all" (160). Ricoeur notes that symbols are often uprooted from myths; with respect to evil, myths usually function to provide order; *Symbolism of Evil*, 161.

68. Simkins, *Creator and Creation*, 43–45. He believes myth to be a collection of metaphors in narrative form.

69. As well as simple similes; Macky, *Centrality of Metaphor*, 58–86.

are now viewed as conceptual, capable of illuminating reality in ways literal language cannot. Thus, like symbols, they are an essential tool used by biblical writers for conveying truths about transcendent realities. Caird emphasizes the cognitive function of religious language, "illumination of the unknown by the known."[70] Soskice stresses the semantic function of metaphor and believes its explanatory nature is particularly applicable to religious language. Metaphor is the primary way in which we speak about God and the set of meanings associated with such metaphors can in fact improve our comprehension of the "unknowable" God. Her assertion that not all metaphors are dual-directional is helpful in this regard, since our knowledge of divine reality is limited. Soskice is cautious regarding reality depiction; metaphors can point to divine reality, but do not provide comprehensive descriptions. She has a helpful hermeneutic: "sacred literature . . . both records the experiences of the past and provides the descriptive language by which any new experience may be interpreted."[71] Macky believes metaphor is powerful, especially with respect to theological discourse. Some things can be said literally about reality, but language about supersensible realities usually requires nonliteral language, and metaphorical language can be understood without translation into literal language.[72] For example, biblical authors assert that God is real, immortal, and eternal, but these "literal" statements are very general; metaphor is often needed for elucidation. Kevin Vanhoozer, in discussing hermeneutics, agrees: "To discern the fittingness between biblical and contemporary performances requires the creativity of metaphor as well as a good grasp of Scripture's literal sense."[73]

There have been many recent studies of biblical metaphors.[74] Although most do not reference metaphor theory, some have invoked it. Nelly Stienstra, for example, uses a conceptual view of metaphor in her

70. Caird, *Imagery of the Bible* 16.

71. Soskice, *Metaphor and Religious Language*, x, 141, 148, 160.

72. Macky, *Centrality of Metaphor*, 145, 183–85, 240; see also Soskice, *Metaphor*, 152–53,.

73. Vanhoozer, *Drama of Doctrine*, 261. Metaphors have a "surplus of cognition"; "relatively determinate meaning without being exhaustively specifiable" (88); metaphorical imagination allows us to see similarities between "then" and "now" (261, 317). J. B. Russell uses the term "metaphorical ontology" noting that, in the ancient world, metaphor was understood to express a "deeper reality than can be attained through the overt sense"; *History of Heaven*, 8.

74. E.g., Jäkel, "Mortal Man," 55–86; Van Hecke, *Metaphor in the Hebrew Bible*; Burke, *Adopted into God's Family*; Gan, *Shepherd in the Hebrew Bible*.

study *YHWH is the Husband of His People*. When applied to an ancient text, "careful analysis of a metaphorical concept is a good way of bridging the gap between two cultures." However, she points out the limitations of conceptual metaphor theory with respect to theology, since the field of meaning around God is unknown. Hence one domain may be rich with meaning in order to describe another, which is lacking in meaning.[75] Gunton, in his study on the atonement, believes "the world can only be known indirectly, and therefore metaphor, being indirect, is the most appropriate form that a duly humble and listening language should take."[76]

Models

Barbour notes that religious models incorporate noncognitive dimensions (awe, mystical union), are personal, and thus may be more influential; such models arise from belief, but may lead to different beliefs. He concludes that "thinking in models may be a useful point of entry into theological reflection."[77] McFague asserts that, unlike science, which aims for new discovery, the goal of theology is "comprehension of all reality by means of a root metaphor and its dominant models." "Theological models are dominant metaphors with systematic, comprehensive potential for understanding the many facets of the relationship between the divine and the human."[78] They survive if they succeed in making human experience understandable. In fact, religious models are only effective if they have explanatory power. McFague suggests that metaphors and models can bridge the gap between religion and theology. Macky's definition is interesting: "A model is a symbol that is established enough in its use with a particular subject (e.g., father with God) for some of the parallels to have

75. Stienstra, *YHWH*, 32, 234. She concurs "that metaphors express truths that cannot be expressed otherwise" (19). S. Dille believes "the literal meaning of 'God' is an unknown apart from metaphor or analogy" and concludes metaphors are best understood when viewed in relationship to each other: "By the interweaving of metaphors, *the text creates coherence* not previously evident"; *Mixing Metaphors*, 15, 18.

76. Gunton, *Atonement*, 17, 37. He laments that theology has been dominated by a literal view of metaphor precluding biblical metaphors being viewed as depicting the reality of God (42) and claims "metaphor . . . operates in the space between what has happened and what is promised" (82).

77. Barbour, *Myths, Models*, 119–21, 179.

78. McFague, *Metaphorical Theology*, 104, 125. She believes that religious models are particularly prone to idolatry if one model becomes dominant at the expense of others (130).

been worked out and become conventional."[79] Like others, he notes the interrelationship of metaphor, model, symbol, and analogy, but adds the feature of conventionality to models. This last factor is problematic because it precludes the development of new models, which in fact is inherent to scientific research and helpful to theological research. Models have been utilized in theological research, although not as commonly as metaphors.[80]

Summary

Evidently, symbols, metaphors, and models are invaluable to theological endeavors. They occur frequently in the Bible, offer richer information than literal language, illuminate sacred reality, can aid our comprehension of the world, and assist in interpretation of new experiences. Such language is particularly useful for discussing supersensible reality, but also needs to be considered in relation to truth and reality.

Models, Metaphors, History, Truth, and Reality

Language is meaningful only if it points to reality beyond itself. But, how and if this happens is not simple. The preceding discussion has touched on the correspondence between figurative language and reality but it is worth expanding on this point, especially the relationship between literal and historical, and the nature of truth and reality.

Literal-Historical

Literal is often defined as that which is obvious to most people, is in common usage, can be found in a dictionary, and requires no further explanation. Unfortunately, the term is inherently ambiguous. Literal can be equated with the empirical, observable sense of a term, or with the conventional, traditional sense. Ambiguity is worsened by the neglect of many authors to define the term. Ricoeur is one exception; he equates literal with the conventional sense of a word.[81] Macky disagrees with defining

---

79. Macky, *Centrality of Metaphors*, 55.

80. E.g., Brümmer, *The Model of Love*; Goldingay, *Models for Scripture*.

81. Ricoeur, *Rule of Metaphor*, 291. Soskice similarly equates literal with accustomed usage and suggests that literal terms, unlike metaphors, may appear in dictionaries; *Metaphor and Religious Language*, 68, 83.

literal as empirical or conventional because this is imprecise and does not account for neologisms or established metaphors. He argues instead for literal as the communicable, independent use of a term.[82] Avis points out that many literal words are dead metaphors. He suggests not making the distinction at all, but to consider language on an imaginative continuum.[83] D. H. Aaron, in his work on divine imagery, notes that "most figurative rhetorical devices thrive on ambiguity." He points out the errors that metaphor theorists make in omitting guidelines for determining whether language is figurative or not, and that biblical scholars make in their assignation of texts as literal or nonliteral. Aaron suggests that instead of assuming a binary attribution (literal/nonliteral), the gradient nature of meaning in biblical texts should be recognized.[84] Clearly, the definition of literal is unclear, and Avis and Aaron are perhaps correct that it is unhelpful and/or unnecessary to choose between literal and figurative language. To add to the confusion, there is often a truth assumption underlying literal language; "literal truth" is automatically considered superior. As Caird rightly notes, "any statement, literal or metaphorical, may be true or false, and its referent may be real or unreal."[85] As discussed above, many scholars believe metaphors provide more truth than literal language, particularly with respect to religion. Avis states it well: "The greatest truths can only be expressed in imaginative form."[86]

Perhaps a more helpful distinction than literal/nonliteral is between metaphor and history. Biblical literary criticism determines the genre of a text (e.g., historical, mythical) to aid in interpretation. However, frequently history and metaphor overlap. Macky points out that "twice true metaphors" are common in the Bible; for example, the Good Samaritan story is quite possibly historically true, but more importantly has a deeper symbolic, pedagogical truth.[87] Avis similarly argues that myth and history are intertwined. Myth can be used to interpret history and vice versa (e.g., the resurrection is both mythical and historical).[88] Others have

82. Macky, *Centrality of Metaphor*, 32–39.

83. Avis, *Creative Imagination,* 101–2.

84. Aaron, *Biblical Ambiguities*, 1, 110–12. He specifies a gradient, which moves towards increasing ambiguity: literal meaning, weakly figurative, strongly figurative, and nonsense.

85. Caird, *Imagery of the Bible,* 131.

86. Avis, *Creative Imagination*, 8, 11.

87. Macky, *Centrality of Metaphor,* 68.

88. Avis, *Creative Imagination,* 60. Forsyth agrees that myth should not be

noted how ancient Israel reinterpreted ANE myths historically and did not feel compelled to distinguish between history and myth.[89] Thus, if a text is considered primarily metaphorical, it may be simultaneously historical. Discussion of a model, or symbolic representation of reality, is possible without making any historical assertions. Metaphorical assertion does not preclude truth assertion. Since the literal/nonliteral dichotomy is unclear and perhaps on a continuum, it is arguably not necessary to make this distinction. And since symbols, metaphors, and models can depict reality at least as well as literal language, it is not critical to distinguish between literal and metaphorical.

Truth and Reality

Although truth can have a simple sense of honesty, it can also be equated with the broader term reality. Truth should have explanatory power and can be viewed as correspondence with reality, even if indirect.[90] The philosophical literature is vast on this topic. Briefly, reality can be known through observation or inference. Inference incorporates knowledge of unseen realities that have observable effects (e.g., particle physics) and education through experts (e.g., geography). Divine reality is known through general or natural revelation (creation), authoritative, inspired, historical revelation (the Bible), and experiential revelation (like visions). Revelation through the Bible, which is inferential, is the prime focus of this study.

Linguistics and postmodernism have both complicated and clarified our understanding of reality. Two general theories can be described: universalism—the view that reality is known objectively and can be expressed through language (sometimes called the correspondence theory of truth), and relativism—the belief that everyone's reality is determined by their language. A similar approach is realism (the belief that there is something "out there" to be known) versus nominalism or anti-realism (the belief that language consists of arbitrary tags unattached to reality, typical of postmodernism). Realism can be further divided into naive realism (objective reality is perceived as is) and critical realism ("reality is apprehended by the human mind, which attempts to express and accommodate that reality

---

pitted against history; *Old Enemy,* 9; Coloe notes that in John symbol and history are intertwined; *Household of God,* 17.

89. E.g., Anderson, *Creation versus Chaos,* 15.

90. Russell, "Barbour's Methodological Breakthrough," 46.

as best it can with the tools at its disposal—such as mathematical formulae or mental models").[91] Critical realism both responds to an existing reality and offers an explanation of that reality.[92] Interestingly, science draws conclusions about reality without clear evidence (e.g., scientists cannot see quarks, but assert their existence based on experimentation). Some aspects of reality may exist but not be observable.[93] This is especially relevant to a study of transcendent realities. Critical realism allows for a diversity of descriptions, incorporates imaginative language, and resists the notion that there is only one correct view.

Recall that metaphors and models have semantic power and are proficient at depicting reality, thus are compatible with critical realism. Many theologians adopt a critical realist position. Soskice advocates cautious realism in that metaphors offer only indirect, sometimes general and vague, perspectives on reality.[94] I concur that critical realism is the most viable alternative: it offers a middle ground between the extremes of naive realism and anti-realism, is easily and intuitively understandable, and is applicable to biblical interpretation. Language has an effect on how we view reality and can provide fresh perspectives on reality, but language does not construct reality. If we acknowledge that there is a reality that is separate and distinct from language, then figurative language can be used to understand or provide a framework for understanding that reality.

Furthermore, reality can be described as stratified or multi-leveled.[95] Metaphors, symbols, and models can provide different views of the many dimensions of reality. This is particularly applicable to multidimensional, transcendent realities. The spirit world, being unseen, is often neglected

91. McGrath, *Science of God*, 141. He claims realism is ontological, epistemological, and semantic; *Scientific Theology*. 1, 75. Barbour is often credited with originating the concept of critical realism as a bridge between science and theology; Russell, "Barbour's Methodological Breakthrough," 45. Russell summarizes aspects of critical realism: the ubiquitous role of metaphor, hypothetico-deductive methodology, a hierarchy of disciplines, a commitment to referentiality and a theory of truth combining correspondence, coherence, and pragmatism (53).

92. McGrath, *Science of God*, 153. The "thing known is something other than the knower" but our access to this reality is only through dialogue between the knower and the thing known"; Wright, *NTPG*, 35.

93. E.g., McGrath, *Science of God*, 145.

94. Soskice, *Metaphor and Religious Language*, 136, 141. Macky uses the term "critical metaphoricalism" in association with critical realism; metaphors, with proper interpretation, can give insight into reality; *Centrality of Metaphors*, 183–85.

95. E.g., McGrath, *Science of God*, 146–52 (he uses the term stratified), McFague, *Metaphorical Theology*, 5.

as a layer of reality, but it is important to include it. Symbols and metaphors are the primary (not the only) manner in which these realities are described in the Bible. Understanding biblical figurative language can enhance our comprehension of this reality. Furthermore, there is a subtle interplay between the development of biblical models and the comprehension of reality. If new metaphors are found, new conceptions of reality are possible. Gunton notes: "It is not that metaphor *precedes* discovery, helping to make it possible but rather that new language and discovery happen together, with metaphor serving as the *vehicle* of discovery."[96]

Summary

Given the difficulties inherent in differentiating literal/nonliteral language, I suggest it is not necessary to do so but rather to emphasize that nonliteral language provides better access to supersensible reality. It is also unnecessary to make an historical/nonliteral distinction because many biblical truths can be both historical and metaphorical. Furthermore, it is important to recognize that reality is multidimensional and a critical realist position offers the best perspective on reality; this correlates well with a metaphorical approach to theology.

Metaphors, Models, and "Spiritual Warfare"

Recalling the discussion in chapter 1 regarding the problems with "spiritual warfare" and viewing it in the context of metaphor theory, it should be apparent that "spiritual warfare" both biblically and extra-biblically is in fact a metaphorical system or model. Since most language about God is metaphorical, it makes sense that language about other spiritual realities would be metaphorical. Given the chaotic, dis-creative and ungodly nature of evil, metaphors are likely the only way it can be depicted. However, "spiritual warfare" literature seldom mentions the term "metaphor"; when it does, the understanding of metaphor is usually outmoded. Boyd, for example, insists that demons and cosmic forces are "real" spiritual beings, and not "mere metaphors."[97] Often "spiritual warfare" is either assumed to be literal (not usually claimed) or assumed to be the only

96. Gunton, *Atonement,* 31. Stienstra agrees: "changing a metaphor involves changing the concept it structures"; *YHWH,* 66.

97. Boyd, *God at War,* 89, 91. He appears to think that "spiritual warfare" is not a metaphor or model.

available model with which to discuss demonology and deliverance. As discussed above, the danger of having only one metaphor is that it can be overused and the original referent forgotten. With common metaphors, like "legs" of a table, there is little concern if they become conventional. With biblical metaphors, however, there are potential problems: original insight is lost, the term overreaches its intent, and alternative metaphors are neglected. I believe this is what has happened with "spiritual warfare." The model has been so assumed in contemporary Christianity that its original use as a metaphor has been forgotten. "Spiritual warfare" has become the primary, perhaps *only*, way in which encounters with demons are described, as opposed to being only one snapshot of a complex reality. The dangers are similar to those of dead metaphors with the added concern that warfare language has socio-political implications. Metaphors are helpful, but potentially dangerous if they are used unconsciously. As Anthony Thistleton warns, "what misleads us is not simply the power of a model or metaphor as such, but the fact that all too often our way of seeing a particular problem is wholly dictated by a *single controlling* picture" which exercises a spell over us.[98] I believe it is essential that "spiritual warfare" be used with full awareness of the limits of metaphors. Using more than one model can guard against the overuse of warfare language, and enrich our understanding of evil spirits.

Conclusion and Application

A broad goal of theology is the comprehension of reality. Recall that demonology is an important if somewhat neglected topic in academic theology, and there are many problems associated with "spiritual warfare" literature. The aim of this study is to increase our understanding of unseen evil reality through developing an alternative model to "spiritual warfare." Since the Bible contains abundant figurative language, and since symbol, metaphor, and model offer depictions of supersensible realities not possible with literal language, it makes sense to utilize this methodology. My intent is to use a thematic approach to find meaning in the biblical texts based on linguistic studies, particularly metaphor theory.[99] Using metaphors/models as a hermeneutical tool does not discount the importance

98. Thistleton, *Two Horizons*, 432.

99. Others who have used a thematic approach (not explicitly metaphorical) and whose work I will draw upon include Boyd, *God at War*; Beale, *Temple*; and Dumbrell, *Search for Order*.

of biblical exegesis and theological reflection on biblical texts. The process can be seen as a "dialectical movement between theology and Scripture," involving a "progressive hermeneutical spiral."[100] Although I am emphasizing unity and continuity, I am not unaware of the diversity within the Bible. As mentioned, there is often a need for more than one model on any particular topic. My model may complement the current "spiritual warfare" model.

To reiterate, I am adopting a critical realist position assuming reality can be known but not perfectly; language may influence our conception of reality, but is not determined by it. Furthermore, reality is multi-layered and there are aspects of it which are not accessible to the senses but which can be known through imagery. In fact, symbols, metaphors, and models (given the overlap between terms, sharp distinctions between them are unnecessary) are the primary way in which this reality can be known and may be easier to understand than literal or abstract descriptions of unseen reality. Symbols are "more real" than "literal" descriptions and can be viewed as revelatory. Biblical metaphors are complex, cognitive, and conceptual, offering an indispensable tool for understanding transcendent reality. They are multivalent, typically originating from universal experiences, and illuminate the unknown via the known. Hence the spiritual realm can be described using images from the physical realm; for example, spatial metaphors like "outside" or visual metaphors like "darkness." Metaphors can provide new information regarding an unknown reality and act as a vehicle for discovery. They offer a partial picture of reality, which can be enhanced through using multiple metaphors within one semantic domain (related by synonymy and antonymy). Hence evil can be understood through metaphors such as darkness, chaos, and sin, as well as its opposite metaphors such as light, order, and obedience, which describe the domain "holy." Multiple metaphors offer multiple snapshots of super-sensible realities.

Models incorporate symbols and metaphors and offer an imaginative perspective on reality, an organizing network of images or tool for ordering reality. Like symbols and metaphors, they move from the familiar to the unfamiliar and provide a semantically rich representation of reality. They are especially helpful in elucidating supersensible reality. Models not only aid in understanding biblical reality, but can provide a framework for interpreting new experiences. They should be simple, consistent, and coherent, concurring with both tradition and experience. Like symbols

---

100. Hart, "Tradition, Authority," 191.

and metaphors, models make some ontological claims. They can provide a useful point of entry into theological reflection and a bridge between biblical studies and theology.

The aim of this study is to enhance our conceptualization of evil through the development of a biblically-based model. Although models of God have been proposed, there are no explicit "models of evil spirits"; if "spiritual warfare" is considered a model, it is the only one available. I plan to construct a model that depicts supersensible reality not only according to the Bible but that would also be compatible with contemporary experience as well. The universality of some metaphors such as space and light/dark as well as the idea of semantic domain can provide a starting point for finding alternate metaphors. The following chapter seeks insight from theology, anthropology, and science before we embark on a canonical search of the biblical texts for non-warfare themes relating to evil. Perhaps by looking at multiple and diverse biblical imagery within a semantic domain using non-warfare lenses, and creating a biblically-based model, our conceptualization of evil can be enhanced, which may subsequently aid our ministry with respect to evil and evil forces.

3

CHAOS: EVIL IN OPPOSITION TO GOD

> A certain worm of wondrous size ... was full of sores and pus ... the ancient
> serpent overflows with blackness—unfaithfulness and deceit—
> and with sores—uncleanness—and with pus—madness.[1]

EVERYONE HAS EXPERIENCED EVIL, either directly or indirectly. In a
post-WWII and post-9/11 world, ignoring it is not an option. Most
people have also sought to understand evil, crying out to God in their
distress. Definitions and theories abound. But evil, both experientially
and biblically, is complex and can be considered chaotic. Some theologians incorporate this concept in their descriptions of evil, for example,
Henri Blocher, "it is neither really something . . . nor really nothing[;]
. . . it is disharmony . . . ambiguous, unstable, variable,"[2] and N. G. Wright,
the "essential reality" of powers of darkness is "chaotic, non-relational,
depersonalizing and non-ontological."[3] Chaos has three somewhat
related meanings: in common usage it means complete disorder; in
ancient literature, including the OT, it is juxtaposed to cosmos, and is
a metaphor for evil; in science it is used to describe phenomena that
appear disordered but are actually governed by simple rules. Chaos in the
OT will be discussed in the following chapter; this chapter explores the
nature of evil/chaos from a variety of perspectives that will assist subsequent discussions of evil in biblical literature.

1. Hildegarde of Bingen, *Scivias* II.7.3, 7.

2. Blocher, *Evil*, 129–30.

3. N. G. Wright, "Charismatic Interpretations," 158.

"Spiritual warfare" considers evil in opposition to God, but only in terms of action, namely battle. Contemporary linguistics has shown that all language contains structure; elements exist in relationship to each other, including opposition, and provide a way of understanding the world.[4] Metaphor theory in particular insists that metaphors depict reality and are the best, if not the only, way of describing unseen realities. Many metaphors are universal, including spatial and container metaphors, which incorporate the opposition "in/out." Thus evil can be considered in opposition to God not just in terms of warfare, but in spatial/linguistic/metaphorical terms. Subsequent chapters examine the biblical metaphors for evil and how they illuminate our understanding of evil. From this a model is constructed to provide a framework for conceptualizing evil. However, first it is worthwhile to consider alternate metaphors for evil in other fields of study. This chapter therefore explores the definition and nature of evil using insights from anthropology, theology, and science. Some anthropologists and historians of religion consider evil in terms of binary opposition to divine reality. Theologians and philosophers have long struggled with the problem of evil, particularly its ontology. In some ways their insights can be viewed in terms of binary opposition. Finally, contemporary science, especially chaos-complexity theory, can suggest models which may be applied to evil.

Despite its prevalence, evil is challenging to define. Biblically, evil can be considered in binary opposition to goodness.[5] The Lord hides his face because he cannot look upon evil (Deut 31:18; Hab 1:13; 1 Pet 3:12), God's people are advised to hate evil and love good (Job 2:3; Ps 97:10; Amos 5:15), and the fear of the Lord is hatred of evil (Prov 8:13). Evil is the antithesis of holiness and hated by God, who loves righteousness and hates wickedness (Ps 5:5, 45:7; Zech 8:17). It can be overcome by good (Rom 12:21) and whoever does evil has not seen God (3 John 11). Evil is often portrayed as darkness in opposition to light and associated with direction verbs (e.g., "do not walk in the way of evildoers," Prov 4:14). Biblical studies are usually limited to specific aspects of evil: OT studies focus on forces of chaos or pagan nations; NT studies discuss demons in the Gospels and powers in the Pauline Epistles. Philosophical studies tend to dichotomize evil as abstract/concrete or moral/natural; they

---

4. Ferdinand de Saussure, sometimes called the father of linguistics, is generally credited with originating the idea that all language comprises systems of related elements; this structure is usually unconscious; *General Linguistics*.

5. Forsyth notes both the OT Satan and the NT devil have opposition as their root meaning; *Old Enemy*, 4.

seldom mention demonology. There is a need for integration of biblical and theological examinations of evil. The above definition of evil as opposition is broad, potentially encompassing both philosophical and biblical categories, but more importantly not necessitating conceiving evil in such categories. The metaphor "chaos" can incorporate this definition. It is elaborated on through an examination of biblical metaphors for evil and subsequent construction of a model other than "spiritual warfare," both of which can illuminate our understanding of the ontology of evil.

Chaos and Biblical Metaphors

The Bible contains abundant metaphors for evil, but no clear, consistent demonology. Numerous terms are used to describe spiritual forces of evil, some fairly straightforward (e.g., demons), others more obtuse (e.g., powers), some metaphorical (e.g., darkness), others more personal (e.g., Satan). The relationship between metaphors varies greatly. Some are used synonymously (e.g., Satan and the devil), some represent part of a larger group (e.g., Azazel and demons), some apparently overlap (e.g., demons and spiritual forces), some are specific (e.g., Abaddon), and others more general (e.g., darkness). Many metaphors are multivalent. For example, darkness is mostly associated with evil, but sometimes God appears in darkness (storm theophanies). Biblical writers layer metaphors thickly. The psalmists frequently employ parallelism in their descriptions of evil and suffering: darkness, wild animals, pestilence, waste, and terrors of the night (Pss 44:19; 91:5, 6). Isaiah (34:9–15), in a prophecy against the nations, associates chaos, the wilderness, the desert, demons, Lilith, and wild animals; Ezekiel (26:19–21) similarly clusters waste, desolation, the deep, great waters, the pit, and death. In the Gospels, the story of the Gerasene demoniac contains an overabundance of metaphors: demons, death, unclean/wild animals, wilderness, the sea, and the abyss (Matt 8:28—9:1; Mark 5:1–20; Luke 8:26–39). Paul mentions Beliar, darkness, lawlessness, and idolatry in binary opposition to Christ, light, righteousness, and the temple (2 Cor 6:14–16). John also uses multiple metaphors—devil, Satan, dragon, serpent—to describe the ultimate evil being (Rev 12:9, 20:2). Notably, in the new creation, metaphors for evil (darkness, death, sin, the sea) are absent. Biblical authors use images creatively and flexibly, sometimes using a term abstractly, elsewhere personifying it. Most metaphors appear in both OT and NT to varying degrees: the serpent/dragon winds its way through Genesis to Revelation; sin is a perpetual problem;

darkness and chaos continually threaten the good creation; and the nations, the waters, sin, and the demons all tremble at the rebuke of the Lord. The cluster of metaphors within the semantic domain of evil is large and can be summarized as "chaos."[6] Even if terms that have only one reference or are ambiguous are removed, a large number remains; the cluster is sufficiently strong to be unaffected.

The importance of using figurative language to describe unseen realities was discussed previously. Surprisingly, this is usually ignored with reference to evil spirits. Philosopher John Hick argues that it is not even possible to study spiritual beings: "No one can say what the devil is or is not in absolute reality, because we have no propositional access to realities beyond the human mind."[7] He fails to recognize that metaphorical truth is at least as valid as, if not better than, propositional truth. Conversely, others claim much knowledge about demonology, speculating about the precise nature, number, and order of demons. "Spiritual warfare" literature, perhaps because of its inattention to the metaphorical nature of biblical descriptions or ignorance of contemporary metaphor theory, has tended to do this. Some of the difficulties inherent in the multiple and varied biblical metaphors for evil are exacerbated when writers attempt to make clear distinctions between terms, or focus on a few terms (usually NT) to the exclusion of others. Many scholars *do* recognize that multiple terms are needed to describe the complex biblical reality of evil, but do not employ metaphor theory: OT scholar Walter Brueggemann uses the concept of semantic domain implicitly when he claims that the different OT terms for chaos, such as *yam* and Leviathan, can be summarized as death or *nihil*;[8] Pauline scholar Arnold does not refer to the concept of a semantic domain, but in a table listing "the powers of darkness in Paul's letters," includes Satan, devil, evil one, prince, spirit, Belial, the enemy, the serpent, the tempter, the god of this world, angel, principalities, powers, dominion, thrones, world rulers, spiritual hosts, elemental spirits, and de-

---

6. Somewhat similarly, N. G. Wright uses the phrase "powers of darkness" to express the "pervasive and nonhuman aspects of this reality"; *Dark Side,* 41.

7. Hick, *Evil,* 5.

8. Brueggemann, *Theology of OT,* 534. Forsyth similarly notes the cluster of ideas for adversary in the Bible: devil, Satan, something in the way, slander, and accusation; *Old Enemy,* 288. He points out that, late in the Second Temple Period, Semihazah, Azazel, Gadreel, and Sammael all blend to become the devil and Satan in the Adam Books (234). Of the many names associated with the evil one, Azazel, Belial, Lucifer, Sammael, Beelzebub, Apollyon, "god of this world," and "father of lies," Forsyth argues that "Satan," or its Greek equivalent "devil," is the dominant term (4).

mons.[9] Boyd also observes the various terms for evil beings in the Bible, although does not consider metaphors and semantic domains.[10]

Metaphor theory can be invaluable in providing an approach to demonology. Contrary to both those like Hick who claim little can be known and those like popular "spiritual warfare" writers who are overly speculative, metaphor theory asserts that much can be known about evil spiritual realities, but only through multiple metaphors. These do not give precise and detailed descriptions but provide snapshots of a complex reality. OT and NT metaphors can be considered collectively, which may guard against the danger of generalizing from individual metaphors. It is essential first to recognize the value and descriptive power of metaphors, and second, the wide range of biblical metaphors for evil. This can broaden our understanding of evil forces as well as provide alternate non-military language. Using the semantic domain of evil in the Bible plus considering antonyms to evil can help with otherwise confusing biblical evidence. It addresses the problem of the overlap in meaning between terms like powers and demons, darkness and death, or sin and impurity. They all swirl together in the murky waters of evil. Rather than asserting one image over another, learning to live with a variety of metaphors can further our understanding of evil. Terms are fluid and flexible, intertwining but nonetheless exhibiting cohesion. All these metaphors point towards a nebulous reality that is difficult to explain without figurative language. This approach allows us to see the forest, not just the trees, and helps guard against over-speculation while providing valuable insight into the unseen world.

Chaos and Theology

It could be argued that some aspects of theology (e.g., redemption) are pointless apart from the context of evil. However, those who study demonology and those who study theology are often disconnected: theologians seldom consider evil spirits, and "spiritual warfare" advocates seldom consider philosophical aspects of evil. Theology has addressed evil

9. Arnold, *Powers of Darkness,* 218. He uses the Second Temple form of Beliar.

10. He states Leviathan, Rahab, Yamm, hostile waters, the prince of Persia, and Satan are all ways of portraying the sinister force that threatens creation. The terms "Satan," "the devil," "Belial," "Beelzebub," "the evil one," "the enemy," and indirectly, "the great dragon," "the serpent," "Leviathan," and "Azazel" all refer to a supreme angel who rebelled and was cast down to earth where, for a limited time, he seeks to oppose the triune God and his followers; *God at War,* 171, 270.

largely through the lens of philosophy, not metaphor, including the issues of theodicy and the ontology of evil. In this section, I overview and evaluate the differing theodicies in order to contextualize the current study, and then examine the views of Karl Barth in more detail for possible contributions to understanding the ontology of evil.

Theodicy

Despite the myriad biblical metaphors for evil and evil beings, most theological discussion on evil has focused on the justice of God rather than the nature of evil. This dialogue can be conceptualized in two categories: optimism and dualism. There are three variations of an optimistic, monistic view. First, the belief that evil is ordained by God and under his control. This was the classical Augustinian view, perpetuated by Aquinas and Calvin. Evil is seen to serve a greater good and contributes to the perfection of creation.[11] God is completely sovereign and created a world with the optimum balance of good and evil. Hick, following Irenaeus, believes God designed the world with evil as a part of it in order to promote human maturity, or "soul-making."[12] Proponents of this view do not usually consider the ontology of evil or demonology. A second variation of optimism sees evil as "nonbeing," or the absence/privation of good. This view seemed to originate with Aristotle and Plotinus, followed by Origen, Augustine, Aquinas, and Barth. A third variation of optimism is the view that evil is not real but mythological, or a human construct. Wink, and his interpretation of the Pauline powers as the evil interiority of social structures, is a well-known representative of this view.[13] In this perspective, ultimately God is responsible for evil, though many theologians attempt to minimize this conclusion. Optimism minimizes the myriad biblical metaphors for evil, minimizes the biblical portrayal of God's opposition to evil, does not address the anecdotal evidence in "spiritual warfare" literature, and seems inadequate to explain extreme or dysteleological evil, and demonization.

11. To be fair, Augustine's view is more complex and includes the notions of privation of good and free will. This optimistic view was epitomized by Leibnitz's "best possible world" theodicy (he also coined the term "theodicy," referring to the justice of God); Hans Schwarz, *Evil*, 92–115; Blocher, *Evil*, 20–30; Hick, *Evil*, 43–95.

12. Hick, *Evil*, esp. 279–400; see also Blocher, *Evil*, 51–54.

13. Wink's work will be discussed further in chapter 7. Yong has a somewhat similar view although he also is sympathetic to a privation view; *Spirit of Creation*, 219.

Although *some* evil may be beneficial for spiritual growth, it does not logically follow that evil is *necessary* for good to occur.[14]

Dualism is present in the theologies of Luther, Bonhoeffer, Kierkegaaard, and Brunner. Because humans have autonomous freedom, evil is a real possibility and a force that opposes God. God practices self-limitation (kenosis), thus allowing the possibility of evil.[15] This view better incorporates demonology. Edwin Lewis is one theologian who emphasizes the role of Satan as an explanation for evil. He argues against any association of God with evil, since they are "absolute opposites." Evil is greater than sin or free choice, because it is structural "in the very nature of created existence." Instead, Lewis posits three eternal forces: the divine creative, the demonic *dis*creative, and the *un*creative, neutral residue, each limited by the other. Dualism, or the conflict between Creator and Adversary, is fundamental to all aspects of life, even though God is greater than his adversary and has won a victory through Christ.[16] The demonic is immoral, irrational, passive, and parasitic, always seeking to destroy aspects of creation. Humans are influenced by both sides and have the power to choose; they stand "where necessity, history and actuality meet possibility."[17] Lewis is helpful to the study of evil because of his emphasis on the role of evil spirits, and his realistic perspective on experiential evil. However, his assumption of metaphysical dualism greatly undermines the sovereignty of God, making his view untenable for most Christian theologians.[18] He also frequently phrases this dualism in military language, thus is subject to the critiques discussed in chapter 1.[19] Boyd follows a dualistic theology in his "spiritual warfare worldview." Although he avoids the eternal dualism of Lewis, insisting that dualism is limited, his warfare language nevertheless leads to stronger dualistic implications than perhaps Boyd

14. In this I concur with Mallow, *The Demonic*, 160.

15. Blocher, *Evil*, 37–49. The degree of God's self-limitation or sovereignty varies with different theologies: process thought (e.g., Whitehead, Griffin) claims God has persuasive power only; open theists emphasize God's loving limitation and the temporary or provisional nature of the dualism; e.g., Pinnock et al., *Openness of God*; Boyd, *God of the Possible*.

16. Lewis, *Creator and Adversary*, 16, 23, 26, 110, 131, 133, 156, 176, 183, 259.

17. Ibid., 48, 52. He states that "God and the Adversary strive through man for the possession of man" as in a "tug-of-war" (125, 253).

18. To be fair, in labeling the demonic as discreative, he suggests it is lesser than the divine, not having creative ability. Lewis's work has been surprisingly neglected, but see critique in Mallow, *The Demonic*, 1–44. N. G. Wright follows Mallow; *Dark Side*, 45–47.

19. E.g., "life is a conflict and the world is a battlefield"; Lewis, *Creator*, 16.

himself would like. Boyd defines evil as "evil precisely because God hates it."[20] This definition is simplistic and somewhat circular: surely God hates evil because of what it is? I believe it is more helpful to conceive of evil generally as antithetical to God, and particularly in terms of the myriad biblical metaphors for evil, summarized by "chaos."

Dualistic views have the advantages of disassociating God and evil, potentially incorporating biblical metaphors of evil in opposition to God, and accounting for extreme evil and experiential descriptions of demonization. The problem with dualism, particularly "spiritual warfare," is the tendency to ascribe excessive reality and power to evil beings. However, to affirm the reality of evil, validate the experience of sufferers, and affirm the sovereignty and goodness of God, some sort of dualism is required.[21] Part of the solution perhaps lies in the ontology of evil—monists tend to be minimalists, dualists tend to maximize the ontology of evil. An ideal view might be partially dualistic by considering evil as a lesser reality: chaotic.

Ontology

The question of whether evil has any actual being has been much discussed. A creative attempt to explain evil and chaos in the world, while emphasizing the sovereignty of God and minimizing the ontology of evil, was made by renowned theologian Karl Barth. He coined the term "nothingness" to describe the chaos and evil in the world that is antithetical to God. This nothingness exists in "opposition and resistance to God's world-dominion."[22] It is sinister and alien, a malignant, perverse entity that is equated with darkness, evil, chaos, demons, and Hades.[23] It is the "adversary with whom no compromise is possible, the negative which is more than the mere complement of an antithetical positive," the antithesis "to God Himself [and] to the totality of the created world." Nothingness is always "invading and attacking" and offers only "menace, corruption and

20. Boyd, *God at War*, 46.

21. In this, I agree with Mallow who, after analyzing the theologies of E. Lewis, K. Barth and P. Tillich, concludes that some form of dualism is necessary; *The Demonic*, 156–57.

22. Barth, *CD* III.3.289. The German term, *das Nichtige,* implies *nihil,* null, or non-existence. The editors chose "nothingness" with the proviso that its meaning is as explained by Barth.

23. Barth, *CD* III.3.289, 352, 523. Barth appears here to have some awareness of the semantic domain of evil.

death"; it refuses and is denied God's providence.[24] This nothingness is not created; it comes from neither God nor his creatures, but arises from the left hand of God when he created the good world. It is all that he did not will, that he said "No" to, "that from which God separates Himself."[25]

In terms of ontology, Barth famously claims "nothingness is not nothing."[26] It has no intrinsic value or substance but exists only in negation to good. It has "no substantive existence," it is a shadow "not consisting anywhere" but "lives only by the fact that it is that which God does not will."[27] It is an "inherent contradiction," an "impossible impossibility." Nothingness has reality only at the frontier of creation, and is real in a "third fashion peculiar to itself." It is the antithesis of both being and nonbeing; "as negation, nothingness has its own dynamic . . . of damage and destruction."[28] Yet nothingness has no power of its own, only that allowed by God. Despite its desire to the contrary, it is a servant of God, under his control. Barth insists that God is not responsible for evil, but neither is it an independent force. Paradoxically, nothingness both opposes God and serves him; it is dependent on him and only has as much power as given by God.[29] Barth claims that nothingness is not to be feared as it has been judged and defeated by Christ; it has no perpetuity. Indeed, it is primarily through knowledge of Christ that nothingness can be identified as such. In the light of Jesus, nothingness has no objective existence; it is merely an "ancient menace, danger and destruction, that ancient nonbeing which obscured and defaced the divine creation of God but which is consigned to the past in Jesus Christ, in whose death it has received its deserts, being destroyed."[30] However, nothingness seeks to deceive us by irrupting in creation and interfering with the relationship between God and humans. Therefore, "the power of nothingness should be rated as low as

24. Barth, *CD III*.3.290, 302, 523.

25. Barth, *CD III*.3.292, 351, 360. Barth's views on creation will be discussed further in the following chapter.

26. *Barth, CD III*.3.349, Barth acknowledges the apparent contradiction in this statement.

27. Barth, *CD III*.3.302, 352, 523; *CD III*.1.108. Somewhat confusingly Barth also uses the term shadow to describe the negative aspects of creation, such as purposeful suffering or soul-making; he clearly distinguishes this from nothingness; *CD III*.1. 371–77. In this he improves upon Hick and others in distinguishing between the two.

28. Barth, *CD III*.3.351; *CD III*.1.102, 310, 350.

29. Barth, *CD III*.1.123–24, 358, 366. These are some of Barth's most confusing claims.

30. Barth, *CD III*.3. 293, 302, 305, 312, 360–61, 363.

possible in relation to God and as high as possible in relation to ourselves." The realm of nothingness is "usurped and not legitimate, transitory and not eternal; yet a real kingdom, a nexus of form and power and movement and activity, of real menace and danger within its appointed limits"; but God "confronts nothingness and contains it within its frontiers."[31] In fact, the main purpose of God's preservation is to prevent the overthrow of the world by nothingness. Nothingness is primarily counteracted through truth as revealed in Christ.

Although nothingness lacks ontological status, Barth claims that nothingness, sin, evil, death, the devil, and hell are very real. Nothingness attains reality, or a concrete form, through death, sin, and the devil. "When the creature crosses the frontier from the one side, and it is invaded from the other, nothingness achieves actuality in the creaturely world."[32] Sin, like nothingness, is opposed by God and never allowed an ontological status. Nevertheless, through sin, humans can become both victims and agents of nothingness. Nothingness exists "behind God's back"; however, creatures can look away from God, therefore nothingness can be dangerous. Through sin, "the chaos separated by God becomes a factor and secures and exercises a power which does not belong to it in relation to God but can obviously do so in relation to His creature"; humans are not able to effect this separation.[33]

Interestingly, Barth equates demons with nothingness. He especially does not want to put angels and demons in the same category, believing those creatures that are opposed to God have nothing in common with heaven. Like nothingness, demons are "null and void, but they are not nothing"; they are "non-divine and anti-divine."[34] Barth insists that

31. Barth, *CD III.*3. 295, 524, 528–29.

32. Barth, *CD III.*3.300, 307–8, 310, 350; akin to sin as an "entry-point" in popular literature, discussed in chapter 1; Smith, *Willful Intent*, 300. T. F. Torrance, from a scientific perspective, views evil as existing at the edge of contingent realities but breaking into the created order; *Divine and Contingent Order*, 118–20. F. Tupper, following Barth to a degree, locates chaos at the boundaries of creation. "Since chaos exists, at least in part, on the frontiers of creation, when we violate these "natural boundaries" that impinge on our finitude, various degrees of self-destruction occur. The abuse of the limitation of our human creatureliness unleashes the ruinous forces of chaos against us"; *Scandalous Providence*, 138. Tupper also helpfully distinguishes between *meonic* (akin to the shadowside of creation) and *oukonic* nonbeing; the latter is always hostile to God and radically evil (142).

33. Barth, *CD III.*3.108, 352, 355, *CD IV.*1.139.

34. Barth, *CD III.*3. 520, 523. They exist only in binary opposition to angels. Barth is cautious with respect to angels, pointing out they are peripheral to Christian

demons are not created by God, but arise from nothingness. (Unfortunately, he fails to explain exactly how.) Like nothingness, demons are dynamic; they have form and power, movement and activity. Chaos manifests through demons, and demons can take on form when they break into creation. They operate through falsehood, by mimicking the kingdom of God; their powers of deception are "like the tentacles of an octopus." Like nothingness, the truth of God exposes and negates them; they are "unreal beings unmasked as falsehood and thus robbed of their powers."[35] Like nothingness, they have been defeated at the cross, and lack perpetuity.

Barth's "nothingness" has received much critique. An obvious objection is his confusing language and ambiguous ontology.[36] R. Scott Rodin points out many inconsistencies in Barth: the confusion inherent in God both controlling and opposing nothingness, the absence of the fall of humanity (central to the rest of Barth's theology) in his discussion of nothingness, his failure to address why God allows the nothingness to continue to exist, his ultimate failure to explain the origin of evil, and his failure to "consider a temporal separation between the cross, where the sentence of death was passed upon evil, and the execution of that sentence in the final parousia."[37] Barth's terminology is clearly inadequate; nevertheless, there is much in his theology that can be salvaged. His idea of evil being linked with chaos, nothingness, and demons fits well with evil being described biblically as opposition to God. Evil can be considered real but without "ultimate ontological standing."[38] Although he does not use the term, his ideas are similar to Lewis's description of evil as parasitic. "Nothingness" perhaps makes more sense as a metaphor for evil rather than a metaphysical category; Barth's work might be improved if he considered metaphori-

---

theology and that the Bible is silent with respect to their nature, origin and relationship to the world (410). We should only take a "quick, sharp glance," but neither must we ignore them (519).

35. Barth, *CD III*.3.526–30.

36. W. Krotke believes it to be "an ontological impossibility" and an absurdity; *Sin and Nothingness*, 39, 42, 48–51; Mallow critiques the "ontological impossibility" of nothingness; *The Demonic*, 46, and the "impossible possibility" of sin (71), and believes Barth underrates the effects of sin and evil (98); N. G. Wright describes Barth's theology of evil as "mental gymnastics"; *Dark Side*, 51.

37. Rodin, *Evil and Theodicy*, 166–67, 191, 195, 197, 202. N. G. Wright also notes Barth's inconsistencies: either God created evil through his "No," or he is powerless to prevent it; *Dark Side*, 52. Mallow points out that even though nothingness is a "negative" side of creation, in Barth's view, God is still responsible for evil; *The Demonic*, 97.

38. Mallow also comes to this conclusion; arguing that evil is parasitic, only existing upon God's creation; *The Demonic*, 158–61. N. G. Wright (*Dark Side*, 51–52) and Noble concur ("The Spirit World," 215, 217).

cal rather than propositional truth. Nonetheless, Barth's insights impact our understanding of evil, particularly in relation to the themes of creation and Christ, and will be revisited.

Chaos and Anthropology

The discipline of anthropology, which has described metaphors for evil that persist across time and culture, can also shed light on chaos. Anthropological structuralism was originated by Claude Lévi-Strauss, who linked linguistic and anthropological studies and suggested human cognition and societies are structured in terms of opposites and similarities.[39] Structuralism is a linguistic model, based on the assumption that "where there is meaning, there is structure."[40] The goal is to find the hidden or underlying configuration, commonalities within apparent discrepancies; the "aim is to reach by the shortest possible means a general understanding of the universe—not only a general but a *total* understanding." The intermediaries between the opposites are important, and myths can function to reconcile contradictions.[41] Furthermore, the structure of the human mind, particularly in its conceptualization of binary oppositions, is universal; "there is a simultaneous production of myths themselves, by the mind that generates them and, by the myths, of an image of the world which is already inherent in the structure of the mind." Structuralism is neither a philosophy nor an exegetical technique but relies on "the principle that every concept in a given system is determined by all other concepts of that system and has no significance by itself alone."[42] It has been attacked by poststructuralist/postmodern philosophies, which tend to deny underlying universal structure or meaning in society.[43] Structuralist techniques have been used in biblical studies with varying degrees of success.[44] Structuralism fits well

39. His views are developed in his classic *Mythologies* (*The Raw and the Cooked, From Honey to Ashes, The Origin of Table Manners, The Naked Man*); see also *Structural Anthropology*. Lévi-Strauss has been much misinterpreted and his theories extended beyond what was intended; Hénaff, *Claude Lévi-Strauss*, 3–5.

40. Greenwood, *Structuralism*, 6.

41. Lévi-Strauss, *Myth and Meaning*, 8–9, 17; *Table Manners*, 489–90; *Structural Anthropology*, 229; Greenwood, *Structuralism*, 9.

42. Lévi-Strauss, *Raw and the Cooked*, 341; Greenwood, *Structuralism*, 2.

43. E.g., Sheriff, *Fate of Meaning*, 28–30.

44. Although Lévi-Strauss never intended it to be so used. Holistic approaches, like structuralism, likely developed in reaction to disintegrative approaches like form-criticism and historical-criticism. The first to use such an approach was E. Leach who

with metaphor theory, especially the idea of the universality of binary oppositions, and applies to a study of biblical metaphors for evil. However, the idea of oppositions needing to be reconciled does not mesh with the theological perspective of evil being antithetical to God.

Mircea Eliade develops the idea of evil in binary opposition to good by examining diverse religions and using a variation of structuralism. He emphasizes the value of myths and symbols, which are transcendent and archetypal, able to reveal ultimate reality, and argues against reductionism, emphasizing the integration of multivalent symbols.[45] Eliade believes a symbol retains its message even if it is no longer conscious. Water is especially symbolic, often having dual meanings: death and rebirth, emersion (cosmogony) and immersion, purifying and regenerating.[46] In an early work, *The Myth of the Eternal Return*, Eliade claims that myth and symbol are a "complex system of coherent affirmations about the ultimate reality of things." He notes the importance of the symbolism of the center; sacred mountains, for example, represent the meeting place between human and divine. The world is duplicated on a higher cosmic-level (e.g., heavenly Jerusalem), but notably, the surrounding desert, seas, and monsters are not duplicated but assimilated into chaos.[47] Most rituals involve a repetition of the primordial creation act in which chaos is banished or ordered; repetition confers reality. The center is the "zone of absolute reality" and the road leading to it is difficult; "from the profane to the sacred, from the ephemeral and illusory to reality and eternity, from death to life, from man to the divinity . . . chaos to cosmos."[48]

applied it to Genesis 1 with questionable conclusions; Greenwood, *Structuralism*, 16–21, 118–19. More recently, E. Malbon has applied structuralism to the Gospel of Mark; *Narrative Space*. Greenwood laments that there is no clear and consistent definition or use of structuralism by biblical scholars; *Structuralism*, 107.

45. Eliade, *Sacred and Profane*, 129. History may add new meaning but the basic structure of the symbol is unchanged (137). Myths seek to discern original meaning; they are paradigmatic models, which are intertwined with ontology, or the "real" (95). Myths in contemporary, secular society are evident in novels and films (205–7). Eliade stresses the importance of myth: through it the "idea of reality, truth, and significance first dawn, to be later elaborated and systematized by metaphysical speculations." Christianity "cannot be completely separated from mythical thinking"; *Myth and Reality*, 139, 164; see also Marino, "Mircea Eliade's Hermeneutics," 37–45.

46. Eliade, *Sacred and Profane*, 129–30. Elsewhere, Eliade emphasizes the primacy of symbol over ritual. Symbols are multivalent and function together to form a system; *Comparative Religion*, 9, 448–56.

47. Eliade, *Eternal Return*, 3, 9. The idea of the symbolic sacred center is "archaic and widely disseminated"; *Sacred and Profane*, 47.

48. Eliade, *Eternal Return*, 17, 18. Eliade similarly refers to bridge and narrow gate symbolism; *Sacred and Profane*, 179–84.

Eliade continues his ideas in *The Sacred and the Profane*. He believes attempts to desacralize the cosmos are unsuccessful because humans cannot live without the sacred, which is like a universal key. The sacred is partly defined in terms of its opposite, the profane. This sacred/profane polarity can also be expressed as real/unreal.[49] It relates to the cosmos/ chaos polarity; the term chaos is often applied to uninhabited land, foreigners, and demons. Eliade uses the term "hierophany" to express the manifestation of the sacred: "something of a wholly different order, a reality that does not belong in our world."[50] Creation "implies a superabundance of reality . . . an irruption of the sacred into the world"; "the sacred reveals absolute reality and at the same time makes orientation possible; hence it *founds the world* in the sense that it fixes the limits and establishes the order of the world." The temple (chosen by Israel's God) can be seen as an "earthly reproduction of a transcendent model" that functions to continually resanctify the world.[51] Conversely, the chaos, which continually threatens sacred reality, is symbolized by demons, the primordial dragon, the marine monster, the primordial snake, darkness, night, death, and cosmic waters (note the consistency with biblical metaphors for evil). This view of the cosmos is reflected in both body and house cosmograms, or microcosms of the universe.[52] Religious people tend to be afraid of chaos and nothingness.

Eliade's work has been criticized primarily because of his dubious methodology.[53] However, critics notwithstanding, Eliade's writing could

---

49. Eliade, *Sacred and Profane*, 10–13, 17, 23, 34. "The sacred is saturated with being" (12). He is somewhat inconsistent in his use of "profane"—sometimes it means neutral, or ordinary; other times it signifies evil.

50. Ibid., 11. Space is nonhomogeneous, consisting of sacred, real space surrounded by formless space (20).

51. Ibid., 30, 45, 58–59. He notes the uniqueness of Christianity in that "myth" acquired historical status in the person of Christ who sanctified history; it is no longer located in "original" time, but historical time (110–11).

52. Ibid., 47–48, 53, 64, 172–79. The multiplicity of sacred centers is not a problem because this space is symbolic and existential (57).

53. Eliade's methodology is not explicit and sometimes inconsistent, although he roughly follows a phenomenological approach. He agrees with Lévi-Strauss that meaning and structure are interrelated but believes structure is related to history, and is the "essence" of something. He was inspired by R. Otto's *Idea of the Holy*, the "*mysterium tremendum et fascinans*"; Girardot, "Introduction," 1–16; Rogerson, "What is Holiness?," 3–21. Eliade has been critiqued for his ambiguity and loose handling of empirical data, and has been called speculative, a mystic not a scholar; Dudley, *Religion on Trial*, 3–42, 119–61. However, Dudley remarks that his "paradigm does not lack explanatory power because it is unverifiable" (135). Eliade's methodology

be used as descriptive, not necessarily normative. Furthermore, contemporary metaphor theory may support his ideas—perhaps he is describing universal spatial metaphors. Eliade's work, intuitive and creative, affirms that evil (profane, chaotic) can be perceived in binary opposition to good. His description of chaos and order is particularly relevant to the theme of Creation. Eliade's association of chaos and unreality resonates with Barth's notion of nothingness and Lewis's description of evil as parasitic.

Anthropologist Mary Douglas has pioneered the study of ritual and its application to OT cultic studies.[54] She claims purity is a system and defilement cannot be understood apart from its structure. Container and body metaphors can be used to view overcoming evil as separating and ordering it. Her work affirms some of the tenets of structuralism, but she develops the concept by including actions not just space. Douglas's work, to be discussed further, is especially relevant to the theme of Israel's cult. Anthropological insights regarding evil in binary opposition to good can inform this study. Rather than viewing evil solely in terms of warfare, it can be viewed in spatial opposition to the sacred, which is how it has to an extent been viewed in other religions, as Eliade shows. This view accords with biblical and theological perspectives of evil in opposition to God. One potential problem is that, like "spiritual warfare," it may lead to an overly dualistic worldview. Both the contributions and limitations of anthropological perspectives need consideration.

Chaos and Science

Using science to enlighten us regarding demonology may appear strange; demons are hardly amenable to scientific analysis. Scientific inquiry does not usually examine evil, but includes the polarities of chaos/cosmos and light/dark and therefore can provide analogies for understanding evil. Science also deals with unseen realities and derives conclusions based on observations of known realities. Partly for this reason, the science-religion dialogue has progressed in the last few decades.[55] Science has long

---

has been described positively as a new hermeneutic of intuition and "live" discovery; Marino, "Eliade's Hermeneutics," 20.

54. Her seminal work is *Purity and Danger.*

55. This is welcome after the "great divide" between science and religion, a result of scientific rationalism. Ground-breaking works in the science-theology debate include those of Barbour in America (*Issues in Science and Religion*) who discussed epistemology, language, and methodology, and T. F. Torrance (*Theological Science*) in the UK. Alister McGrath has built upon Torrance's work in his 3-volume *Scientific Theology.*

recognized the value of metaphors and models to gain understanding of both small- and large-scale phenomena. As discussed in chapter 2, models are taken from a familiar realm and applied to an unfamiliar one; one is used as a lens through which to see the other. Models function to understand reality. Scholars increasingly recognize that contemporary science talks more of models than of laws.[56]

Historically, Newtonian physics dominated science for two centuries. Newton's laws describe simple, linear systems (e.g., a pendulum) and claim that, with the correct information, anything can be predicted; the universe operates with stability and reliability. Newtonian physics is reductionistic in that complexities of nature are assumed to have underlying, yet undiscovered, simple laws. Philosophically this led to a mechanistic and deterministic worldview; the "clockmaker" God establishes the laws and lets the universe run on its own. However, science in the past century has radically altered theological views.[57] Newtonian physics has been challenged by quantum mechanics, which shows that certain interactions are inherently unpredictable;[58] by chaos-complexity theory, which claims that many interactions are nonlinear and chaotic; and by the recognition that there is much that remains unknown in the universe, such as dark matter and energy. This section examines chaos-complexity theory and dark matter with respect to their potential as models for conceptualizing evil.

He notes that both science and theology adhere to a realist epistemology; *Nature,* 77.

56. E.g., Cohen and Stewart, *Collapse of Chaos,* 19. Interestingly this view of science as not always empirically verifiable could provide support to Eliade's methodology.

57. R. J. Russell notes several recent scientific discoveries (e.g., DNA, quantum theory, relativity, chaos-complexity theory) which have forced theologians to reconsider the God-world interaction; *Cosmology,* 118. D. Toolan remarks, "the enlightenment view . . . [—]nature as mechanistic and deterministic—is dissolving before our eyes. In its place contemporary science is discovering a world that is irreversibly temporal, dynamic, interconnected, self-organizing, indeterminate, and boundlessly open to evolutionary transformation." This "new cosmic story requires theological repair work"; *Home in the Cosmos,* 2.

58. Quantum physics points out that certain aspects of the universe (primarily the very small and the very large) function in terms of probabilities and uncertainty. The position and velocity of subatomic particles cannot be known simultaneously; they spin in a superimposed state with a 50 percent chance of being either up or down (the Heisenberg Uncertainty Principle), and the act of measurement affects the system. There are multiple potential interactions between subatomic particles and the forces between them. Nature is inherently random and unpredictable. Cohen and Stewart, *Collapse of Chaos,* 44–45, 266; Coles, *Cosmos to Chaos,* 121–35; Hooper, *Dark Cosmos,* 43–58.

There have been some applications of scientific theories to the study of evil. Field theory has been used by Wolfhart Pannenberg, mostly as a model for the action of the Holy Spirit, but he also suggests that evil spirits may operate as fields of force.[59] Robert John Russell has used entropy as a model of evil. Evil is disorder, degeneration, and dysfunction, and entropy theorizes that all matter and energy tends towards increasing disorder. The cosmos continues only because of God's continuing creative participation; miracles, for example, exhibit an unusual decrease in entropy. Russell notes that both evil and disorder increase chaos in the world and both are dependent on being: "As in theodicy, entropy is parasitic to natural processes."[60] He does not discuss evil spirits. Yong has used emergence theory (the idea that complex levels of reality arise from but supersede lower levels) to suggest that the human spirit, angelic spirits, and demonic spirits emerge from embodied relationships. These are irreducible to their material substrates. With respect to the demonic, Yong believes "they lack their own being or onticity and thus emerge only parasitically in and through the moral behaviors . . . of free creatures."[61] Not only is he speculative and perhaps unnecessarily complex, but, in suggesting emergence theory as an explanation for the origin of evil, Yong appears to contradict much biblical evidence. Chaos-complexity is a more recent theory that may elucidate our understanding of evil.

Chaos-Complexity Theory

Chaos-complexity is a scientific model that is being increasingly applied to many fields of study. Three types of systems can be described: simple (e.g., a recipe that follows an easy formula), complicated (e.g., a rocket ship, requiring multiple formulae and expertise), and complex (e.g., interpersonal relationships—unpredictable and not amenable to formulaic analysis). It is this last category, highly intuitive but only relatively recently studied, that is of interest. Chaos-complexity, based on observations that

---

59. Pannenberg, *Systematic Theology.* 2, 79–129. See discussion and critique in Worthing, *God, Creation and Contemporary Physics,* 117–23. Yong also describes both the work of the Holy Spirit and evil spirits as force fields; *Discerning,* 127.

60. Russell, *Cosmology,* 233; also 226–41; see chapter 8, "demonology."

61. Yong, *Spirit of Creation,* 219. He follows Philip Clayton's philosophy of emergence and focuses on eschatology and teleology rather than origins (133–72); he admits his proposal is speculative. Yong's idea could perhaps function as a model for some, not all, instances of evil, although he does not specify that he is suggesting it as a model; this is discussed further in chapters 4, 7, and 8.

many systems are nonlinear and do not obey simple laws, has challenged Newtonian science. Chaos theory developed from the pure sciences in the past half century; complexity theory, although related to chaos theory, is a more recent development. They are similar enough to be combined.[62] In chaos theory, simple laws can have complicated consequences; in complexity theory, complex causes can produce simple effects, or complex systems can exhibit simple behavior. Chaos can be defined as a system in which small changes in the initial conditions of processes produce big changes in the outcome; complexity can be defined as a system that is chaotic and develops through a process of feedback on itself. A complex system is "a system that is made up of several simpler components interacting with one another."[63] The weather is a well-known example of a chaotic system in that it is highly sensitive to changes in initial conditions and results from an interaction of multiple factors such as collisions of millions of miniscule molecules of air and water.[64] There are multiple characteristics of chaos-complexity, nonlinearity and self-organization being most relevant here.

NONLINEARITY

Both chaos and complexity are nonlinear, arising from interactions of small numbers of simple components, and challenge the assumption that complicated phenomena arise from complicated rules. In nonlinear dynamic systems, interactions are disproportional, often following exponential growth curves with consequent growth of uncertainty. Relationships between variables are unstable and as the number of components increases, the number of interactions between them increases faster. Complex systems are extremely sensitive to small changes in initial conditions (two points starting out close become exponentially farther away)

62. Chaos-complexity theory evolved in diverse ways. Some classic experiments include the pendulum (if there is one, it obeys Newtonian laws; if a second is attached, it exhibits chaotic behavior), dripping faucets (at first regular, then if opened, irregular), and simple computations which diverge greatly if decimal points are rounded off differently. For a scientific textbook, see Cencini et al., *Chaos;* for lay level accounts see Gleick, *Chaos;* Cohen and Stewart, *Collapse of Chaos;* Stewart, *Does God Play Dice?;* Gribbin, *Deep Simplicity;* Polkinghorne, *Exploring Reality,* 7–37; Coles, *From Cosmos to Chaos;* Smith, *Chaos;* Fisher, *Perfect Swarm.*

63. Gribbin, *Deep Simplicity,* 143, 255.

64. E. Lorenz, a meteorologist, postulated the now famous "butterfly effect": the title of presentation in 1972 was "Does the flap of a butterfly's wing in Brazil set off a tornado in Texas?" Quoted in Gribbin, *Deep Simplicity,* 60.

and on-going feedback. Minor changes produce maximal effects, e.g., "the straw that broke the camel's back." Although we can observe the effects, we cannot know all the variables or discern the "seed of instability." Furthermore, continuous positive feedback into a system results in exponential and complex behavior. Common examples include traffic jams, stock markets, and population growth.

SELF-ORGANIZATION

Aspects of self-organization in chaos-complexity theory include self-similarity, attractors, boundedness, stretching and folding, bifurcations, and self-organized criticality. Self-similarity describes repetitive and similar patterns within complex systems, known as fractals—"geometric form[s] with fine structure on all scales of magnification."[65] These non-smooth and ubiquitous geometrical structures appear to be an inherent characteristic of nonlinearity, can be produced by simple mathematical formulae, and are evident in a variety of natural phenomena (e.g., a coastline). Attractors are theoretical components of complex systems to which other aspects are drawn. They are postulated to explain the convergence of components in a system close to a particular point. There may be one attractor or several attractors within a basin of attraction. In the long term, the system selects the simplest set from all possibilities (e.g., a marble in a bowl settles down to a position of minimal energy, water on the top of a cliff will run to either side). Any complex system settles at the equilibrium point between forces of attraction and repulsion. It can also be described as bounded (all points remain within certain boundaries) and adaptive (components respond collectively to changes in circumstances). Another characteristic of complex systems is the notion of stretching and folding. Systems expand to a certain point then fold into the basin of attraction. When exponentiality and uncertainty get too large, the system folds back on itself, increasing its stability. A related aspect is the phenomenon of bifurcation. Systems that are developing in a nonlinear manner become unstable; once they reach a critical point will often split into two more-stable systems. These successive bifurcations "nest" into each other and become self-similar fractals (e.g., the flow of a tap represents an endless process of bifurcation). The binary oppositions of anthropological structuralist theory have been postulated to be similar to the process of bifurcation.[66]

65. Cohen and Stewart, *Collapse of Chaos*, 23.
66. Mosko, "Introduction," 15.

Following from bifurcations are the self-organizational tendencies of chaotic-complex systems. As systems extend far from equilibrium they tend to self-organize into states of greater stability, often at critical bifurcation points. Thus the emergence of simplicity on a large scale; dynamical systems are able to generate stable structures. This is sometimes known as self-organized criticality because the system arranges itself at a certain critical point (e.g., a pile of sand topples when only one more grain is added). Self-organization can be observed in "swarm intelligence," insects that organize without a leader, especially if they have similar goals. Paradoxically, order exists within most forms of chaos.

APPLICATIONS

Chaos-complexity theory has been applied to and transformed many fields and subfields of diverse disciplines including anthropology, biology, economics, and psychology. It provides a new framework with which to understand many aspects of life. Interestingly, this shift in scientific worldview, from linear/deterministic to nonlinear/chaotic, has coincided with a similar shift in sociology, from modern to postmodern.[67] Both contemporary sociology and science recognize the contribution of multiple variables to a system, and that most phenomena in life are irreducibly complex. Chaos-complexity theory can be seen as a paradigm shift, although critics are concerned about its over-application (e.g., as an explanation for evolutionary processes; a sand pile may change but never becomes a cube).

Not surprisingly, many scientists have noted the philosophical implications of chaos-complexity theory. They generally agree that reductionism is no longer an adequate way of viewing reality.[68] The whole is greater than the sum of its parts and nonreductionist strategies need to be employed; the context as well as the content is important. Newtonian science viewed the universe as a web of causalities; now scientists consider it more helpful to look for patterns, not isolated steps of causality; they emphasize convergence not contingency.[69] Ian Stewart rephrases Einstein's famous assertion that God does not play dice into a question and suggests a better question: "Given some particular subsystem for the real world, is it best modeled by a deterministic mathematical system or a random one?" He further notes that there can be no truly fundamental theories,

67. E.g., Hayles, *Chaos and Order*.
68. E.g., Barbour, *Issues in Science*, 8; Cohen and Stewart, *Collapse of Chaos*, 221.
69. Cohen and Stewart, *Collapse of Chaos*, 246, 400–401.

only approximations within a defined domain; the result is a "pluralistic patchwork of locally valid models."[70] Leonard Smith remarks that this increases human responsibility as we need to distinguish between models and reality and decide whether they are similar enough; having the wrong model leads us to ask the wrong questions.[71]

Chaos-Complexity and Theology

Chaos-complexity theory has been applied to theology mostly with re-spect to the God/world relationship and the determinism/freewill debate. Many scientist-theologians stress the openness of creation and believe that God acts in the world through the small changes characteristic of chaotic-complex systems. Polkinghorne, perhaps representative, claims that God interacts through "information input" into dynamic processes. With respect to evil, he believes God respects the freedom of both the creature and the creation and is self-limited by the degree of openness in the process.[72] Polkinghorne does not address demonology. Boyd follows Polkinghorne in arguing that God is sovereign but can tolerate risk in creation. As chaos-complexity theory describes how the world can be overall predictable without every detail being known, so God is not neces-sarily omni-controlling. This reconciles with the idea that God can accom-plish his purposes but still allow his creatures significant freedom. Boyd also points out that sensitivity to initial conditions may explain the un-predictability of evil "natural" events. Uniquely, he suggests that, because demons have free will, they can influence so-called "natural" evil events, like tornadoes.[73] However, as discussed earlier, he describes evil spirits using linear, deterministic language and does not consider that they may *be* a complex system.

Sjoerd Bonting more deliberately develops a "chaos theology." He equates scientific chaos with primeval chaos, which he claims is uncreated and morally neutral, but is a source of creativity and evil. In creation, God orders this chaos, but some remains and continues to threaten the world

---

70. Stewart, *Does God Play Dice?*, 281, 376.

71. Smith, *Chaos*, 15, 154–57.

72. Polkinghorne, *Quarks, Chaos*, 62, 69–79, 89; *Exploring Reality*, 136–46. God's activity may be discernible only in hindsight as it is hidden "within the unpredictable flexibility of cosmic process"; *Science and Providence*, 52. Polkinghorne uses aspects of both quantum physics and chaos-complexity theory.

73. Boyd, *Satan*, 151–58, 218–19, 282–84.

in the form of evil (this explains "natural" evil arising from the chaotic behavior of complex systems). He thinks God can act through chaos events: "What the scientist observes as chaos events, the theologian . . . may experience as the love of the Creator for his creatures."[74] Bonting briefly dismisses Satan as having no relationship to evil.

The application of chaos-complexity to theology is still in its infancy, and there are other potential applications, such as to demonology. Previous scholarship has likely been operating within a Newtonian worldview, viewing demonology as a linear system and using rules applicable only to complicated systems, not complex ones. Hence there have been assertions of demonic organization and hierarchies. Recognizing that demons cannot be described with precise formulae may explain the diversity of the biblical verses, and the problems with classification attempts. With Stewart we should question, are evil spiritual forces best modeled by a linear, deterministic system, or a chaotic-complex one? We need to recognize though that the ancient world would not have used contemporary scientific theories as models, and that not all aspects of chaos-complexity are applicable to demonology (e.g., there is no biblical suggestion, fortunately, that the number of demons is increasing at an exponential rate).

Nevertheless, chaos-complexity theory as a model for evil accords with biblical metaphors such as chaos, theological metaphors like nothingness, and anecdotal descriptions in "spiritual warfare" literature. Specific aspects of chaos-complexity may elucidate demonology. The concept of "boundedness" fits well with Barth's view that "nothingness" is limited and can attain reality through sin. Perhaps evil spirits cluster around a basin of sin. The idea of self-organization may contribute to an understanding of the ontology of evil—if demons are like insects, they can cluster and appear to have greater ontology than they actually do. The different facets of chaos-complexity theory will be considered in relation to biblical themes explored in later chapters.

74. Bonting, *Chaos Theology,* 35; *Creation and Double Chaos,* 95–101. N. G. Wright has a similar view; *Dark Side,* 77; and Yong thinks that chaos represents both disorder and the "primordial plenitude"; *Spirit of Creation,* 156. Recall that Barth, like Bonting, claims that evil arises from chaos, except that Barth views chaos/nothingness as evil, not neutral.

Dark Matter and Nothing

A second aspect of science that can elucidate demonology is the recent discovery of dark matter in the universe. Theologian Thomas Noble believes a "structured doctrine of . . . evil to complement our theology of God . . . is impossible, as impossible as constructing a physics of darkness to complement our physics of light."[75] However, contemporary physics is indeed doing this. Scientists estimate that 90–95 percent of our world is composed of dark matter and energy, infiltrating visible reality.[76] Visible matter is only a small portion of the universe. This unseen dark matter is theorized from astronomical observations (e.g., unexplained radiation, gravitational and other forces), which can only be explained by the presence of invisible matter. Related to dark matter is empty space. Physicists assert, in words hauntingly reminiscent of Barth, that nothingness is not nothing. Empty space is composed of radiation, energy fields, and virtual particles. Space is dynamic: new subatomic particles appear and disappear continually, "the line that separates *something* from *nothing*, matter from empty space is blurred."[77] Most of the universe's energy resides in empty space. Paul Davies notes that "existence" is difficult to define: "Atoms . . . inhabit a shadowy world of half-existence"; quantum fields consist of "quivering patterns of invisible energy."[78] Similarly, an electron is "like a wavy cloud of existence."[79] Thus the unseen world, though very real, is less structured than previously thought. Reality is flexible, multi-layered, and intertwined.

To my knowledge, there have been no applications of the theory of dark matter/energy to theology. However, similar metaphors have been used. Hans Schwarz compares evil to antimatter (somewhat similar to dark matter) that "destroys those parts of the creation with which it comes into contact, producing a radiation, the effects of which are felt in other

75. Noble, "The Spirit World," in Lane, *Unseen World,* 218.

76. Hooper, *Dark Cosmos,* 1–17. Dark matter is estimated to account for one third of this and dark energy the rest. Speculative explanations for dark matter/energy include subatomic particles and parallel universes.

77. Genz, *Nothingness,* 305, italics original; see also 1–10; Hooper, *Dark Cosmos,* 58–62; 157–71.

78. Davies, *Mind of God,* 85; see also Barbour, *Religion and Science,* 165–84.

79. Hooper, *Dark Cosmos,* 50. Toolan notes, "lawfulness at the macroscopic level . . . rides in fact on a wildly chancy underworld of vibrating, oscillating, aleatory clouds"; *At Home,* 181.

parts of creation."[80] Robert Cook states, "Black Noise reverberates around the universe as the legacy of the primordial chaos."[81] Dark matter as a model for evil accords with biblical metaphors of darkness, theological metaphors of nothingness, and anthropological metaphors of unreality. This can help reconcile differing views on the ontology of evil. Evil can be conceived of like subatomic particles and energy fields; a shadowy reality, a *lesser* reality, a chaotic, disorganized, unstable existence that continually seeks to become more real.

Conclusions

Chaos is an apt description for evil from biblical, theological, and anthropological perspectives, and can be modeled after scientific chaos. Understanding evil forces as a complex system can explain the diversity of both biblical metaphors and experiential reports. The cluster of biblical metaphors in the semantic domain of evil can be broadened to incorporate Barth's notion of nothingness; Eliade's ideas of the profane; and scientific theories of chaos, nothingness, and dark matter. Chaos, a biblical metaphor for evil, is also chaos, used in theology to describe the nature of evil. Darkness, another metaphor for evil, is also dark matter/energy. Nothingness, Barth's term for evil, is also nothingness, the science of empty space. Chaos is also chaos, the scientific term for nonlinear dynamic systems.

As suggested previously, demonology is best discussed using metaphorical truth rather than propositional truth. Chaos as a metaphor can incorporate evil both in an abstract and a personal sense, and thus help bridge the gap between philosophical and "spiritual warfare" literature, as well as incorporating OT and NT metaphors. Curiously, few scholars associate chaos with demons, Barth being one exception, as discussed above.[82] However, from a biblical, theological, and logical perspective, there is good reason to connect the two. Both chaos and demons exist in opposition to God and divine reality. Both provide different snapshots of a complex evil reality. Evil as opposition to God can be variously expressed. Lewis, Barth, and Eliade all describe it as antithetical to the divine, with the

---

80. Schwarz, *Evil*, 74. Jürgen Moltmann similarly describes evil "potencies which do not belong to the human sphere but . . . have a destructive effect on that sphere"; *God in Creation*, 169; see also N. G. Wright, *Dark Side*, 72–74, 79–81.

81. Cook, "Devils and Manticores," 182.

82. Tupper, not engaging metaphor theory, notes that the lines between sin, chaos, and the demonic are blurred; *Scandalous Providence*, 137.

assumption of some degree of dualism. This opposition is defined linguistically and spatially, spatial metaphors being universal (further evidenced by the work of Eliade and Douglas). Warfare imagery is notably absent in Barth's and Eliade's work. Eliade particularly defines the sacred in terms of opposition to the profane. It is reasonable, therefore, to define and further understand the profane in terms of its opposition to the sacred, which will be endeavored in the next four chapters. However, as mentioned, a potential problem with dualistic views is the attribution of a high degree of ontology to evil spirits. This can be mitigated by the proposals of Barth and Eliade as well as by scientific analogies. Lewis, albeit overly dualistic, describes the discreative demonic as parasitic on creation. Eliade's real/unreal dichotomy fits well with Barth's notion of nothingness plus some aspects of chaos-complexity theory and dark matter. Evil can be viewed as existing in binary opposition to God, but having a lesser reality— a shadowy existence akin to subatomic particles. Chaos-complexity theory in some ways confirms that "nothingness is not nothing." Barth's theology of evil is greatly hindered by his terminology; rather than describing a "not nothing" nothingness, we can consider a chaos/evil that is a *lesser* something. This chaos exists at the boundaries of divine reality (as Barth and Eliade claim in different ways) and can attain reality when it crosses the frontier, through sin for example. Evil/chaos/demons exist in a quasi-real manner, only at the edge of God's good creation; they are parasitic, seeking to infiltrate and harm this creation. Eliade's views not only describe the profane as "unreal" but as existing at the periphery of reality.

In the next four chapters, I examine the biblical themes of creation, cult, Christ, and church in order to develop a model for conceptualizing evil. From the results of the above exploration of theology, anthropology, and science, this model can be constructed using a spatial framework and the categories of profane space, sacred space, and sacred actions. In each chapter, the cluster of biblical metaphors for evil is explored; especially facets that exist in binary oppositions to holiness. In creation, the dichotomies are primarily light/dark and cosmos/chaos; in the cult, they are clean/unclean and life/death; in Christ and the church, they include the above plus creation/new-creation and truth/lies. Hence the profane can be viewed through the lens of the sacred; evil understood in antithesis to God and holiness. As a subtheme, the above discussion on the ontology of evil will be considered in relationship to the biblical metaphors for evil. A non-warfare model for conceptualizing evil may provide further insight into the nature of chaos/evil.

4

CREATION: A CIRCLE ON
THE FACE OF THE DEEP

There was this great circle of gold colour—similar to the dawn—stretching out
from this person who was sitting on the throne and was so full of light.[1]

CREATION THEOLOGY HAS BEEN immortalized, and sometimes restricted, by the opening words of the Bible: "in the beginning." Yet
creation is about much more than beginnings. It is about the glorious
gift of a loving Creator, the continuous offer of protection from anti-
creational forces, each and every newborn baby, spring that perennially
returns, each new sunrise at the dawning of every day, personal renewal
by the Spirit of God. The biblical theme of creation can be mined indefinitely; it influences and is influenced by other themes. Nevertheless, the
beginning is a good place to start.

There is no single theology of creation in the OT.[2] Stories of the
beginning are not limited to the beginning; poets and prophets have much
to say, creation and covenant are interdependent. Francis Watson believes
"creation, the beginning of the story of God's dealings with the world and
with humankind, establishes the framework within which the history of
the divine-human covenant can unfold, the foundation upon which all
subsequent occurrence takes place."[3] Creation is also often conceived of

1. Hildegarde of Bingen, *Scivias* III.1.9.

2. E.g., Clifford and Collins "Introduction," 1–15.

3. Watson, *Text and Truth*, 232, 242; C. Dempsey notes "the phrase 'in the beginning' starts a process that continues throughout the rest of Genesis 1–2 and the biblical

in terms of eschatology as Löning and Zenger do: A "theology of creation . . . is not simply a prelude to salvation history, but sustains, pervades, and embraces the entire biblical witness to God."[4] An understanding of creation is essential for developing a model for conceptualizing evil. I agree with Bonting that the "solution of the problem of evil must rest on an adequate creation theology."[5]

Biblical creation texts contain abundant imagery, therefore suit a metaphorical methodology. Furthermore, God's good creation is portrayed as antithetical to evil forces, which allows understanding through the examination of binary oppositions. Recall from chapter 2 that spatial metaphors are universal, and from chapter 3 that the center as a symbol for the sacred is universal. One such spatial image portrays the creation of sacred space as God drawing a circle on the face of the deep (Job 26:10; Prov 8:27). In this chapter, I examine the nature of the deep, the evil that surrounds creation, then the nature of the circle, sacred space in creation. Next I discuss and evaluate sacred actions in creation with respect to divine responsibility (ordering and limiting evil), angelic responsibility (the "fall"), and human responsibility (and the results of disobedience). I then review numerous microcosms of creation depicted in the OT, and finally develop and evaluate a preliminary model for conceptualizing evil.

Profane Space

As argued previously, evil can be thought of as being in binary opposition to good. Thus chaos can be understood in comparison with creation; indeed this was how the ancient Hebrews conceived of creation.[6] In the OT,

---

text and world as a whole"; "Creation, Evolution," 13; F. Gorman asserts "creation and cult cannot be separated: they are dynamically interrelated aspects of the Priestly worldview"; *Ideology of Ritual*, 39.

4. Löning, and Zenger, *To Begin with*, 3. Moltmann similarly thinks creation theology should not be limited to a theory of origins, but should incorporate history and eschatology; *God in Creation*, 53–56.

5. Bonting, *Creation*, 136. Yet "spiritual warfare" literature seldom includes discussions on creation.

6. Unlike the traditional doctrine of creation *ex nihilo* most OT scholars affirm that Genesis compares chaos and cosmos, life and death, good and evil, not "something" and "nothing"; e.g., von Rad, *Genesis*, 49; McCarthy, "Creation Motifs," 88; Levenson, *Persistence of Evil*, xiii. C. Westermann points out that the creation narratives represent "not the philosopher inquiring about his origins . . . it was man threatened by his surroundings;" "an existential, not an intellectual problem"; *Creation*, 11. The doctrine

creation theology functions in the tension between cosmos and chaos, life and death. Furthermore, the ancient world did not conceive of space abstractly; mythical space was indistinguishable from its contents.[7] The symbolic portrayal of evil/chaos is found primarily in the opening chapters of Genesis as well as in some poetic, wisdom, and prophetic biblical literature. Chaos can be understood as symbolizing evil through the meaning of key terms plus by its relationship to ANE terms, and its activity in posing a threat to creation. Profane space, albeit sometimes interpreted as common/ordinary, is used throughout to refer to "evil" metaphorical space in binary opposition to sacred space. First, I examine the metaphors for evil in creation passages, then the nature and origins of chaos.

Chaos, Darkness, Desert, Deep, Sea-Monsters . . .

The opening two verses of the Bible are among the most discussed and debated within biblical scholarship.[8] They contain sinister, chaotic elements: *tōhû wābōhû, ḥōšek* and *tĕhôm. Tōhû* and *bōhû* are used elsewhere, separately or combined, in connection with chaos, waste, and void (Deut 32:10; Job 12:24; 26:7; Isa 24:1; 34:11; 45:18; Jer 4:23). *Tōhû wābōhû*, has been interpreted as "without form," "abyss," "nonbeing," "nothingness," "undifferentiated," "background noise," "turbulence," or even "hodgepodge."[9]

---

of creation *ex nihilo* developed in response to Gnosticism, polytheism, and Platonic dualism. G. May questions the common acceptance of this doctrine, noting that in the ancient world, *ex nihilo* was simply an "unreflective, everyday way of saying that through the act of creation something arose which did not previously exist"; *Creation Ex Nihilo,* 21. Copan and Craig recently published a vehement defense of creation *ex nihilo,* claiming that May does not distinguish between words and concepts; *Creation out of Nothing,* 12. The issues (conceptual, biblical, scientific, and theological) with the doctrine of creation *ex nihilo* are summarized well by Bonting; *Creation,* 70–73; *Chaos Theology,* 15–19; see also Welker, *Creation and Reality,* 6–20; McGrath, *Nature,* 156–70.

7. Löning and Zenger, *To Begin with,* 9, 11, 18–20; Childs, *Myth and Reality,* 84–85; see also Brinkman, *Perception of Space,* 45, 51.

8. There are numerous interpretive issues, e.g., the lack of an article; ambiguity whether Genesis 1.1 is an independent or dependent clause (most view it as a summary statement, e.g., B. Anderson, *Creation versus Chaos,* 111; Waltke, "Initial Chaos Theory," 216–28; Blocher, *Beginning,* 63; Jewett, *God, Creation,* 466; Fretheim, *God and World,* 36; Smith, *Priestly Vision,* 44–45). Genesis is frequently misunderstood, due to a tendency to impose contemporary thought onto an ancient text, and failure to recognize the mythopoetic genre of Genesis 1; Brueggemann, *Genesis,* 11.

9. It is translated as unseen/invisible and unformed (LXX), formless and empty (NIV), or a formless void (NRSV); Jewett, *God, Creation,* 462–67; Keller, *Face of the*

The definitions themselves are chaotic. The term chaos conveniently summarizes this concept and accords with chaos-complexity as a model for evil as suggested previously.[10] Darkness (*hōšek*) is another metaphor for evil. It can be viewed as independent of God's good creation and is associated with death and nonbeing.[11] Darkness, since it is not created but only separated and limited by God, is arguably not good.[12] *Tĕhôm* connotes the sea or, more precisely, the deep, and is typically portrayed as evil.[13] Although these metaphors can be multivalent, considered together and in context (discussed below), they are best understood as multiple metaphors within the semantic domain of evil.

Similar metaphors for evil occur in wisdom, poetic, and prophetic literature. The sea needs to be guarded, rebuked, and controlled by the Creator (Job 7:12; 26:12; 38:8; Pss 33:7; 74:13; 89:9; 106:9; 107:29; Prov 8:29; Isa 50:2; Jer 5:22; Nah 1:4). The deep is gathered and placed in storehouses, and the raging sea is calmed (Pss 33:7; 89:9; 107:29). This sea is sometimes indwelt by monsters (or chaos personified as monsters), such as Leviathan (Job 3:8; 41:2–14; Ps 74:13, 14; Isa 27:1) and Rahab (Job 9:13;

Deep, 183–89. Keller remarks, this "churning, complicating darkness . . . wedged between the two verses which everyone knows . . . refuses to disappear" (9).

10. Although chaos is borrowed from Greek, meaning a yawning chasm, it later was associated with disorder; *DDD* 185–86; Batto, *Slaying the Dragon*, 76. Note that this is in complete contrast to much of the "spiritual warfare" literature, which describes evil spirits as highly organized.

11. E.g., Ps 88:6. *DCH* 3:331–32; Childs, *Myth and Reality*, 33; Dumbrell, *End of the Beginning*, 173. Prophets warn repeatedly about a return of creation to darkness (see below); John 1:5 implies the presence of darkness prior to creation.

12. Löning, and Zenger; *To Begin with*, 20; Noort; "Creation of Light," 3–20. One verse (Isa 45:7) suggests that God creates darkness, however, it is written in the context of God ordering chaos (Isa 42:15; 43:16) as well as likely intended to console Israel regarding God's sovereignty and their future deliverance; see also Boyd, *God at War*, 149. Given the multivalency of metaphors, it is possible that this darkness is referring not to the primordial reality of Genesis 1 but to an aspect of creation; McGrath, *Nature*, 148; Smith, *Priestly Vision*, 73. A. Motyer suggests Isa 45:7 is better translated as "I create disaster" (NIV), since most other occurrences of the word *ra* mean trouble or calamity; *Isaiah*, 359. Curiously, Copan and Craig claim that God creates both darkness and water, perhaps because of their agenda to prove creation *ex nihilo*; *Creation out of Nothing*, 33.

13. *DDD* 737–42. Batto points out that the sea in Genesis 1 is "overladen with mythic tones" suggesting its associations with evil; *Slaying the Dragon*, 110. Interestingly Genesis 1:2 contains both desert and water imagery, both seemingly in opposition to godly reality. Smith observes the multivalency of water imagery in Genesis: it can "evoke both the potential threat of destruction from the periphery and its positive life-giving capacity within creation"; *Priestly Vision*, 61.

26:12–13; Ps 89:9–10, 20; Isa 51:9–11).[14] The association of evil with these terms is clearer than in Genesis 1; these passages can shed light on metaphors for evil in Genesis 1. Furthermore, there are parallels between Genesis and poetic/prophetic literature, such as the strong linguistic affinities between Genesis 1 and Psalm 104.[15] The Genesis 2 creation account differs from the Genesis 1 account but the symbolism is similar.[16] The desert, not the sea, is now the predominant metaphor for evil. Christopher Barth points out that three cosmic phenomena manifested activity of these "superhuman, demoniacal, and destructive forces" that threatened Israel and all creation: ocean, desert, and night.[17]

Further insight into chaos can be obtained from other ancient religions. This is especially needed with respect to Genesis 1 because there is no immediate context for interpretation. In the ancient world, evil was frequently associated with darkness, chaos, the sea, the desert, the waste, death, and the wilderness.[18] Most of these concepts were personified in ANE literature: *yām* (the Hebrew word for sea) was a Canaanite sea-monster, Yamm; Tiamat, an evil Babylonian sea-goddess, is etymologically related to *těhôm* (the deep); Mot (related to the Hebrew for death) was lord of death and sterility, often depicted with a large throat; Leviathan

---

14. Also Behemoth (Job 40:15–24). Boyd claims these are "real" evil forces; *God at War*, 94–100. Conversely, Yong thinks these are somehow archetypical manifestations of evil; *Spirit of Creation*, 218. C. Barth believes Rahab and Leviathan are symbols, but indicate reality and are important despite few references; *God with Us*; 14. Batto notes the "chaos monster" is always lurking despite YHWH's sovereignty; *Slaying the Dragon*, 98. The last two scholars make the most sense given my previous argument regarding the reality-depicting nature of metaphors and symbols.

15. E.g., God creating heaven and earth, dividing earth and water, creating animals. Anderson believes they reflect an Israelite liturgy (*Creation versus Chaos*, 73); see also Day, *Yahweh and the Gods*, 51.

16. Genesis 1 (actually Gen 1:1—2:3 but referred to here as Genesis 1 for simplicity) has typically been called the priestly account (P), and Genesis 2 (actually Gen 2:4–25) the Yahwist account (J), based on the presumed authors. This "documentary hypothesis," expounded by J. Wellhausen in the late nineteenth century and primarily applied to the Pentateuch, has been influential in OT studies. It posits four independent sources for the biblical texts: Yahwist, Elohist, Deuteronomist, and Priestly; *History of Israel*, 6–13, 34–35, 52–54, 99–116. It is not widely accepted but can be helpful as a heuristic device; Brueggemann, *OT Theology*, 8, 9; Batto, *Slaying the Dragon*, 41.

17. Barth, *God with Us*, 14. Batto thinks there are only two symbols of chaos: the ocean/primeval-flood/dragon-like monster and the barren desert; *Slaying the Dragon*, 47.

18. Eliade, *Sacred and Profane*, 47–48; Russell, *Devil*, 62–68.

was a dragon with seven heads who ruled the sea.[19] The struggle with dangerous waters was a common theme in ANE literature; the sea and the primeval waters were viewed as mingling together as a river encircling the world.[20] Parallels between biblical and ANE literature are uncontested, but there is debate regarding the degree to which Israel was influenced by or transformed these texts. The commonest argument is that biblical authors wrote polemically against ANE religions, mostly evident in Genesis 1.[21] However, the association between evil and chaos can be discerned in the background, given the multiple ANE terms in the text. John Day uses the term "afterglow" to describe the presence of ANE images in OT texts. These images lived on but were transformed by Israel's monotheism.[22] Recall that in the ancient world myth and history were intertwined. As Mary Wakeman points out, "the distinction that we try to make between the sea as a symbol and Yam as the name of a mythical monster would have been incomprehensible to the myth-makers . . . the sea was not *like* the monster; the correlation was immediate and complete."[23] Consequently, the biblical

---

19. *DDD* 737–42, 867–69, von Rad, *Genesis,* 50; Wyatt, *Mythic Mind,* 204. Leviathan means "twisting one"; also called Lotan, *DDD* 511–15. The period of interest is the mid to late Bronze Age (2000–1250 BCE) and regions/nations included Mesopotamia (Sumer, Assyrian, Akkad, Babylon), Elam, Levant (Canaan, Ugarit, Ebla), Egypt, and Anatolia (Hittite). There is overlap between these areas, e.g., Hittite religion contained elements from both Canaan and Mesopotamia. Most ANE religions were polytheistic; Hallo, *Context of Scripture*; Walton, *ANE Thought* , 43–83; Smith, *History of God*; Day, *Yahweh,* 4–6, 30, 74.

20. Forsyth, *Old Enemy,* 63.

21. Creation in Genesis 1 occurs simply and effortlessly compared to the complicated battles of ANE stories. Furthermore, the sun and stars (ANE astral deities) are created by God, undermining their divinity; Waltke, "Theology of Genesis 1," 328–30; Routledge, *OT Theology,* 126. Arnold, however, believes the polemical nature of Genesis 1 has been overstated and that Genesis 1 "transcends competing theologies"; *Genesis,* 32. Brueggemann argues that Israel borrowed, but radically transformed ANE religious beliefs; *Theology of OT,* 652, but Walton suggests biblical authors did not necessarily borrow from ANE literature, but reflected beliefs common in the ancient world; *ANE Thought,* 85.

22. Day, *Yahweh,* 232–33. Similarly, Levenson believes that the OT has its roots in the Canaanite world; *Sinai and Zion,* 113; Löning and Zenger think the Genesis "precreation" material (chaos, the primal ocean, darkness, endlessness, and hiddenness) is derived from Egypt and Mesopotamia; *To Begin with,* 9–13.

23. Wakeman, *God's Battle,* 104. Similarly, R. Simkins thinks myth and history are interrelated, therefore cannot be used to distinguish between biblical and ANE creation stories; *Creator and Creation,* 86–88. Batto claims primeval stories are vehicles of truth; *Slaying the Dragon,* 99, 118.

metaphors for evil would have been readily associated with ANE concepts. The precise nature of chaos/evil, however, is not simple.

The Nature of Chaos

Typically, chaos and darkness are viewed as evil, a threat to creation, and are generally depicted as ominous and sinister. They are neither created, nor nonexistent. Brevard Childs describes chaos as a reality rejected by God that remains a threat to creation; Bruce Waltke concludes that chaos in the OT always has a sinister, eerie connotation and darkness is cloaked in mystery.[24] The identification of chaos with evil is strengthened by correlations with ANE literature. Neil Forsyth believes the OT places YHWH's enemies in parallel with ANE cosmic enemies: Yamm (and his counterpart Nahar, meaning river) "embodies the chaotic, disintegrating power of water, whether as raging sea or flooding river."[25] Joel Burnett, in his examination of divine absence, notes that chaos (associated with divine absence) is somehow separate from God's good creation. Divine absence is a result of cosmic structure, and the boundaries of creation: "God's ability to manage and limit the powers of chaos and death lie not in their divine origins but rather in their exclusion from God's realms of activities."[26] This view connects chaos with evil and locates it outside of God's good creation, although always a potential threat to creation (note the similarities to Barth's idea of nothingness as being outside of creation).

However, some scholars have attempted to dispense with chaos by assigning it a neutral interpretation or claiming agnosticism. Thus Blocher suggests that chaos is simply the raw material of creation.[27] Elsewhere he states that the Genesis creation "contained not the slightest embryonic presence of evil."[28] Terence Fretheim, in his OT creation theology, also

24. Childs, *Myth and Reality*, 35, 42; Waltke, *OT Theology*, 181. Brueggemann agrees that the chaos of Genesis 1:2 represents forces of evil, which "must repeatedly be rebuked and swept away"; *Theology of OT*, 529, 656–57; *OT Theology*, 159, 326–31. From a theological view, Cook agrees chaos is evil; "Devils and Manticores," 181.

25. Forsyth, *Old Enemy*, 47, 62.

26. Burnett, *Where is God?* 64, 75, 84. In particular, YHWH is not associated with the realm of the dead, which by definition is remote from divine presence (66–67). "Though God has access to death's realm, it lies outside the normative realm of God's presence in the ordered cosmos" (176).

27. He argues that the text gives little information; Blocher, *Beginning*, 65–66.

28. Blocher, *Evil and the Cross*, 128. Yet he does not provide a satisfactory explanation for evil.

denies any presence of evil prior to creation, claiming the chaos of Genesis 1:2 refers to raw materials in existence prior to creation, "which are of no apparent interest or simply assumed to have had their origins in prior divine activity." He believes chaos is neutral, representing disorderly parts of creation.[29] David Tsumara assigns a neutral interpretation to chaos by emphasizing the OT polemic against ANE literature; arguing that *tĕhôm* simply means ocean, and *tōhû wābōhû* emptiness, a neutral state of affairs.[30]

It is possible though, given the multivalent nature of metaphors, to view chaos as symbolizing *both* a neutral, formless mass *and* forces of evil.[31] Or, as Bonting suggests (discussed in chapter 3), to view chaos as potentially giving rise to evil. Regardless, the association between chaos and evil cannot be ignored. Elsewhere in the Bible, and especially in ANE literature, darkness, the deep, waste, and void are all associated with evil. Furthermore, Genesis states neither that darkness is created, nor that it is pronounced good; this darkness/chaos exists before the divine fiat. If chaos is neutral, it also does not make sense for it to be confined, separated, and ordered at the beginning of creation (discussed below). This association of chaos and evil fits better with later texts describing creation as overcoming evil forces, as well as the presence of the snake and the command to subdue the garden (Genesis depicts an imperfect creation, discussed below). A neutral interpretation of chaos ignores the multiple texts that associate chaos with evil. Although the issue is complex, biblically and philosophically, it seems that the initial unformed state of creation is not an ideal situation, and perhaps antithetical to God (recalling the previous chapter's discussion on the definition of evil). It can be viewed as the malevolent mysterious reality that exists prior to the creation of the

---

29. Such as sea monsters which can hurt people; Fretheim, *God and World*, 13, 36, 236. Yet disorder is associated with evil. Fretheim relates "chaos" more to sin, noting the frequent association between moral and cosmic order (97, 108, 135, 175). Cf. Powlison who thinks moral and situational evil are separate; *Power Encounters*, 66–69.

30. Tsumara, *Creation and Destruction*, 43, 65. John Walton follows Tsumara in his assertion that chaos represents not an enemy of YHWH, but a non-functional, non-productive state; "Creation in Genesis 1:1—2:3," 48–63. Jewett argues that Genesis 1:2 is a portrayal of the nonbeing or nothingness that precedes creation; *God, Creation*, 466; however, nonbeing and nothingness themselves can have evil connotations.

31. McGrath suggests two paradigms: chaos as an inert formless mass that requires shaping (Gen 1) and chaos as personal forces such as a dragon; *Nature*, 146. He notes that darkness and the deep exist before creation, but creation can also be seen as first calling the universe into existence then ordering it (156).

good world, the deep on which God draws a circle. As William Dumbrell concludes regarding the Genesis account, "we are forced to deal with the possibility that evil was present at the very beginning of creation."[32] As I acknowledged earlier, however, chaos is quite possibly a multivalent metaphor, at times meaning a neutral state, other times evil.

The interpretation of chaos has implications for the ontology of evil. It is possible to find a compromise between viewing chaos as a pre-existent, powerful enemy of God and viewing it as neutral. As discussed in chapter 3, chaos/evil can be considered a lesser reality. Since this chaos is rejected by God (so Childs and K. Barth), or outside the realm of creation (so Burnett), it is denied the blessing of God that gives life and reality. In the OT, as discussed above, ANE demonic forces are greatly brought down to size, but their influence is apparent but in the background. Even though chaos is evil by nature, it is not equal to God (thus discounting any views of metaphysical dualism). Conceiving of this realm as quasi-real affirms the presence of evil at the beginning of creation, but minimizes its power.

The Origins of Chaos

Unfortunately, the Bible is imprecise regarding the origin of this evil/chaos. In the Genesis account, it is not stated to be created, although elsewhere it is clear God creates heavens and the earth and all that is in them (Gen 1:1–27; Pss 89:11, 12; Isa 40:26; Neh 9:6; John 1:3; Acts 4:24; Col 1:16; Heb 1:2; Rev 4:11). There have been many attempts to address this dilemma; four views are apparent.[33] First is to accept the mystery. Many OT scholars simply observe that chaos pre-existed without explanation. Claus Westermann, for example, concludes that the "origin of evil cannot be explained" and we "must live with the reality of evil."[34] Second is a

32. Dumbrell, *Search for Order*, 17.

33. Note that I am referring specifically to primordial chaos/evil. Other views of the origin of evil include within a "shadow side" of God (which most Christian theologies reject) and as a by-product of human sin (which does not explain prehumanoid suffering, or the presence of the "evil" serpent in God's good creation). This last view is held by Wink (based on Jungian psychology and the "shadow" side of humanity) and Yong (evil "emerges" from "sin;" although he is unclear how "archetypical" evil emerges prior to the creation of humanity), *Spirit of Creation*, 218. I agree that sin is important as an explanation for evil but insufficient alone; to be discussed further.

34. Westermann, *Creation*, 98. Although he implies that God creates evil since there is dissimilarity built into creation (43). Waltke concurs the origin of the primordial waters, the angels and Satan is unknown; *OT Theology*, 180, 230. Childs

two-stage theory of creation proposed by Augustine and others: God first creates chaos, or a formless mass, then creates the heavens and the earth from this.[35] Robin Routledge, who associates chaos with evil, follows the two-stage theory but questions why God would create emptiness. He suggests that since chaos is the opposite of creation, it allows for the possibility of sin and rejection of God, and the return of chaos.[36] Third is to view chaos as a by-product of creation, albeit not usually articulated as such. K. Barth appears to suggest a simultaneous creation (or non-creation) of chaos in the Genesis account; he views "nothingness" as coming from the left hand of God when he creates the world.[37] Although Barth's terminology is confusing, this idea has some merit in that it avoids metaphysical dualism but affirms the association of chaos and evil. Moltmann similarly believes that, in creating the world, God first makes room by creating an empty space from which he withdraws himself (divine kenosis) and restricts his power; alternatively stated, he first creates nothingness or nonbeing which he then calls into being; God creates by "letting-be" or "making room."[38] However, this space from which God has withdrawn, "God-forsaken space," is consequently evil. (Moltmann is perhaps more poetic than soundly theological, and confusing with respect to omnipresence and divine kenosis: if God is present everywhere, how can there be God-forsaken space? He is unclear regarding the timing of creation—is he advocating a two-stage theory, or does kenosis occur simultaneous with creation?) Fourth is to view chaos as having *become* evil secondary to a primordial angelic fall. Boyd is a strong advocate of this view. He adopts a "restoration" theory of creation, suggesting that Genesis 1 provides not

---

vehemently rejects chaos as pre-created or having become so by an angelic fall, but unfortunately does not offer an alternative explanation; *OT Theology,* 222–26.

35. This follows Wis 11:17: God "created the world out of formless matter." Josephus was one of the first to suggest this theory; *Antiquities,* 1.1. Early church fathers concurred, e.g., Justin Martyr, *First Apology,* 10, 59; Tatian, *Discourse* 4, 5. Augustine suggested that God first created a formless, unstructured universe ("near nothing"), then created the heavens and earth out of this; *Confessions,* XII, 15.

36. As in the flood; Routledge, *OT Theology,* 32–33.

37. Barth, *CD III.I,* 360; discussed further below.

38. Moltmann, *God in Creation,* 86–93; *Science and Wisdom,* 119–20; Moltmann follows the Jewish Kabbalistic idea of *zimsum,* the contraction of divine presence. (Polkinghorne follows this view, "Kenotic Creation and Divine Action," 90–106). Moltmann's ideas of "God-forsaken space" have been deemed "unconvincing and unbiblical" (Copan and Craig, *Creation,* 20), and "materially unfounded mystification" (Pannenberg, *ST,* 15). Interestingly, his ideas concur with Burnett's suggestion that evil is outside creation.

an account of creation, but an account of *restitution* of a world that had become formless and chaotic as a result of corruption of a previously good creation by evil spirits: "It is an account of God's restoration of a world that had . . . become formless, futile, empty and engulfed by chaos." He concludes that evil is an "intrusion into the cosmos," and humanity "birthed in an infected incubator."[39]

In sum, the possible explanations for the origin of evil are that primordial chaos was created as a first-step, arose simultaneously with creation, or developed as a result of a primordial angelic fall. Boyd's theory is intuitively attractive and cannot be dismissed outright, but neither can it be uncritically accepted. Barth and Moltmann's ideas, which I see as similar, are also speculative but accord well with the thesis in this study that evil exists in opposition to God, and is not blessed by divine presence. A two-stage theory is unnecessarily complicated and poorly compatible with the biblical text. Viewing evil metaphorically and as a complex system can help reconcile the views of evil as both chaos existing outside the structure of creation and as consisting of "fallen angels." Evil is perhaps simultaneously a nebulous force and a quasi-personal particulate reality (which concurs with the nature of some scientific realities such as light being both a particle and a wave). The important point is that evil is not part of God's good creation, and is populated by evil spiritual forces that need to be confined. I agree we need to accept some degree of mystery and be cautious with conclusions; nonetheless, theories and models are invaluable for conceptualization, especially for the difficult topic of evil. Furthermore, conceiving of evil as a lesser reality can guard against metaphysical dualism.

39. Boyd, *God at War*, 103–10; *Satan*, 313–17. He claims this view explains the presence of the "ancient serpent" in the garden; the command to guard Eden (Gen 2:15), "fill" and "subdue" the earth (Gen 1:28); the linguistic difficulties of Genesis 1:2; is more compatible with the cosmic conflict creation accounts; and accords with scientific evidence regarding the age of the earth and pre-humanoid suffering. This theory postulates a "gap" between Genesis 1:1 and Genesis 1:2; was popularized by the Scofield Bible, but is not well accepted. Blocher concludes it to be imaginative with no textual support; *Beginning*, 41–43; Waltke deems it false on linguistic and theological grounds; "The Restitution Theory," 136–42; and Dumbrell notes it merely puts the problem of evil a step back plus casts scientific precision on a poetic text; *End of Beginning*, 173–74. Boyd admits his theory is speculative; *God at War*, 112–13.

Summary: The Threat to Divine Reality

Metaphors for evil in biblical creation texts include darkness, the desert, the deep, sea monsters, and chaos (which can encapsulate the others). Their origin is unexplained. Although these metaphors may be multivalent, mostly they are employed to depict evil as a force in opposition to God's good creation. This chaos can be understood further through an examination of its binary opposition, sacred space, as depicted in creation passages.

Sacred Space

Biblical authors did not treat space as an independent topic, but included much description of such space within other topics.[40] In this section, I examine Eden as the first sacred space, plus the borders of this space.

The Circle of Eden

Recall Eliade's assertion that sacred space is universal, frequently symbolized by the center, and defined by divine presence. Ronald Simkins, following Eliade, relates sacred space to biblical descriptions of creation; the two are mutually dependent: "People's perceptions of sacred space affirm their particular views of creation, and creation myths explain and ascribe significance to their awareness of sacred space."[41] Such symbolic space reflects reality.

The first such sacred space described in the Bible (Genesis 1) is symbolized by light, life, and land, all of which are pronounced good. God begins the creative process by calling forth light, followed by separating the waters and creating dry land. He fills creation with all kinds of life (Gen 1:3, 9, 11–27). When creation is complete, he rests. In the ancient world, deities usually rested after their work, signifying there was now order in the cosmos; this rest usually occurred in a temple.[42] Hence, symbolically, creation is God's temple. This is affirmed by later texts that conflate

---

40. Brinkman, *Perception of Space*, 73; we need to "read between the lines" to discern OT concepts of space.

41. Simkins, *Creator and Creation*, 133. Walton describes Eden as cosmic geography, real but not the same as physical, literal geography; *ANE Thought*, 124–25.

42. Walton, "Creation," 60–61; *ANE Thought*, 197–99; Batto, "Creation Theology in Genesis," 33; *Slaying the Dragon*, 78.

creation of cosmos and construction of the temple (Ps 78:69; Isa 66:1).[43] In the second creation account, sacred space is symbolized by the mythical and mystical Garden of Eden. Eden means bliss or delight, and is filled with symbols of life: rivers of fresh water, fruit-bearing trees, and specifically the tree of life. *Gān* (garden) implies a covered or surrounded space, like a walled garden.[44] It is more like a park, which in the ancient world was associated with great kings. The most important characteristic of Eden is that it is purely a gift from God to his creatures; creation is a result of his generosity and sovereignty." God delights in his creation (Ps 104:26; Prov 8:30–31), blesses it (Gen 1:22, 28; 2:3), and all creation in turn praises him (Job 38:7; Pss 8; 19; 65; 97; 104; 145; 148).[45] Furthermore, God is personally present—he walks in the garden with the humans (Gen 3:8).[46] Moltmann summarizes: "The space of the world corresponds to God's world-presence, which initiates this space, limits it and interpenetrates it."[47] It could be concluded that the very purpose of creation is to provide a space for divine-human interaction. Eden is considered holy because of God's presence, and consequently is guarded by cherubim. The Genesis 2 account complements the Genesis 1 account and portrays an immanent and personal Lord God, who lovingly shapes humans and places them in a world in which he can relate to them. As Simkins notes, "it is God's presence in the creation that ascribes the creation with value."[48]

The first creation is an ideal world, but not perfect. Puzzling elements in the story include the command to subdue creation, and the sudden appearance of a malevolent snake in the garden. Furthermore, humans are not specifically pronounced good (breaking the poetic cycle of other days), perhaps foreshadowing sin. The rainbow, usually symbolic of a pledge to maintain order, is only hung up after the flood.[49] Some authors view the original creation as perfect, but they do not discuss the above

---

43. Smith, *Priestly Vision,* 16. Discussed further below and in the following chapter.

44. As in royal gardens (2 Kgs 25:4; Neh 3:15; Jer 39:4; 52:7); *DCH* 2:366; Dumbrell, *Search for Order,* 24; von Rad, *Genesis,* 53. On Eden see *DCH* 6:283; Blocher, *Beginning,* 112; Arnold, *Genesis,* 58; Batto, *Slaying the Dragon,* 49.

45. Brueggemann, *Theology of OT,* 528; *Genesis,* 27–28, 36. Arnold, *Genesis,* 43. Israel also praised God for his on-going sustenance (Ps 104:27–30; 145:15–16; Brueggemann, *Genesis,* 39).

46. Beale points out that the same word is used to describe God walking with his people as a reward for obedience in Lev 16:12; *Temple,* 66.

47. Moltmann, *God in Creation,* 149–50, 157.

48. Simkins, *Creator and Creation,* 144; von Rad, *Genesis,* 53. "*Yhwh ĕlōhîm*" is used for the first time, unlike *ĕlōhîm* alone in Genesis 1; Arnold, *Genesis,* 56.

49. Batto, "Creation Theology," 35–36.

issues or the meaning of "good."[50] But many biblical scholars note that *ṭôb* means purpose and order, rather than perfection. Dumbrell for instance believes *ṭôb* implies *functional* goodness, not perfection. It reflects a correspondence between divine intention and the universe. Creation needs controlling, and so is not perfect.[51] Original creation can be considered metaphorical space—it is ideal, good (very good) but not perfect in a Western rationalistic manner; there is potential for evil. Genesis offers a brief glimpse into this original ideal sacred space, symbolized by light, life, and a luscious garden. This sacred space, admittedly not perfect, is filled with divine presence. It can be illustrated thus:

Figure 4.1: A Circle on the Face of the Deep

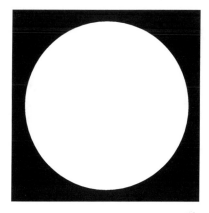

The Boundary

However, this picture is inadequate. Life, biblically and experientially, is more complex than black and white, good and evil. Even Genesis contains

50. E.g., M. Erickson claims "there was nothing evil within God's original creation"; *Christian Theology*, 1, 375. Pannenberg claims creation was originally perfect, although he notes the tension inherent in the idea of Christ as the completion of creation; *Systematic Theology*, 2, 163. This approach, perhaps wanting to emphasize divine sovereignty and perfection, has difficulty explaining the origin of evil, and/or places excessive weight on human sin.

51. Dumbrell, *Search for Order*, 20–22. See also *DCH* 3:351–56; von Rad, Genesis, 52; Batto, *Slaying the Dragon*, 91. Good can also mean "free" (Fretheim, *Creation Untamed*, 16) and "peaceful" (Ps 104:28; Isa 45:7; Smith, *Priestly Vision*, 62). Bonting believes that since *ṭôb* refers to a functional goodness, it is conceivable that evil was present in the Genesis creation account; *Creation*, 54.

hints of this. For example, in the second creation account, the human is created outside the garden *then* placed inside (Gen 2:15);[52] and, following their disobedience, Adam and Eve are placed outside the garden, not into darkness, the deep, or chaos, but presumably into an intermediary place. In anthropological terms, the intermediate space between two opposing spaces is called liminal. It forms a bridge and is potentially dangerous or creative. Liminal space, usually seen to bridge or mediate between the sacred and the profane, in cultic theology is transformative: those in this space must move towards either the center or the periphery.[53] This space can be depicted as grey; it still receives the light emanating from the sacred center, but is also influenced by the black periphery. The divine blessing extends into this intermediary area; God's provision and protection remain with humans despite their rebellion. This space becomes better defined through Israel's cult (discussed in chapter 5).

Simkins describes two models of sacred space and its boundaries, which were common in the ancient world, including Israel. The more primitive horizontal model locates holy land and order at the center, the originator of creation; Jerusalem for example is at the center. The periphery is symbolized by the sea, the desert, and chaos.

Figure 4.2. Simkins's Horizontal Model of Sacred Space[54]

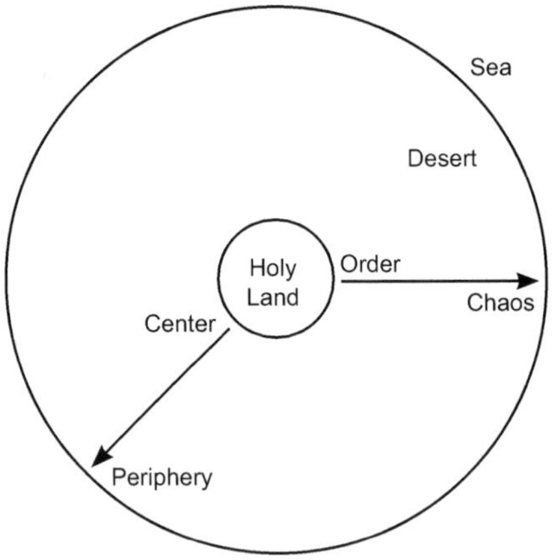

52. Dumbrell, *Search*, 23.

53. Anthropologist Victor Turner (*The Ritual Process*, 94–97) developed the term "liminal." Kunin cites the sacrifice of Isaac (Gen 22) and the ascension of Elijah (2 Kgs 2:11–14) as examples of liminality; *God's Place*, 30–37.

54. Simkins, *Creator and Creation*, 134; reproduced with permission.

The vertical model, which Simkins believes is the dominant one in biblical stories, relates sacred space to the cosmic mountain, the place of divine-human interaction (discussed further in the following chapter).

Figure 4.3. Simkins's Vertical Model of Sacred Space[55]

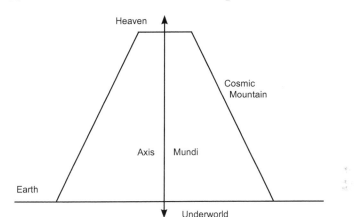

Simkins thinks both models are essential to describe Israel's "symbolic understanding of the structure of God's presence in the creation."[56] I believe these models can also be helpful in understanding the relationship of sacred space to peripheral or profane space. They note the presence of divine reality while incorporating the presence of evil forces that threaten God's good creation, but are broader and less dualistic than "spiritual warfare" models (discussed further below).

Conceptualizing Evil

Characteristics of sacred space can inform our understanding of profane space, especially through the use of binary oppositions. Sacred space is symbolized by light, life, and land; evil is symbolized by darkness, death, and seas.[57] This concurs with other biblical descriptions of the nature of evil/chaos. Furthermore, since sacred space is described as central, profane

55. Simkins, *Creator and Creation*, 139; reproduced with permission.

56. Ibid., 144.

57. Wilderness/the desert—profane space—does not fit as well into this classification, because its binary is not as obvious. However, it is associated with death, barrenness, and demons which are opposed to life, fertility, and the divine. The desert could also be contrasted with Jerusalem, the "sacred city."

space can be seen as peripheral. Sacred space is a gift from God, blessed and filled with divine presence; therefore, profane space is perhaps not a gift from God, cursed and characterized by divine absence. These factors further inform the ontology of evil. Lacking divine blessing and presence, and existing peripherally to divine reality, evil is likely to be somewhat less real, affirming suggestions from the previous chapter regarding the ontology of evil.

Sacred Actions

Sacred actions are as important as sacred space in aiding our conceptualization of evil. Actions in creation are obviously primarily related to the divine. However, angels and humans appear to have some responsibility. These are discussed in turn.

Divine Initiative

There is no doubt that God alone creates the world and is thus worthy of praise; however, the manner in which he does so has been debated. Mark Smith describes three models of creation in the Bible, noting they are interrelated: divine power (creation due to God's victory over cosmic enemies), divine wisdom (creation as craft), and divine presence (creation imbued with divine holiness, as discussed above).[58] The categories used more commonly are creation-through-conflict and creation-without-conflict. Examining similarities between these views may provide further information. This section first evaluates warfare interpretations of creation, and then examines alternate metaphors and concepts that may contribute to a non-warfare model of creation.

---

58. Smith, *Priestly Vision*, 12–14. He stresses that non-Genesis texts need to be incorporated and believes the third model is based on the first: a space for divine dwelling is created after the victory over enemies (27–31). These models provide both insights and limitations: the first is the least satisfying due to its violence, but has the advantage of explaining chaos in the world; the second model is appealing for today, but may be too optimistic; the third model is the most difficult for today, but appeals to the intuition that life is not simply power struggles; this model affirms that the transcendent can become immanent (32–37).

Many biblical verses imply that God creates by battling chaos, sometimes personified as a monster. The view of God creating by overcoming chaos was first discussed by Hermann Gunkel over a century ago, following the discovery of documents describing Babylonian myths—all depicting creation as a battle between opposing forces.[59] He argues that many biblical passages portraying creation as involving conflict originated with ANE creation myths; this is known as the *Chaoskampf* tradition (or the combat myth) and has been supported by documents found at Ugarit in the early twentieth century. The combat myth was widespread in the ancient world and almost certainly known to biblical authors.[60] Many verses are thought to follow *Chaoskampf* (Job 3:8; 26:12; 38:8; Pss 74:13; 89:9; 106:9; 107:29; Isa 27:1; 50:2; Hab 3:15; Nah 1:4).

Longman and Reid, in their examination of the "divine warrior" motif in the OT, emphasize the battle imagery of *Chaoskampf*. They point out God's victory over the "evil" sea and his continual battle with forces of chaos. *Chaoskampf* texts "reflect a cosmological conflict that is reflected in historical warfare but ultimately reaches its origins in the spiritual realm."[61] Boyd has capitalized on the *Chaoskampf* motif in his claim that God is at war with evil forces. He believes "this theme constitutes one of the oldest [and] most profound elements of the cosmic warfare motif" in the OT. This conflict between order and chaos is both primordial and

---

59. Gunkel, *Schöpfung und Chaos*. Ancient creation stories focused more on the creation of gods, not earth. In the Babylonian cosmogony, *Enuma Elish*, Apsu (sweet, male water) and Tiamat (bitter, female seawater), the primordial couple, dwell happily until their noisy progeny disturb them. Apsu plots to kill them, but they hear of the plan and appoint Ea to kill Apsu. Tiamat is enraged and produces hoards of demons to fight for her. However, Marduk (or Bel, Ea's son and leader of the lesser gods) kills Tiamat splitting her body: half becomes the heaven, half the earth. Tiamat continues to exist in the form of threatening primeval waters; Hesiod, *Theogony*; Foster, "Mesopotamia," 161–213; Walton, *ANE Thought*, 43–83. In Canaanite cosmogonies, Baal, son of El and Asherah, is depicted as a fertility god and warrior who ascends to the throne through his conquest over the sea (battle with Yamm and sea dragons), and his conquest over death (Mot). Some versions depict Baal and Mot in eternal combat; Smith, *Ugaritic Baal Cycle*. On the association between these myths and Genesis, see Batto, "Creation Theology," 16–38; *Slaying the Dragon*, 44–48; Anderson, *Creation versus Chaos*, 15–20.

60. Batto, *Slaying the Dragon*, 77; Forsyth, *Old Enemy*, 6. Batto claims both Isa 51:9–11 and Jer 31:35 reinterpret the combat myth; *Slaying the Dragon*, 80–83, 112.

61. Longman and Reid, *God is a Warrior*, 78. They believe this warrior theme begins in Genesis 3 and ends in Revelation.

perennial. The OT appropriated the ANE conception of "the world as being surrounded by hostile monsters that forever seek to devour it." Boyd claims that belief in demonic realities was behind the association between water and evil; thus Leviathan is a formidable foe that YHWH subdues. Moreover, "a very real battle took place when God created the world, and it is still taking place as Yahweh (not Baal or Marduk) preserves the world from chaos."[62]

Some scholars have argued against using *Chaoskampf*, partly out of concern for warfare imagery and to deemphasize the influence of ANE mythology on the OT. Richard Middleton expresses concern about the violent imagery in *Chaoskampf* passages. He emphasizes the socio-political context of those texts as well as their polemical intent—to demythologize pagan creation accounts. He accepts their occurrence but believes they are uncommon. Middleton summarizes:

> If the portrayal of God's exercise of non-violent creative power in Gen 1 is taken in conjunction with its claim that humanity is made in the image of *this* God, this has significant implications for contemporary ethics. This opening canonical disclosure of God and humanity constitutes, not only a normative framework for interpreting the rest of Scripture, but also a paradigm or model for exercising of human power in the midst of a world filled with violence.[63]

Tsumara, discussed above, uses linguistic analysis and concludes there is no evidence for *Chaoskampf* in the biblical creation stories.[64] He argues that "chaos" can mean "emptiness" or "waste," and that "water" and "sea" carry no connotations of evil monsters. Furthermore, the poetic passages that refer to monsters or storm theophanies are only metaphorical. Tsumara's primary weakness is his focus on Genesis 1 and minimization of poetic/wisdom/prophetic literature. He also appears unaware of contemporary metaphor theory's claim that metaphors depict reality. As discussed above, I believe that chaos does symbolize evil; however, the appropriation of ANE myths by biblical authors does not have to be interpreted through warfare imagery. One can find a middle ground between the denial of ANE imagery and its excessive appropriation.

62. Boyd, *God at War*, 84, 87, 91, 93–96.

63. Middleton, "Violent God?" 341–55. Middleton expands on this idea in *Liberating Image*.

64. Tsumara, *Creation and Destruction*. 182–85. Fretheim follows Tsumara in denying the presence of *Chaoskampf* in the creation texts; *God and World*, 43–46.

AUTHORITY

A first way is to emphasize authority instead of power. Written in the context of ANE religions, the polemical nature of Genesis 1 is readily apparent. Many have noted that creation occurs without conflict, in obedient response God's will. The Genesis account portrays God as creating simply and effortlessly with a word; he issues a divine command and it is so.[65] In stark contrast to the weapons used by ANE heroes to defeat their enemy, YHWH uses only his voice.[66] Most creation passages emphasize God's authority over evil and indeed all creation. Emphasizing authority over power not only offers alternative non-warfare language but also helps reconcile the various creation texts (e.g., authority is common to both conflict and wisdom models of creation).

THE HOLY SPIRIT

Second, attending to the role of the Holy Spirit in creation may be helpful. The interpretation of *rûaḥ ʾĕlōhîm* (Genesis 1:2b; "Spirit of God," NIV, "wind from God," NRSV) has been debated. If it is simply a wind, this could be seen as compatible with the chaotic situation described in the rest of the verse.[67] However, this phrase elsewhere in the Bible is interpreted as "Spirit of God" making it more likely to be the case here.[68] This supports the idea that the Spirit is involved in creation generally, and perhaps specifically by keeping chaos at bay. Thus the Spirit anticipates God's action in creation. Dumbrell believes the *rûaḥ ʾĕlōhîm* portrays a "picture of order

---

65. McBride, "Divine Protocol," 9; Batto, *Slaying the Dragon*, 79; Brueggemann, *Genesis*, 24; Jewett, *God*, 457–58. C. Koester points out that Genesis 1:3a is translated *egeneto* in the LXX: the same word used in the prologue to John's Gospel; *Word of Life*, 30.

66. Forsyth, *Old Enemy*, 64. In other creation texts, YHWH rebukes the sea (Pss 104:7, 106:9) again indicating authority.

67. E.g., Bonting, *Creation*, 53.

68. T. Wardlaw argues *rûaḥ ʾĕlōhîm* is the Spirit of God because the exact collocation is used in Gen 41:38, Exod 31:3, and Num 24:2 where the meaning is "Spirit," and it is appropriate for the Spirit to be associated with chaos since God brings order; *Words for God*, 291–93; Childs believes the Spirit is present over chaos because chaos is a threat to creation; *Myth and Reality*, 35, 42; see also Blocher, *Beginning*, 68. However, Ancient Hebrews did not clearly distinguish between wind and spirit. Fretheim believes the ambiguity should be retained; *Creation Untamed*, 20, and Smith thinks *rûaḥ ʾĕlōhîm* should be considered as both divine breath and wind; *Priestly Vision*, 55–56.

imposed upon an unruly element in creation."[69] The Spirit protecting creation supports the idea that chaos symbolizes evil.

Creation can also be viewed as effected by the Holy Spirit. The Spirit signifies the presence of God, and is elsewhere associated with creation ("By the Word of the Lord the heavens were made, and all their host by the breath of his mouth," Ps 33:6).[70] The first humans are given life through the breath of God (Gen 2:7); indeed all new life is attributed to the Spirit (Job 33:4; Ezek 37:1–14). By contrast, if God withdraws his Spirit, death often results (Job 34:15; Ps 104:30; Hos 13:15).[71] Life is generally considered to be dependent on the presence and activity of the Holy Spirit. Moltmann believes "God always creates through and in the power of his Spirit, and that the presence of his Spirit therefore conditions the potentiality and realities of his creation."[72] Significantly, the Spirit is not typically associated with warfare imagery; instead, images of wind (Gen 1:2; Exod 14:21; John 3:8; Acts 2:2), breath (Job 27:3; 32:8; 34:14; Pss 18:15; 33:6; John 20:22), a dove (Matt 3:16; Mark 1:10; Luke 3:22; John 1:32), and even silence (1 Kgs 19:12, 13) are used.[73] Theologian Michael Welker specifically notes that the Spirit is not a Spirit of war or "military enthusiasm", "but delivers out of distress and helplessness as a Spirit of righteousness and mercy."[74] Hence emphasizing the Creator Spirit may provide alternative non-warfare language for understanding evil.

69. Dumbrell, *Search for Order,* 17; see also Arnold, *Genesis,* 39.

70. See also Job 26:13; Ps 104:30; Routledge, *OT Theology,* 114. On the breath of life tradition see Edwards, *Breath of Life,* 35–39, 47–49.

71. Although Ps 51:11 would seem to imply that death is not necessarily a result of the Spirit's withdrawal; Welker, *God the Spirit* , 159–64.

72. Moltmann, *God in Creation,* 10; also 55, 66, 95–103, 206–14, *Spirit of Life,* xii, 5–8. He notes that God's Spirit is present everywhere, sustaining and preserving creation; since the world is threatened by nonbeing, it must be continually preserved from annihilation; *Source of Life,* 117–18. The role of the Spirit in creation has a long tradition: e.g., Basil of Caesarea, Athanasius; Hildegarde of Bingen; Kärkkäinen, *Pneumatology,* 37–65; Burgess, *Holy Spirit;* 47–49; Pinnock, *Flame of Love,* 49–77; Cole, *He Who Gives Life,* 73, 103.

73. The story of Elijah emphasizes the nonviolence of the Spirit of God; he is found not in wind or earthquake but in silence. Admittedly, there are some examples of the wind/Spirit of God inciting war and/or violence: Saul (1 Sam 11:6), Gideon (Judg 6:34) and Samson (Judg 14:6, 19). However, it could be argued that these examples serve a specific divine purpose and are exceptions. And, as Welker notes, the Spirit is only ever *indirectly* involved in violence, the result of which liberates God's people; *God the Spirit* , 52–60.

74. Welker, *God the Spirit,* 54–57.

ORDER, SEPARATION, AND BOUNDARY-SETTING

Finally, the creation metaphors of ordering, separating, and establishing limits can be emphasized over warfare imagery. In the Genesis 1 account, the verb *badal* (separate or divide) occurs with respect to the divisions between light/dark, sky/sea, and earth/sea. It has been suggested that in this creation account, order is more important than formation, and that this focus on separateness is unsurprising given the priestly origins of Genesis 1.[75] The verb *bārā* (typically translated "create") similarly connotes cutting, or separating and ordering.[76] Thus, as many biblical scholars point out, in Genesis 1 darkness is limited by "wholesome order"; it is not created, but only separated by God; primordial chaos is limited and contained by God, but not eliminated; chaos/evil is ordered in creation.[77] It has also been noted that this separation is not a one-time event: the *rûaḥ* "hovering" over creation implies continual activity over chaos.[78] Furthermore, as discussed above, God's rest after completion of creation symbolizes order. The Genesis 2 account has similar imagery: there is no hint of struggle but a focus on ordering.[79] Prophetic and wisdom literature describes YHWH assigning a limit to the seas, a boundary they may not pass (Job 38:10, 11; Prov 8:27–9; Isa 50:2; Jer 5:22; Nah 1:4). The "deep" is gathered and placed in storehouses (Ps 33:7), the raging sea is calmed (Pss 89:9, 107:29), and sea monsters are tamed (Job 40:15–24; 41:2–14;

75. The author was most likely one of Israel's priests; Arnold, *Genesis*, 29–30. Smith notes that *habdēl* is a priestly word and no other creation account has the obvious order of Genesis 1; *Priestly Vision*, 79, 87–89.

76. Arnold, *Genesis*, 37. Westermann describes the Genesis 1 account as involving a series of interventions: God divided, named, made, set, created, and blessed; *Creation*, 39–43 Walton notes that *bārā* has organizational implications, and is used only of God although its subjects include people, places, and abstractions; *ANE Thought*, 183. Van Wolde argues *bārā* means separate based on linguistic, exegetical, and comparative evidence; "The Verb *bārā*," 3–23; however, Becking and Korpel believe her argument is weak; they use an historical approach to suggest that create is the primary meaning of *bārā*; "To Create," 2–21. Perhaps it is a multivalent metaphor.

77. von Rad, *Genesis*, 52; Noort, "Creation of Light," 3–20; Arnold, *Genesis*, 64; Gibson, *Language and Imagery*, 97–99.

78. Waltke notes the Hebrew form is a participle, meaning continuity; *OT Theology*, 182. The Spirit "hovering" prior to the creation of the world also implies the pre-existence of chaos. The persistence of evil/chaos requires the continual creating/ordering of creation. Tupper makes a similar point from a theological perspective, noting that preservation and creation cannot be easily distinguished. God "sustains humanity in its sinfulness" but does not preserve chaos/sin; *Scandalous Providence*, 32.

79. McCarthy, "Creation Motifs," 90, 91.

Ps 74:13, 14). In the Psalms, divine sovereignty is emphasized: God is in control and creation is a manifestation of divine rule; "everything has its provender, its place and time" and the "centrality of order and purpose in creation" is underscored.[80] Frequently God is praised because he has set boundaries on evil (Pss 33, 89, 104, 107). Thus creation involves a simultaneous construction of sacred space and separation from profane space.

The *Chaoskampf* motif affirms that God's good creation exists in binary opposition to forces of evil, however, many of these texts allow for non-warfare interpretations, which accords better with the Genesis 1 account of creation-without-conflict. Although there are some violent images, such as crushing or piercing the dragon, other metaphors are available. Even the ANE creation myths can be viewed with non-warfare imagery. Egyptian cosmogonies, for instance, likely viewed creation as differentiation.[81] Simkins describes the Babylonian story thus: "Creation in the *Enuma Elish* entails the establishment of order, classification, and differentiation. . . . Tiamat is . . . confined within set boundaries."[82]

Many biblical scholars have discussed the combat myth without recourse to warfare language. Bernhard Anderson uses language of boundaries and order and argues that this motif was reinterpreted historically in the OT: "The raging, unruly waters of chaos symbolize the powers which threaten to destroy the meaningfulness of history. . . . Creation continues, precisely because at each moment of time, darkness must be dispelled and the raging waters of the abyss kept in their place by the creative word of God." He notes the common belief of a cycle of creation, lapse, and restoration, which Israel interpreted as stories of God's deliverance. Chaotic, demonic powers, symbolized by the sea, are "subdued by the Creator but not finally vanquished." Creation is thus a continual process. Anderson believes creation involves cosmic order: the waters are assigned limits and all creatures have their proper place, being radically dependent on the Creator.[83] Wakeman, in her examination of mythical monsters, points out that the evil monster in ANE cosmogonic myths either devours or separates (death/life, dark/light, dry/wet), and has to be captured, confined, bound, and ordered. Similarly, the biblical monster swallows (Exod 15:12; Jer 51:34), is cursed (Gen 3:14; Job 3:8; 41:1), rebuked (Ps 106:9;

---

80. Mays, "Maker of Heaven and Earth," 84; Miller, "Poetry of Creation," 96; C. Barth, *God with Us*, 18.

81. Clifford and Collins, "Introduction," 3.

82. Simkins, *Creator and Creation*, 194–95.

83. Anderson, *Creation versus Chaos*, 132, 134; "Biblical Creation Faith," 12–15.

Isa 50:2; Nah 1:4), trampled upon (Job 9:8; Hab 3:12, 15; Amos 4:13), killed (Pss 74:13, 14; 89:10; Isa 51:9), and/or confined (Job 38:8–11; Ps 104:9; Prov 8:27, 29; Jer 5:22). "One of the ways of dealing with the conquered monster is to establish a boundary to his legitimate sphere of activity . . . and thereby incorporate him in the cosmos."[84] This border separates chaos from cosmos (Mic 7:11). In the future, the cosmos or Israel's boundary will be extended. Hence Wakeman sees boundaries and battle as equivalent metaphors. Jewish scholar Jon Levenson also emphasizes the ordering of creation. He notes that the main difference between Genesis 1 and the Babylonian myths is that God creates without opposition; God's mastery is stressed. Primordial chaos is not eliminated but transformed; water and darkness are confined. Thus what emerges from the creation stories is "an environment ordered for peaceful human habitation and secure against the onslaughts of chaos and anarchy." Evil is not annihilated but continually transformed and bounded. Evil is experienced because "God's ordering of reality is irresistible but not constant or inevitable."[85] Levenson summarizes: "The confinement of chaos, rather than its elimination is the essence of creation."[86] Smith likewise stresses creation as separation and differentiation; creation results not from destruction (as in battle imagery) but from construction, which results in a divine temple.[87] He brings together ideas of sacred space and sacred actions of ordering.

These scholars have been quoted at length to underscore the point that most creation passages can be interpreted without using warfare language. Boundary metaphors of *Chaoskampf* are at least as prevalent as

84. Wakeman, *God's Battle,* 39, 133. She believes one monster concept underlies both ANE and biblical literature (2). Day agrees that creation involves limiting chaos and concludes that "chaos monsters" were subdued and deprived of power in the OT; *God's Conflict,* 74–87, e.g., Leviathan is portrayed with only one head, not seven; mythical creatures which threaten creation are best understood as demonic beings. God controls the sea in creation, echoing ANE cosmogonies, and reflected in the exodus story. Day asserts that God creates without conflict (7, 23, 50–55).

85. Levenson, *Persistence of Evil,* 14, 47, 121–23. God's victory is meaningful because his foe is formidable and still present (27).

86. Ibid., 17. Brueggemann follows Levenson in his assertion that the creation of Genesis 1 reflects an imposition of order on chaos; it is an on-going process due to the resilience of chaos which "must repeatedly be rebuked and swept away"; *OT Theology,* 159, 326–27. Creation is completely dependent on divine ordering (333). Routledge also affirms the ordering aspects of *Chaoskampf* and emphasizes the continual nature of creation: "mythological imagery thus enables the OT writers to show God's victory in creation as a past event, a present reality and a future hope"; *OT Theology,* 130; see also Batto, *Slaying the Dragon,* 119.

87. Smith, *Priestly Vision,* 51–71.

warfare metaphors. If creation is viewed as ordering and assigning limits to evil, these metaphors function both to explain the persistence of evil and as polemical against the complex warfare of ANE myths. Biblical "chaos" is a modified and diminished version of ANE "chaos." YHWH has more authority than pagan "gods" and need only speak a word to order "chaos." The biblical authors accepted some of the aspects of ANE myths, but fashioned their own theology from them. This view could satisfy Middleton's concerns about violent imagery as well as Tsumara's and Fretheim's concerns about the polemical nature of the creation texts. It is unnecessary to abandon ANE motifs in order to remove violence from creation stories. Rather chaos/disorder/anti-creational forces can be used as a collective metaphor for evil. Evil that needs to be continually confined, separated, contained, and put in its proper place.

Many theologians have discussed creation using metaphors of order and boundaries (albeit not usually explicitly). Barth describes creation in terms of separation from "nothingness." He views Genesis 1–3 as prehistory. The chaos of Genesis 1:2 refers to a "primal and rudimentary state ... of evil and nothing good can come from these primeval waters.[88] Chaos is not created, but rejected by God; it is that which God "has already rejected, negated, passed over and abandoned even before He utters His first creative Word"; "the unwilled and uncreated reality which constitutes as it were the periphery of His creation." Creation involves "a separation and the demarcation of a frontier in face of the element of chaos." The basic separation between light (good creation) and darkness (evil, non-creation, nonbeing) at creation relates to the eternal separation as God says "no" to darkness. In creation, God pushes back chaos "outside the limits of the world willed and determined by Him." As a result of this separation, there arises a frontier of chaos. The separated elements remain as a "memory of chaos in the cosmos."[89] Although Barth's exegesis of Genesis is questionable, his ideas have some merit, especially his focus on separation and ordering as opposed to warfare.[90] Moltmann's views are again similar to those of Barth. He highlights ordering in creation: "God introduces order

---

88. Barth *CD III*.1.81, 105, 108. The Spirit over this chaos functions to reveal its dark nature. He also argues against a "Golden age" in creation because the first humans were sinners immediately; *CD IV*.1.508.

89. Barth, *CD III*.1.102, 122, 133, 142; *CD III*.3.352.

90. N. G. Wright accuses him of eisegesis; *Dark Side*, 51; Blocher believes he introduces a dualism foreign to Genesis; *Beginning*, 64. Keller points out his anti-warfare polemic: "Barth's God does not need to fight," "He dominates not with sword but with word"; *Face of the Deep*, 92.

through separation" and creation "extends the work of God against chaos, nothingness and death." God's work in creation is the restraint of chaos; "the forces of chaos—night and sea—thrust themselves into creation, even though they are excluded and confined by God."[91]

Simkins, in keeping with his models of sacred space, notes that, in the ancient world, the human body was often seen as a microcosm of creation.[92] Conception, gestation, and birth are internal activities; order and boundaries are external ones. He argues that metaphors of procreation are more common in both ANE and biblical literature than metaphors of conflict. In fact, in the Bible, images of separation and differentiation are primary; conflict only occurs when creation is threatened. Simkins also discusses agricultural metaphors of creation and notes that both internal (birth, plant growth) and external (order, differentiation) metaphors exhibit unity. With respect to Genesis 1, he points out that most elements are described in terms of God separating or making. Furthermore, the cycle of catastrophe and new creation, common in ANE myths, provides an understanding of evil for Israel. "God's redeeming work is described as a new creation . . . God defeats but does not annihilate chaos. God merely confines or restricts chaos to fixed bounds."[93] Other theologians who emphasize boundary-making aspects of creation include Löning and Zenger[94] and Alister McGrath.[95]

The scholars discussed above emphasize the process of creation as involving separation, division, and ordering; they employ *spatial* imagery. Divine action in most creation texts involves placing limits on evil, in order to protect the good creation. Most scholars do not explicitly refer to spatial metaphors, but these actions in creation fit well with the spatial model presented earlier. Creation, as a circle on the face of the deep,

91. Moltmann, *God in Creation*, 77; *Crucified God*, 193; *Science and Wisdom*, 39.

92. Simkins, *Creator and Creation*, 75–79.

93. Ibid., 91–116, 195.

94. They believe creation involved an organization of chaotic elements (*tōhû wābōhû*, darkness, primeval waters). "A boundary is laid for chaos that it is not able to cross, but only because the creator God daily summons up the divine chaos-taming might"; Löning and Zenger, *To Begin with*, 18–20, 39.

95. He views creation as the subjugation of chaos, and imposition of order. Creation does not result from battle but from a free decision of God to create an orderly world. In the Psalms, kingship is a stabilizing force that promotes "social and political order in a potentially chaotic world"; "divine ordering of creation sets boundaries for all the forces contained within its bounds"; McGrath, *Nature*, 146–55. He also suggests that disorder (sin perhaps) is related to chaos-complexity theory (288–89).

is produced first by separating out the deep; because chaos continually threatens creation, this separation and ordering is reapplied continually.

Angelic Responsibility

Another "sacred action" is the behavior of created spiritual beings. This topic is included here for thematic purposes, but incorporates both OT and NT verses. There is no clear biblical evidence regarding the nature or autonomy of angelic beings. It appears they are created spiritual beings (explicit in Ps 33:6; implicit in Rom 11:36; Eph 3:9; Col 1:16), albeit details are lacking regarding their creation.[96] They were present to rejoice in the creation of the earth, and therefore, were probably created sometime prior to the Genesis account (Job 38:7). Angels function as servants of God; giving messages (Gen 16:7–11; Judg 6:11–21; 13:3–21; Matt 1:20; 28:2–7; Acts 8:26; Rev 1:1), accompanying and protecting God's people (Exod 25:20–22; Pss 34:8; 46:7, 11; Dan 6:22; Acts 8:26; 10:22), worshiping (Ps 148:2; Luke 2:13, 14; Heb 1:6; 12:22; Rev 5:11, 12; 7:11, 12), ministering (Matt 4:11; Heb 1:14), and judging (Mark 8:38; 13:27; Acts 7:53; 12:23; 2 Thess 1:7, 8). In the OT, these spiritual beings form a divine assembly or council that surrounds God and appear to have consultant roles (Gen 19:1, 13; 1 Kgs 22:19–22; Job 1–2; Pss 82:1; Jer 23:18).[97] There is some suggestion that angels are assigned care of the nations (Deut 32:8; Dan 10:13; Mic 4:5), and there are implications that divine beings can be punished for failing in their duties (Ps 82:6, 7; Isa 24:21–22).[98] All of this suggests that angels have some degree of moral autonomy, or the ability to defy God. In addition, there are hints that some angels rebelled; typically discussed as the angelic fall.

This fall is alluded to in the judgment of gods who are doomed to fall (Ps 82:6, 7) and fallen stars that were associated with angels in ancient times (Dan 8:10–11; Matt 24:29; Mark 13:25; Rev 9:1). In the Gospels, an

96. Waltke, *OT Theology,* 273.

97. E. T. Mullen summarizes: the functions of the assembly of gods: aid in warfare, carry out decree, act as heralds, and honor and adore; *Divine Council,* 279; see also Miller, *Divine Warrior,* 66–70. This council is also implied by the term "us" in divine speeches (Gen 1:26; 3:22; 11:7; Isa 6:8).

98. Given the few obtuse references, conclusions about "territorial spirits" should be extremely tentative. On punishment, see Mullen, *Divine Council,* 232–42; Page, *Powers,* 54–62. With respect to Isaiah 24, Twelftree points out two stages to the defeat: they are first imprisoned then punished; suggested also in 1 En 10:4–6, and Jub 5:5–10; *Christ Triumphant,* 25.

angelic fall is implied in Luke's description of Satan falling like lightning in response to the proclamation of the kingdom of God, which indicates a present, continual fall.[99] John 12:31 also mentions the "ruler of this world" being "cast out," which suggests a fall of Satan as a result of the incarnation.[100] There are four primary clusters of biblical texts that are used in support of an angelic fall: the serpent of Genesis 3, the sons of God in Genesis 6, the fall of an exalted one (Lucifer) in Isaiah and Ezekiel, and the apocalyptic expulsion of the dragon/devil from heaven. There are numerous exegetical difficulties with these texts: allusions to an angelic fall are oblique, frequently isolated and sporadic; often occur in mythopoetic passages, appearing to reflect extra-biblical myths; and there is no consensus regarding who fell (Satan, angels) or when this occurred. The angelic fall also leads to questions regarding the nature of angels, particularly their autonomy. J. B. Russell comments on the biblical ambiguity surrounding this topic. First, the nature of the fall (moral, loss of dignity, literal ejection from heaven, voluntary departure), second, geography (heaven to earth, heaven to underworld, earth, or air, to underworld), and third, chronology (primordial, after the creation of humans due to envy, with the watchers at the time of Noah, at the advent of Christ, at the passion of Christ, at the parousia, a thousand years following). The only point that is completely consistent is that the new age of Christ conflicts with the old age of Satan.[101] The four primary "angelic fall" passages are discussed in turn.

The Serpent

Most OT scholars point out that the snake of Genesis 3:1–5 is merely an animal.[102] However, they admit that there is much strange about this creature (it talks and appears to have preternatural knowledge) and recognize its relationship to evil.[103] This serpent seems malevolent and opposes God;

---

99. Luke 10:18. This could also be a prophetic statement, but the tense of the verb suggests more a continuous action, not necessarily a "defeat"; Page, *Powers*, 110; Twelftree, *Name of Jesus*, 140.

100. There is an apparent contradiction to an angelic fall in the Johannine Christ's statement that the devil was a murderer "from the beginning" (John 8:44). Christ's omniscience could perhaps explain this.

101. Russell, *Devil*, 241–42.

102. E.g., von Rad, *Genesis*, 87; Brueggemann, *Genesis*, 47; Arnold, *Genesis*, 62.

103. E.g., Page, *Powers*, 13. However, the imagery is multivalent, sometimes symbolizing good (e.g., the serpent that Moses raise up provided healing, Num 21:9). J.

it distorts and contradicts his word, and leads the humans to disobey. In addition, it is cursed by God (Gen 3:14–15), implying that is has moral responsibility.[104] The snake is associated with the dragon of ANE mythologies and is identified as the devil in later texts (Rev 12:9).[105] This has led to a general, if sometimes reluctant, acceptance of at least an association between the serpent and Satan, although Blocher criticizes those who minimize the nature and role of the snake: "Scripture itself leaves us in no doubt; the snake is the devil."[106] Boyd too asserts that the serpent in Eden is Satan.[107] I think we can confidently conclude there is at least an *association* between the serpent and the devil: both exist in the semantic domain of evil, in antithesis to holiness and goodness. As Eliade (and Barth to a lesser extent) have suggested, chaos, the devil, the dragon, and the snake are all related. The serpent's appearance in the garden requires explanation, and some sort of a primordial angelic fall is a reasonable, if speculative, option.

The *Běnê 'Ělōhîm*

There has been much discussion surrounding the interpretation of Genesis 6:1–4. This passage, due to its unique and mythic nature, is notoriously difficult to translate. It appears isolated from the remainder of Genesis 6,[108] and the meaning of *běnê 'ělōhîm* ("sons of God") has been debated. Some have suggested that they represent humans (Sethites)[109] and not heavenly beings, however, the majority of scholars view them as angels or

---

Charlesworth claims the serpent appears to tell the truth because the humans do not die; *Good and Evil Serpent*, 310, but he misses the symbolic nature of death.

104. Page, *Powers*, 14.

105. Wakeman, *God's Battle*, 84. Also, through the devil's envy death entered the world (Wis 2:24); Satan took the form of a snake in order to deceive Eve (Ap Mos 7:2). There is an implied association in Paul's reference to God crushing Satan under the feet of believers (Rom 16:20).

106. Blocher, *Beginning*, 151.

107. Based primarily on NT assertions as well as ANE parallels; *God at War*, 154–58. Waltke also asserts that the Genesis serpent embodies Satan, citing John 8:44 and 2 Cor 11:3; *OT Theology*, 273–74. He is inconsistent in saying that the origin of the primordial waters, the angels, and Satan is unknown (180, 230).

108. Although W. VanGemeren argues that Genesis 6:1–4 is not as isolated as it seems but bears linguistic and conceptual relationships to Adam and Noah; "Sons of God," 333–36.

109. Augustine held this view; VanGemeren, "Sons of God," 333–36; Page, *Powers*, 47–49.

lesser gods.[110] Elsewhere, *běnê ʾělōhîm* always refer to heavenly beings and the interpretation of this story in Second Temple Judaism affirms their identity as rebellious angels. These angels, by coming down to earth and mating with humans, violate boundaries between heaven and earth that were established in creation (Gen 1:6–10). Fretheim suggests that Genesis 6:1–4 depicts "the crossing of boundaries between the heavenly and earthly realms."[111]

The literature of the Second Temple Period elaborates on this story (in the Watcher Tradition), primarily in the pseudoepigraphal book of 1 Enoch, but also in Jubilees.[112] The watchers and/or their progeny destroy things, harm or eat humans, and lead them astray to idolatry and demonic sacrifice.[113] Archie Wright believes the *běnê ʾělōhîm* have autonomy as members of the divine council. He concludes that these angels "crossed the boundaries of the cosmos, which resulted in the corruption of the world and everything in it."[114] Annette Reed also notes the importance of the Enochic literature and asserts that the interpretation of Genesis 6:1–4 cannot be understood apart from the Watcher Tradition. Like Wright, she thinks this literature demonstrates concern with proper epistemological boundaries between heaven and earth; angels violated these boundaries and the angelic descent became an etiology for evil.[115] Although this

---

110. E.g., von Rad, *Genesis*, 113; VanGemeren, "Sons of God," 328, 345–48; A. Wright, *Origin*, 93–94, 103.

111. Fretheim, *God and World*, 79; Brueggemann, *Genesis*, 72. Page also points out that the angels were not content to "live within the parameters established by Yahweh" and sinned by "rejecting the order created by God"; *Powers*, 53.

112. Enoch being the faithful albeit mysterious figure who "walked with God" (Gen 5:24). This book, also known as Ethiopian Enoch, was composed from 200–260 BCE. Chapters 6–16, the Book of the Watchers (BW), are most relevant. A. Y. Reed believes 1 Enoch/BW should not be dismissed as non-canonical, as it was used by later biblical writers and was esteemed in the early church, often functioning as Scripture; *Fallen Angels*, 57, 136, 152–55. There are also allusions to this story in multiple DSS, e.g., CD, 4QEnGiants. There is much inconsistency.

113. Jub 11:4, 5; 1 En 19:1–2. The leaders of the Watcher angels are Shemihazah/Semyaza and/or Asaʾel/Azazel, and the progeny of the illicit mating are called evil spirits, demons, giants, Gibborim, and/or Nephilim(1 En 15:8–11; Jub 10:5). Nephilim (from the Hebrew root *npl* meaning to fall) is translated as giants in the LXX. They are referred to in Num 13:33, and described as giants; Hanson, "Rebellion in Heaven," 221–22.

114. Wright, *Origin of Evil Spirits*, 103, 137. Wright's analysis places the origin of evil outside of creation.

115. Reed, *Fallen Angels*, 116. There was also an association between the watchers, idolatry, and demons (46–49).

literature is extra-biblical, it was highly regarded and is nonetheless helpful to our understanding of the idea of an angelic fall. The theme of the
Watcher Angels is picked up by NT texts that refer to angels who sinned
and left their proper dwelling; they are bound in chains and cast into deep-
est darkness, or Tartarus, until the eschaton (2 Pet 2:4–9; Jude 6).[116] The
interpretation of this passage in the Second Temple Period affirms previous suggestions of evil as boundary violation.

Because of this transgression, God is grieved and destroys all
humankind, save a few. There are multiple conceptual and linguistic similarities between Genesis 1 and Genesis 6–8 (often seen as a new creation;
see below). This "angelic fall" might inform our understanding of a primordial fall: after the flood, itself a result of the sin of angels, the "evil/
chaotic" waters are separated and God creates again. Therefore, the angelic
fall of Genesis 6:1–4 could possibly be also referring to a primordial angelic fall. This myth appears to assign moral responsibility to angels and
implies that they violated boundaries; unfortunately, it is not conclusive.

Lucifer

The association between Lucifer, or Satan, and the mythic stories in Isaiah
and Ezekiel has been around since early Judaism. Isaiah 14:3–21 refers to
the king of Babylon but incorporates mythic language. This *hêlēl benšāḥar*
("Day Star, son of Dawn," NRSV; "Morning Star, son of the Dawn," NIV)
aspires to ascend to heaven, above the stars and clouds, on Mount Zaphon, like the "Most High," but is doomed to the pit and Sheol. The Vulgate translated *hêlēl* as Lucifer (light-bearer), solidifying the connection
with Satan. Ezekiel 28:2–19 describes the prince of Tyre who is violent and
proud, thinking he is a god, but is judged a mere mortal. Before his punishment (cast from the mountain of God, exposed, burned), he was perfect, wise, and beautiful, adorned with precious stones, and living in Eden,
the mountain of God. There is suggestion here of an angelic being that fell
far, however, the connection with Satan in these myths is not conclusive;
for instance, Christ is also referred to as the morning star (2 Pet 1:19; Rev
22:16).[117] They have likely been influenced by ancient extra-biblical myths:

116. Both authors appear to follow 1 Enoch. Jude 9, 14 and 15 quote almost directly from 1 En 1:9; Reed, *Fallen Angels*, 106; Skaggs, *1 Peter*, 114, 117–22, 154, 159, 168.

117. Kelly, *Satan: A Biography*, 93, 94, 164–67. Boyd, I believe, is too confident in
his conclusions regarding the association with Satan; *God at War*, 157–62.

there is an association with Venus,[118] Greek mythology,[119] ANE myths of gods aspiring beyond their status,[120] stories of a revolt of gods or cosmic rebellion, and myths of stars falling.[121] The Isaiah and Ezekiel myths probably represent a mingling of mythic traditions.[122] These myths can also be described in spatial terms: the "reversal of fortune that results from inappropriate boundary crossing."[123] Overall, there is consensus that the Isaiah and Ezekiel passages are more than simply historical, probably reflecting a myth of cosmic rebellion, but the identification of Satan with *hêlēl* is not clear-cut and cannot be used as definitive evidence for an angelic fall.

THE DRAGON

Finally, in the Revelation 12:4–27 story, the devil/dragon/Satan throws down stars from heaven then seeks to devour the new-born child/ruler from the woman. He is battled by the angel Michael and thrown to earth. Because of this expulsion, Satan can only exercise power on earth.[124] He knows his time is short and wages war on the rest of the woman's children. Eventually the dragon is bound. Adela Yarbro Collins suggests that the war in heaven reflects *Chaoskampf*. She argues that the dragon, Leviathan, and Satan are the same; Satan's rebellion against God in heaven parallels other ancient myths.[125] The expulsion of Satan and his angels from heaven

118. McKay, "Helel and the Dawn-Goddess," 451–64.

119. The myth of Phaethon, "morning star," the son of Helios (sun god) and Eos (dawn goddess), in pride begged to drive the sun-chariot but failed and was struck down; Hesiod, *Theogony;* Mckay, "Helel."

120. A story in Akkadian mythology relates a god, Athtar, the "shining one," who aspired to ascend Mount Zaphon but fell or was cast down from on high; Day, *Yahweh,* 166–84. Day points out that Isaiah refers to a star who was originally in Eden and perfect; whereas Ezekiel describes an arrogant human who aspired to ascend to Eden.

121. 1 En 86:1–6; 2 En 29:4; Mullen, *Divine Council,* 232–44; Forsyth, *Old Enemy,* 134–40.

122. Prinsloo, "Isaiah 14:12–15," 435–36. They also perhaps demonstrate an interesting intertwining of human and spiritual rebellion.

123. Page, *Myth of Cosmic Rebellion,* 218.

124. Lichtenberger, "Down-Throw," 119–47. Interestingly, other texts suggest Satan's realm is in the air or heavens (Eph 2:2, 6:12).

125. Collins, *Combat Myth,* 83. Skaggs and Benham agree the dragon and Satan are one, but point out the highly symbolic and ambiguous nature of the text; *Revelation,* 128–30. Reed believes the Revelation text about the war in heaven reflects the Watcher Tradition, but was transferred to the beginning of time and Satan named instead of Asael; *Fallen Angels,* 116. Historical associations with Rome in this passage have also been noted.

is perhaps the clearest text suggesting an angelic fall. However, given its eschatological and mythic nature, interpretation is complex. As discussed, it relates to other biblical (the Watcher Tradition, the combat myth) and extra-biblical myths. Although this story appears to be referring to a future event, there is no reason it cannot also refer to a primordial time or the time of the incarnation. Overall, this passage implies but does not provide conclusive evidence for an angelic fall.

SUMMARY AND THEOLOGY

Auffarth and Stuckenbruck, introducing their volume on the angelic fall, note that this doctrine, despite its immense influence on Christianity and Judaism, is only hinted at in the Bible. It receives its most complete treatment in the literature of the Second Temple Period and offers an attractive solution to the problem of evil in that God does not have to be blamed.[126] Despite ambiguous biblical support, the doctrine of the angelic fall has been widely accepted. It developed with church fathers,[127] and Augustine affirmed the angelic fall, which he transposed to the beginning of creation.[128] Belief in an angelic fall persisted into the Middle Ages and beyond. The Fourth Lateran Council (1215 CE) affirmed that Satan and the demons were created good, but sinned of their own free will, and are eternally damned. Thomas Aquinas believed Lucifer fell almost immediately after his creation.[129] The angelic fall remains an official doctrine of the Roman Catholic Church.[130]

126. Auffarth and Stuckenbruck, "Introduction," 1, 10. Lichtenberger notes the "down-throw" tradition appears in early Jewish texts and the Gospels; "Down-throw," 119–47.

127. Justin Martyr followed the Watcher Tradition and attributed much evil to fallen angels; angels had originally been appointed to mediate God's providential rule, but had disobeyed; 2 *Apology* 5; Tertullian emphasized the free will of angels; *Against Marcion* 5:17, *Apology* 22; Origen connected Satan, Lucifer, the Prince of Tyre and the Dragon; *Exhortation*, 18; Lactantius blended two traditions, suggesting there were two classes of demons: heavenly (Satan and the fallen angels) and earthly (the offspring of the Watcher angels); *Divine Institutes*, 2:8, 14, 15, 17, 7:24.

128. Augustine, *City of God*, 22:1, 15:23; Reed, *Fallen Angels*, 219–21.

129. Other angels cannot sin: once they do one good act, they are confirmed to grace; Aquinas, *Summa Theologicae I*, 62–64. Luther followed traditional beliefs regarding the angelic fall: Satan was expelled from heaven because of his sinful pride, where he corrupted Adam and continues to corrupt all humanity; *Weimer Ausgabe* 1.269, 15.473, 25.456, 37.286.

130. Cunningham, "Satan," 359–66.

Boyd argues for a "literal prehistoric fall of angels and cosmic forces."[131] He thinks that the autonomy of angelic beings, depicted in the divine council and elsewhere, is biblically supported, and attributes the origin of evil to the angelic fall. Their freedom allowed for rebellion. Since God is holy and does not create evil, angels must have "made themselves evil."[132] Boyd points out that because evil has an end, it must have had a beginning. In fact, his basic thesis is that the primary explanation for cosmic evil is the freedom of spiritual beings. Boyd's approach is logical but he minimizes the biblical ambiguities and interpretive challenges associated with the "angelic fall." He also associates this fall with the "gap" theory, itself tenuous. I think his confidence is unwarranted. Conversely, Yong appears to deny any angelic fall or even existence of spirit beings prior to the creation of humanity; he does not wrestle with the concept which, despite its ambiguity, has much support.[133]

Probably the majority of contemporary scholars recommends caution with respect to the doctrine of the angelic fall because of the ambiguity of the biblical evidence.[134] Blocher believes that being true to the Bible requires acceptance of the notion of an angelic fall but cautions against giving it a key position.[135] Noll affirms that the mythic "rebellion in heaven" leads to the conclusion that evil originated with the unaccountable sin of Satan. Interestingly, he states that angels violated "the created barrier of the firmament."[136] Another approach is through logic. Nigel G.

131. Boyd, *God at War*, 101. He believes the Genesis 3 serpent, the Genesis 6 *běnê ʾĕlōhîm*, and the Isaiah and Ezekiel myths all refer to Satan and demons. Boyd does not appear to recognize that metaphors can depict reality, which results in his insistence on distinguishing between "literal" and "metaphorical."

132. Isa 45:18, Boyd, *God at War*, 99, 284–87. He garners support from the post-apostolic fathers; *Satan*, 40–48.

133. He states that "without . . . human and relational substrates, there are no angels"; *Spirit of Creation*, 217. He later states that fallen angels are one way the demonic may manifest but does not explain in what manner these emerge (219). I think Yong seriously undermines the divinity and goodness of angelic beings by suggesting they emerge from human substrates.

134. E.g., Cook, "Devils and Manticores," 165–84. He points out some intriguing questions that result from the premise of demons arising from an angelic fall, e.g., can one be possessed by an angel (169). Erickson accepts the angelic fall, and believes it must have been sometime between the end of creation and the fall; *Christian Theology*, 1, 448. This perhaps reflects his commitment to creation as perfect.

135. Blocher, *Beginning* 42. However, since he argues that there is no evil in Genesis 1–3, and that the Isaiah and Ezekiel texts cannot be used to support an angelic fall, it is not clear where he thinks the angelic fall is described in the Bible (64).

136. Noll, *Angels of Light*, 56, 122.

Wright describes the biblical references as elusive and oblique, but thinks that there are theological, if not exegetical, reasons for tentatively accepting the angelic fall.[137] He notes that this fall locates evil within creation, and is likely due to abuse of creaturely freedom, although the Bible does not discuss why angels would choose to sin.

I agree with Wright and others that the angelic fall is the most logical way to explain the origin of evil spirits. I also agree with Barth's association of demons with chaos, but his explanation of them somehow arising from this chaos is difficult to support biblically. We cannot know details regarding the angelic fall, but the concept is helpful. If angels, at least at some point in the primordial past, had the capacity to rebel against God, their creator, then maybe these "fallen" angels continue to pose a threat to creation. Considering the above-mentioned passages together and recognizing their mythical/metaphorical nature can provide more insight than each can alone, and may guard against dogmatic conclusions. Metaphors depict reality but not usually in a linear, rationalistic manner. In terms of the timing of the "angelic fall," perhaps one does not have to choose between options but conceive of it as simultaneously primordial, pre-flood, concurrent with Christ, and eschatological. A common theme that emerges in the preceding discussion is boundary violation—angels disregarding the created barrier between heaven and earth. This idea accords with the description of chaos/evil/fallen-angels as outside the good creation, needing to be separated and confined, but continually seeking to cross the border and intrude upon divine reality. When they succeed, evil is experienced (perhaps most evident in the serpent story). Evil can be understood not as a result of cosmic war but as a result of disobedience and boundary violation on the part of spiritual beings. However, some evil is also a result of human rebellion and misuse of responsibility.

Human Responsibility

A final "sacred action" is human responsibility, which becomes a more prominent theme later in the OT, but is present in the Genesis creation

137. N. G. Wright, *Dark Side*, 70–74, 156. T. Noble similarly believes logically we have to accept it since God is good and all he created is good; "The Spirit World," 205. Waltke also supports the angelic fall from a purely logical perspective; *OT Theology*, 273–74. Satan, like other angels, is a created being and part of the divine council. However, since he is not good and works in opposition to God, he must have rebelled. Waltke concludes that sin originated in the heavenly council prior to the beginning of Genesis 1.

stories. As Boyd, Fretheim, and others point out, the freedom God gives his creatures entails risk: the possibility of rebellion.[138] Viewed from a spatial perspective, humans living in the intermediary zone between the light and the dark can choose to turn towards the center or the periphery. The first humans are only given one prohibition, one boundary: they are not to eat from the tree of the knowledge of good and evil. They choose, however, to follow the deception of the snake and disobey God, with tragic consequences for all creation. The humans mistrust and assert themselves over God.[139] They choose to believe the lies of the devil over the truth of God. This story has been much discussed. Brueggemann thinks that Genesis 3 has been misunderstood: It is not an account of the "fall" and does not address abstract questions regarding how evil or death came into the world. Rather it is about the "reality of God and his resolve for life in a world on its way to death."[140] When the humans disobey, a prohibition is violated, permission is perverted, and vocation is neglected. Bill Arnold concurs that Genesis 3 is more interested in the nature of human rebellion than the explanation for evil. He believes "evil was present in potentiality in the Garden of Eden because of the inherent libertarianism of creation." The divine command implies the possibility for a return to chaos, symbolized by death.[141] Brueggemann and Arnold are correct that the nature of the "first sin" is complex; it involves more than simple disobedience but has spatial as well as moral aspects.

The results of this sin are manifold and can be portrayed through spatial imagery. Primarily, the humans are separated from their Creator; this loss of intimacy with God is evidenced by the fact that they are ashamed to be in his presence.[142] They do not die in a literal sense but experience what seems like death because of their separation from God.[143] Since sacred space is filled with life, profane space can be viewed as

138. Fretheim, *God and World*, 69; Boyd, *Satan*, 85–115; Pinnock et al., *Openness of God.*

139. Fretheim, *God and World*, 74; Biddle, *Missing the Mark*, 12–14. M. Boda notes that the Genesis 3 sin foreshadows covenant disloyalty; *Severe Mercy*, 517.

140. Brueggemann, *Genesis*, 41–44, 48.

141. Arnold, *Genesis*, 64–65. Blocher suggests the language of covenant breaking instead of fall, which Hos 6:7 uses in comparing Israel's transgression with Adam's *Beginning*, 136.

142. Arnold, *Genesis*, 67. There is also separation from each other and within themselves, evidenced by blame and shame; Blocher, *Beginning*, 174–75; Fretheim, *God and World*, 75.

143. Madigan and Levenson note that the ancient Hebrews did not make a

associated with death. In spatial terms, once the humans are cast from the presence of God, they fall under the influence of the evil periphery. As Blocher points out, the humans through their disobedience "perverted the order of the Creator."[144] By eating of the tree of the knowledge of good and evil, humans gain moral autonomy, when they should be completely dependent on God. Simkins summarizes the association between human obedience and order in the cosmos: "When humans follow the covenant, the order of creation is maintained. The established boundaries remain fixed. If humans neglect or reject the covenant, however, the creation itself suffers. The order of creation disintegrates, and the world reverts to its original chaotic state."[145] Evil can thus be conceptualized in terms of boundary violation. In contemporary theology, the doctrine of "original sin" and the notion of a moral "fall" are being increasingly questioned.[146] Therefore, it may be helpful to understand "sin" in spatial terms.

As a consequence of their rebellion, the humans are sent out of the circle of Eden; there is spatial separation. Once out, they are closer to chaos and further under the influence of the outer darkness. Unsurprisingly, evil escalates. Interestingly, the first occurrence of the word "sin" appears in relationship to Cain, where it is described in language reminiscent of an ANE demon.[147] Some scholars have hinted at, although not expounded, the relationship between sin and evil forces in Genesis 3. For example, Hellmut Frey, "the woman opened the doors to the dark power, and now as a penalty the doors are always to remain open," and Bernard Batto, "it was because of human sin that the divine sovereign's archenemy, Abyss, was able to regain entry into God's 'perfect' world and nearly undo it."[148]

---

distinction between literal death and a feeling of being dead which accompanies isolation; *Resurrection*, 54; like Burnett, discussed above.

144. Blocher, *Beginning*, 141.

145. Simkins, *Creator and Creation,* 198. Interestingly, Calvin believed that order is disrupted through the fall, and creation is now dependent on its Creator for the maintenance of order; *Institutes* I.xvi.2–4. Dumbrell also uses spatial terms: sin is "a deliberate human assault upon the established order of creation"; *Search for Order,* 27, as does McGrath: sin is not primarily a moral concept, but a failure to accept limitations placed on human existence; *Nature,* 287.

146. E.g., C. Barth believes there is no OT reference to a "fall" although rebellion is common; *God With Us,* 31–33; Van Wolde notes the "fall" is an anthropocentric doctrine and in fact the earth benefits from humans being driven out of the garden; *Stories,* 44–45.

147. Genesis 4:7 describes sin as "crouching," reminiscent of Rabisu, an ANE crouching demon; *DDD* 682–83; Boyd, *God at War,* 82; Fretheim, *God and World,* 72.

148. Frey, *Geschichte des Altertums,* quoted in von Rad, *Genesis,* 93 (similar to the

They seem to be suggesting that sin violates a boundary, which then allows evil beings to violate their boundaries. However, they perhaps overemphasize human responsibility and do not consider the initial transgression of the serpent.

Barth has also related sin and evil. Sin, like nothingness, is opposed by God and never allowed ontological status. Through sin though, humans can become both victims and agents of nothingness. Nothingness exists "behind God's back"; however, creatures can look away from God, therefore nothingness can be dangerous. Through sin, "the chaos separated by God becomes a factor and secures and exercises a power which does not belong to it in relation to God but can obviously do so in relation to His creatures."[149] Nothingness becomes real through sin. Similarly, Moltmann, in his discussion of "God-forsaken space," believes that created beings contribute to the evil nature of this space by isolating themselves from the Creator; conversely, those who sin and turn away from God fall under the influence of this evil space.[150] Moltmann and Barth appear to advocate a bidirectional model of boundary violation: evil occurs both as a result of human sin and demonic disobedience.

By employing spatial imagery, it can be seen that disobedience to the Creator has cosmic effects. By choosing to face the periphery rather than the center, humans violate their boundaries. (It could be argued that this choice was influenced by the snake, which had violated its own boundaries.) This results in cosmic disorder, which then encourages evil forces to overstep their boundaries, with consequent escalation of evil. Hence boundary violation can be considered not only dual-directional but continual and exponential (humans sin—open door to demonic—demons further incite to sin . . .).

Counteracting Evil

In sum, although the establishment of boundaries on evil is primarily a consequence of the grace of God, humans (and angels initially) perhaps have some responsibility in maintaining the order and boundaries of godly reality, mostly through obedience to God's commands. Understanding sin

---

idea of sin as an "entry point" for the demonic in popular literature); Batto, "Creation Theology in Genesis," 36.

149. Barth, *CD III*.3.108, 352, 355; *CD IV*.1.139. Barth's ideas are interesting but somewhat speculative.

150. Moltmann, *God in Creation*, 88–91.

as boundary violation accords well with previously discussed metaphors of order, separation, and boundary-setting in creation, and the nature of evil as disorder and chaos. Emphasizing divine authority, the role of the Holy Spirit, and creation as involving the limitation of evil provides alternative language to warfare.

Microcosms of Creation

The theme of sacred space, a circle on the deep, is referred to repeatedly throughout the OT; microcosms of creation can be discerned. Three primary ones are presented here.

The Flood

The first obvious one is the flood narrative (Gen 6:1—9:17). Floodwaters are like primordial waters—the deep, which was confined, is now allowed to cover the earth again. This can be viewed as an undoing or reversal of creation and boundary language is prominent. The flood "unleashes the force of chaos"[151] and "there is a collapse of the principal boundaries of creation."[152] God removes the boundaries on the deep, which results in it encroaching on and destroying most of creation. However, one person is saved. As Adam is commanded to tend the garden, Noah is commissioned to build an ark. The ark is like a mini-circle on the deep. After the flood, God re-enacts creation, or re-creates; he sends a wind (reminiscent of the *rûaḥ ĕlōhîm*), dry land appears, animals are called out of the ark, humans

---

151. Brueggemann, *OT Theology,* 334; Gage, *Gospel of Genesis,* 9–20. Brueggemann places Gen 1–11 in chiastic formation, with the flood narrative as central; *Genesis,* 22–23; *OT Theology,* 539–45; Waltke, *OT Theology,* 292. This story has many parallels with ANE literature; Holloway, "What Ship Goes There," 215, 222, Walton, *ANE Thought,* 177.

152. Simkins, *Creator and Creation,* 203. Batto views the flood as an extension of the battle against chaos and loss of order; the "power of chaos gradually reinfiltrated the earth . . . until eventually it overwhelmed creation." There are two sides to chaos: a meta-historical force and an historical reality; the waters of the primeval ocean merge with the waters of the flood; *Slaying the Dragon,* 86–87. Walton similarly notes that since creation involved setting boundaries on cosmic waters, in the flood restraints were removed, leading to destruction; *ANE Thought,* 177; see also Lohfink, *Theology of Pentateuch,* 154–203.

are blessed, and their commission renewed. There are also many linguistic and conceptual parallels between creation and flood stories.[153]

The Exodus

A second microcosm is the Moses/Exodus story (Exod 2:1–10; 7:14–15:21). Moses's basket (perhaps a mini-Eden surrounded by water) is described with the same terms as Noah's ark, and Pharaoh can be seen as the embodiment of chaos, or the chaos monster; he exhibits anti-creation behavior by ordering the murder of infant boys.[154] The plagues represent an undoing and distortion of creation—water becomes blood, light and dark are no longer separate, and the world reverts to chaos. Similar themes are apparent in the story of the Red Sea crossing. This inaccurately named body of water, *yām-sûp,* is better interpreted as a sea at the edge of the world thus corresponding to the primeval waters of creation.[155] The Lord sends a strong wind—a "blast from his nostrils" (Exod 15:8; Ps 106:9), supporting the Spirit/wind connection—or a rebuke, which blows away the waters and divides the sea, creating dry land so that Israel can cross. When the Egyptians cross, the boundary is removed, creation is undone, and the waters of chaos drown the Egyptians. This association is particularly evident in the worship of Israel (Pss 66; 74; 77; 89; 114; 136; Isa 51:9–11; Hab 3:2–16); the exodus is seen as a new creative act, hence creation and redemption are brought together and even viewed as a continual process.[156] YHWH is praised and the Sabbath commemorates both the "liberation of

153. As above plus Genesis 1 concludes with "God saw"; Genesis 6 begins, "God saw"; there are seven days of creation—the same before the flood starts and before Noah exits the ark; the wind that subdued the flood waters is like the wind hovering over creation; Van Wolde *Stories,* 121–3; Batto, *Slaying the Dragon,* 87.

154. Fretheim, *Exodus,* 38, 106, 109–11, 159; Brueggemann, *OT Theology,* 539–45; Dumbrell, *Search for Order,* 40–42; Anderson, "Biblical Creation Faith," 12–15; Waltke, *OT Theology,* 292–94. Pharaoh is explicitly compared with a dragon of the sea in Ezek 32:2. Batto sees Egypt as an extension of the chaos monster and believes Pharaoh and the sea merge as a single entity; *Slaying the Dragon,* 113–14.

155. *Sûp* means border; *DCH* 6:133–34; Simkins, *Creator and Creation,* 136; Batto, *Slaying the Dragon,* 115.

156. The Red Sea crossing was also applied to personal deliverance (Ps 14). C. Barth thinks that "primeval and historical events" are interwoven in Ps 74 and Isa 51; *God with Us* 14. Batto sees the splitting of the Red Sea and God's original victory over the chaos monster as one act in Isa 51; the creation of Israel is equal to or more important than original creation and the exodus is most significant as a continual act; *Slaying the Dragon* 82, 110–11, 116. See also Boyd, *God at War,* 88–89.

cosmos from lifeless chaos to ordered life and the liberation of Israel from Egyptian bondage"; Israel clearly connected their celebration of YHWH's lordship over the Egyptians with his mastery over chaos: "The historical event of the crossing and the mythological combat . . . become identical . . . Deep, Rahab, Red Sea—all are parallel forms of the cosmic and historical adversary."[157]

The Tabernacle/Temple

The wilderness tabernacle is an obvious microcosm of creation (Exod 25–28; 35:30–38). It is a basic paradigm of sacred space.[158] In its construction, the same attention is given to order, shape, and design as in creation; the cherubim of Eden reappear. Most importantly, the tabernacle, like Eden, provides a place for God to dwell among his people.[159] The tree of life and the light of God, central to creation, are symbolized by the lampstand (Exod 25:31–40; 27:20, 21).[160] The tabernacle provides tangible assurance of the divine presence, a sanctuary in the midst of chaos, order within disorder: "At this small, lonely place in the midst of the chaos of the wilderness, a new creation comes into being."[161] Furthermore, the divine filling of the tabernacle is like the divine filling of the cosmos.[162] There are similarities between the tabernacle and Noah's ark. Both Moses and Noah receive a divine commission and both places provide a sanctuary. The Promised Land can also be viewed as a return to Eden: Canaan is likened to the Sabbath, and the crossing of the Jordan has parallels to the exodus story.[163]

157. Waltke, *OT Theology*, 187; Forsyth, *Old Enemy*, 104.

158. Fretheim *Exodus*, 268–76, *God and World*, 128–31; Beale, *Temple*, 32–39; Levenson, *Sinai and Zion*, 90–112, 128–44; Arnold, *Genesis*, 59; Dumbrell, *Search for Order*, 105–13. This association is not surprising given the priestly origins of Genesis; von Rad, *Genesis*, 47.

159. *Miškān* (tabernacle) is related to *mš* (to dwell); *DCH* 5:527–31; Brueggemann, *OT Theology*, 663, although the more commonly used terms were house of the Lord/ house of God; Haran, *Temples*, 13.

160. Which is always lit; Beale, *Temple*, 34; Levenson, *Sinai and Zion*, 132. Walton describes the garden as an antechamber to holy of holies; *ANE Thought*, 124–25.

161. Fretheim, *Exodus*, 269–73; *God and World*, 131.

162. Exod 40:34–38; Pss 33:5; 72:19; 119:64; Isa 6:3; Jer 23:24; Fretheim, *Exodus*, 276.

163. Josh 3–5, esp. 4:23; Batto, *Slaying the Dragon*, 128, 136–44). Batto notes the river Jordan is personified as the chaos dragon (151). See also Dumbrell, *Search for*

Solomon's temple similarly reflects the original sacred space of creation. It is connected with both Eden and mythic Mount Zion.[164] All function to keep chaos at bay. Eden can be viewed as an archetypical temple, or a microcosm of the temple, symbolic of God's presence in creation. Both have tripartite structure: outside the garden (all of God's creation) corresponds to the court, the garden to the holy place, and the tree of life to the most holy place.[165] "The entire cosmos may be viewed as a temple for God's sovereign rule. Conversely, Israel's sanctuaries, both the wilderness tabernacle and Solomon's temple, may be seen as microcosms of the universe."[166] Furthermore, God establishes order through speech-acts: seven speeches in creation (Gen 1:1—2:4a), seven speeches for the construction of the tabernacle (Exod 25–31), seven acts of Moses in the construction of sacred space (Exod 40:17–33), seven instructions for sacrificial activity (Lev 1–7), and seven acts in the ritual for ordination (Lev 8).[167]

Finally, there is cosmic/temple symbolism in some OT eschatological passages. Prophets warn of the consequences of Israel's disobedience: a reversion of the world to chaos, or a step-by-step undoing of creation (Isa 24:1–13; 34: 8–15; Jer 4:7, 20–25; 25:11, 12, 18, 38; 49:33; Ezek 6:5, 14; 33:27–9; Hos 2:12; Zeph 1:13).[168] More optimistically, Ezekiel connects the holy mountain with the Garden. His visionary temple is built on a high mountain with streams flowing from it, connecting Eden and heaven; it contains no ark, God's presence is sufficient (Ezek 28:13, 14; 40:1—47:12).[169] G. K. Beale believes OT "tabernacle and temples were symbolically designed to point to the cosmic eschatological reality that

---

Order, 54; Gage, *Gospel of Genesis,* 21. The story of Jonah could also be seen as a microcosm—he is kept safe from the sea/evil and enclosed in a God-given space.

164. 1 Kgs 6:1–38; Levenson, *Sinai and Zion,* 91, 128, 133–35, 170. He follows Eliade's notion of centrality and cosmic symbolism. The temple, at the center, sustains the world and all other space relates to it (139).

165. Beale, *Temple,* 26, 73, 74. Adam is then the archetypal priest, tending and guarding the garden (68).

166. Arnold, *Genesis,* 48. Smith believes the Jerusalem temple reflects God's victory over sea, and is also like Eden in power and beauty; "Like Deities," 3–27.

167. Gorman, *Ideology of Ritual,* 32, 47–50. Seven of course representing perfection.

168. Childs, *OT Theology,* 223; Brueggemann, *OT Theology,* 333.

169. Levenson, *Sinai and Zion,* 128. Isa 2:2 claims that God's future home will be on the highest mountain, Joel 3:18 mentions streams of water coming from the divine dwelling. This vision occurs after the prophecies of destruction of those opposed to God; Dumbrell, *Search for Order,* 105–6.

God's tabernacling presence, formerly limited to the holy of holies, was to be extended throughout the whole earth."[170] The theme recurs: sacred space is threatened by chaos but kept in its proper place through divine authority.

Preliminary Model for Conceptualizing Evil

Given the preceding discussion, a preliminary model based on creation theology can be constructed, and an approach to understanding evil using spatial metaphors can be described. First I summarize the argument thus far.

Summary

Recall that figurative language is the best way to comprehend supersensible realities. Metaphors are conceptual, providing information beyond that offered by literal descriptions and offering multiple snapshots of multi-layered reality. Good models should be comprehensive, intelligible as a unit, supported by biblical texts, consonant with tradition, adequate for life, and provide a means for understanding new experiences. With respect to OT creation texts, the preceding discussion has demonstrated that spatial imagery is readily apparent. Creation is orderly, filled with light and life, and is a dwelling place for God, a place for divine-human interaction. God's good creation is set in opposition to forces of evil—chaos, darkness, void, the deep, death, the sea, sea monsters, and a malevolent snake—that threaten creation. ANE demons have been much reduced in the OT, but the imagery lurks in the background. It is not explained but assumed that this evil, or parts of it, pre-existed or arose simultaneously with creation, and is populated by evil angels, those who abdicated their responsibility, violated a boundary, and now oppose God and creation. Consequently, when God begins to create, his actions involve separation, ordering, and placing boundaries on evil. Biblical scholars and theologians have emphasized creation as a process of separation and ordering. As shown, delimiting evil does not necessarily entail warfare. Humans are also given a boundary; when they disobey, the results are spatial separation—they are cast from the sacred center into a world influenced by forces of evil.

170. Beale, *Temple*, 25.

Finally, there are many microcosms of creation that reflect the same spatial imagery of creation.

Model

Considering the preceding discussion and diagrams in figures 4.1–4.3, the spatial imagery of creation and chaos can be depicted as follows:

Figure 4.4: A Model of Creation

This model portrays the mythical space depicted in biblical creation texts and the actions relating to this space. It can also be envisioned in three dimensions, in conical shape, which blends the imagery supplied in Simkins's horizontal and vertical models. The center corresponds to the ideal creation symbolized by Eden. It is the dwelling place of God, filled with light and life. The intermediary zone, the world, is where humanity dwells; it is depicted as grey since it still receives the blessing of God. Humans retain their ability to image their Creator. However, the world can be influenced by the evil forces at the periphery, symbolized by darkness. Consequently, humans remain dependent on God for protection and deliverance from these forces, as evidenced in the exodus story. This model bears some similarities to E. Lewis's idea of three eternal forces: the divine creative, the demonic discreative, and the uncreative, neutral residue, discussed previously. But a primary difference is that Lewis views these spaces as equal and co-eternal. My model places divine reality clearly at the center with other space peripheral to and dependent on it. The grey area is somewhat neutral but benefits from sacred space. Lewis's views of the demonic as irrational and parasitic, and his stress on human choice, accord with this model.

Most discussions regarding creation and sacred space have, quite rightly, focused on the center, the light and life of God. Yet, the same model can be used to understand the periphery, the realm of chaos and evil and its effects on the intermediary zone, the world in which the first and subsequent humans live. In addition to metaphors already discussed, evil space can be understood as characterized by divine absence (in binary opposition to divine presence). Since chaos is space that is rejected by God, and in turn rejects him, it is necessarily evil (God-forsaken). And because it lacks divine presence, it can be understood as qualitatively less real. However, it seeks to attain reality by intruding upon creation. Consequently, it remains a continual threat to creation and requires continual reapplication of boundaries. It is put in its place through divine action, assisted by human obedience. Chaos as less real is consonant with the metaphors darkness, waste, and void. Intuitively, darkness and emptiness seem not as real as light and abundance. It also accords with theological metaphors like nothingness, as well as chaos-complexity and dark matter as models for evil. Chaos can be seen to be characterized by disorder. This makes sense since it lacks the presence of the God of order. It accords with other metaphors for chaos such as such as sea monsters, a snake that seeks to disrupt creation, and the *běnê ĕlōhîm* who disturb the order of creation.

This model can provide insight into the world, the grey space between good and evil. First, there are implications for understanding the origins of evil in the world. There appear to be three agents that can loosen boundaries on creation: God (as in the flood), humans (as in sin), and evil spirits (because they need controlling, and can at times transgress their boundaries as evidenced by the serpent). When boundaries are violated, evil results. Second, because these evil forces can influence humans (e.g., the snake), there are implications for human responsibility. In this spatial model, humans can turn in two directions: towards the center in worship and obedience to God, or towards the periphery and evil. There can be seen to be interplay between sin and evil. When humans choose evil, the boundaries on the forces of evil are loosened, and evil can attain reality.

Evaluation

This model is simple yet comprehensive. It fits with biblical creation passages and offers a framework for understanding them. It is consonant with theological understandings of creation. More importantly, it offers an alternative approach for the conceptualization of evil and evil spirits. Even though preliminary, it appears to be applicable to experience. The reality of evil in the world and the limitation of it through divine grace are intuitive, as is the human experience of sin and its consequences. This model is able to reconcile original and continual creation. It fits with creation accounts in Genesis and poetic/prophetic passages plus microcosms of creation. One could imagine the circles to vary in size at different times; for example, prior to the flood, darkness was prominent; afterwards it was pushed back, creation renewed, and the circle of light enlarged. This model accords with creation theology's emphasis on the world as dependent on God. Without his provision, his boundaries on evil, and his light, the darkness would quickly overtake creation. This model allows for the role of the Holy Spirit in creation. It is the wind or breath of God that keeps the waters at bay, the Spirit of God that gives and sustains life, the Spirit that maintains order in the cosmos.

This model has several advantages over a warfare model. First, it is more comprehensive; not limited to creation-through-conflict verses but able to incorporate other texts. It includes both spatial and action metaphors. Warfare only considers action. A spatial model allows for a conceptualization of reality that can guide our actions within it. Second, this model perhaps provides a more balanced perspective on evil. Perceiving evil at the periphery, or outside the world, affirms its potentiality while minimizing its power. Warfare imagery implies a battle with an equal and opposite force whereas boundary imagery can allow for a view of evil as having reduced ontology. Existing outside the world in a quasi-real state, it can only be parasitic on creation. Sacred space is ultimate reality; evil is only semi-real. In this model, God is at the center of the cosmos, the source of all life, and the means by which creation is preserved and order maintained. Evil forces are relegated to the outer realms, and although they have some power for destruction, it is minimal. Third, this model affirms the sovereignty of God. Warfare imagery tends to result in a diminished view of sovereignty; God has to fight a formidable foe. Adopting boundary metaphors allows for a greater view of God's sovereignty. He does not necessarily battle chaos, but merely assigns limits. He does not angrily fight an enemy but calmly maintains order. He simply rejects that which rejects him. There can be no doubt as to who is in overall control. Fourth, this model is less dualistic than a warfare model. Warfare imagery lends itself to a view of a battle between equal and opposite forces; a black and white view that ignores the shades of grey. Yet the light is always stronger than the darkness; it extends into creation to protect against forces of darkness. This model incorporates grey and better fits the biblical portrayal of evil as a complex interplay between human sin and diabolic evil. Fifth, this model emphasizes human responsibility. Living in the grey area, humans can be influenced by evil forces but can choose which direction they face. This model can incorporate human responsibility while affirming the potential reality of evil forces, and thus has pastoral implications. Sixth, this model allows for an increased role of the Holy Spirit. Warfare imagery focuses on the divine warrior, seldom associated with the Spirit of God. Seventh, this model, by emphasizing ordering and boundary-setting as a method for dealing with evil forces, avoids the difficulties inherent in a warfare model and provides alternative nonviolent language. Finally, this model provides some insights into the nature of evil spirits—they are characterized by chaos, darkness, disorder, and divine absence. In suggesting the above advantages of a spatial over a warfare model, I do not intend to deny that warfare imagery is present in some creation passages and elsewhere in the OT, but that spatial/boundary metaphors are a viable alternative to a warfare model which specifically can inform our ministry with respect to deliverance.

This model will be developed in subsequent chapters. The focus on sacred space, with its accompanying actions, appears to be a helpful framework in which to conceptualize evil. It also has implications for counteracting evil, which will be discussed further. One concern with this model is that, albeit less dualistic than warfare, it is still somewhat dualistic; there is only one shade of grey, unlike most human experience, which includes varying shades. Another issue relates to the exact nature of the boundaries and the circumstances in which they can be violated. These concerns may be addressed through the examination of other biblical themes, which we turn to next.

5

CULT: A TABERNACLE IN THE WILDERNESS

The white cloud has a royal throne placed upon it.
This royal throne has a circle around it ... there is a ...
living person ... covered with a light of wondrous glory.[1]

THE HEART OF ISRAEL's culture was its legal and ritual systems. But many cultic texts read more like an anatomical dissection manual than divine revelation. Prohibitions appear arbitrary and sometimes harsh. Few sermons are preached on Leviticus. It is unsurprising that biblical scholarship in this area, especially among Protestant Christians, has been slow to develop.[2] Although typically limited to the Pentateuch, priestly themes are present throughout the Bible. Cultic themes (actually most of the OT) are neglected in popular "spiritual warfare" literature; therefore, examining an area not typically associated with "spiritual warfare" may provide an alternative model for understanding evil, and may elucidate theologies of evil. Furthermore, investigating texts based on

---

1. Hildegarde of Bingen, *Scivias* III.1.2, 3, 9, 12.

2. Many scholars have noted that academic study of priestly writings is minimal. Brueggemann thinks that it has been inhibited by "Christian supersessionism and Protestant cult aversion"; *Theology of OT*, 651–53. G. Klingbeil, who found only four studies from 1990–99 done by evangelical Christians, suggests reasons for this neglect: the perceived "barbaric" nature of these texts, the apparent lack of contemporary relevance, the NT bias in study, the prophetic critique of ritual, and the influence of modernity; *Bridging the Gap*, 50, 118–24.

themes, symbols, metaphors, and models may avoid many of the challenges inherent in cultic studies.[3]

Israel's cult can be viewed as functioning to mediate the presence of the Lord. This was achieved through sacred places (tabernacle, temple), sacred actions, (sacrifice, ritual washing, obedience to covenantal laws), sacred personnel (priests), and sacred times or seasons (feasts, celebrations).[4] These four were often intertwined. Sacred space and actions are the most pertinent to this study. In terms of definition, cult (derived from Latin, signifying care or adoration) pertains to the practices within a system of religious belief, in this case, the worship life of Israel.[5] Most biblical literature pertaining to the cult is presumed to have been written by Israel's priests, hence the designation priestly theology. Cultic concepts incorporate both sacred space and sacred actions, or ritual, a frequently misunderstood term. Roy Gane defines ritual as "a privileged activity system that is believed to carry out a transformation process involving interaction with a reality ordinarily inaccessible to the material domain."[6] Ritual, because it deals with unseen reality, relates to metaphors, symbols, and worldview, as in Frank Gorman's definition: "A complex performance of symbolic acts, characterized by formality, order and sequence, which . . . has as one of its central goals the regulation of the social order."[7]

3. Klingbeil suggests ritual studies are challenging because ritual texts are not easily dated, multiple meanings are common, rituals are often abbreviated in the Bible, and comparative material, although helpful, cannot be used exclusively; *Bridging the Gap*, 52–66. He advocates a multidisciplinary, holistic approach to cultic studies; "ritual connects us back to the past, enlightens our present, and can help prepare for the future" (244). Jenson describes two approaches to ritual study: kerygmatic (focusing on socio-historical background) and theological. He believes the latter are more fruitful partly because they are more comprehensive. Jenson is unique in incorporating metaphor theory, noting that symbolism is intrinsic to priestly material and often complex. He suggests conceptual metaphors of purity may or may not have had material counterparts and may have become conventional, losing their metaphorical association; *Graded Holiness*, 26–34, 61–69, 152–53.

4. Many biblical scholars have noted these divisions, often also including a fifth category, sacred objects, like the Ark of the Covenant; e.g., Childs, *OT Theology*, 161–67; Waltke, *OT Theology*, 458–65.

5. Waltke equates cult and liturgy; *OT Theology*, 448.

6. Gane, *Cult and Character*, 15.

7. Gorman, *Ideology of Ritual*, 19. Klingbeil comments on the relationship between aspects of priestly theology: "cult describes the entirety of religious actions, which in turn consists of a specific number of rituals comprising subrites and distinct symbols"; *Bridging the Gap*, 8. He also discusses the interdependence of cult and worldview; cultic beliefs reflect an underlying frame of reference (12). Jenson also equates worldview,

This chapter examines cultic texts (defined thematically) through the lens of metaphor theory, particularly the themes of sacred/profane space and actions, in order to further our understanding of evil spiritual forces. First I examine profane space, including the demonic, impurity, and immorality, and their relationship to sin; then describe sacred space (tabernacle/temple) in terms of binary oppositions and graded holiness. Sacred action is discussed next and rituals interpreted as ordering, cleansing, and boundary-setting. Finally, the model described in the previous chapter is further developed and evaluated.

Profane Space

Cultic texts contain many of the same metaphors for evil as creation texts: demons, darkness, chaos monsters, and the desert. Some are developed further and new ones, such as impurity, appear. Although some scholars claim the OT contains few references to Satan and demons (e.g., theologian Stanley Grenz: "Ancient Hebrews were largely unaware of" the demonic[8]), if evil is examined from a metaphorical perspective (e.g., darkness, demons, wilderness, chaos, sea monsters, wild animals, pagan gods, uncleanness, death) the semantic domain of evil is quite large. In this section I examine demonology, one evil figure (Azazel) in particular, then impurity and immorality, the relationship between sin, impurity, and the demonic, and conclude with discussions about "de-demonization" and the ontology of evil.

Demons, Wilderness . . .

The wilderness is an apt metaphor for evil in cultic theology. Israelites, for instance, frequently complain about the wilderness; it is filled with *šiyyîm* (wild and unclean animals) as well as demons, and is associated with death (Isa 34:14; Num 20:4, 5). The psalmists, in their pleas for deliverance, use multiple metaphors for evil: darkness, pestilence, wild animals, destruction, deep mire or bog, deep waters, death, the pit, and Sheol (Pss 13:3; 28:1; 30:3; 40:1; 44:19; 55:4, 15; 69:2, 14; 74:19; 91:3, 5, 6; 116:3; 143:3).

---

symbol-system, root-metaphor, and classification system that he believes underlies priestly theology; *Graded Holiness*, 2, 58–59.

8. Grenz, *Theology*, 223. He does not discuss the multiple metaphors used for evil in the OT. Later, however, he acknowledges that Leviathan and Lucifer are related to Satan (225).

Death, as in Genesis, is usually interpreted metaphorically as separation from God, or personified as an evil force (Jer 9:21).[9] Sheol is associated with death and is antithetical to divine presence (Deut 32:22; 2 Sam 22:6; Job 11:8; 17:13–16; Prov 5:5; 7:27; Jon 2:2, 3; Isa 7:11; 38:18; Ezek 31:15).[10] Some specific evil creatures are described: sea-monsters (discussed in chapter 4), goat-demons (2 Chr 11:15; Isa 13:21), Dagon (1 Sam 5:1–5), Lilith (Isa 34:14), Molech (Lev 20:2-5), and Azazel (Lev 16:8–10). These beings are not well explained but appear to exist in opposition to God. There are only three references to Satan in the OT (1 Chr 21:1; Job 1:6–11; 2:1-7; Zech 3:1-5) and he is an ambiguous figure. There is some sugges-tion he is merely a servant of God, but his character is malevolent and he works in opposition to goodness, therefore warrants placement in the semantic domain of evil despite lack of details.[11] There is no Hebrew term that can be precisely equated with "demon." Interestingly, the LXX translates several Hebrew terms as *daimon*: *šēdîm* (Deut 32:17; Ps 106:37;

9. C. Barth views death in the OT as a two-sided reality: a "boundary of life that God has fixed" and a "power of destruction that menaces us on our path in world" (e.g., illness, persecution); death is not meant literally but used to emphasize the ter-rible nature of suffering; *God with Us*, 277.

10. Madigan and Levenson describe it as a "grave, pit, underworld, engulfing waters, subterranean city, prison, lifeless, remote, inaccessible, cut off from the living, and life-giving worship"; *Resurrection*, 53–54. God is mostly absent from Sheol (Lev 20.27; 1 Sam 28.3; 2 Kgs, 23.24; Pss 88:3–5; 115:16). The exceptions (Ps 139:8; Amos 9:2) perhaps prove the rule; Burnett, *Where is God*, 65–67. It is depicted as a place of no return (2 Sam 12:23; Job 7:9) and a place where God cannot be praised (Ps 6:5). However, at times it seems that those in Sheol may be redeemed (1 Sam 2:6; Ps 30:3; Hos 13:14). Madigan and Levenson explain this discrepancy by noting that Sheol is not the destination for all who die, but only those who die outside of God's grace. Furthermore, the faithful can be rescued from Sheol; *Resurrection*, 67–79.

11. *DDD* 726–31. P. Day, in her study of Satan in the OT, notes that the noun generally only meant adversary or legal accuser and could refer to human or celestial beings. Occurrences are so diverse that we should speak of "satans," not Satan; there is "neither a single meaning nor a sole referent." She suggests the use of the definite article does not imply a proper name, but "a certain accuser"; *Adversary in Heaven*, 15, 43, 63, 147. H. A. Kelly argues that much of the "Satan" myth has been retro-fitted into the Bible and he aims to "rehabilitate Satan's reputation." He dislikes the term "evil" because "it has been so infused with later philosophizing" that it suggests a "fathom-less iniquity" and prefers the term "troubling" spirit. Satan in the OT is no more than a servant of God who functions to observe and test humanity; *Satan: A Biography*, 18, 23–31, 328; see also Ma, "Exorcism in the OT," 27–44. By contrast, Boyd points out many statements in Job that refute this conclusion: God asks Satan where he has been, implying Satan is not completely under God's control; Satan seems eager to inflict pain, suggesting a sinister nature; the intent of the Job prologue is not to blame God for evil, but to demonstrate the complexity of the cosmos; *God at War*, 144–49.

demon in most English translations) is related etymologically to lordship, *śirim* (Lev 17:7; 2 Kgs 23:8; goat-demon, goat-idol) means "hairy one" or "he goat," *ĕlîlîm* (Ps 96:5; "idols") are regarded as worthless, and *qeteb* is translated as destruction (Ps 91:6).[12] Worship of demons and pagan practices (e.g., child sacrifice to Molech) were strictly forbidden, indicative of Israel's awareness of and participation in such evil (Lev 18:21; 20:2–5), and there are clear injunctions against consulting demons (1 Sam 28:3–25; Lev 19:31, 20:27; Deut 18:10–11).[13]

Many of these terms are better understood against their ANE background: Dagon was a Mesopotamian god with ties to the underworld; Mot, lord of death and sterility; Resheph, a god of plague and pestilence; Molech, a god of the underworld whom people consulted regarding ancestors; Gad, the god of fortune; Belial, the personification of wickedness; Azazel, a desert demon; Siyya, likely a collective term for demonic desert dwellers; Lilith, a particularly evil demon who roamed at night seeking men to destroy; and Sheol, a being with a wide mouth looking to devour souls.[14] OT translations frequently neutralize these names; for instance, Mot becomes merely death. ANE literature contains multiple exorcism rites; ancestor worship and cults of the dead were common.[15] The literature of the Second Temple Period likewise provides insight into OT demonology. Generally, evil spirits were thought to roam in abundance over all the earth tempting, accusing, and punishing humankind.[16]

12. *DDD* 127–28, 673–74, 732–33; Unger, *Biblical Demonology*, 58–61.

13. Specifically witchcraft, divination (obtaining knowledge though ungodly means), magic, necromancy (consulting spirits of the dead), cleomancy (accepting a fatal word or omen), cleromancy (divination by casting lots), and oneiromancy (divination from dreams); Nigosian, *Magic and Divination*, 5–11, 39–56, 76–84; Unger, *Biblical Demonology*, 107–64.

14. *DDD* 216–19, 598–602, 700–703, 581–85, 339–41, 169–71, 128–31, 897–98, 520–21, 768–70 respectively; Russell, *Devil*, 92–95; Milgrom, *Leviticus*, 197. Interestingly Belial is translated more frequently in the Vulgate OT than current English versions.

15. E.g., a Hittite incantation for house-purification solicits deities to carry uncleanness back to the underworld; Hallo, *Context of Scripture*, 168–69. Milgrom summarizes the premises of pagan religions: its deities are themselves dependent on and influenced by a metadivine realm, this realm spawns a multitude of malevolent and benevolent entities, and if humans can tap into this realm they can acquire magical power to coerce gods to do their will; *Leviticus: Ritual and Ethics*, 8; following Kaufmann, *Religion of Israel*, 21–59.

16. Jub 48:9–15; 50:5; 1 En 15:11; 16:1; 40:7; 53:3; 69:6. Specific evil spirits include Sammael, Asmodeus, Belial/Beliar (mentioned twenty-four times, also an ANE god, the personification of wickedness), Mastema, from the root *stn* meaning

Cosmic dualism is prominent in the DSS; opposing spirits of good and evil are thought to battle for the world and for individual souls.[17] "Spirits of angels of destruction," "spirits of the bastards/giants," "demons," "Lilith," howlers, and yelpers/wild animals are some of the evil beings listed.[18] There are also multiple prayers of protection, magical incantations, and exorcism rites.[19] Considering the background of ANE and Second Temple literature and using metaphor theory opens conceptual space for understanding demonology in the OT.

Azazel

This mysterious sin-receiving desert creature, unique to Leviticus 16, has produced much scholarly debate. Azazel is part of the ritual, *Yom Kippur*, which occurs annually and involves two goats—one sacrificed to the Lord; the other loaded with Israel's sins and sent into the wilderness to Azazel. This ritual is often called the "day of atonement," but Jewish scholars Jacob Milgrom and Baruch Levine have persuasively argued that it is better translated "day of purgation," based both on the interpretation of *kippēr* and the function of it (purging the sins of Israel).[20] There are three views regarding Azazel's identity: a supernatural demonic being, a rocky precipice or place of destruction, and a term meaning "the goat that went away."[21] This last interpretation was followed in the LXX and the Vulgate,

enmity; Semyaza/Shemihazah, and Satan; *DDD* 106–7, 169–71, 244–49, 553–54, 726–31 respectively; Forsyth, *Old Enemy*, 182–88. Although there was diversity, much of the literature of early Judaism seemed preoccupied with eschatology and apocalypticism, especially the tension between good and evil spiritual forces; Nickelsburg, *Jewish Literature*. Beale believes ANE and Second Temple texts can be viewed like commentaries; *Temple*, 31.

17. Evident especially in "The Scroll of the War of the Sons of Light against the Sons of Darkness" (1QM); DSS references enumerate the cave number in which the scroll was found, Q for Qumran, and the document title or number; Wise et al., *DSS*; Russell, *Devil*, 212–14.

18. Lists in 4Q510, 4Q511, and 11Q11; Alexander, "Demonology of DSS," 333.

19. The Songs of the Maskil (Sage) aim to "frighten and terrify" evil spirits (4Q510–11); demons and the diseases they cause are named (4Q560); see also 11Q5 19.15–16; 11Q11.

20. Levine argues that *kippēr* is best translated as "to wipe clean" (as in Jer 18:23); *Presence of the Lord*, 56; see also Milgrom, *Leviticus 1–16*, 255–56, 524, 1079–84. However, J. Sklar argues that linguistically it can mean both cleanse and ransom; "Sin and Impurity," 18.

21. See Milgrom, *Leviticus 1–16*, 1020; Gorman, *Ideology*, 97; Douglas, *Jacob's Tears*, 45–47.

and the term "scapegoat" has commonly been applied.[22] However, the goat that carries the iniquities of Israel to Azazel is not a goat that becomes an unwitting victim (as scapegoat implies); rather the goat is merely a transport animal. Gane's suggestion, "tote-goat," is better.[23]

The view of Azazel as a demon is the most widely accepted based on the following evidence: First, the wilderness and the demonic are commonly associated; second, linguistically, the unnamed goat is sent to someone or something (the fixed preposition *le* is translated either "to" or "for" Azazel); third, also linguistically, the phrasing suggests two beings; there are two goats, one goes to a personal being, the Lord, therefore the other must also go to a personal being;[24] fourth, the opposition in location and recipient of the two goats implies that Azazel is the complete antithesis to holiness;[25] fifth, Second Temple literature includes references to Azazel/Asael (see previous discussion on the Watcher Tradition); and finally, in NT studies, Azazel has been equated with Satan.[26] Milgrom notes that this view is the most common in midrashic literature but believes the name has survived beyond having significance. Furthermore, ANE elimination rites were similar to the Azazel ritual, frequently involving banishing evil to its place of origin.[27] Levine thinks that in *Yom Kippur*, sin is returned to where it came from; this sin is forced onto Azazel through the power of the priest since this being is unlikely to willingly accept such a "gift."[28]

Mary Douglas is one of the few dissenters. She claims that Azazel is simply a name for the goat; "there is no need to invent a gift for a Goat-Lord of the wilderness" especially since sacrifice to demons is prohibited.[29] However, I believe Douglas misses the point: First, there is no evidence that

22. The LXX intentionally edited out demonic references; Maccoby, *Ritual and Morality*, 90–91.

23. Gane, *Cult and Character*, 243. Furthermore, linguistically, since the goat is sent to Azazel, it makes no sense to send a goat to a scapegoat.

24. Gorman, *Ideology*, 98.

25. Gane argues that since Azazel receives such a noxious gift, he is clearly the enemy of the Lord, the extreme opposite of God's presence in the holy of holies; *Cult and Character*, 250–51.

26. As in the expulsion of the sinner in 1 Cor 5:5; Shillington, "Atonement Texture," 46.

27. Milgrom, *Leviticus: Rituals and Ethics*, 166.

28. Levine, *Presence of Lord*, 81, 82. G. Anderson agrees, arguing that the physical weight of sin had to be removed (Ps 103:12, Mic 7:19); *Sin: A History*, 23.

29. Douglas, *Jacob's Tears*, 45–47. Maccoby also minimizes the being of Azazel, believing it to be a "residue of remembrance of the demon"; *Ritual and Morality*, 90–91.

sin is regarded as a gift, second, there is no sacrifice to Azazel mentioned, and third, Azazel has no active role in the ritual. Levine, conversely, is being somewhat speculative in stating that the "noxious load of sin" has to be forced onto Azazel. There is no evidence that Azazel resists this "gift"; it is possible, as Gane suggests, that demonic beings actually like sin. The text gives insufficient information. Although Azazel is only mentioned once, the *Yom Kippur* ritual is central to Israel's cult (and later Christian theology), implies an association between sin and the demonic, and provides further evidence of the continuing presence of evil forces within cultic theology.

Impurity and Immorality

Biblical cultic passages focus on impurity and immorality, which are associated with profane space. Israel is separated from her neighbors to be holy, and purity is required for participation in cultic life (Lev 19:2; 20:24, 26). Sources of uncleanness (impurity or pollution) include certain types of animals, some bodily discharges, skin diseases,[30] dead bodies, and house "disease."[31] Impurities are divided into severe (primarily corpse contact, skin disease, genital discharge, and childbirth) and lesser (primarily menstruation and sexual activity). Impurity can also be divided into moral (usually deliberate, e.g., idolatry, incest, murder) and ritual (usually inadvertent, e.g., corpse contact, bodily fluids). It cannot come into contact with holiness; if it does, ritual reparation is required.[32] Milgrom offers an explanation for the apparently arbitrary sources of uncleanness: there is a common denominator in the regular sources of impurity—death.[33] Loss of semen or vaginal blood can be seen as loss of the life force. Skin disease often appeared white, or death-like. Holiness, in contrast, represents life, explaining why blood is used in many rituals. However, Saul Olyan points out that the clean/unclean dyad exists in gradations and doubts it is possible to find a single underlying principle to explain sources of defilement.

---

30. The Hebrew, *šāra*, has often been mistranslated as leprosy. Biblical scholars and physicians agree that the skin disease described does not match the known symptoms of leprosy, a neurological disease. Milgrom and others use the more precise term scale disease; *Leviticus: Rituals and Ethics*, 127.

31. Probably mildew; Neusner, *Idea of Purity*, 18–22.

32. Num 19; Lev 12–15 generally; Lev 7:20–21; 15:31; 16:16 specifically; Sklar, "Sin and Impurity," 26–27.

33. Milgrom, *Leviticus: Ritual and Ethics*, 12.

Along with animals, corpses, skin disease, and genital discharges, he notes that alien lands and idols are unclean too. Much prohibited behavior is similar to that endorsed by the Canaanites.[34]

Immorality, or sin, in the OT is a multivalent concept. There is no exact Hebrew word for sin, but *ḥaṭṭāt* (to miss the mark or deviate from the norm) is most commonly used.[35] Iniquity, transgression, and sin are often used in parallel (Exod 34:7, 9; Job 10:6, 14; Ps 51:2, 3; Prov 5:22), as are sin and wickedness (Ps 104:35; Prov 21:4; Isa 13:11; Jer 18:23; the wicked are diametrically opposed to the righteous [Ps 97:10; Prov 10–15; Mal 3:18], and the wise [Dan 12:10]; they are associated with the nations [Ps 9:5, 17] and darkness [1 Sam 2:9; Prov 4:19]). Sin and idolatry are related, and rebellion and stubbornness are likened to divination, idolatry, and iniquity (2 Kgs 17:7–18; 1 Sam 15:23).[36] Sin is viewed as a "thing" that God can remove (Ps 103:12), "put" away or "crush" (2 Sam 12:13), and "cast" into the sea (Mic 7:19); it can be loaded onto a goat (Lev 16:10); and is a weight to be dragged (Ps 38:4; Isa 1:4; 5:18) or a snare (Prov 5:22).[37] It can be described as an "organic continuum" that can "twist and pervert" reality.[38] Penalties for disobedience are harsh and include disease, famine, infertility, exile, and death (Exod 26:16, 19, 22; Lev 17:8–10; 20:9–21; 24:13–25), all associated with the semantic domain of evil.[39] Divine absence is also a consequence of disobedience. Sometimes God withdraws, abandons Israel, or departs from the sanctuary; typically, waste and desolation

34. Gen 35:2; Lev 18:24–30; 20:22–23; Ezek 4:13; 36:18; Hos 9:3–4; Olyan, *Rites and Rank*, 40, 48, 49.

35. Although the meaning is broad and varied; *DCH* 3:198–200; Ricoeur, *Symbolism of Evil*, 72–73.

36. Turning away from the one true God to other gods/idols is a grave sin (Exod 32:31; Jer 16:10–12), as is disobeying the covenant (Lev 24:13–21; Num 14:28–38; Ezek 18:24).

37. Anderson notes some metaphors for sin: stains that need cleansing, burdens to be removed, debts to be repaid, a weight to be born; sins are like "things"—God can wash, cover, or crush them; *Sin: A History*, 13–22; Biddle points out the ubiquity of sin, which has violation of relationship at its root; *Missing the Mark*, 30–33.

38. E.g., Isa 59:8–10 describes sinners as unable to walk straight. Biddle notes that OT concepts of sin include deed, guilt, and consequence; sin creates a "perverted condition that can twist the perceptions and decisions of subsequent generations"; thus sin is not a debt but a heritage; *Missing the Mark*, 118–20.

39. The prophets include destruction, famine, pestilence (Isa 34:9–16; 51:19; Jer 4:23–28; 9:20; 14:12–18; cf. Deut 28:20–25; 1 Kgs 8:35; Job 18:13, 14). Boda lists the consequences for sin as death, "cutting off" (exile), bearing guilt and destruction of objects for severe sin, and ritual, sacrifice and reparation for less severe sin; *Severe Mercy*, 57–59.

ensue (Deut 28:20–25; Isa 34:9–16; Jer 4:23–28; Ezek 8:6, 10:18).[40] God occasionally sends an evil spirit as punishment; however, God's Spirit leaves first, perhaps indicating incompatibility between the divine and the demonic (1 Sam 16:15–16; although God can be present to evil and use it for his purposes, he is not present *within* evil; discussed further in chapter 8). Pagans are also sometimes inflicted with evil (e.g., the Egyptian plagues include blood, pestilence, skin disease, famine, darkness, and finally, death; Exod 7–12).

There is a complex association between immorality and impurity.[41] Douglas notes that "a polluting person is always in the wrong," but the category of sin is larger than the category of impurity. This association is often indirect (e.g., Miriam is punished for her sin with the infliction of an unclean skin disease; Num 21:1–16).[42] Douglas summarizes: "Treatment of purity as symbol, metaphor, or allegory involves the assignment to purity of a value extrinsic to the cult. To be impure is to be guilty of something, normally, though not always, having to do with ethics."[43] Milgrom points out that deliberate sin incurs a harsher penalty than inadvertent sin, but voluntary repentance can transform a deliberate sin into an inadvertent one and reduce the penalty. Both repentance and feelings of guilt are needed.[44] Impurity, the effects of sin on the sanctuary, differs from iniquity, the effect on the sinner. The relationship between sin and impurity is graded: the "severity of the sin or impurity varies in direct relation to the depth of its penetration into the inner sanctuary." Milgrom believes that at times sin can pollute the sanctuary without leaving a mark on the sinner.[45]

40. Psalmists plea that YHWH not leave them, or hide his face (Pss 22:11, 19; 27:9; 38:21; 44:23, 24; 55:11; 69:17; 102:2; 143:7); Jonah "flees from the presence of the Lord"(1:3); the name Ichabod means divine absence (1 Sam 4:21); recall discussion in chapter 4 on divine absence.

41. There is also a connection between impurity, or defilement, and sin (Ps 51:2; Isa 6:6–7; Zech 13:1). Sklar notes that sin and impurity both endanger (having severe consequences) and pollute; "Sin and Impurity," 23–31.

42 . Similarly the priest confesses the sins of the people (Lev 16:18–21); Douglas, *Purity and Danger*, 21–24, 113.

43. Douglas, *Purity and Danger*, 25. Neusner similarly believes impurity's can be seen as a metaphor for morality and ethical behavior, evidenced by the frequent allusions to idolatry as uncleanness; *Idea of Purity*, 1, 11–15, 108, 118–28. Furthermore, illicit sexual relations are regarded as defilement.

44. Lev 5:1–6; 6:1–7; Milgrom, *Cult and Conscience*, 84–123; *Leviticus: Ritual and Ethics*, 46–50, 171–72. Although Boda argues that "feelings of guilt" is not a necessary translation; recognition of guilt is; *Severe Mercy*, 62–64.

45. Stage 1: inadvertent sin pollutes the courtyard; Stage 2: the priest's inadvertent

Jonathan Klawans similarly observes that moral impurity was usually considered more severe than ritual impurity, resulting in defilement of the sanctuary, defilement of the land, profaning of the divine name, departure of the divine presence, battle with the nations, and ultimately exile from the land.[46] In sum, morality trumps purity. Not all impurity is sinful, but all sin is impure. This is important when considering the relationships between purity, morality, sacred space, and sacred actions.

Impurity, Immorality, and the Demonic

As impurity and immorality are related, so are impurity and the demonic (Ps 106:35–9; Isa 34:14; Jer 2:23; 19:13; Ezek 23:30), and immorality and the demonic (Deut 32:17; Lev 18:21; 20:2–5; Ps 106:36–38), especially with respect to idolatry. Those who sacrifice to demons, pagan gods, and idols become unclean (Gen 35:2; Ps 106:35–9; Jer 2:23; 19:13; Ezek 23:30; 36:25). All three—sin, impurity, and evil spirits—are explicitly connected in Zechariah's vision and the Azazel ritual. The connection becomes well established in Second Temple literature, which associates impurity and immorality as well as implicating idolatry and evil spirits as a cause of uncleanness.[47] At Qumran, sin and impurity were associated, and impurity was at times considered a malevolent force; there is a prayer that the spirit of humankind be purified "from all the abominations of falsehood and from being polluted by a spirit of impurity."[48] Skin disease was sometimes attributed to evil spirits. Philip Alexander, examining demonology in the DSS, observes that the term "unclean spirit" is common. In fact, parallels

---

sin pollutes the shrine; Stage 3: wanton sin pollutes the holy of holies; Milgrom, "Israel's Sanctuary," 390–99; *Leviticus 1–16,* 257. Olyan (*Rites and Rank,* 40–48) and D. Wright ("Spectrum of Priestly Impurity," 150–82) also note the gradations of impurity and their correspondence with morality but Finlan criticizes Milgrom for making totalizing claims about temple purification; *Atonement Metaphors,* 35.

46. Ritual impurities in the Bible had only a temporary effect and required minor cleansing such as washing or waiting. In contrast, moral impurity resulted in defilement of sinners, the land, and the sanctuary, and required atonement, punishment, or exile (Lev 18:24–30); Klawans, *Impurity and Sin,* 26–27, 119, 127–28. Maccoby also notes that morality is more important than impurity (e.g., David eating the holy bread in 1 Sam 21:1–7); "ritual is about holiness, not about morality; yet . . . holiness is for the sake of morality;" *Ritual and Morality,* 193, 204.

47. 1 En 10:18–22; Jub 7:20–21, 11:4; 1 Macc 1:21–4; 4:42–59; 2 Macc 5:21; 10:3–8.

48. S1QS4:20–22; similarly, the spirits of Belial are "cursed for all their service of unclean impurity" (1QSM 13:5); cf. 11Q19:45–51; CD 11:19–21; 1QS 3:8, 9; 4:5; 4Q272 1:1–16; Klawans, *Impurity and Sin,* 75–78.

between demons and impurity are impressive and it is impossible to draw sharp distinctions between sin, impurity, and evil, "the concepts merge into each other." He describes the community at Qumran as a "sectarian group defending the boundaries of . . . its holy space from the encroachment both of encircling impurity and of encircling demons."[49]

Interestingly, impurity is sometimes described using language suggestive of evil spiritual forces. For example; Milgrom: an "aerial miasma which possesses magnetic attraction for the realm of the sacred";[50] Maccoby: "an effusion that signifies the supernatural in its despised, rejected, and yet lingering form; banished to a region outside the influence of the Temple, and yet attached somehow to the Temple ceremonies by an indissoluble link";[51] Klawans: a "potent force unleashed by certain human actions."[52] Levine more explicitly equates impurity and the demonic. He views impurity as an active force that endangers the people of God. It is an external force that enters and/or attaches itself to persons. Sin especially can introduce "demonic contagion into community."[53] The primary purpose of purification rituals is to expunge this alien force. Jenson also associates impurity, immorality, and the demonic with respect to *Yom Kippur*: the domain of Azazel is "a coalescence of the demonic, the impure, and the sinful."[54]

It should be clarified that although there is an association between sin, uncleanness, and the demonic, it is complex. Not all sin is demonic, and not all impurity is demonic (e.g., it is difficult to associate evil spirits with childbirth). Extreme unclean states (e.g., idolatry, death) are associated with sin and more likely to have a demonic association. Not all sin and impurity is demonic, yet all evil forces probably incorporate both sin and uncleanness. Recognizing the metaphorical association can nonetheless prove helpful. There is sufficient evidence to include uncleanness, impurity, and sin as metaphors within the semantic domain "evil." This does not mean that all impurity or sin is evil, but it adds to our conception of evil.

---

49. Alexander, "Demonology of DSS," 331–53. Klawans also points out the clear connection between impurity and the demonic in the Second Temple Period; *Impurity and Sin*, 88.

50. Milgrom, *Leviticus 1–16*, 257; Milgrom, "Israel's Sanctuary," 392–95.

51. Maccoby, *Ritual and Morality*, 91.

52. Klawans, *Impurity and Sin*, 29.

53. Levine, *Presence of the Lord*, 63, 75, 77. Levine's translation of *kippēr* as "wipe away" supports his view of impurity as an external force (56, 57).

54. Jenson, *Graded Holiness*, 203.

Summary: The Threat to Divine Reality

In addition to metaphors for evil in creation passages, cultic passages include demons (Azazel particularly), impurity (itself a demonic-like force), and immorality. These evil forces threaten sacred space, requiring continual reapplication of boundaries. Prophets point to a future "day of the Lord" when evil will escalate, but this is followed by hopes of a new creation and elimination of evil (Isa 13:1—23:18; 49:1—55:13; Amos 5:18–20; Zeph 1:14–18).[55]

A contested issue in cultic studies is the extent to which the OT "de-demonized" creation or the degree to which Israel followed, or was opposed to, the views of the surrounding cultures. Douglas believes biblical writers precluded belief in demons and sacrifice to them. "Demons are the primitive element rejected by Israel; the stable, moral relation with God is true religion." In Leviticus, "belief in the maleficent power of demons has been demolished." Instead, Douglas argues, uncleanness is used as an explanation for affliction. Hence Leviticus functioned primarily as polemical to other religions. Douglas thinks that "religions which explain evil by reference to demonology or sorcery are failing to offer a way of comprehending the whole of existence."[56] Milgrom similarly denies any contribution of demonology to Israel's thought, claiming that in Israel, "the world of demons is abolished; there is no struggle with autonomous forces because there are none. With the demise of the demons, only one creature remains with "demonic" power—the human being."[57] Free will explains the power of humans who can in fact drive God out of his sanctuary. Demonology evolved into ethics, sin replaces the demonic, and thus evil resides in humans. Milgrom admits that demons are in the background of the biblical texts; as discussed, he affirms Azazel as a demon. He appears to be somewhat inconsistent here—if demons lurk in the background, they have not been abolished in the OT. Neither Douglas nor Milgrom considers the strong affirmation of the demonic in ANE or Second Temple literature. By contrast, Levine emphasizes ANE influence on Israel. The presence of the demonic is taken for granted by the cultic community and the cult functioned primarily to eliminate evil forces, which are equated

---

55. Interestingly, Ezekiel prophesies that God will *cleanse* rebellious Israel, and give her a new heart and spirit (36:25, 26). For discussion of the prophetic "day of the Lord" motif see VanGemeren, *Prophetic Word*, 214–24; Motyer, *Isaiah*, 138–45, 196–201, 242–75.

56. Douglas, *Leviticus*, 2–5, 9–10, 11, 17, 107, 122–23, 149, 174, 189.

57. Milgrom, *Leviticus 1–16*, 1079; *Leviticus: Ritual and Ethics*, 9.

with uncleanness.[58] He also believes that blood sacrifices were offered to demons and accepted in lieu of life. This last point is poorly supported and many others take a more moderate view.[59]

Perhaps part of the reason for the discrepant views is that many scholars confuse literal and metaphorical or insist they are mutually exclusive. Those who look only for the existence of clearly defined evil spirits in the OT will likely conclude that they were either eliminated or extremely minimized. They have difficulty explaining the multiple metaphors for evil; the odd occurrence of a figure like Azazel; the association between immorality, impurity, and the demonic; and the resurgence of demonology in Second Temple Judaism and the NT. However, if evil forces are examined through the lens of conceptual metaphor theory, the picture is very different. Including symbolic representations of evil (e.g., uncleanness, wilderness), as well as ANE demons used in the OT (e.g., Resheph, the Canaanite demon usually translated as pestilence), and evil spirits in ancient Judaic literature results in a much larger category of evil forces. Even if one argues that a specific term like Resheph had no association with evil forces, the category is still large enough to continue without that term. Some terms like uncleanness, which occur outside as well as within the category of evil, can nevertheless elucidate our conceptualization of evil. Consideration of the semantic domain of evil, rather than one element of it, like demons, is much more fruitful. It addresses the problem of the overlap of meaning between terms like god and idol, sidesteps the issue of whether a term is meant literally or metaphorically (usually both), and allows for a more comprehensive view of evil. Douglas insists that unclean and demonic are unrelated perhaps because she is viewing them within small, separate categories. As discussed, they are not necessarily synonymous, but related, and can be seen as items within the larger category of evil.

However, even though the semantic domain of evil is quite large, the OT seriously undermines and minimizes ANE "gods": When the ark is

58. Levine, *Presence of the Lord*, 56, 68, 75, 78. Nigosian similarly remarks that the abundant evidence of occult activities in the OT means that Israel was no different from her neighbors; *Magic and Divination*, 88. F. Gaiser thinks that demons are absent in the OT because they cannot remain in the presence of God; they exist among the nations but dare not show their face in Israel; *Healing in the Bible*, 149.

59. E.g., Unger claims "the category of demons was already well known to Hebrew thought, and that heathen idolatry was interpreted as initiated and energized by demonic activity and deception"; *Biblical Demonology*, 13–14; however, compared with its pagan neighbors, biblical demonology was devoid of exaggeration and superstition (23).

captured, Dagon cannot survive in the presence of the Lord (1 Sam 5:1–5); Bel falls down without resistance (Isa 46:1; Jer 50:2); Elijah taunts his opposition suggesting Baal is taking a trip or asleep (1 Kgs 18:27).[60] The OT attests that "gods"/demons exist, but are not to be feared; they are no match for the one true God. Israel has advanced views compared with her polytheistic neighbors, but has not eliminated the demonic. These gods are in opposition to YHWH but no competition. I agree that many of the biblical texts are polemical with respect to ANE religions. But, unlike Douglas, I believe the demonic is not demolished in the OT, merely diminished. The supreme God of Israel sets boundaries around evil, and puts it in its proper place. He teaches his people that he alone is to be worshiped. Demons are named far less frequently in the OT than in ANE literature, but this is most likely because their existence was so assumed, they did not need mentioning. What was needed was to focus attention away from them and onto the one true source of life, YHWH. I agree that appealing to the demonic as a sole explanation for evil is inadequate, but I would argue that religions which fail to incorporate evil spirits as a causative factor are not offering a comprehensive view of existence. A holistic, systematic view of evil should in fact incorporate the evil spirits that the Bible attests to. Although I agree with Milgrom about the importance of human responsibility, I disagree that this requires elimination of demonic forces. Both need consideration for a comprehensive perspective on evil. To reiterate, the OT did not "de-demonize" cultic life; evil forces, depicted by multiple metaphors, were assumed to be present but were brought down to size and given proper perspective.

Cultic metaphors for evil can also give insight into the ontology of evil. Many of the metaphors for evil suggest a "less than real" status (recall Eliade's real/unreal dichotomy). This "unreality" is evident in the manner in which ANE "gods" are treated in the OT. Noll remarks that compared with pagan literature there is a notable absence of names of gods in the Bible. When they do appear, biblical texts "radically undermine their reality."[61] Milgrom and Douglas conclude that demons are absent

---

60. The gods of the nations are markedly inferior to the God of Israel (2 Kgs 18:33–35; 19:12; Ps 96:5; Isa 36:18; 37:12; 40:17; Jer 14:22) and tremble in his presence (Isa 64:2). Motyer, *Isaiah*, 368; Noll, *Angels of Light*, 33–34. Boyd, using somewhat different arguments, also notes that the OT "toned down" the demonic compared with the ANE; *God at War*, 75–80.

61. Noll, *Angels of Light*, 33–34. Russell notes historically that demons are "seldom clearly distinguished from one another" and have a "strange and blurry quality"; *Devil*, 73.

from the OT perhaps because these scholars do not include the category, "semi-real" (even though Milgrom's "miasma" sounds suspiciously like a nebulous reality or a demonic force). Alexander notes the ambiguity in the description of demons in the DSS; multiple terms are used and there is no technical precision with respect to classification.[62] Chaos and disorder also carry connotations of unreality. Perhaps part of the reason for the multiple, often ambiguous, terms for evil spirits is the nebulous nature of demons. If these beings are somehow ontologically "less real" it makes sense that they would be difficult to describe clearly, and why metaphors provide a better picture. Douglas, for example, although she argues for "de-demonization," focuses on disorder as the force that threatens cultic life (see below). It is logical to make a connection between disorder and evil, which are both polar opposites of order and holiness. This concurs with conclusions in chapters 3 and 4 about the nature of evil as chaotic and quasi-real.

Sacred Space

Cultic sacred space is similar to the sacred space of creation. It is character-ized by centrality, light and life, holiness, and purity. It is clearly separated from profane space (qōdeš, "holy," connotes separateness) and is filled with divine presence.[63] Cultic biblical studies often focus on time not space, yet the concept of sacred space, literally and metaphorically, is old.[64] Notably there is no warfare involved in the construction of sacred space; perhaps explaining why cultic passages are ignored in popular "spiritual warfare" literature, and perhaps illustrating how a "dead" metaphor can lead to ne-glect of other metaphors. This section discusses the metaphorical theology

---

62. Alexander, "Demonology in the DSS," 336, 350. He seems to suggest that demons are put in their proper place in the DSS. In light of Douglas's work on catego-rization (see below), he remarks that demons do not fit in the world; they are out of place as they belong properly in the abyss.

63. *DCH* 7:190–95; C. Barth points out various forms of divine presence (a pillar of cloud, an angel, the ark, the tent, the priestly tabernacle) and believes separation relates to covenantal holiness; *God with Us,* 100–105, 140; H. Harrington also notes the description of holiness as a consuming fire which can refine and separate the pure from the impure, creating a boundary around the sacred; *Holiness,* 1, 11–13.

64. E.g., Josephus viewed the tabernacle and temple as symbolic of the universe; *Jewish War,* 5.5. For studies on biblical space, see Cohen *Shape of Sacred Space* and Dozeman, "Biblical Geography," 87–108. Dozeman notes that biblical geography is multivalent, both historical and symbolic (102–3).

of holy places, first the temple, then the binary oppositions that elucidate sacred space, and finally the concept of graded holiness.

Temple Cosmology

The original and prototypical constructed sacred space is the wilderness tabernacle. Moses received detailed instructions regarding the construction of the tabernacle, illustrated thus:

Figure 5.1: Plan of the Tabernacle[65]

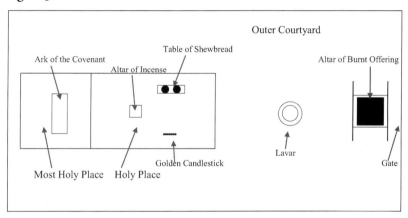

The tabernacle is located in the center of camp, and there are three "zones": the Most Holy Place (Holy of Holies), the Holy Place (together these are also called the sanctuary), and the Courtyard. The Holy places contain the ark with the Sinai covenant, the lampstand, the cherubim, and the bread of divine presence. Significantly, the tabernacle is the dwelling place of God. This holy space is so powerful that those who come in contact with it can contract holiness (Exod 29:37; 30:29), and encounters with sacred space could cause death (Exod 19:12). The successors to the tabernacle—Solomon's temple (1 Kgs 6:1–38), the second temple (Ezra 3:8–10; 5:1, 2; 6:13–18), and Ezekiel's visionary temple (Ezek 40:1—47:12)—albeit somewhat different, are similar in important symbolic respects (including three zones and divine presence).[66] Solomon believed God could not be

65. Exod 25–31; 35–40. However, as M. Homan points out, biblical texts do not allow precise determination of the tabernacle's shape; *To Your Tents,* 129–84.

66. Temples can also be described at Shiloh, Gilgal, Bethel, and Hebron; Haran, *Temples,* 26–39. Note that metaphorical conceptualizations of sacred space do not

contained by a mere temple. The post-exilic temple appears less opulent than Solomon's; the Ark of the Covenant is missing, likely not recovered after the destruction of the temple. Ezekiel's visionary temple is elaborate, built on a high mountain with streams flowing from it, and contains no ark; God's presence is sufficient. Morality is a prerequisite for divine presence, and temple access is restricted to the obedient and pure (Ezek 43:7–9; 44:5–14; 47:1–12).[67] Zion and Jerusalem also describe sacred space and are associated with centrality, creation, the exodus, the temple, and a meeting place with God, as well as symbolizing the coming kingdom of God (2 Kgs 19:31; Pss 2:6; 9:11; 69:35; Isa 1:27; 51:3; 60:14; Zech 8:3).[68]

The temple was conceived both symbolically and literally in Israel (a twice-true metaphor). The psalmists when praising or petitioning God used multiple spatial metaphors to refer to the presence of the Lord: tent, sanctuary, temple, throne, holy hill, strong tower, fortress, stronghold, city, Mount Zion, and heaven (Pss 2:4; 15:1; 18:2; 28:2; 31:3; 46:4, 5; 48:1, 2; 53:2; 61:3; 63:2; 74:2; 80:14; 87:1–3). They worshiped God "in his holy temple" and "in heaven," clearly associating the two (Ps 11:4; cf. Isa 6:1–13).[69] The temple is linked to life and often discussed in opposition to death or Sheol (Pss 6:5; 9:7, 17; 55:14, 15; 63:2, 9). Divine presence is associated with rest (Exod 33:14; Josh 1:12–15; Ps 95:11; Isa 63:14) and peace (Lev 26:6; Pss 4:8; 29:11; 85:8; 122:7; Isa 9:6, 7). There are boundaries set around sacred space (YHWH tells Moses to put limits around Mount Sinai [Exod 19:10–24] and only priests have access to the holy of holies [Exod 28:1—29:46]).

---

preclude historical existence, but consideration of it from a symbolic perspective is more fruitful. There is some debate regarding the historicity of the tabernacle as described in Exodus (e.g., Haran argues the wilderness tabernacle was largely imaginary and that Solomon's temple was projected onto the tabernacle; *Temples*, 189–94).

67. Divine presence is also associated with hope and the face/glory of God (Exod 20:3; Pss 42:2; 80:3; Ezek 39:29). There is no Hebrew word for divine presence; "face" is used instead; Terrien, *Elusive Presence*, 65.

68. G. McConville notes that there is no single OT view of Jerusalem; it is sometimes a people, sometimes a place; there is a fine line between literal and metaphorical (Zion is primarily metaphorical and associated with worship); the link between Zion and Jerusalem led to assimilation with covenantal theology; "Jerusalem in the OT," 21–51; C. Barth remarks, the "coming kingdom of God is but one, and the symbol and center of this kingdom is the new Jerusalem"; *God with Us*, 234–303; Dumbrell summarizes: "Jerusalem becomes a major biblical symbol uniting city and saved community; combining sacred space and sanctified people"; *End of the Beginning*, 5–19; see also Dow, *Images of Zion*, 43–67.

69. Terrien notes that the tension between divine presence in creation and in the temple is never resolved; *Elusive Presence*, 405.

The relationship between temple and creation was discussed in the previous chapter. Sacred space in cultic passages is further associated with the sanctuary, the temple, the throne, a holy hill, a city, heaven, holiness, purity, centrality, light, life, and fertility. It is frequently symbolized by the cosmic mountain, through which communication between heaven and earth is possible. The temple (chosen by Israel's God) can be seen as an "earthly reproduction of a transcendent model," which functions to continually resanctify the world.[70] Richard Clifford examines the cosmic mountain motif in ANE and biblical literature, noting that mountains are frequently venerated because they are thought to be the dwelling of the high god, a meeting place for gods, the source of water, the meeting place between heaven and earth, and the place where divine decrees are issued.[71] He suggests that, during the Sinai revelation, Moses may have seen and then copied the heavenly tent. In a similar vein, Levenson discusses the cosmic symbolism of the temple, which he relates to the mythic Mount Zion and Eden. The temple is a "visual vehicle for the knowledge of God"; it functions as a connecting point with heaven. The nature of sacred space (and holiness) is qualitatively different; there is a barrier between the temple and ordinary reality. "The sanctuary is an enclave of ideal reality within the world of profanity."[72] Furthermore, the temple functions to keep chaos at bay; it sustains the world, and all other space relates to it. Levenson also points out the analogies between creation and temple in the priestly account, summarizing, "It is through the cult that we are enabled to cope with evil, for it is the cult that builds and maintains order, transforms chaos

70. Eliade, *Sacred and Profane*, 36–39, 58, 59. K. Wennell similarly describes the tabernacle as "the closest of the earthly models to the heavenly ideal;" she notes the temple as "dynamic sacred space becomes static centralized sacred space, and the temple is now the center of the promised land which is characterized by holiness"; *Jesus and Land*, 24, 27; see also Barker, *On Earth*, 8–10.

71. Clifford, *Cosmic Mountain*, 3, 5, 123. Ugaritic myths believed mountains were the location of meetings between the gods, and between heaven and earth; El, Baal, and Anat all lived on mountains (34–90).

72. Levenson, *Sinai and Zion*, 91, 95, 115–25, 127–28. Cohen, following Eliade, notes that the center, also symbolized by a mountain, tree, pillar, vine and ladder, provides a link between heaven and earth, and is a place around which the world is organized. Mountain imagery includes security, height (close to heaven and authority), and fertility, and accommodates the paradox of God dwelling both on earth and in heaven; *Shape of Sacred Space*, 29–39, 63. Kunin points out the liminal nature of mountains; a raised space bridging earth and heaven such as the tower of Babel (Gen 11), the sacrifice of Isaac (Gen 22), and the Sinai covenant (Exod 20); *God's Place in the World*, 31–32. Anderson also observes the Hebrew belief in the temple as an entry point to heaven, e.g., Isa 6; "Praise of God," 15–33.

into creation, ennobles humanity, and realizes the kingship of God who has ordained the cult and obedience to the directives of the divine master that his good world comes into existence."[73] Steven Holloway, comparing the temple in OT and ANE texts, proposes the following: The temple is the architectural embodiment of the cosmic mountain; it is associated with the waters of life that flow forth from springs within the temple; it is built on the waters of chaos and prevents eruption of those waters; the world is recreated annually through the temple that represents abundance, prosperity, and a safe haven from chaos; the temple is a place where humans can interact with the divine through sacrifice.[74]

Sacred space is also associated with purity. Milgrom points out that God will not dwell in a polluted sanctuary (Lam 2:7; Ezek 11:22), hence the importance of purity rituals. Furthermore, the sanctum has the power to sanctify others (Exod 29:37; 30:26–29; Lev 6:18, 27) or cause their downfall (Num 9:13, 20; Lev 23:29, 30; Exod 31:14), especially with respect to neglect of ritual and idolatry (Lev 20:2–6; Ezek 14:8).[75] Sacrilege against sacred space is related to covenantal violation, because the sanctuary represents God himself. Holiness is defined by separation from the pagans, but the lines are not clearly drawn since all people are called to be holy. Milgrom describes sacred space in concentric circles with the sanctuary in the center, followed by the land, with the earth outside the circle.[76] Again, the divisions are not absolute; God dwells in the land as well, therefore it needs to be kept pure. Gorman stresses the importance of order and boundaries for the creation and preservation of sacred space. The conceptual categories of space and time allow the intersection of cult and cosmos; participation in the cult maintains order in the universe. Gorman believes the tabernacle is the basic paradigm of sacred space.[77] Cosmos, sacred space, and sacrificial activity are closely related. D. Wright

73. Levenson, *Persistence of Evil*, 127, 133, 139, 170.

74. Holloway, "What Ship Goes There," 328–55.

75. Milgrom, *Leviticus 1–16*, 258; *Leviticus: Ritual and Ethics*, 32, 52, 62–67.

76. Milgrom, *Leviticus: Ritual and Ethics*, 102, 109, 252. Olyan notes that any space where the divine is present is holy: Moses at the burning bush (Exod 3:5), Joshua at Jericho (Josh 5:15), Mount Sinai (Exod 19:23), the desert tabernacle (Exod 25–30), the temple of Solomon (1 Kgs 6–7), and the visionary temple of Ezekiel (Ezek 40–48); *Rites and Rank*, 17–22. Klingbeil agrees that sacred space is defined by divine presence and is therefore flexible; *Bridging the Gap*, 161.

77. Gorman, *Ideology of Ritual*, 16, 17, 32; see also the previous discussion in chapter 4.

uses the term "cultic topography" to refer to the symbolism of the tabernacle in Israel.[78] He diagrams three concentric circles with the sanctum (holy) in the center, the habitation (generally pure but with some non-communicable impurity and restricted communicable impurity) in the middle, and outside the habitation (pure and impure) as the outside circle. Beale similarly emphasizes the cosmic aspects of the temple, viewing it as a microcosm of the universe. He describes its symbolism thus: The outer court is where humanity dwells, the holy place corresponds to the visible heavens, and the holy of holies to the invisible heavens.[79]

To summarize, sacred space, particularly as a metaphorical concept, is prevalent in biblical cultic passages. It is characterized by holiness, purity, and divine presence and represented by the tabernacle, the temple, the cosmic mountain, and heaven. Sacred space can also be defined in terms of its oppositions, the unholy, the unclean, and the profane.

Binary Oppositions

Saul Olyan expresses surprise at the lack of study of binary oppositions in the OT, given their prevalence. He examines the dyads holy/common, clean/unclean, Israel/alien, and whole/blemished with respect to social status and hierarchy, concluding that binary oppositions function to generate hierarchy and communicate totality.[80] Olyan argues that the holy/common contrast is primary; all other cultic binary oppositions presuppose it. It is essential for the maintenance of sacred space; without this distinction, the divine presence may depart. Like holiness, the clean/unclean opposition is ubiquitous in cultic writings: "The holy/common distinction establishes a boundary around the sanctuary; the unclean/clean distinction deter-

---

78. D. Wright, *Disposal of Impurity*, 231, 244.

79. Beale, *Temple*, 25, 32. "The Old Testament tabernacle and temples were symbolically designed to point to the cosmic eschatological reality that God's tabernacling presence, formerly limited to the holy of holies, was to be extended throughout the whole earth." Eden is an archetypical temple and Sinai can also be seen to have three divisions: the foot where the Israelites were; half way up, where priests were allowed; and the top where Moses met the Lord, surrounded by a cloud (105). Beale also points out similarities in symbolism between biblical imagery and that in ANE and Second Temple literature (51–54, 76–78).

80. The first two dyads are often found in close proximity (e.g., Lev 10:8–11; Ezek 44:23); Olyan, *Rites and Rank*, 4, 15. The term common (sometimes called profane in a usage different from this study) is confusing: it can be divided into clean and unclean; Milgrom, *Leviticus 1–16*, 732; Boda, *Severe Mercy*, 51–52.

mines who or what may cross it."[81] Others have commented on binary oppositions in cultic texts: Gorman believes the categories, clean/unclean, holy/not-holy, life/death, and order/chaos interact and intersect,[82] and Douglas follows a binary model particularly in her body cosmogram, with categories being inside and outside. She relates these oppositions to those under the covenant and those outside it.[83] Binary oppositions, however, do not give a complete picture and can lead to dualistic views (see chapter 1). Moreover, cultic metaphors are complex (e.g., profane, in opposition to holy, includes common, not necessarily sinful, aspects of life). There is often a more nuanced relationship between categories than binaries imply; as Douglas remarks, "the picture is not black and white."[84] Opposite dyads, though, can be helpful in explaining reality. We can appreciate a concept better by examining the contrary notion. Grey is best understood through knowledge of black and white. An approach that incorporates binaries plus the graded areas in-between is likely most helpful.

Graded Holiness

Gradations of holiness have been discussed in cultic theology. The tabernacle consisted of three zones, the symbolism of which has been interpreted in various ways. Some (e.g., Eliade) emphasize the dualities holy/unholy, but miss the nuances of cultic theology and are subject to previously mentioned criticisms of dualism. Others follow the tripartite temple structure in describing gradations of holiness and purity. Milgrom, Wright, and Gorman may be summarized as describing the three parts as holy (God, tabernacle, sanctuary), semi-holy (Israel, the habitation), and unholy (humanity). Tripartite models, however, miss the cosmic metaphors within cultic theology, especially the symbolism of evil, chaos, the

---

81. Olyan, *Rites and Rank*, 17, 38.

82. Gorman, *Ideology of Ritual*, 232. Anderson notes the relationship between life/death and the divine presence: "Just as life was experienced in the cult as being before the very presence of God in the (heavenly) temple, so 'death' was experienced in the cult as being cut off from that presence outside the temple"; "Praise of God," 28. D. Wright similarly argues that a common goal of purification rituals was to keep the sanctuary holy; divine presence is incompatible with impurity; *Disposal of Impurity*, 273.

83. Douglas, *Purity and Danger*, 120–22; *Leviticus*, 152.

84. Douglas, *Leviticus*, 152; see also Gorman, *Ideology of Ritual*, 192; Wright, *Disposal of Impurity*, 246.

demonic, and disorder that Eliade and Levenson point out. Like the model developed in the previous chapter, they do not reflect shades of grey.

Philip Jenson, not necessarily intentionally, provides a balance between dualistic and tripartite temple cosmology models. He claims that the idea of holiness is most clearly evident in the spatial dimension (not personal, ritual, or temporal) and "reflects a graded conception of the world."[85] Specifically there is a range encompassing very holy, holy, clean, unclean, and very unclean. The sacred (very holy) is associated with God, temple, life, being, and order and the profane (very unclean) is associated with the Gentiles, the wilderness, death, nothingness, and chaos.[86] The holiness spectrum provides a framework for understanding the various concepts of purity and holiness both in an idealist sense (human categorization of the world) and a realist sense (human dealings with death). Jenson believes these two aspects are complementary. The structure of the tabernacle provides the clearest example of the spatial dimension of the spectrum of holiness. Unlike others who usually note three zones, Jenson includes five zones: 1—the Holy of Holies, 2—the Holy Place, 3—the Court, which includes a Holy Place and the entrance of the Tent of Meeting, 4—a clean place, which could be in or outside of the camp, and 5—an unclean place, usually outside the camp. The tabernacle gives concrete expression to the deeper symbolism of cultic life; for instance, gold, abundant in holy zones and on priestly garments, is precious and stable, reflecting the presence and character of God. Gradations of sacred space correlate with human experience of space and give orientation to life. Jenson believes Eliade's dichotomy misses many of the nuances of the priestly material (e.g., the concepts of holiness and cleanness are closely aligned but not identical).[87] Kunin follows Jenson but modifies the binary oppositions of structuralism (e.g., camp/world, Israel/nations) and uses a model of concentric circles (also five zones), with variations.[88] He describes two biblical models of

85. Jenson, *Graded Holiness*, 36. He follows Douglas and other anthropologists in using a structural and conceptual approach. Order and its associated concepts, structure, classification, and grading, can be seen as the central theme in the priestly writings (210–15). He views the holiness spectrum as a classification system, or worldview (58–9), which incorporates a complex symbol-system (61–62).

86. Jenson, *Graded Holiness*, 63, following Davies, "Interpretation of Sacrifice," 387–99.

87. Jenson, *Graded Holiness*, 43–44, 90, 112. He follows Haran's gradations of holiness with respect to materials within the tabernacle and taboos regarding approaching the tabernacle; Haran, *Temples*, 158–87. Unlike others, Jenson actually includes the "unholy" in his spectrum.

88. Kunin, *God's Place in the World*, 11–42. He further develops segmentary

sacred space, static (Solomon's temple) and dynamic (the tabernacle), suggesting the latter represents an idealization of the former. These models do not conflict but are used conceptually to relate categories of space. Kunin's dynamic model is more amenable to symbolic conception, but he only includes the nations in the periphery, not evil forces. Jenson's model incorporates both binary oppositions and gradations of holiness present in cultic texts, plus includes the dimension of evil.

Conceptualizing Evil

Understanding sacred space can provide insight into profane space. This study of sacred space confirms other observations that evil is characterized by darkness, impurity, immorality, pagans, the wilderness, and a lack of divine presence. And, since sacred space is characterized by order, reality, and rest, its opposite is likely characterized by disorder, unreality, and unrest. Evil, like holiness, can be considered in spatial terms. Gorman, for instance, relates morality to cosmic structure: "Sin and its resulting impurity, then, may be said to cause the breakdown of the divinely created order."[89] Hence evil can be seen as a destructive and disorganizing force. Burnett, discussed previously, suggests that divine absence is related to cosmic structure; he implies that evil exists outside of godly reality, which accords with a spatial conceptualization of evil.

Sacred Actions

How we conceive of space, physically and metaphorically, determines our actions towards it. Furthermore, sacred actions are necessary to maintain sacred space. Although God primarily gifts creation by limiting evil, humans have responsibility too. This section examines divine initiative and human responsibility in cultic theology. The latter can be viewed as ordering and setting boundaries on sacred space. Obedience and worship are

---

models which he believes are more accurate than concentric models; the latter only depict graded holiness and not the structural relationships between different categories or parts to whole (15–18). These variations may be more accurate but are somewhat confusing and do not aid in conceptualization. Kunin criticizes Jenson for some of his concepts not fitting within a concentric model. He believes the concentric model implies an extension of graded holiness beyond the camp. However, this is not necessarily the case, especially if one places the model on a background of black/evil.

89. Gorman, *Ideology of Ritual*, 80.

also important for the maintenance of such space. All are related to the action of purification, or cleansing.

Divine Initiative

There are three aspects to the work of God in maintaining sacred space. First, he dictates the expectations of Israel for her part in the covenant. This includes obedience to the commandments as well as various rituals, which can make reparation for intentional and inadvertent impurity (e.g., grain offering, burnt offering, exile from camp for certain periods). The Israelites, especially priests, are charged with distinguishing between holy/ common and clean/unclean, and conducting purity rituals as proscribed (Lev 10:10; 20:25).[90] Rituals are best understood metaphorically (see below), even though some, like Barker, believe rituals "actually inaugu- rated and brought about whatever it was they represented."[91] Second, God offers forgiveness for sin. Because of the relationship between morality and purity discussed above, confession and reparation are required prior to sacrifice, and forgiveness is offered in response to confession (Lev 5:5, 6; 6:1–6; 26:40–45).[92] The penitential psalms witness the importance of repentance; David famously prays for forgiveness and a clean heart (Ps 51:1, 2, 7; also Pss 32; 38; 65; 130). Elsewhere purity is interpreted meta- phorically to mean repentance (Isa 1:16; Prov 20:9). Ultimately, it is the Lord who purifies from sin and uncleanness as well as offering healing and renewal (Ps 51:2, 7; Zech 3:5).[93] Third, God offers his Spirit. The Holy Spirit empowers certain people for specific tasks, such as building the tab- ernacle (Bezalel and Oholiab, Exod 31:1–6), and indwells some leaders and prophets (e.g., Samson, Judg 13:25; 14:6, 19; 15:14; Saul, 1 Sam 10:6, 10; 16:13; the elders of Israel, Num 11:25). The Spirit can activate goodness

90. Leviticus provides the most comprehensive regulations regarding cultic purity, with echoes in Exodus and Numbers. This book divides into three sections, commonly designated as: the priesthood (1–10), ritual pollution and purification (11–17), and holiness (18–26).

91. Barker, *On Earth*, 6. "Words, actions, and places were used both to express and to realize temple theology" (2). Gane also believes ritual is thought to change reality; *Cult and Character*, 15.

92. Although, as Boda notes, forgiveness is complex in Leviticus, sometimes oc- curring simply as a consequence of ritual, not divine will; *Severe Mercy*, 71–75.

93. "I am the lord your healer" (Exod 15:22–27; cf. Num 21:4–9); Gaiser, *Healing in the Bible*, 3–126.

(Ezek 36:27), and conversely can be grieved by Israel's sin (Isa 63:10).[94] Finally, there are implications, discussed above, that God has structured the world such that evil is separated from holiness.

Human Responsibility

As in creation, humans have responsibility to be obedient to God's commands. Cultic texts expand upon this notion and add the ideas of worship and ritual, especially the maintenance of purity. These can be interpreted as setting boundaries on evil.

OBEDIENCE, WORSHIP, AND PURIFICATION

Covenantal obedience is an essential responsibility of Israel, and morality is generally considered superior to ritual. Sometimes praise and obedience are preferred to burnt offerings. The psalmists substitute praise, prayer, and raised hands for sacrifice (Pss 50:14; 51:16, 17; 141:2; cf. Prov 15:8; 21:3; Eccl 5:1). There is a clear association between sacred space ("holy place"), purity ("clean hands"), and morality ("pure heart," honesty, fidelity) in Psalm 24:3, 4. Directional metaphors of obedience are also evident: people can choose the ways of righteousness or wickedness (Deut 5:33; Pss 27:11; Prov 2:12–15; 10:17; 15:19–24), and God promises to separate sin "as far as the east is from the west" (Ps 103:12).[95] Morality is usually considered more important than purity. The prophets critiqued cultic rituals only if they were performed with a wrong attitude: Isaiah is only against sacrifice if it is hypocritical and Hosea insists that covenant love is more important than ritual. Overall, the prophets condemn hypocrisy, not ritual law per se (Isa 1:15; Hos 6:6).[96]

---

94. Welker, *God the Spirit*, 66–83, 102–5; Harrington, *Holiness*, 43; Gabriel, *Lord is the Spirit*, 125–30.

95. Jäkel, in his study of biblical journey metaphors, points out that God's way is the good way, a straight path that is holy and leads upwards, to eternal life; evil ways are crooked, dark and slippery, full of obstacles, and lead to death. The righteous keep to a straight path and delight in God's way. The good way is lit by God's word and he guides, teaches, and watches over them; the wicked are ignorant of God's way and refuse to be informed; they run to evil and lay traps for the righteous; "Mortal Man," 55–86. Recall that journey metaphors are universal.

96. Jeremiah denounces the immoral behavior of the Israelites who think being in the temple will make all things right (Jer 7:1–34); Amos exhorts social justice over religious festivals (5:22–24). Milgrom stresses that prophets were more concerned with

Sacred space is dependent on divine presence and God's ability to order and cleanse creation. However, impurity, closely related to sin, results in disorder. Human actions are therefore important as well. The biblical texts underline the importance of obedience (to the law), sacrifice, worship, and social justice, with confession and reparation being required for transgressions. Sacrifice ("to make sacred") is related to the ordering of creation and cultic life, and is associated with praise. Covenant, cult, and cosmos are intertwined. Covenantal obedience is directly related to the maintenance of sacred space. As discussed above, disobedience leads to disorder. Klawans believes sacrifice functions to invite and maintain the divine presence; by contrast, sin repels it.[97] This explains why idolatry is so abhorrent; turning away from the one true God to other gods negates both divine presence and blessing; it violates a boundary and leaves an opening for disorder and evil. The cult provides ways in which immorality, whether inadvertent or deliberate, can be purified (recalling that some sin cannot be purified, but results in death or exile). Sin, which results in disorder and impurity, can be confessed and, consequently, the Lord restores order and purity (although severe sin sometimes resulted in death—separation of evil rather than its purification). Sacred actions are required for the maintenance of sacred space (ritual laws follow immediately after construction of the tabernacle), and humans carry responsibility (the Decalogue comes before the tabernacle instructions and is reiterated throughout the OT).[98]

---

moral behavior than mere rituals; "ritual piety is vitiated by their immoral behavior"; "Jeremiah's Repudiation," 274–75; see also Barton, "Prophets and Cult," 111–22.

97. Klawans, *Purity, Sacrifice,* 68–71. Harrington similarly notes, "Israel lives between the two poles of (1) holiness/life, i.e., a blessed, ordered, and significant existence which leads to eternal bliss, and (2) evil/death, i.e. a cursed, chaotic, and meaningless life which will end in destruction"; there is choice between obedience (leading to holiness, God, life) or rebellion (leading to impurity, false gods, death); *Holiness,* 42.

98. Fretheim notes the eight "negative" commands focus on boundaries (although he does not consider evil forces) and aim to protect the community; *Exodus,* 221. The Decalogue, rather than being viewed as prohibitions, can be seen as boundaries on creation, ways to maintain order; e.g., worshiping other gods violates a holiness boundary; murder violates a body boundary, adultery violates a social boundary; all can create a break in cosmic structure and allow the intrusion of evil spiritual forces. This is similar Barth's ideas of sin providing an opening for "nothingness" and Burnett's notion of evil being outside cosmic structure.

ORDERING, BOUNDARY-SETTING, AND PURIFICATION

Holiness and purity, characteristic of sacred space, are attained via cleansing as well as separation, or setting boundaries on "un-holiness." Sacred space is achieved via sacred actions. Although there have been various interpretations of the ritual passages, many scholars believe these are best understood holistically and metaphorically. [99] In her ground-breaking work, *Purity and Danger,* Douglas challenges the assumption that rituals related to purity are primitive, arguing that the concepts of dirt and pollution are similar in all cultures: dirt is seen as "matter out of place." "Dirt is essentially disorder" and all human rituals relating to dirt involve efforts to eliminate it and thus organize an otherwise chaotic environment. Humans are naturally ritualistic creatures. It is "impossible to have social relations without symbolic acts."[100] Douglas applies this anthropological insight to biblical cultic texts insisting on unity in interpretation: "Defilement is never an isolated event. It cannot occur except in view of a systematic ordering of ideas"; it is a "basic condition of all reality." Underlying ritual behavior is a need for order. "Ideas about separating, purifying, demarcating and punishing transgressions have as their main function to impose system on

99. Earlier interpretations of cultic texts, some of which are still contemporary, included symbolic views (the proscribed rituals were not meant literally, e.g., Origen, *Homilies on Leviticus*), hygienic theories (avoidance of animals as disease carriers, e.g., Harrison, *Leviticus*), humanitarian theories (sparing certain animals), and cultural theories (avoiding things associated with pagan religions, e.g., the admonition not to "boil a kid in its mother's milk" [Deut 14:2] is against a Canaanite fertility rite; Levenson, *Sinai and Zion,* 52). Some claim these laws were arbitrary or cannot be meaningfully interpreted (propagated by twelfth-century Jewish scholar, Maimonides, *Mishnah Torah*). In the nineteenth century, psychological approaches to cultic studies appeared, e.g., Freud compared ritual taboos with psychotic obsession; *Totem and Taboo*. Anthropologists also started investigating biblical rituals, although often dismissing them as primitive and irrational (e.g., Robertson Smith, *Religions of the Semites,* 439, 446, 449; he uses the word savage liberally). These approaches have largely been rejected (e.g., Douglas insists that Moses was a great spiritual leader, not an "enlightened public health administrator"; *Purity and Danger,* 1966, 29). Similar ideas on purity are found in extra-biblical literature; Milgrom, *Leviticus: Rituals and Ethics,* 163–65; Gordon and Rendsburg, *Bible and ANE,* 154–56; Levenson, *Sinai and Zion,* 26–29. The community at Qumran extended and interpreted purity rules stringently; ritual and moral impurity were intertwined (1QS 3:8, 9; 4:5; CD 11:19–21; 4Q266–73; 11Q19:45–51); Harrington, *Purity Texts,* 19–27; "Purity and DSS," 397–428; Haber, "*They Shall Purify*," 166–69.

100. Douglas, *Purity and Danger,* 40, 62. When humans encounter anomalies, we create a system that can account for them. "In a chaos of shifting impressions, each of us constructs a stable world in which objects have recognizable shapes" (36).

an inherently untidy experience."[101] The purity laws, otherwise puzzling, should be understood both systematically and symbolically. Defilement is a structure and its parts should not be analyzed separately. Dirt relates to the dyads of order/disorder, being/nonbeing, form/formlessness, and life/death. Prohibitions relate to categorization, therefore animals that do not fit their class are considered unclean.[102] Pollution or defilement occurs when the boundaries are transgressed, the categories violated. Douglas notes that there are both external and internal boundaries. The first relate to the social and religious functions of the ritual laws, thus social pollution occurs when boundaries are violated. The second relates to morality; sin transgresses a boundary and subsequent pollution can be cancelled through repentance.[103] The reason for obedience to these symbolic and systematic regulations is primarily practical: it results in God's blessing and the consequent sustainability of the land. Conversely, the withdrawal of God's blessing is the source of all dangers. It is God who keeps order in the world. "In the Bible the Lord is credited with power which keeps the universe in good state. If the Lord's power is withdrawn it unleashes climatic disorders, drought, plague, and famine." The priests are charged with maintaining order by cleansing, separating, judging, and forgiving.[104] Hence, sacred space is kept sacred through the grace of God, and through the actions of God's people. Holiness involves separation, order, wholeness, and completion. Douglas relates holiness to body imagery; bodily discharges are defiling because they break the boundaries of the body. The Hebrews viewed blood as the source of life, therefore all bodily margins are potentially dangerous.[105] In later works, Douglas utilizes a structural approach to interpretation, suggesting for example, that in Leviticus sacrifice becomes a "framework for the philosophy of life." Part of the function of rituals is to "organize space and time in conformity with established cosmic analogies" and to relate society to the universe.[106] Although some

101. Douglas, *Purity and Danger*, 4, 41; *In the Wilderness*, 21. Wenell similarly states, "separation (i.e., between God's people and the nations) and distinction (i.e., between clean and unclean animals) is part of a system of thought which also established boundaries for purity"; *Jesus and Land*, 64.

102. E.g., creatures in the water without fins or scales (Lev 11:10); Douglas, *Purity and Danger*, 5, 55; similar to Eliade's views, discussed in chapter 3.

103. Douglas, *Purity and Danger*, 136, 158.

104. Num 15, 18, 19; ibid., 32, 151. Similarly, "God's work through the blessing is essentially to create order, through which men's affairs prosper" (50).

105. Ibid., 51–53, 120–22.

106. Douglas, *Leviticus*, 66, 135. Douglas uses the concept of microcosms, which make a "model of the universe, based on established similarities" (134).

aspects of her original work have been challenged,[107] Douglas continues to be influential with respect to viewing the cultic texts as systematized. Part of the reason for her success is her broad meaning-oriented approach, which accords with the methodology used in this study.

Like Douglas, Gorman views rituals symbolically as the sacred actions necessary for the ordination, maintenance, and purification of sacred space. Rituals are a "means of holding back social confusion, indeterminacy, and chaos because they provide patterns for enacting an ordered existence." Gorman thus associates sacred space and actions. He considers cultic categories broadly, applicable to all creation. "The created order, which includes the established order within which human existence takes shape, is understood to exist only insofar as clear lines of distinction between various conceptual categories are maintained." When categories are violated (e.g., sin, defilement), there is a collapse of order and chaos ensues. Impurity potentially causes the departure of divine presence with consequent collapse of order and eruption of chaos.[108] God's grace is required for the maintenance of creation. Many others have observed the importance of order in the maintenance of sacred space.[109] Kunin adds the ideas of liminality (elements which do not fit into a category must either be purified or removed) and directionality (movement towards the east is typically associated with sin).[110] The spatial symbolism of *Yom Kippur* is also significant. Jenson notes the opposition of the two goats: one is sacrificed to sacred space, the other sent to Azazel in profane space.[111] *Yom Kippur* is a good example of setting boundaries on evil. Gorman explains it as a ritual of restoration, required annually to reestablish the order of both

107. E.g., her rigid classification system and unclear definitions; Jenson, *Graded Holiness*, 78–79. Douglas later modified her position, admitting she was too extreme and that biblical uncleanness does not always apply cross-culturally; *Jacob's Tears*, 124–25.

108. Gorman, *Ideology of Ritual*, 29, 20–28, 42, 59, 79.

109. E.g., Milgrom relates separation and ordering to the ideas of holiness and purity; adherence to ritual laws leads to holiness; *Leviticus: Ritual and Ethics*, 179; Klingbeil believes sacrifice "is definitely a way to create, maintain, and restore a specific order" and "structure, order and sequence, space, and time are all significant elements of ritual"; *Bridging the Gap*, 140, 173.

110. Adam and Eve (Gen 3:24), Cain (Gen 4:16), and the builders of Babel (Gen 11:19); there is also upward movement towards heaven (e.g., cosmic mountain imagery, Elijah's ascent) and downward movement towards the underworld/death (e.g., the spirit of Samuel raised by the witch, 1 Sam 28:3–5); Kunin, *God's Place*, 14, 34–37.

111. The domain of Azazel is personal and the antithesis of holiness; Jenson, *Graded Holiness*, 202–3.

cult and cosmos;[112] Gane suggests that the purpose of placing sins on the goat "is to transfer moral evils back to where they ultimately came from in the first place."[113]

It is apparent that ordering is as important to Israel's cult as it is to creation. Keeping appropriate boundaries in the cosmos is closely related to purification, cleansing the cosmos. The spatial categories of holiness and purity are related and in opposition to evil and impurity. And impurity and immorality are related. Cultic activities can thus be viewed as divinely ordained ways in which Israel can be purified from sin and evil, and order can be restored. God purifies both by setting boundaries on evil, and by offering forgiveness for sin. Although Israel is responsible for covenantal faithfulness, ultimately it is the Lord who maintains purity.

Counteracting Evil

Understanding sacred actions improves our understanding of evil actions. Interestingly, disobedience results in consequences which are in binary opposition to holiness: disease, exile, and death. Appropriately, most scholars emphasize holiness and blessing; they discuss obedience, sacrifice, ritual purity, and social justice. Many of them do acknowledge the presence and influence of evil forces, but they seldom elucidate their nature, their relationship to the cult and the cosmos, or the correct response to them. As mentioned with regard to binary oppositions, understanding both extremes can help inform the middle. The above examination of sacred actions can help understand ways in which evil can be counteracted. Building on Douglas's theory of dirt, one could conceive of evil as household dust and clutter. It tends to accumulate and requires regular cleansing, "holy housekeeping." Evil can be understood in spatial terms (as opposed to warfare): it occurs when boundaries are violated, and needs to be repeatedly separated and returned to profane space where it belongs.

112. Kunin, *God's Place*, 61. Leviticus 16 "reflects a coherent, intelligible conception of ritual action as an enactment of world through the ritual breakdown and re-establishment of the categorical distinctions of holy/profane, pure/impure, and order/chaos" (62). Gorman points out that because sin is a cause of disorder, it makes sense that it be sent to the realm of disorder; *Ideology of Ritual*, 99.

113. Thus it is an elimination ritual, not a sacrifice; Gorman, *Ideology of Ritual*, 247, 264. Israel, by sinning, becomes an accomplice of Azazel, God's enemy. He relates the "gift" of sin to Azazel to the Genesis 3 notion of a tempter who delights in sin and the wilderness goat-demons (263–64). Azazel deserves this "gift."

A CULTIC MODEL FOR CONCEPTUALIZING EVIL

The preceding examination of cultic theology allows further development of the model suggested in the last chapter. First, I summarize the findings thus far.

Summary

With respect to priestly theology, most scholars agree that Israel's cult included a symbolic dimension related to cosmic reality, and some view the cult as primarily metaphorical (e.g., Gerald Klingbeil concludes, "the sacrificial cult functioned as a model of a bigger and more relevant reality").[114] The cosmic significance of the temple is well established. Sacred space is central, holy, pure, and the dwelling place of God. Some scholars focus on binary oppositions: sacred/profane (Eliade), order/disorder (Douglas), order/chaos (Levenson), and clean/unclean (Olyan). These have the advantage of incorporating the dimension of evil, but miss the subtle variations of holiness. Others follow the tripartite tabernacle structure in describing cultic life, which allows for some gradations, but tends to exclude the opposite of holy, namely, evil. Jenson, who suggests five gradations of holiness, incorporates both the nuances in the cultic texts and the dimension of evil, therefore is most applicable. The manner in which people relate to sacred space is also described metaphorically: ordering, cleansing, and setting boundaries. It is primarily God who keeps order and purifies, but human responsibilities include distinguishing between "clean" and "unclean," covenantal obedience, repentance, and worship. Rituals are ways in which order and purity are restored. Appropriately, scholarly discussion has focused on the sacred dimension of space. Little attention has been given to avoiding infiltration of evil and unclean spirits from the profane realm. Although most acknowledge the existence of evil as a threat to cultic life, the nature of it and the divine and human response

---

114. Klingbeil, *Bridging the Gap*, 237. He applies this mostly to the NT but also believes it functioned as such in the OT, to a lesser degree. Many scholars use metaphorical language implicitly, e.g., Unger, although he does not engage with cultic literature, provides a summary that employs spatial and purity metaphors: "In the call of Abram, and the creation of the nation Israel, God purified and separated a small stream from the vast river of humanity. His purpose was to keep this branch pure and separated, that with it He might eventually cleanse the great river itself. Its purity consisted in its clear-cut separation to the one true God in the midst of universal idolatry" (Deut. 6:4; Isa 43:10–12); *Biblical Demonology*, 22.

to it has not received much study. One exception is the Azazel ritual, which nicely fits into Jenson's spatial model of the cult. Jenson claims that his model of graded holiness allows for both an idealist/conceptual and a realist perspective on reality.

Model

A modified version of Jenson's model can be used to conceptualize sacred and profane space, and the grades of holiness in between (figure 5.2). It can also be depicted in three dimensions, reflecting cosmic mountain symbolism (figure 5.3).

Figure 5.2: Spatial Model of the Cultic view of the Cosmos (Horizontal).

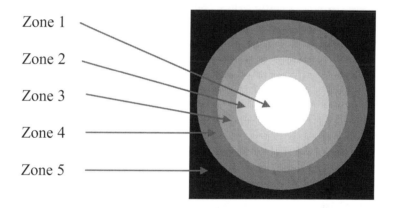

Figure 5.3: Spatial Model (Vertical)

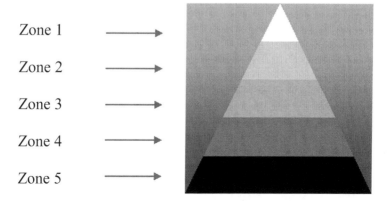

Zone 1 is central, at the apex; all other space is dependent on it. The metaphors within the semantic domain "holy" include personal (the Lord), spatial (heaven, sanctuary, tabernacle, temple, Zion, Eden, mountain), ethical (perfection, cleanness, purity), and symbolic (order, life, light, real). By contrast, Zone 5 is not well delineated; it is in the outermost and lowest regions of metaphorical space. Cultic metaphors within the semantic domain of evil also incorporate personal (Satan, demons, Azazel), spatial (wilderness, desert), ethical (unholy, unclean, impure, sin), and symbolic (unreal, disorder, darkness, nothingness, unreal, chaos, death). In the cultic texts, Zone 2 includes the most holy place, Zone 3 the courtyard, and Zone 4 Israel's camp. These spaces are sustained by the grace of God, but require cooperation on the part of Israel. Cultic rituals take place in Zones 2 and 3. Extreme sin can result in the departure of the divine presence with consequent intrusion of chaos and evil from Zone 5.

In continuity with the model developed in the previous chapter, this model emphasizes profane space in opposition to sacred space, obedience and boundary-setting as a way to maintain order, and evil as a result of boundary violation. The main differences between this model and the "creation" model are the inclusion of purity/cleansing metaphors and expanded "grey" zones. The cultic model incorporates cosmic dualism and binary oppositions, but is not limited to them. There are three buffer or neutral zones between the extremes of holy and evil. This makes sense of biblical texts that suggest that God cannot abide evil, and that evil is incompatible with holiness. There is space that separates the polarities of holiness and evil. The middle zones allow for the extension of God's grace from Zone 1 (therefore are perhaps not strictly neutral). Moreover, this model allows for overlap and subtle variations between categories evident in the cultic texts. Middle zones can incorporate sin that is not unclean, impurity that is not sin, and sin or impurity that is not demonic. The extreme zones, 1 and 5, can be seen as fixed, whereas the in-between zones are more flexible, dependent on divine blessing, and affected by human actions.

This spatial model can also account for the downgrading of the demonic in the OT, in comparison with ANE literature. The forces of evil are not eliminated but are put in their proper place. They do not run rampant in all zones of reality, but are relegated to the outer reaches of metaphorical space. However, they are able and desire to transgress their boundary, and infiltrate Zone 4 and possibly Zone 3. The primary means by which this occurs is through human disobedience. Sin, though not equated with evil, has sufficient relationship to the demonic that it can be understood as one of the ways in which the boundaries can be violated;

sin perhaps "invites" the demonic into Zone 4. As discussed, moral impurity (especially idolatry, being associated with the demonic) was always considered more severe than ritual impurity. Consequences included disease, famine, exile, and death—not surprisingly associated with Zone 5. Disobedience is frequently associated with intrusion of evil into neutral space; "death has come up into our windows, it has entered our palaces" (Jer 9:21).

At times God appears to use "evil" directly. He punishes disobedience by letting evil forces out of their bounds, opening the gates and allowing them to reap destruction.[115] Other times (the distinction is not always clear) the infliction of Zone 5 forces appears to be simply a natural consequence of sin, and not directly ordained by God. In this spatial model, when Israel turns away from holiness, she is automatically turning towards evil; in a sense inviting it in. Rejection of God, obvious in idolatry, results in implicit acceptance of the demonic and its associated evil. In addition, the Lord's blessing is required to maintain sacred space. With blatant disobedience, he withdraws his presence with a natural consequence of evil forces being let loose. Often the God of the OT is portrayed as angry and vengeful, but when viewed through a spatial model, many of the results of sin can be understood as simple boundary loosening, or consequences of withdrawal of divine blessing. There are also occasions in which evil forces appear to have the ability to defy their God-ordained boundaries and enter neutral zones. The psalmists' frequent pleas for deliverance from various Zone 5 afflictions imply that evil forces have some independence. The fact that Israelites were aware of the existence of evil spirits is evidence that these did not remain in Zone 5; the frequency of idolatry implies that demons crept out of their space at times.

The sacred actions required for the maintenance of sacred space take place within Zones 2 to 4. Whereas the actions at Zone 1 (e.g., blessing) and Zone 5 (e.g., demonic infliction) are unidirectional, the actions in the middle zones are bidirectional. Humans can choose to turn towards God or towards evil. It is God who primarily maintains order in the world; his light and life flow out from Zone 1 into all reality, and he establishes a loving relationship with his covenantal people through whom he works to maintain order and purity in creation. Covenantal obedience is a primary way in which boundaries can be maintained. If disobedience results in the

115. E.g., God sends an evil spirit (1 Sam 16:15, 16), punishes Egyptians by sending a variety of "Zone 5" afflictions (Exod 7–12), and punishes the wicked with darkness, terrors, poisonous serpents, skin disease, famine, drought, and exile (Num 21:6, 8; Job 18:13, 14); all unleashed from Zone 5; see Boyd, *God at War*, 81.

loosening of the boundaries on evil, then obedience should result in these boundaries being strengthened. God, however, provides opportunities for restitution when sin occurs. Confession and repentance can reverse the process and result in evil being returned to its divinely ordained zone, and the world being purified. This model in fact emphasizes human responsibility; because of the middle, neutral zones, it protects against a "devil-made-me-do-it" attitude. Moreover, it can elucidate the complex relationship between sin and evil. Although sin can loosen the boundary between Zones 4 and 5, it is not synonymous with evil. Cultic rituals can be seen as a way to maintain or restore order, *Yom Kippur* being a prototypical example: sacrifice is given to the Lord in Zone 1, sin is given to Azazel in Zone 5, and the boundaries are restored. In addition, sacrifice was often viewed metaphorically as praise. Worship of the one true God is also required for maintaining sacred space, especially in light of the results of its opposite, idolatry. Finally, humans have responsibility in distinguishing between clean and unclean, or good and evil, i.e., discernment. Conceptualizing holiness and evil in terms of a graded spatial model can inform how we act within this space. Awareness of the outside darkness and evil cultivates dependence on the one true God and highlights the need for participating with him in ordering divine reality by continually reapplying the limits on evil, returning it to the outer regions of chaos and consequently cleansing the cosmos.

Evaluation

This spatial model provides a framework for understanding reality and is applicable to demonology. Multiple metaphors offer information that is unavailable through simple literalistic language. This model is comprehensive yet uncomplicated and fits with OT cultic texts. It has the same advantages over a warfare model that were discussed in chapter 4. In particular, this cultic model, with its gradations of holiness, is less dualistic than a warfare model. It emphasizes human responsibility perhaps even more than the "creation" model. This model incorporates biblical texts and symbolism that are central to OT theology. The focus on sacred space places God at the center of the cosmos, as the source of all life, and the means by which creation is preserved and order maintained. Furthermore, sacred space is ultimate reality; evil is quasi-real. This model emphasizes ordering and setting boundaries as a method for dealing with evil forces, thus providing alternative nonviolent language. It affirms the existence and threat of evil forces, but emphasizes their limitations and location within peripheral metaphorical space. This model accords with theological conceptualizations of evil as "nothingness," anthropological ideas of evil/unreality in binary opposition to God/ultimate-reality, and scientific models of evil as dark matter and chaotic. This model of the gradations of sacred space and unholy space can be helpful in our conceptualization of evil, and offers a perspective on the perennial problem of our experience of evil and disorder in the world. It can also assist our understanding of how to respond to evil.

However, there are some challenges associated with this model. First, with regard to the degree of dissimilarity to a warfare model, one could argue that "defending the boundaries" is warfare language. I agree this model could incorporate some warfare metaphors, but I believe it allows for a broader understanding of dealing with evil forces. Second, generally foreigners and outsiders were included in the category of evil. The OT hints at future inclusion of the nations into divine reality, but this problem may need to be deferred. Third, the exact nature of the boundaries is unclear: How one can tell where one is within metaphorical space? How does movement between zones occur? The next issue to be discussed is whether this model is supported by biblical texts in the NT.

6

CHRIST: A LIGHT IN THE DARKNESS

All the living sparks are rays of his splendour,
just as the rays of the sun proceed from the sun itself.[1]

J ESUS IS OFTEN DESCRIBED in evangelical Christianity as a "personal
savior." Metaphors for Jesus are seldom used, and discontinuity
between Old and New Testaments is usually emphasized.[2] Furthermore,
studies of exorcism in the Gospels are often done in isolation; when they
are incorporated into the larger theological picture, it is typically within a
warfare framework. The trinitarian aspect of Jesus' ministry is also minimized in "spiritual warfare" literature; Jesus alone is depicted as engaged
in a battle with evil spirits. Yet there is so much more to understanding
the person and work of Christ: the Gospels present Jesus as God incarnate, the hope of Israel, the new creation, the new temple, the light, the
life, and the truth, and the way in which the world is once again ordered
and cleansed from evil forces. There is much radically new in the Gospels
but there is much repetition of OT themes. Metaphors familiar to Israel
reappear, and spatial imagery is apparent, with Jesus now the sacred center. As in the OT, evil is defined in binary opposition to holiness.

---

1. Hildegarde of Bingen, *Divine Works*, 4.11

2. J. D. G. Dunn remarks that NT studies have been dominated by synchronic
approaches. Diachronic, thematic approaches allow for continuity between the two
testaments; *NT Theology*, viii–ix. Gospel studies have also focused on socio-political
(e.g., Pagels, *Origin of Satan*), and historical (e.g., Twelftree, *Exorcist)* approaches.

This chapter examines the Gospels with respect to understanding evil, using the thematic approach discussed in chapter 2. Issues addressed include continuity between Christ, creation, and cult, as well as apparent discontinuity. These writings are examined for cultic metaphors of cleansing and boundary-setting as a way to conceptualize evil. It is hoped that alternative images can assist in understanding evil. First, I examine the demonology of the Gospels, and then sacred space with reference to divine presence, the kingdom of Heaven, plus Jesus as the new temple, and the light, life, and truth. Sacred actions are discussed in terms of the authority of the Holy Spirit, cleansing and setting boundaries on evil, the atonement, and the eschatological separation of evil, in contrast to "spiritual warfare." Sacred actions also include human responsibility in terms of belief and authority over evil. Finally, the model developed in previous chapters is refined in light of the results of this investigation.

Profane Space

As with cultic studies, scholarly work on the Gospels usually, quite rightly, focuses on the sacred center, Christ. But knowledge of the periphery, in binary opposition, is important too. A cursory reading of the Gospels reveals a radical change with respect to evil. In the OT, references to *personal* evil forces are rare, but, as discussed, they were evident in the background. However, the literature of Second Temple Judaism reveals an active faith community with a prominent demonology (detailed in the previous chapter). Archie Wright summarizes: "By the turn of the Common Era there was in place a worldview within Judaism in which the activity of autonomous or semi-autonomous evil spirits was regarded as a reality."[3] The Gospels were written in the larger context of the Greco-Roman world, which also exhibited a strong belief in evil spirits.[4] The Greek Magical Papyri, for instance, contain multiple lists of incantations and exorcism techniques, there are appellations, "unclean demon Satan" and "serpent-faced god," and demons are associated with disease, chaos, blackness, and the underworld.[5] Darkness and chaos still symbolized evil, but evil was primarily

---

3. Wright, *Origin of Evil Spirits*, 1.

4. E.g., Philo of Alexandria thought evil spirits filled the air; *On Giants*, 6–31; Cole, "Greek Religion," 266–317; North, "Religions in the Roman Empire," 318–63; Arnold, *Powers*, 35–47; Sorensen, *Possession*, 75–115.

5. PGM IV: 1231–50; PGM XII: 153–60; PGM IV: 1227; PGM IV: 2699; PGM I: 96–116; and PGM IV: 1231–50 respectively; Betz, *Greek Magical Papyri*; abbreviated

personified as demons. Another religion prevalent during this time was Zoroastrianism, which taught metaphysical dualism: the existence of two equally powerful and independent sources of good and evil.[6] Although the relative influence of Judaism, Greco-Roman culture, and first-century Palestine culture on Christianity is debated, it is helpful to understand the context in which the Gospels were written. The changing culture led to religious syncretism, but the majority of Jews, Greeks, and Romans believed that spirits populate the heaven, earth, and underworld and that the "supernatural realm exercises control over everyday life, and eternal destiny."[7] In this section I examine metaphors for evil in the Gospels, followed by examinations of whether demons are organized or disorganized, and whether Satan is a ruler or intruder into divine reality.

Darkness, Demons . . .

In the NT, especially the synoptic Gospels, the devil and demons appear quite prominently.[8] They are always depicted in opposition to Jesus. In the synoptic Gospels, Judaic and Greco-Roman terms are evident plus metaphors for evil that were prominent in ancient Israel. Satan (retained from the Hebrew and used as a proper noun), *diabolos* (devil; Greek translation of Satan, meaning opponent; the LXX translated Satan as *diabolis*),[9] and Beelzebul seem to be used synonymously (Matt 12:27; Luke 11:18–19;

PGM, based on the Latin. These date from the second to the fifth centuries BCE, although practices are likely older than texts. Many also included Jewish magic and Egyptian deities, along with traditional Greek gods. The fourth book contains many descriptions of exorcisms. Sometimes demons were summoned for assistance (PGM 1.96–116; 11.2), and aids such as special sounds (PGM V: 83–89), an olive branch whip (PGM IV: 1231–50), or an amulet (PGM IV:1254) were used. Magic was not a pejorative term in antiquity, and was not distinguished from religion. Demons were thought to live in the air (PGM I: 96–194) and were often viewed as spirits of departed humans; Josephus, *Antiquities*, 8.46; Homer, *Odyssey*, 11, 24; Bolt, "Jesus, the Daimons," 75–102; Twelftree, *Christ Triumphant*, 39–43.

6. Ohrmazd and Ahriman respectively; Russell, *Devil*, 98–121.

7. Arnold, *Powers*, 19, 36. Twelftree similarly notes that it was "widely believed that the world was infested with beings hostile to man, against which protection or relief was sought"; *Christ Triumphant*, 50–52. W. Carr describes this world as "one of old gods, exorcisms, magicians, and philosophers"; *Angels and Principalities*, 21.

8. In the Gospels, there are forty-eight references to Satan and 102 references to evil spirits.

9. Forsyth also notes the connection with *skandalon*, slanderer or obstacle (Matt 16:23); *Old Enemy*, 113, 267.

"Beelzebul" is not easily translated [see below] but is definitely associated with Satan). He acts as a stumbling block (Matt 16:23), causes illness (Luke 13:16), and can "enter into" someone (namely Judas; Luke 22:3; John 13:27). The devil is portrayed as the enemy (Matt 13:25–28, 39; Luke 10:19), the "ruler" of this world (John 12:31; 14:30; 16:11), a liar (John 8:44), and a murderer (John 13:2), who incites sin.[10] *Daimonion* (demons) is the most common term used to describe evil spirits, but *akatharton pneuma* (unclean spirit) is also used (especially by Mark [5:1–13; 7:25; 9:25]; also Luke 8:26–32; 11:24). Evil spirits are sometimes associated with the sea,[11] the desert,[12] birds,[13] snakes, and scorpions.[14] They recognize Jesus for who he is (Luke 4:33–35) and seem to have superhuman strength (Mark 5:4; Luke 8:29).[15] These spirits appear to be able to enter animals and people (the pigs and the man in the Gerasene demoniac, Matt 8:28–34; Mark 5:1–20; Luke 8:26–39; the man with an unclean spirit, Mark 1:23–26; Luke 4:31–36; the boy with a demon, Matt 17:14–20; Mark 9:14–29; Luke 9:37–43), causing illness at times (muteness, Matt 9:33; deafness and muteness, Mark 9:25; seizures, Matt 17:15–18; Luke 9:42; physical handicaps, Luke 13:11; and mental illness, Mark 5:5, Luke 8:27). Afflicted people are described as *daimonizomai* ("demonized").[16]

Abstract metaphors are also used to portray evil spiritual forces in the Gospels. Darkness in John is a multivalent metaphor, as Koester observes: "darkness connotes sin, evil, falsehood and death."[17] Some scholars have

10. Murderer could be a reference to the serpent in Eden (Rom 5:12, 15; Wis 2:24) who brought death into the world; it is less likely a reference to Cain, the first murderer; Page, *Powers*, 125–26.

11. Twelftree notes, with respect to the Gerasene demoniac, that water was a known abode for demons; *Name of Jesus*, 86; see also discussion in chapter 4.

12. In the temptation narrative (Matt 4:1–11; Mark 1:12, 13; Luke 4:1–13) and the story of the restless spirit (Matt 12:43–45; Luke 11:24–26).

13. In the parable of the sower (Matt 13:3–8, 18–23; Mark 4:1–9, 13–20; Luke 8:4–8, 11–15). Birds were also associated with Satan in ancient literature, e.g., Satan disguises himself as a bird (Apoc Abr 13:3–8; cf. 1 En 90:8–13; Jub 11:11); Marcus, *Mark 1–8*, 309; Page, *Powers of Evil*, 115.

14. Luke 10:17–19. Snakes and scorpions were commonly associated with the demonic in the ancient world (Deut 8:15; Ps 91:13; Ezek 2:6); Page, *Powers*, 111; Twelftree, *Exorcist*, 122–27, *Name*, 140.

15. Page, *Powers*, 150–55.

16. Literally "has a demon." However, as Page points out, this term is imprecise and broadly applied; *Powers*, 138.

17. John 1:5; 3:19; 8:12; 12:46; John's imagery is complex; darkness usually signifies evil but sometimes ignorance; Koester, *Word of Life*, 189.

noted the perpetuation of OT "chaos" in the NT. For example, Elizabeth Struthers Malbon believes that Mark uses *thalassa* ("sea" as opposed to *limnē*, "lake") to emphasize the association between chaos and evil,[18] and Gene Davenport thinks that darkness in the NT shares the power of chaos, noting that at times personal terms for evil are appropriate, but at other times, chaos dominates.[19] Although evil forces in the NT are depicted with more clarity, there is continuity with OT metaphors for evil. Satan continues acting in opposition to God albeit to a greater extent, darkness is opposed to the light of Christ as it was opposed to the light of creation, impurity is associated with the demonic, and the sea and desert are also places of evil.

Demons: Organized or Disorganized?

However, the Gospels do not present a cohesive demonology; there is overlap of terms and ambiguity. For instance, the unclean spirit in the Capernaum synagogue is singular but refers to itself as "us" (Mark 1:21–27; Luke 4:31–37).[20] Similarly, in Acts 10:38, Jesus is described as healing those afflicted by the devil, whereas the Gospel accounts describe people as afflicted by demons, implying overlap between the devil and demons; and the woman healed on the Sabbath is crippled by a "spirit" and bound by "Satan" (Luke 13:11, 16). Many statements about demons appear only once: request for a demon's name (in Mark and Luke's version of the Gerasene demoniac, Mark 5:9; Luke 8:30), reference to a "kind" of demon (in the story of the boy with seizures, Mark 9:29), and reference to "more evil" demons (in the story of the restless demon, Matt 12:45). Despite these inconsistencies, many scholars make confident claims regarding the number and nature of demonic forces. Boyd, for instance, states that the NT belief is that the world is saturated and infested with a large number of demons;

18. Malbon, *Narrative Space*, 100. Similarly Boyd (*God at War*, 205–7) and Bonting (*Creation and Double Chaos*, 98) suggest that chaos persists in the sea that has to be subdued.

19. Davenport, *Into the Darkness*, 23, 34. Similarly, L. Newbigin views darkness as a menacing reality in the background; *Light has Come*, 105.

20. The demon says "what have you to do with us"? The plural either indicates that the demon was both one and many or speaking on behalf of all unclean spirits. There is similar confusion with the pronouns used in the story of the Gerasene demoniac (Matt 8:28–34; Mark 5:1–20; Luke 8:26–39).

this "army of demons" exists in a hierarchy (although he admits details are lacking).[21]

Yet there is no conclusive evidence that demons are unified: there is no recorded dialogue between demons, or any detailed description of structured relationships between demons. In the story of the Gerasene demoniac (Matt 8:28–34; Mark 5:1–20; Luke 8:26–39), a large group of spirits afflict one man; however, a cluster of demons does not necessarily mean they are unified (admittedly there is also no evidence of disunity or disharmony; they could be loosely associated but there is insufficient information).[22] The behavior of this man hardly indicates demonic organization, and the actions of the demons when in the pigs can easily be explained by the swarm behavior characteristic of chaotic-complex systems (discussed in chapter 3). There are no passages in which Satan and demons as characters appear together.[23] There is no evidence that demons follow Satan's commands, in fact they repeatedly are described as following Jesus' commands. Never do the demons ask Satan's permission to do anything, but in fact ask Jesus' permission. On one occasion, a demon brings other demons along, implying that they can act without Satan's permission. There is no proof that demons have individuality and personality (as commonly assumed in popular "spiritual warfare" literature). Satan is the only evil spirit that is named. On one occasion when a demon is perhaps named ("legion" in the Gerasene demoniac), the term is metaphorical, meaning a large number.[24] Demons are quite consistent in the few words they do say,

21. Boyd, *God at War*, 182, 186, 191, 194, 271. Similarly Sorensen refers to a hierarchical structure (lesser demons are accountable to Satan) of demonic beings that have individual personality; *Possession*, 119, although he later notes that the Gospels' primary interest was in the exorcist, not the nature of demons (125); Grenz believes demons "form a unified kingdom of evil"; *Community of God*, 224, 227. Recall the popular notion of demonic hierarchies, discussed in chapter 1.

22. Much is made about the military significance of the term legion (e.g., Boyd, *God at War*, 194–95). A Roman legion of soldiers comprises 5,000–6,000 men, but, in Mark's version, the herd of pigs number only 2000. Furthermore, the term "legion" is likely figurative (see below). It is a stretch to conclude from the "legion" metaphor that demons exist in an organized, hierarchical army.

23. J. Fitzmyer notes that demons are never associated with Satan; *Luke*, 545. There are two vague references to some sort of association between Satan and the demons, but this is not elaborated on and does not necessarily mean a hierarchy exists (Satan as "ruler of demons" to be discussed below, and the "devil and his angels" [Matt 25: 41]).

24. Only named in Mark and Luke's version. The term is similar to "myriad"; *DDD* 507–8. Fitzmyer suggests that the name given, "legion," is probably a trick in that a number, not a name was given; *Luke*, 734. Twelftree points out that by the time the Gospels were written the term would have lost its military significance, and was

which are formulaic in nature (their most common utterance is to name Jesus the "Holy One of God"). Their "emotions," if any, are limited to fear, and their behavior is limited to tormenting people. Once Jesus refers to "this kind" of demon, but this does not warrant concluding a hierarchy of many kinds. Once we hear of "more wicked" demons; again this is not irrefutable evidence for organized structural relationships. Demons are often described by the effect they have on a person (muteness, seizures) but this does not mean there are particular demons with individual "disease" names. There is no evidence of Jesus casting out individually-named demons one by one. The disciples are given authority over evil spirits, not detailed instructions for getting to know the name, personality, or rank of the demon (as commonly advised in some "spiritual warfare" literature).

Given the above discussion, N. G. Wright's conclusions appear more accurate: "It is surely mistaken to conceive of the demonic realm as well organized and highly structured. Its essence is not reason but unreason, not organization but chaos"; "accounts that outline the shape of the demonic organization are to be treated with extreme scepticism."[25] Joel Marcus similarly points out, "we should not look for too much consistency when dealing with things as ambivalent and protean as demonic spirits."[26] There is no way we can know the number of demons in the world, and, particularly since they are described in metaphorical terms and are likely chaotic by nature, even speculation about numbers and nature is unproductive. Part of the confusion could be that many scholars view evil forces through the lens of scientific rationalism and literalism. However, as argued in chapters 2 and 3, evil forces are best viewed metaphorically and as nonlinear, complex systems. Demons are real, but depicted metaphorically and chaotic by nature. Viewing them so is compatible with OT depictions of evil and reconciles differing depictions of evil in the Synoptics (demons) and John (darkness). Emphasizing metaphors for evil may allow for improved comprehension of their nature and how they are dealt with. It is perhaps best to consider the NT terms (Satan, devil, demon, evil spirit, unclean spirit, enemy, darkness, chaos) as a cluster of metaphors for forces of evil in binary opposition to Christ. Admittedly the problem

---

therefore metaphorical, meaning a large number; *Name of Jesus,* 108–9. He may be overstating his case; there is no certainty whether the term had military connotations or not. I suggest that the metaphorical nature of the term be emphasized.

25. N. G. Wright, *Dark Side,* 116. He uses the term chaos with its common meaning, but chaos and disorganization are not necessarily the same; the scientific definition may provide more precision.

26. Marcus, *Mark 1–8,* 342.

of the relationship between Satan and evil spirits remains unresolved. There is clearly some sort of a distinction made, but it is unclear; perhaps through the use of chaos-complexity theory, Satan could be likened to the "queen bee" in the demonic "insect colony" (as opposed to a commander-in-chief of an army).

Satan: Ruler or Intruder?

As discussed in chapter 1, popular "spiritual warfare" literature and some scholarly literature tends to overrate and overstate the power of Satan. Biblical scholars also often assume that Satan is a ruler with his own kingdom. For example, Joachim Jeremias in his NT theology claims that Satan is a "commander of a military force" who "rules over a kingdom"; demons are his soldiers and servants.[27] Susan Garrett summarizes her thoughts regarding the devil in Luke's writings: "The dark regions are the realm of Satan, the ruler of this world, who for eons has sat entrenched and well-guarded . . . the sick and possessed are held captive by his demons."[28] The pervasiveness of the term "kingdom of Satan" in secondary literature is quite surprising given its few biblical references; it appears in many biblical dictionaries and commentaries.[29] With respect to theology, Oscar Cullman applied a WWII analogy to Christ's victory over evil. He argued that the ministry, death, and resurrection of Christ was equivalent to D-Day, and that the parousia and final judgment of evil is equivalent to V-Day. The decisive defeat of evil has been accomplished, but the final defeat is still to come; we live in the battleground between the two ages.[30] Boyd

---

27. Jeremias, *NT Theology*, 93–94. J. Weiss similarly describes a "well organized kingdom of Satan" which is set against the kingdom of God; *Jesus' Proclamation*, 77, 101. This assumption is based on interpretations of the Beelzebul controversy (Matt 9:34; 12:24–29; Mark 3:23–7; Luke 11:17–23) and John's description of Satan as the "ruler of the world" (12:31; 14:30; 16:11). In some Second Temple literature, evil spirits were thought to be organized in a kingdom, e.g., "kingdom of the enemy" (T. Dan 6:4).

28. And both Gentiles and Jews are "in bondage to the devil"; Garrett, *Demise of Devil*, 101. Jesus "initiates a series of incursions into Satan's domain, robbing him of his captives by releasing them from illness, demon possession, and sin," but the war is not over and the devil still has potential authority to work harm (43, 54).

29. E.g., Marcus, *Mark 1–8*, 273; Telford, *Gospel of Mark*, 158; Sorensen, *Possession and Exorcism*, 119; Ladd, *Theology of NT*, 46–50; Grenz, *Theology*, 224, 227; Ott et al., *Theology of Mission*, 249.

30. Cullman, *Christ and Time*, 198. C. S. Lewis popularized this analogy, stating we are living in "enemy-occupied territory" in which God has landed "in disguise" to give us a chance to join his side; *Mere Christianity*, 46, 64.

somewhat similarly claims that the underlying assumption of Jesus' ministry is that Satan has "illegitimately seized the world and thus now exercises a controlling influence over it." Furthermore, the kingdom of Satan is a correlative concept to the kingdom of God, and these two are engaged in warfare.[31] Boyd is correct to emphasize that Satan's rule is illegitimate, but by correlating the "kingdoms" of Satan and God, I believe that he overemphasizes the extent of this rule. His commitment to warfare language likely leads to this assumption; as noted in chapter 1, warfare language can imply that opposing sides are equal and opposite.

An important question is whether Satan has legitimate rule over the world or whether he is an intruder into godly reality, a pseudo-ruler over those who follow him. The answer to this question is critical to understanding the ontology of evil. Discussion in previous chapters suggested that evil forces are a threat to divine reality, not that they rule over that reality, and the picture is similar in the Gospels. Although the above authors imply that Christ is the invader of Satan's domain, others are more moderate: Koester notes that, since God creates and gives life, he is clearly the superior being, and Satan is the intruder;[32] Joel Green describes Satan, when he enters Judas, as gaining a "beachhead from which to attack Jesus"[33] (note that this is opposite to Cullman's claim that Christ gained the beachhead); and theologian Donald Bloesch suggests that the demonic make "repeated forays" into godly territory, "in order to conceal their overall retreat."[34] This controversy regarding the "rule" and "kingdom" of Satan warrants a closer examination of relevant texts.

In the temptation narrative (Matt 4:1–11; Mark 1:12, 13; Luke 4:1–13), Satan offers Jesus a kingdom, implying it is his to offer. Boyd notes that Jesus did not dispute Satan's claim.[35] However, neither did Jesus affirm it. It could be that such a claim was not worthy of an answer; plus, Satan is elsewhere portrayed as a liar. Fitzmyer suggests that Satan merely poses as god of the world, claiming illegitimate authority.[36] Neither in this passage nor elsewhere does Jesus endorse the rule of Satan; neither does

31. Boyd, *God at War*, 181, 185, 196.

32. Koester, *Word of Life*, 76; Arnold similarly states that God is the ultimate sovereign king, although evil spirits exercise "significant influence"; *3 Crucial Questions*, 20.

33. Green, *Gospel of Luke*, 66.

34. Bloesch, *Holy Spirit*, 220–21. I. H. Marshall similarly believes the kingdom of God involves the "recovery of territory" which implicates Satan as the intruder; *NT Theology*, 61.

35. Boyd, *God at War*, 181.

36. Fitzmyer, *Luke*, 516.

he describe himself as involved in a battle to win the world from Satan. The two-kingdom concept is only implied in one passage, the Beelzebul controversy, and the point of this passage is that Jesus operates with the power of the Holy Spirit, not the power of Satan.[37] Although there seems to be an implication that Satan has some power, I am not convinced broad conclusions can be made. As mentioned above, there are no passages where demons clearly take orders from Satan. Elsewhere the kingdom of God is juxtaposed to and antithetical to the earth or world, not Satan (in the parable of the sower, Matt 13:22; Mark 4:19; Luke 12:30–31, and in Johannine dualism, John 15:18–19, 17:1–26, 18:36).[38] Guelich notes that exorcisms occur only as signs of the kingdom and that the kingdom of God is "never juxtaposed to a 'kingdom of Satan.'"[39] John's assertions about Satan as ruler of the world can have alternative interpretations. Significantly, *kosmos* (world) can have multiple meanings, including the created world, or a portion of creation, humanity in rebellion.[40] It is likely John was referring to the latter. Page suggests that Satan's power has arisen as a result of human sin in a world that does not recognize Jesus, not that he has been given a kingdom.[41] Perhaps John named Satan ruler of the world (and those who did not acknowledge Jesus as children of the devil) as a rhetorical strategy to encourage people to follow Jesus.

Satan exists in binary opposition to Jesus and good, but this does not necessarily mean that Satan rules over a kingdom, although he maybe holds sway over those who reject the kingdom of God. It is possible that Jesus acknowledges Satan's "rule" over sinful humanity without advocating its legitimacy. Although the devil's influence over the world is implied, conclusions regarding his "rule" and "kingdom" should be cautious, the extent of this "rule" minimized and its illegitimacy emphasized. Perhaps commitment to warfare language has resulted in the overstatement of Satan's "rule." Military metaphors imply a battle between equal and opposite

37. Twelftree, *Exorcist*, 106. M. Humphries notes that the emphasis is on the character of Jesus not Beelzebul; the image is not of two warring kingdoms but of a robber who has invaded the house of a strong man; *Christian Origins*, 53–54.

38. Satan is described as ruler of the world (John 12:31; 14:30; 16:11) rather than ruler of demons, although he could conceivably, but unlikely, be ruler of both; Ladd, *Theology*, 263.

39. Guelich, "Jesus, Paul, Peretti," 41.

40. Discussed further in chapter 7; Yung suggests that Satan rules "over a limited sphere . . . humankind in rebellion against God"; "Theology that Recognizes the Demonic," 21.

41. And that Satan is a liar; Page, *Powers*, 125–29.

forces, which leads to strong claims regarding Satan's power. Alternate metaphors may illuminate this issue plus provide non-warfare interpretations of key passages. There is evidence that evil spirits do not remain within their space but violate boundaries and encroach upon divine reality (e.g., a man with an unclean spirit is in a usually clean place, the synagogue).[42] Thus I believe that Satan is best viewed as an *intruder into*, not a ruler of, the world.

Summary: The Threat to Divine Reality

From the above discussion, it is evident that Gospel writers affirm the reality of evil spirits and the impact they have on people, but these writers do not describe a detailed demonology. Compared with the demonology of surrounding cultures, evil spirits are de-emphasized in the Gospels; they are not named and there are no elaborate exorcism rituals or prescription of amulets, for instance. Humans are not portrayed as helpless victims but have responsibility. Hence, it appears that, as in the OT account, evil spirits have been brought down to size in the Gospels and are no match for the triune God.[43] However, they are depicted as a threat to the world, and have potential to afflict people. Evil can be further understood through its relationship to Christ. Barth, discussed previously, claims that nothingness attains reality when it crosses its boundaries; furthermore, it is revealed and exposed only through Christ.[44] Somewhat similarly, Bell argues that evil spirits are only real because of the work of Christ: "Satan's fundamental existence is dependent on the fact that Christ (the ultimate reality) delivers us from his power"; Satan is thus demoted to a mythical figure but can still "exercise devastating power in the world."[45] Bell is unclear regarding the ontology of Satan and seems not to consider evil in the OT, or other metaphors for evil, such as darkness, present at the creation of the world. Barth makes more sense: The light of Christ exposes the darkness,

42. Also, with respect to the Gerasene demoniac, T. Klutz notes that Jesus implies the desert is an unsuitable place for humans and it is not good for the evil spirits to be in a man (both spatial images); *Exorcism Stories,* 106.

43. Klutz thinks it is noteworthy that demons, although they converse with Jesus, never affect him in any material way; *Exorcism Stories,* 104–5.

44. Barth, *CD III.*3, 302, 312. Newbigin believes darkness is "what confronts one who turns away from the true source of his being"; *Light has come,* 4.

45. Bell, *Deliver us,* 351–53.

yet evil has a somewhat independent, albeit reduced, existence, compared with the true reality of Christ.

Although evil spirits are diminished in status in the Gospels compared with surrounding cultures, there is evidence they have encroached upon divine reality. As darkness covered the earth prior to creation, the same situation is apparent before the ministry of Christ, evidenced by the preoccupation with demonology in the Second Temple Period, and the multiple references to demons in the Gospels. Evil forces appear to have significant power, have infiltrated God's good creation, and have afflicted many people. The world is unclean and chaotic, in need of healing and reestablishing boundaries on godly reality (as illustrated in Figure 6.1).

Figure 6.1: The World Prior to Christ

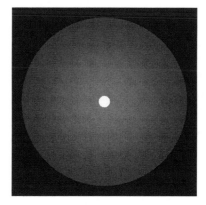

Sacred Space

Most christological studies focus on the Son of God as prophet, priest, and king; Messiah, teacher, and Suffering Servant.[46] This study instead emphasizes spatial images of Jesus and his ministry. It is often noted that, in the Gospels, there is an absence of discussions regarding Israel's land.[47] However, as will be shown, space in the NT is mostly depicted metaphorically. There is both continuity and discontinuity with OT depictions of space. To review, sacred space was symbolized by Eden, the tabernacle, the temple, mountains, and heaven, and characterized by holiness, purity, centrality,

46. E.g., Telford, *Mark*, 30–40.
47. E.g., Bryan, *Jesus and Israel's Traditions*, 168.

light, life, and fertility.[48] Most importantly, it was defined by the presence of God. This section builds on discussions in previous chapters with respect to sacred space. In the OT, sacred space was both symbolic and literal (although the symbolic was likely more significant); with Christ, sacred space becomes entirely symbolic. Jesus is the new creation, the new tabernacle/temple, the location of divine-human interaction, and the dwelling place of God through his Spirit. He is the source of holiness, purity, light, life, and truth. This is evident in Jesus' teachings and actions, and is primarily depicted in the Synoptics through the concept of the kingdom of God/Heaven, and in John through temple imagery. Recall though that there is usually overlap and interrelationship between metaphors.

Divine Presence

As God walked "in the garden" with the first humans, now he walks among humans as the incarnate son. As God dwelt among Israel through the tabernacle and temple, now he dwells among humans through Jesus. God comes down from heaven, out of the holy of holies and into unholy places. His light spreads out into the darkness. The Gospels portray Jesus as both divine and as embodying the presence of the divine, through God the Father and God the Spirit. He can be portrayed, therefore, with spatial metaphors, and cannot be understood apart from his dependence on the Father and the Spirit.[49] First, the Gospels claim that Jesus is conceived by the Holy Spirit (Matt 1:18; Luke 1:35). Luke (1:35) describes Mary as being "overshadowed" by the Holy Spirit (as the Spirit "hovered" over creation).[50] Elizabeth is filled with the Spirit upon meeting Mary, and "Mariam" sings a song of rejoicing as Miriam did after the exodus (Luke 1:41–55). There

48. See summaries in Hoskins, *Jesus as Fulfillment*, 38–106, and N. T. Wright, *JVG*, 204–6.

49. This idea brings up the complexities of Christology and trinitarian theology—beyond the scope of this study. In recent years Spirit Christology, as opposed to Logos Christology, has received renewed attention; e.g., Del Colle, *Christ and Spirit*; Pinnock, *Flame of Love*, 79–111; Edwards, *Breath of Life*, 66–86. This study emphasizes Spirit Christology because, as discussed in chapter 1, the Spirit has been relatively neglected in "spiritual warfare" literature. With Pinnock (80) and others, I consider Spirit Christology complementary to Logos Christology.

50. Luke especially emphasizes the Holy Spirit; Green, *Luke*, 43–46. M. Lodahl notes similarities between this event and the Shekinah spirit overshadowing creation, the tabernacle, Mount Zion, and Israel; *Shekinah Spirit*, 161–62. He states that the Spirit "broods" over Mary's womb as he hovered over the deep. See also Cole, *He who Gives*, 154–55; Witherington and Ice, *Shadow of the Almighty*, 111.

are hints that a new creation, a new exodus, and a new temple are being established in Jesus. Second, Jesus is anointed by the Spirit and the Spirit makes Jesus known (Luke 4:18–19, quoting Isa 61:1).[51] Third, the Gospel writers are explicit about the relationship between God and Jesus. Matthew calls Jesus Emmanuel ("God with us," Matt 1:23, 24, quoting Isa 7:14), describes him as God's chosen servant (Matt 12:18–21, quoting Isa 42:1–3), and has Jesus acknowledge his dependence on his Father, without whom he can do nothing (Matt 11:27). Luke plainly states that Jesus is the "Son of God" (1:35) and, when Jesus heals a demoniac, he tells the man to proclaim what *God* has done (8:29).[52] John identifies Jesus using the name associated only with God: "I am."[53] Jesus comes to make God known, claiming he is the only way to the Father (Luke 10:22; John 1:36; 12:44; 20:28).[54] Finally, actions performed by Jesus (raising the dead, forgiving sins) were previously understood as prerogatives only of God.[55]

The baptism of Jesus (Matt 3:13–17; Mark 1:9–11; Luke 3:21–22; John 1:29–43) is a highly symbolic and trinitarian event: the heavens open, God speaks, and the Spirit descends and remains on Jesus. This validates Jesus as the promised one on whom the Holy Spirit rests.[56] And the one on whom God's Spirit rests has authority to establish God's kingdom through justice, mercy, and release from captivity (evil).[57] In particular, Jesus as bearer of the Holy Spirit is contrasted with unclean spirits who

51. John's Gospel, often associated more with Logos than Spirit Christology, nevertheless records how the Spirit rests on Jesus and makes him known (1:33; 16:13, 14); Koester, *Word of Life*, 134–36; Edwards, *Breath of Life*, 66–75.

52. Klutz points out the parallelism between the actions of God and those of Jesus; *Exorcism Stories*, 150.

53. The self-identification of God (LXX *ēgo eimi*, e.g., Exod 3:14; Deut 32:39) Jesus applies to himself (e.g., Mark 14:62; John 8:24, 28, 58) which sometimes results in him being accused of blasphemy (John 10:33); Koester, *Word of Life*, 41, 103–4.

54. Koester, *Word of Life*, 25. Since God is invisible, Jesus is his vehicle of revelation; Köstenberger and Swain, *Father, Son*, 51.

55. Köstenberger and Swain, *Father, Son*, 111; Brown, *Gospel of John*, 301.

56. Isa 11:2; 42:1; 61:1; 64:1. Witherington and Ice, *Shadow of the Almighty*, 84–85. Marcus describes the event as a "gracious gash in the universe"; *Mark 1–8*, 165. Edwards asserts that the Christ-event is brought about by the Holy Spirit; "the same Spirit who is the Life-Giver, empowering the emergence of the universe . . . now anoints and rests upon Jesus of Nazareth"; *Breath of Life*, 79.

57. Welker, *God the Spirit*, 108–24. Dumbrell believes the baptism should be viewed in cosmic context; the heavens open indicating a new age, the inauguration of the kingdom of God; *Search for Order*, 189. The baptism of Jesus also anoints him for ministry; Lodahl, *Shekinah Spirit*, 163.

are clearly inferior and obedient to Jesus (Mark 1:21–28; Luke 4:31–37). This narrative echoes creation (God speaks, the Spirit is over the water), the flood (the dove symbolizing the end of an evil age),[58] and the tabernacle/temple (there is a direct connection between heaven and earth, and Jesus is the new location of divine presence). In short, "Jesus is anointed by the very presence and power of God, such that wherever Jesus goes and whatever he does the presence and power of God dwell in him and empower his word and deeds."[59] The transfiguration (Matt 17:1–13; Mark 9:2–13; Luke 9:28–36) is similarly symbolic: Jesus, on a high mountain, becomes dazzling white, a cloud overshadows them, and God speaks.[60] There is trinitarian imagery reminiscent of Mount Sinai and the conception and baptism of Jesus, as well as temple/cosmic mountain symbolism. The Gospel writings, with their OT echoes, suggest that divine presence is no longer primarily in the holy of holies, but now located in Jesus. Stephen Barton describes this as a "dislocation and relocation" and an "extension and intensification" of sacred space; God is present in the person of Jesus in whom the Holy Spirit dwells.[61] Jesus, like OT sacred space, is characterized by holiness and purity. He not only is holy, but makes things holy (Matt 23:17–19).[62] Although there are multiple facets to Jesus Christ, the above discussion suggests that one aspect is the portrayal of him as the new locus of divine presence.

The Kingdom of Heaven

The kingdom of Heaven is a similarly complex concept; this discussion focuses on its connection with sacred space. Jesus announces the arrival of the kingdom of God, or kingdom of heaven.[63] *Basileia* ("kingdom") is

58. Marcus, *Mark 1–8*, 159–60. Lodahl likens the wings of the dove to the wings of the Shekinah Spirit, as suggested by rabbinic Judaism; *Shekinah Spirit*, 164. Köstenberger and Swain note that the dove that could not find a resting place now has; *Father, Son*, 138.

59. Witherington and Ice, *Shadow of the Almighty*, 85.

60. Lodahl notes that this event brings together past, present, and future; *Shekinah Spirit*, 176–77. Green points out the constellation of OT images, e.g., Jesus as the Chosen One (Isa 42:1), his face becoming like that of Moses (Exod 34:28); *Luke*, 62.

61. John 1:1–18, 29–34; Barton, "Dislocating and Relocating Holiness," 197.

62. Dunn, "Jesus and Holiness," 170. Even demons recognize him as the "Holy One of God" (Mark 1:24; Luke 4:34).

63. The first words Jesus utters in Mark (1:15), and considered a central message;

both an abstract (denoting sovereignty) and a concrete (implying terri-tory) noun, but the concept is multivalent.[64] There is spatial imagery: the kingdom "comes near" with Jesus (Matt 3:2; 4:17; 10:7; Mark 1:15; Luke 10:9, 11) and is a place some may "enter" (Matt 5:20; 7:21; 18:3; Mark 10:15; 23–5; Luke 16:16–25; John 3:5). However, there has been debate as to whether the kingdom should be conceived spatially or not. Mary Ann Getty-Sullivan argues that it incorporates action as well as space, and is primarily a relational concept, a new reality begun in faith,[65] and Karen Wenell believes that the kingdom is socially constructed, representational space: "the kingdom is a sacred space built out of sayings and beliefs."[66] Conversely, Weiss uses spatial terms: The kingdom of God is "never something subjective, inward or spiritual, but is . . . usually pictured as a territory into which one enters, or as a land in which one has a share."[67] N. T. Wright similarly claims that the kingdom invoked a sense of holy land, but there is no corresponding literal geography.[68] Perhaps some of the confusion arises from the failure of some to consider the kingdom metaphorically—multi-layered and multivalent. The kingdom of heaven can be viewed as a spatial symbol incorporating the concepts of holy land, sacred space, sacred actions, and divine rule.

The kingdom of Heaven fulfills OT eschatological expectations, and can be seen as a new age, a new creation, and a New Jerusalem.[69] When

---

Ladd, *Theology,* 50–125. Matthew uses the term "kingdom of heaven" partly because of the Jewish prohibition on saying the name of God; also because he emphasizes the heavenly origin of the kingdom; kingdom of God and kingdom of heaven can be used interchangeably; Getty-Sullivan, *Parables,* 7.

64. BDAG 168–69.

65. Getty-Sullivan *Parables,* 5, 169. Similarly Bell asserts that the kingdom is un-spatial, referring more to the rule of God; *Deliver us,* 104.

66. Wenell, *Jesus and Land,* 1–2, 14, 102–4.

67. Weiss, *Jesus' Proclamation,* 133.

68. Wright, *JVG,* 206, 216–18; Jewish symbols are missing—there is no reference to geography or race.

69. Exodus 23:20; Isa 35:1–10; 61:1–11; Mal 3:1; Dumbrell, *Search for Order,* 182; Getty-Sullivan, *Parables,* 27; Bell, *Deliver us,* 96, 97. N. T. Wright notes that Jesus affirmed Jewish beliefs about the kingdom and often used OT imagery (shepherd, vine) but that the kingdom was redefined; it now belonged to God and the Messiah; *JVG,* 173–75. The temporality of the kingdom is ambiguous; some verses describe it as future (Mark 14:25), others as immanent (Mark 13:32, 33), and others as a present reality (Mark 1:15, 9:1); Dumbrell, *Search for Order,* 188; Bell, *Deliver Us,* 105. It is often used in an eschatological sense, having implications both for this age and the age to come (e.g., Luke 17:20). Bruce Chilton argues that Jesus' parables indicate the kingdom as a dawning reality, not a completed result; *Pure Kingdom,* 145. However,

Jesus heals the sick, the blind, the deaf, and the lame, he announces the activity of the Holy Spirit in the kingdom (Isa 29:18; 35:5, 6; Jer 31:8). G. K. Beale argues that the miracles of healing inaugurate the beginning of a new creation as evidenced by the reversal of the curse of a fallen world. He claims the "kingdom of creation" is a plausible center for NT theology.[70] In spatial terms, much like heaven breaks into earth, the "kingdom breaks into human life, changing everything."[71] Unlike the temple, however, entry into this kingdom is through belief and ethical behavior, not ritual or ethnicity.[72] The kingdom also relates to holiness, especially evident in the Lord's Prayer (Matt 6:9, 10; Luke 11:2). Bruce Chilton likens the kingdom to the Shekinah—both indicate divine presence and are paradoxically near and far. He also relates it to purity in that unclean spirits are expelled, and, like purity, it can be viewed as a palpable force that radiates to all who are willing to grasp it. As such, the kingdom operates by expelling demons, healing, cleansing, and raising the dead.[73] Hence the kingdom can be understood as dynamic. There are images of it growing and spreading, like a mustard seed or leaven (Matt 13:31–2; Mark 4:30–32; Luke 13:18–19).[74] This makes sense given the multivalent and metaphorical nature of the kingdom of heaven. Jesus embodies the kingdom, but the concept is larger than him.

Jesus' exorcisms especially indicate the presence of the kingdom.[75] This is explicit in the Beelzebul controversy in which Jesus links casting out demons with the arrival of the kingdom of God (discussed further below). This has often been described using warfare language. For example, N. T. Wright believes that Jesus' battles with Satan are indicative of

there is consensus that it is both present and future, or that one can experience the future in the present (inaugurated eschatology); Ladd, *Theology*, 54–56.

70. Beale, *Temple*, 174; "New Creation," 159, 165.

71. Getty-Sullivan, *Parables*, 23. N. T. Wright believes Jesus' mighty works should be seen in the context of prophecy fulfillment, the proclamation of the kingdom and the breaking in of a new order; *JVG*, 191–93.

72. E.g., the kingdom belongs to children (Matt 19:14; Mark 10:14; Luke 18:16), prostitutes and tax-collectors (Matt 21:31), and the poor (Matt 19:23; Luke 6:20, 18:25); it is not limited to Jewish people (Luke 4:43). It has been described as an "upside down" kingdom; Getty-Sullivan, *Parables*, 89.

73. Chilton, *Pure Kingdom*, 27–28, 90–96, 142; the kingdom is an "intense intervention of God that cannot be contained" (70); it is "final, all-pervading, perfect, holy, and radiant" (99). See also Barton, "Dislocating," 198.

74. Jeremias, *NT Theology*, 98; Ladd, *Theology*, 96–97, 109, 122.

75. Exorcism is closely tied to the kingdom in Acts 2:43; 4:30; 5:12; 6:8; Twelftree, *Name of Jesus*, 134.

the arrival of the kingdom, and the exorcisms establish that the kingdom of God will involve the defeat of Israel's enemy.[76] In non-warfare terms, the kingdom of heaven, as sacred space, is incompatible with evil; Jesus therefore cleanses sacred space by removing evil forces that have intruded upon it. In the Lord's Prayer, "your kingdom come" and "deliver us from the evil one" form a type of inclusio,[77] and in the parable of the sower, the enemies of the kingdom are Satan, persecution, and worldly anxiety.[78] This suggests that sacred space, symbolized by the kingdom of heaven, can be viewed spatially in binary opposition to evil, profane space. The person (the locus of divine presence), the teachings (ethics, not ritual), and the actions (separating evil) of Jesus define this space.

The New Temple

Cultic temple imagery persists in the Gospels, and includes the notions that Jesus is the replacement and fulfillment of the temple, and the replacement of temple functions. Such imagery is prevalent in the Fourth Gospel, but present in the other three. Jesus teaches in the temple (Matt 26:55; Mark 12:35; 14:49; Luke 2:46; 20:1; 21:37–38), describes himself as "greater than the temple" (Matt 12:5), and claims he will destroy the temple and rebuild it in three days (Matt 26:61; Mark 14:58; 15:29; John 2:19). He also radically states that he can forgive sins (Matt 9:4–6; Mark 2:5–10; Luke 5:20–24), previously only a function of cultic rituals.[79] In the "temple cleansing" incident (Matt 21:12, 13; Mark 11:15–17; Luke 19:45, 46; John 2:13–22), Jesus admonishes those who have corrupted his "house of prayer."[80] Chilton emphasizes space rather than action in this passage, believing it is better seen as an occupation rather than a demonstration,

---

76. Wright, *JVG*, 195, 226–28. Similarly, Boyd claims the rule of God is primarily about "vanquishing the rule of Satan"; *God at War,* 171–91, esp. 187.

77. Matt 6:9–13. The consensus is that *poneros* refers to evil one, not evil in the abstract, as it is a noun and there are numerous other references to "evil one" (e.g., Matt 13:19); Page, *Powers,* 112–14.

78. Getty-Sullivan, *Parables,* 32–33.

79. Beale believes this shows that Jesus is both a new sin offering and the replacement of the temple; *Temple,* 177. N. T. Wright also notes that Jesus claimed to do what only the temple previously could; "Jerusalem in the NT," 58.

80. The synoptic Gospels quote a blend of Isa 56:7 and Jer 7:11, the prophetic denouncement of hypocrisy. John quotes Ps 69:9, emphasizing Jesus as the eschatological hope of restoration.

representing Jesus' claim on territory.[81] In the Synoptics, this event occurs during Passover, suggesting that Jesus replaces not only the temple, but also its rituals.[82] In John, it takes place earlier and John explicitly equates the temple with the body of Jesus. Mary Coloe believes that this scene is the hermeneutical key to John: the temple as a christological symbol is transferred from a building to a person, Jesus.[83] This highly symbolic action of Jesus is multivalent and depicts Jesus as the fulfillment and replacement of the temple and by extension, a new creation.[84]

In the Johannine prologue, Jesus is described as *eskēnōsen* ("tabernacling") in the world, with obvious allusion to the wilderness tabernacle and creation.[85] There is a link between flesh and glory, and the fulfillment of the prophetic promise that God would dwell in the midst of his people (Ezek 43:7, 9; Zech 2:10).[86] This event exceeds prophetic expectations: God, previously available only through mysterious meetings in the tent, is now accessible in human form, suggesting that Jesus supplants the tent, tabernacle, and temple.[87] Furthermore, worship no longer occurs in the temple, but through the Spirit (John 4:20–24). Jesus now supplies living water, as God did in the wilderness, and the eschatological temple is promised to do (John 7:37–8; cf. 8:12; Exod 17:6; Ezek 47:1–12; Zech 14:7, 8); he walks on water and describes himself as new and better manna (John 6:19–20, 25–40; obvious exodus imagery);[88] Jesus is the new locus of divine provi-

---

81. Chilton, *Pure Kingdom,* 118. N. T. Wright views this incident as a judgment on Jerusalem for her misuse of the temple and rejection of God and Jesus; it is related to eschatological expectation in that the present temple is becoming redundant; *JVG,* 423–27. Beale notes that since the temple's purpose in sacrifice is no longer needed, this clears the way for the eschatological temple; *Temple,* 179, 192.

82. Hoskins, *Fulfillment,* 176.

83. Coloe, *God Dwells,* 65–84.

84. Hoskins, *Fulfillment,* 109. A. Kerr believes the temple cleansing can be seen as a new creation, since it follows the Cana miracle that occurred on the seventh day; *Temple,* 69–70.

85. Exod 33–40; 25:8 is specific; BDAG 928. Koester notes that "*skēnē*" was used for tent, tabernacle, and a human body; *Dwelling,* 20.

86. Hoskins, *Fulfillment,* 117–18; Kerr, *Temple,* 148–50; Coloe, *God Dwells,* 20–25. Although Solomon questions whether God will dwell on earth (1 Kgs 8:27); Koester, *Word of Life,* 204.

87. Hoskins, *Fulfillment,* 123; Kerr, *Temple,* 112. Jesus as the new temple, the place where heaven and earth connect, is reinforced by the claim that angels descend upon him (John 1:51; Gen 28:12); Hoskins, *Fulfillment,* 126–33.

88. Hoskins, *Fulfillment,* 136–39, 160–66, 184; Kerr, *Temple,* 168, 214–23, 239; Koester, *Word of Life,* 62; Coloe, *God Dwells,* 93–99; Beale, *Temple,* 196. Hoskins

sion. John 14:1–14 also portrays Jesus as the only way to the Father (whose "house" has many rooms); access to divine presence is no longer through the temple, but through Jesus.[89] Jesus as the new "temple" is now inclusive in that access is not restricted to the Jewish nation.[90] There is also a suggestion in the Gospels that Jesus replaces Jerusalem: his ministry begins and ends in Jerusalem, and many important events occur there.[91]

From the above discussion, it is evident that Jesus can be viewed as the new metaphorical temple. Kerr notes that Jesus' saving presence is "represented by images from the history of Israel—bread, light, door, shepherd, resurrection, way, and vine"—all of which are linked with the temple.[92] Beale extends the symbolism, claiming that Jesus as the new temple is another way of referring to him as the new creation, since the temple was symbolic of creation.[93] Jesus is now the means of communication between earth and heaven, the locus of divine presence, the new temple, tabernacle, and creation. He can be conceived of as replacing and redefining OT sacred space.

Light, Life, and Truth

Given the view of Jesus as the new temple, it is unsurprising he is also considered the source of light and life, which characterized sacred space in the OT. Matthew (4:16) describes Jesus as beginning his ministry by quoting Isaiah 9:2: "The people who sat in darkness have seen a great light," and Luke (1:78) has Zechariah echo the prophetic promise of dawn

concludes that Jesus simultaneously fulfills the Passover, feast of tabernacles, dedication, and the temple; *Fulfillment*, 175, 181

89. Coloe (*God Dwells*, 159–60; *Household of God*, 108–9) and Kerr (*Temple* 277, 294) claim that "house" symbolizes temple, not heaven, given the reference in John 2:16. However, given that the temple was symbolic of heaven, the difference is likely not significant.

90. The previous temple of course denied access to Gentiles; Dunn, "Jesus and Holiness," 116; Bryan, *Israel's Traditions*, 207–8.

91. The idea is also implied in Matt 5:25; 7:24–27; 23:37; 27:53; John 19:20. Dow believes the Zion tradition continues but is detached from the earthly city; Jesus replaces Zion as the dwelling place of God; *Images of Zion*, 139, 142–78.

92. Jesus is the new Eden and the new holy of holies; Kerr, *Temple*, 345. Köstenberger and Swain similarly think that Jesus can be seen as the fulfillment and replacement of God's previous dwelling places; *Father, Son*, 138.

93. Beale, *Temple*, 176, 196–97. He notes this is also explicit in the Johannine prologue (192). Löning and Zenger view Jesus as the origin of world, and the goal and meaning of creation; *To Begin with*, 190.

breaking and giving light to those in darkness. Davenport notes that the setting of the Sermon on the Mount is Galilee, which was identified with Gentiles, lost tribes, death, and darkness. Thus, "the light of God invades the darkness."[94] The transfiguration unambiguously portrays the association between Jesus and light: Jesus shines like the sun, symbolizing a new creation. Margaret Barker points out that, in the Gospels, light and life are depicted in opposition to darkness and death. "The coming of the light was the coming of life and the effect of the light was to purify and transform."[95] Light/dark imagery is particularly prevalent in John. The light of Jesus is hated by those who love darkness; light exposes evil (John 3:19–21). John's prologue contains Genesis imagery: as God pushes back darkness in creation, so Jesus dispels darkness. Newbigin believes that the coming of Jesus is a fresh creative act; he is the "light of the world" who gives life.[96] As in creation and temple imagery, light and life are associated. Jesus is also the giver of living water (John 4:10, 11, 7:38), and the bread of life, which, like manna, comes down from heaven but which, unlike manna, gives eternal life (John 6:35, 48–51; cf. Exod 16:1–36).[97] Ladd comments that in John, "the world below is the realm of darkness, of Satanic power, of sin and of death"; in Jesus' mission "light and life have invaded the darkness to deliver people from darkness, sin, and death, to give them the life of the Spirit."[98] Barker connects creation, Johannine imagery, and the Holy Spirit: "the flowing of life into the creation was the flowing of the Spirit."[99] Finally, the Spirit, life, and love are associated; life is attained by knowing God through Jesus and the Spirit (John 3:1–16; 6:63; 20:31).

In John, Jesus is further defined as the truth. *Alētheia* connotes real, authentic, and genuine.[100] Jesus is described as "full of grace and truth" (John 1:14, 17) and the "way, the truth, and the life" (John 14:6). Jesus

94. Davenport, *Into the Darkness*, 21.

95. Barker, *On Earth*, 25.

96. John 8:12; cf. Zech 14:7, 8; Newbigin, *Light has Come*, 4, 91–102. Jesus also brings light by healing the blind; this association is explicit in John 9:5–7 (117). *Zoē* ("life") occurs thirty-six times in John.

97. This is the living water that Israel forsook (Jer 2:13; 17:13), is promised on the "day of the Lord" (Zech 14:8), and is associated with the Spirit (Isa 44:3); Barker, *On Earth*, 32–34; Hoskins, *Fulfillment*, 163–66; Kerr, *Temple*, 188; Newbigin, *Light has Come*, 117. Koester notes that Jesus' actions follow his teachings: he claims to be the bread of life, and feeds the 5,000; he is the light of the world, and heals the blind; he is the resurrection and the life, and raises Lazarus; *Word of Life*, 164.

98. Ladd, *Theology*, 165.

99. Barker, *On Earth*, 34.

100. BDAG 42; Newbigin, *Light has Come*, 9; recall Eliade's real/unreal dichotomy.

brings the truth and the truth frees his followers (John 8:32); truth is associated with life and the Spirit (John 3:21, 14:17, 15:26, 16:13). As Newbigin states, "the life of God is also the light of truth."[101] Truth is contrasted with Satan who is named a liar (John 8:44–46). With respect to deliverance from evil, Twelftree concludes that, in John, "*demon possession is combated through knowing the truth: Jesus.*"[102] It is often noted that John does not record any exorcisms, but by viewing evil metaphorically, it is evident that Jesus, through word and deed, opposes darkness. Interestingly, Boyd describes John's light/dark imagery using warfare language;[103] however, although light/dark is associated with warfare imagery in some Judaic literature, it is difficult to see military metaphors in John's description of Jesus as light, life, and truth. Ladd notes that Johannine dualism is vertical, contrasting the world above with the world below; thus Jesus comes down from heaven, the realm of light and truth, into the world below.[104] Heaven/earth and light/dark dualisms do not carry warfare connotations.

Light/dark language can have the concerns with dualism discussed in chapter 1, but it is also possible to see shades of grey in light/dark imagery, since the world of darkness is variable. As Newbigin helpfully says, light and dark are not separated by a fixed boundary: e.g., a lamp casts shadows, but its purpose is to fill the room with light.[105] Darkness and light are not necessarily black and white; boundaries are blurred. As the kingdom is understood as a dynamic concept, so light can be perceived dynamically as extending into the darkness.

---

101. Newbigin, *Light has Come*, 4. Ladd describes truth as the "full revelation and embodiment of the redemptive purpose of God" received through the Spirit, and acceptance of the word and person of Christ (e.g., John 18:37); *Theology*, 303–5.

102. Twelftree, *Name of Jesus*, 204, italics original, perhaps as a polemic against the "power encounter" movement. He points out that the truth Jesus teaches relates to the accusation of him being demon possessed, although readers are likely to conclude the opposite: that Jesus' opponents are demonized since Jesus also claimed the Jews had the devil, a liar, as their father (200–203).

103. Boyd, *God at War*, 227–28.

104. John 8:23; 16:11. He also notes that John's dualism is different from Qumran dualism, which posits a conflict between good and evil spirits; John contrasts God and the world; Ladd, *Theology*, 259–60, 71.

105. Newbigin, *Light has Come*, 133.

Conceptualizing Evil

The above overview affirms the similarities between sacred space in the OT and the Gospels. And our understanding of sacred space can inform our understanding of profane space. Jesus can be viewed as the embodiment of sacred space—the light of the world, the new temple, the kingdom of heaven, the new creation, and the locus of divine presence. He is the new center, holy space in opposition to the periphery, profane space. Conceptualizing the kingdom spatially provides a non-warfare framework for understanding evil and, since the kingdom is dynamic and nonlinear, evil in binary opposition can also be understood as such, confirming previous suggestions of evil as a chaotic-complex system. Sacred space is characterized by divine presence; therefore, profane space can be defined by divine absence, perhaps endorsing its nature as disorganized and evil. Jesus is the new temple—his holiness and light radiate outwards revealing and dispelling the darkness. Jesus is the light, life, and truth, in opposition to darkness, death, and lies. Truth, which connotes reality, confirms the idea that evil, in binary opposition, is unreal, or less real. Jesus represents ultimate reality. Spatial imagery locates evil at the periphery, diminishing its ontological status. Temple imagery does not picture Christ as sneakily establishing a small "beachhead" in a world ruled by Satan; it shows Christ bursting into the world to reestablish and extend the sacred center (Figure 6.2).

Figure 6.2: The Advent of Christ

Sacred Actions

Understanding sacred space can elucidate the behavior required for its maintenance. Following suggestions in previous chapters, Jesus' actions can be interpreted as setting boundaries on evil and purifying sacred space. His words and deeds can be described with cultic, spatial metaphors as opposed to warfare ones. The Gospels indicate that Jesus did not just preach the kingdom, but acted on his words by healing and casting out demons. Almost all Jesus' behavior is highly symbolic.[106] Hence metaphor theory is well suited for understanding the Gospels. Jesus' miracles,[107] especially his exorcisms,[108] can be understood as *reestablishing sacred space*. Viewing evil as boundary violation sheds light on Jesus' ministry. In this section I examine sacred actions first in terms of divine initiative in dealing with evil then in terms of human responsibility.

Divine Initiative

The work of Christ, particularly with respect to evil spirits, is often described using warfare language. Although there is little such language in the Gospels themselves, many scholars interpret stories within a warfare framework. Spatial imagery can provide an alternative lens through which to view the Gospels' portrayal of evil. As noted above, Jesus does not come as a divine warrior, but as a new creation, temple, and light that shines in the darkness. This section critiques previous warfare approaches to Jesus' dealings with evil spirits, discusses the authority provided by the Holy Spirit to deal with evil, and suggests alternative interpretations of relevant passages in terms of cleansing and setting boundaries on evil. Jesus' death

---

106. E.g., in the Synoptics, Jesus uses parables; in John the narrative itself is symbolic; Coloe, *Household of God*, 18.

107. The word "miracle" does not occur in the Gospels but is commonly used to describe extraordinary acts of Jesus, "signs and wonders." See Twelftree, *Miracle Worker*, 24–27, for the various definitions of miracle. I concur with N. T. Wright that miracles should be understood as operating within the natural world, and evidencing the work of Christ (unlike the Enlightenment view that miracles are restricted to that which cannot be explained by science); *JVG*, 188; see also Bell, *Deliver Us*, 111–12; Cook "Devils," 190.

108. The word *exorkistōn* (exorcist) occurs once in the NT (Acts 19:13), but is commonly applied to Jesus when he expels demons. Twelftree's definition is helpful: "exorcism was a form of healing used when demons or evil spirits were thought to have entered a person and to be responsible for sickness and was the attempt to control and cast out or expel evil spiritual beings or demons from people"; *Exorcist*, 13.

and resurrection are discussed using spatial imagery, and, finally, Jesus' teachings regarding the eschatological separation of evil are examined.

Warfare?

Warfare imagery is commonly applied to the exorcism stories, and often extended to the teaching and miracles of Jesus plus his death and resurrection. Some OT scholars claim that warfare themes continue into the NT. Longman and Reid, for example, assert that the "divine warrior" theme extends to the NT: Jesus "battles" demonic forces and sends out an "army."[109] Among NT scholars, there is a long tradition of using warfare language to describe Jesus' encounters with evil spirits.[110] Garrett views much of Luke as "spiritual warfare," believing even passing references to exorcism and healing can be interpreted as earthly signs of "victory" over an "invisible enemy."[111] Twelftree similarly sees Jesus' exorcisms as an eschatological battle, arguing that the battles in Mark are cosmic and spiritual, and that John views Jesus' entire ministry as a "battle with Satan or the demonic."[112] These scholars are correct in describing Jesus as opposed to evil spirits, but the issue is whether warfare language is essential. With respect to theology, Boyd's work, as mentioned, contains abundant warfare language. He claims the Gospels portray a world "caught in the crossfire of a cosmic battle between the Lord and his angelic army and Satan and his demonic army," and all miracles, healings, and exorcisms should be interpreted as "acts of war."[113] Conversely, Guelich notes that of all Jesus' references to the

109. Based on Mark 1:23–28; 6:6, 7; Longman and Reid, *God is a Warrior*, 97, 103. Similarly Forsyth believes the combat myth is the "essential forming principle" of the NT," Jesus' exorcisms representing a battle against evil spirits; *Old Enemy*, 249, 285; see also Anderson, *Creation versus Chaos*, 150.

110. Jeremias wrote that Jesus' exorcisms are depicted as battles in the Gospels, especially Mark; *Proclamation*, 85–96; Dumbrell, who otherwise does not emphasize warfare language, states that, in the temptation narrative, God battles Satan; *Search for Order*, 189.

111. Garrett, *Demise of Devil*, 54. She believes this cosmic conflict began in the "shadowy past" (59) and that Satan's challenge to God in the temptation narrative led to his demise (41). N. T. Wright claims Jesus' exorcisms were indicative of his battle with Satan, Israel's real enemy, as opposed to Rome, their perceived enemy; the exorcisms represent implementation of Jesus' initial victory over Satan in the wilderness temptation; *JVG*, 192, 196, 446–72.

112. Twelftree, *Miracle Worker*, 67; *Name of Jesus*, 96, 115, 127, 195–96.

113. Boyd, *God at War*, 19, 172, 180–84. Although he later states that Jesus' only weapons were faith and prayer (203).

devil and demons, none of them have military imagery, and that only once in the Synoptics is Satan referred to as "enemy" and then it is in a personal, not military, context. He concludes, "the phrase 'spiritual warfare' finds no basis in the Gospels' portrait of Jesus' ministry."[114] Concerns with military metaphors have been discussed previously; the issue here is exegetical. Is warfare imagery the only way to interpret the exorcism stories, or has the commitment to such language influenced the way in which the Gospels' portrayal of evil is understood? Examination of relevant biblical passages may reveal alternative interpretations.

AUTHORITY AND THE HOLY SPIRIT

Warfare language typically emphasizes power. However, Jesus is effective primarily because he is sanctioned by the Holy Spirit. As discussed above, Jesus is filled and anointed with the Spirit, and it is this that makes his ministry efficacious. Mark (1:22) and Luke (4:32) specifically point out that Jesus has authority over demons, and John (5:19–21, 30) also emphasizes the importance of the Father's authority.[115] Demons even recognize the authority of Jesus.[116] *Dunamis* typically means power, might, and ability, whereas *exousia* implies authority or the right to act. However, the terms overlap in meaning, with *dunamis* sometimes implying authority, and *exousia* implying power.[117] Andrew Walker points out that *dunamis*, emphasized in charismatic circles, is rarely used in the exorcism stories;

114. Guelich, "Jesus, Paul, Peretti," 37, 40–42; "enemy" in Matt 13:39.

115. Hendrickx, *Miracle Stories*, 52; Newbigin, *Light has Come*, 69. Getty-Sullivan believes Matthew stresses the authority of Jesus evident in his rebuking a fever and forgiving sins; *Parables*, 91.

116. They ask his permission to enter pigs in the story of the Gerasene demoniac; Klutz, *Exorcism Stories*, 92.

117. BDAG 262–63, 352–53. In Luke 10:19, the disciples are given *exousia*, whereas Satan has *dunamis*. Klutz suggests that the authority of Jesus is evident in Jesus' commands to demons, and his power evident in the demons' obedience; *Exorcism Stories*, 48–49. Hendrickx defines *exousia* as an "independent powerful reality"; *Miracle Stories*, 58. Consider also the story of the centurion who understands obedience because he is under authority, not because he is afraid of power (Matt 8:9; Luke 7:8). Interestingly in English there is also overlap in meaning: someone with authority often has power over someone else, e.g., a parent has authority over a child but this is not usually conceived of in terms of power; businesses with good bosses in authority run smoothly, not like a battle. Murphy uses the example of a police officer stopping a truck by holding out his hand—authority not power; *Handbook*, 300.

exousia is used instead.[118] Twelftree uses the term "power-authority," which I prefer to "power" alone, but "authority" could also be used alone, avoiding the warfare connotations of power. Jesus' dealings with demons need not be described in terms of "power encounters," but as the exercising of divine authority.

The Gospels demonstrate that Jesus is authorized by the Father and the Spirit. Immediately on his return from the desert, Jesus, "in the power of the Spirit," begins healing and exorcising wounded people. Lodahl claims that the Holy Spirit is the initiating and sustaining power of Jesus, healing is an expression of the anointing of the Spirit, and the defeat of demons is a result of the animating power of the Spirit.[119] The most explicit example of the role of the Spirit is the Beelzebul controversy, or the Spirit/finger saying (Matt 12:22–32; Mark 3:21–30; Luke 11:14–23).[120] Here it is evident that it is only by the Spirit that Jesus casts out demons and, in contrast to contemporaneous exorcists who employed elaborate techniques, God only requires a "finger." Following this story is a difficult statement that those who blaspheme the Spirit will not be forgiven.[121] Welker believes that blasphemy signifies the refusal of God's gift of deliverance, which can only occur through the Spirit of God.[122] This could also be conceived in spatial terms: the Holy Spirit is present in the realm of God and absent in the realm of evil. As Welker notes, "the Spirit is present in that which is *held together* and *enlivened* by God—but not . . . in

118. Walker, "Devil You Think You Know," 104. I concur with Walker, though he ignores the complexities of the terms.

119. Lodahl, *Shekinah*, 152, 169, 173.

120. Mathew says "Spirit" and Luke says "finger" of God (which recalls the plague narratives, Exod 3:20; 7:4–5; 8:18). This concept frequently refers to the might of God. There is debate over whether finger or Spirit is original; however, both affirm Jesus' source of authority as divine; Page, *Powers*, 105; Twelfree, *Exorcist*, 98–113; *Miracle Worker*, 160, 169.

121. In Matthew and Mark's versions. Mark adds that Jesus was accused of having an unclean spirit. The disobedient Israelites who grieved God's Spirit (Isa 63:10; cf. Exod 23:21) are probably in the background of this statement; Witherington and Ice, *Shadow of the Almighty*, 117; Brandon, *Satanic Conflict*, 67.

122. The so-called "impossible possibility"; Welker, *God the Spirit*, 211–19. This idea is echoed by many: Pinnock uses spatial imagery to describe this sin: "a person standing deliberately outside the circle of love"; *Flame of Love*, 89; Brandon notes that to deny the work of the Spirit is to deny the presence of God; *Satanic Conflict*, 67. Interestingly there is also a connection with impurity; Bryan notes that especially in the Second Temple Period, this "unpardonable sin" is tied to purity; there is no forgiveness for sins which pollute holy people or reject the covenant (Jub 33:17–21; 1QS 8:20–6); *Israel's Traditions*, 157–58.

that which is decaying to dust . . . through falseness and unrighteousness human beings can grieve and banish God's Spirit."[123] Those who reject the Spirit are rejecting divine reality, and choosing life (or lack of life) apart from the Spirit. This statement need not be understood as a harsh judgment, but simply as a spatial reality; it is not possible to exist in sacred space without acknowledging the Holy Spirit. Access to the center is possible only through the Spirit.

Finally, Jesus expels evil spirits through a simple authoritative command without "powerful" mechanical aids.[124] The word commonly used in describing Jesus' actions towards demons is *ekballō* (cast out).[125] This term has spatial connotations: demons are sent *away* from where they do not belong. *Exerchomai* (depart or go out of), another spatial term, is also used.[126] *Epitimaō* (rebuke), commonly used in relation to demons, emphasizes Jesus' authority and can be considered a "technical term for the subjugation of evil powers."[127] Unlike other ancient exorcists, Jesus does not ask the demon's name, or use magical formulae.[128] The summary statement (Matt 8:16), "with a word," highlights simplicity. Sometimes there is no direct command to a demon, but "let it be done" (Matt 15:28) or "it has been done" (Mark 7:29). There is no consistency in Jesus' language, either in form or content, other than the imperative mood. Jesus is successful not because of his words but because he operates in the Spirit; authority, not technique, is emphasized. The simplicity of the process does not lend itself

123. Welker, *God the Spirit*, 161. Yong similarly notes that "the experience of divine absence . . . is properly termed 'demonic'"; *Discerning*, 127. See further discussion in chapter 8, "pneumatology."

124. E.g., Tobit 8:3 describes incense being required for the expulsion of an evil spirit. Although Twelftree notes some similarities between the methods of Jesus and those of contemporaneous exorcists, Jesus' methods were overall simpler; *Christ Triumphant*, 64.

125. BDAG, 299. *Ekballō* is also used in the LXX to describe how God drives away Israel's earthly and cosmic enemies (e.g., Exod 23:30); Twelftree, *Exorcist*, 110; Sorensen, *Possession*, 133.

126. BDAG 347–48; Sorensen, *Possession*, 133.

127. BDAG, 384; Page, *Powers*, 143, 162; Marcus, *Mark 1–8*, 194 (they follow Kee, "Terminology," 232–46). The same word is used in the LXX in God's rebuke of Satan (Zech 3:2) and a similar word with respect to God's rebuke of waters (Pss 18; 104; 106); Hendrickx, *Miracle Stories*, 32; Forsyth, *Old Enemy*, 286–87.

128. The exception being "Legion" in the Gerasene demoniac discussed above; Page, *Powers*, 144–45. Twelftree notes that Jesus did not pray, use incantations, or the word adjure which were common in ancient exorcisms; *Exorcist*, 163; see also Sorensen, *Possession*, 138.

to warfare imagery; rather the language of *authority* dominates. Through a word, Jesus effects a real change in the world. Emphasizing authority over power and simple commands over elaborate exorcism techniques are first steps towards a non-warfare perspective on deliverance in the Gospels. Emphasizing the Holy Spirit further supports non-warfare language, as discussed in chapter 4. The authority of the Spirit over evil can also be understood in spatial terms—through the Spirit, demons are relocated and removed from sacred space into profane space, outside godly reality.

CLEANSING AND RE-ESTABLISHING BOUNDARIES ON EVIL

Recall that metaphors of purification and boundary-setting with respect to dealing with impurity and evil are interrelated in cultic theology. In the Gospels too, cleansing and limiting are ways in which evil is dealt with. Many of Jesus' deeds can be understood in light of cultic theology. Furthermore, in continuity with the OT theme of the exodus as a new creation, involving the overcoming of evil forces, many of Jesus' deeds can be seen as doing the same.

Jesus can be viewed as extending sacred space outward, cleansing it and removing evil. Since he is the locus of holiness, it is unsurprising that he incorporates purity in his teachings and actions. However, Jesus radically changes its definition. First, he emphasizes inclusion, not exclusion, fulfilling the prophetic hope for a universal gathering of all nations (Isa 9:1–3; 42:1–15 [quoted by Matt 12:15–21]; 60:1–22; Zech 2:10–11). Jesus' miracles are shared equally between Jews and Gentiles.[129] Second, Jesus teaches internal rather than external purity (Matt 15:1–20; 23:25–28; Mark 7:1–23; Luke 11:39–41). Cultic purity changes to ethical purity.[130] Third,

129. Jesus not only talks to but offers living water to a Samaritan woman (John 4:1–26); a Samaritan is commended for his love, over a Jew (Luke 10:30–37); Bryan, *Israel's Traditions*, 175–85; Dunn, "Jesus and Holiness," 189; a Canaanite woman is commended for her faith, and her daughter is healed (Matt 15:21–28; Mark 7:24–30); Telford, *Mark*, 100. Jesus dissolves barriers that separate people such as race, gender, and age; Green, *Luke*, 90.

130. Now it is only evil within that can take purity away, not bodily impurity, unlike what the Pharisees thought; Bryan, *Israel's Traditions*, 167. As Dunn remarks, Jesus "set loose" the purity regulations, although he worked within conventions, and outer purity could also be seen as symbolic of inner purity, e.g., a leprous man confesses sin (Mark 1:44); holiness was important to Jesus as a "power which cleanses uncleanness and dissolves impurity"; "Jesus and Holiness," 183–88, 191–92. Brandon thinks that Jesus' exorcisms proved not only his defeat of Satan, but also his ministry of cleansing the nation; both paved the way for the kingdom of God; *Satanic Conflict*, 69.

purity is no longer acquired through ritual action but through the cleansing work of Jesus. In Luke (4:18; 6:20; 7:22; 14:13, 21; 16:20), the lists that previously pertained to exclusion from Israel's camp now refer to inclusion—the blind, the lame, and those with blemishes and scale disease.[131] Jesus heals those with skin disease and, instead of contracting impurity, transfers cleanness (Matt 8:1–3; 11:5; Mark 1:40–42; Luke 17:11–19).[132] A hemorrhaging woman, with a severe form of contagious impurity, is healed by touching Jesus' cloak, and impurity is not transferred to Jesus but purity transferred to the woman (Matt 9:20–22; Mark 5:25–34; Luke 8:43–48).[133] Jesus also raises the dead to life (Jairus's daughter, Matt 9:18, 24, 25; Mark 5:23, 39–43; Luke 8:41, 42, 49–55; the widow's son, Luke 7:11–15; and Lazarus, John 11:1–4.). Since the dead were considered unclean, this can be viewed as another act of cleansing, and since death was associated with evil spirits, resurrections can be seen as exorcisms, albeit indirectly. Jesus goes into the periphery, associated with impurity, death, and evil, cleansing and healing people afflicted by conditions associated with this zone.

As healing and cleansing are intertwined, so are healing and exorcism: The Canaanite woman's daughter is "healed" of her demon (Matt 15:21–28; Mark 7:24–30); a fever is "rebuked" by Jesus and the woman healed (Luke 4:39); and the woman crippled by a spirit is healed by Jesus laying hands on her, thus representing an exorcism as well as a healing (Luke 13:10–13).[134] In summary statements, Jesus is described as healing demoniacs and curing those with evil spirits (Matt 4:24; 15:28; Luke 6:18; 7:21; 8:48).[135] Many biblical scholars have noted this connection. For instance, Twelftree thinks that Luke "recast healing stories as exorcisms" and the boundaries between healing and exorcism are blurred: "all sickness

---

131. Green, *Luke*, 80–81. This was promised by the prophets (Jer 33:8; Ezek 36:22–36; Zech 13:1).

132. Recall that in 4Q272 1:1–16, skin disease was attributed to evil spirits, thus associating this cleansing with exorcism; Marcus, *Mark 1–8*, 209; Dunn, "Jesus and Holiness," 188–90; Klutz, *Exorcism Stories*, 116–17; Haber, "They Shall Purify," 134.

133. Twelftree, *Miracle Worker*, 118–19; Haber, "They Shall Purify," 127–29, 132–36.

134. Page, *Powers*, 118–21; Bell, *Deliver Us*, 70. *Epitamaō* ("rebuke") is elsewhere used with reference to demons as discussed above. Laying hands on and standing over someone was a common practice in ancient exorcisms, highlighting the association; Twelftree, *Miracle Worker*, 148.

135. Explicit in the claim of Jesus healing "all who were under the power of the devil" (Acts 10:38); Page, *Powers*, 133; Twelftree, *Name of Jesus*, 36–53; Bell, *Deliver Us*, 68.

(and healing) is given a demonic and cosmic dimension."[136] However, the relationship between illness and the demonic is complex; only in some cases do demons cause illness.[137] J. C. Thomas, in his study of the devil and disease, concludes that some illness is caused by demonic forces, but there is no simple correlation.[138] As healing and cleansing, and healing and exorcism, are associated, so are cleansing and exorcism.[139] Klutz argues that the connection between unclean spirits and impurity is often overlooked. Yet an exorcism occurs following a teaching on impurity, and once Jesus succeeds in healing only after the person becomes like a corpse, thus unclean (Mark 7:1–30; 9:25–27).[140] But, since many illnesses caused impurity, and impurity was associated with evil spirits, the three can be seen to be intertwined.

Healing, cleansing, and exorcisms can also be seen as manifestations of creation. Both healing and exorcism are indicative of the establishment of the kingdom of heaven, and the renewal of creation. Creation imagery relates to spatial imagery: Jesus' dealings with evil spirits can be viewed as the spatial separation of evil. His miracles, especially exorcisms, reestablish boundaries on divine reality. This connection between sacred actions and sacred space, between exorcisms and the kingdom, has often been noted. Garrett, for example, states: "as the Kingdom of Satan diminishes, the Kingdom of God grows proportionately" (although recall above critique of the "kingdom" of Satan).[141] However, most scholarship has either

136. Twelftree, *Name of Jesus*, 132, 133, 154. Similarly, Bell believes that boundaries between healing and exorcism are blurred; *Deliver us*, 68–69; Green claims "almost every account of healing in the Third Gospel is portrayed as an encounter with diabolical forces"; *Luke*, 78; Klutz thinks that exorcism and healing are two facets of a single ritual; *Exorcism Stories*, 188; and Bell agrees that it could be said that all healings are exorcisms; there is an observable change in the person following expulsion of a demon; *Deliver Us*, 68–69.

137. See above for illnesses caused by evil spirits. Examples in which illness is not connected with the demonic include blindness (Matt 9:27–30; Mark 8:22–23; John 9:1–12), deafness and muteness (Mark 7:31–37), and many of the healing summary statements.

138. Thomas, *Devil, Disease*, 160, 188, 302. Gaiser comes to a similar conclusion noting that healing is usually considered broadly; *Healing in the Bible*, 134–35.

139. E.g., the frequent references to "unclean spirits." Wenell thinks the "battle over impurity is waged against Satanic forces"; *Jesus and Land*, 100–101.

140. Klutz, *Exorcism Stories*, 118–28, 136. Bryan concurs that the language of impurity is always associated with evil spirits, especially in Mark; *Israel's Traditions*, 160. Sorensen similarly believes that since exorcism restores a person to wellness, or a state of purity; it fits into Jesus' revised scheme of purification; *Possession*, 127–28.

141. And every healing is a loss for Satan and a gain for God; Garrett, *Demise of*

interpreted the exorcisms in isolation, or through the lens of warfare. There has been little examination of space. Space in Mark has been explored, although without consideration of evil. Elizabeth Struthers Malbon notes that numerous topographical terms are used; there is symbolic hierarchy from sea to earth to mountain to heaven. Mark incorporates fundamental spatial oppositions (chaos/order, sea/desert, heaven/earth, foreign-land/ homeland, isolated/inhabited) and stresses Jesus as the mediator. Malbon also comments on Jesus' teaching with respect to purity: "the sacred realm is inadequate to contain Jesus' 'new teaching' and it overflows into the profane realm."[142] Her work confirms the spatial symbolism central to this study; however, Jesus does not always mediate between sacred and profane space, but often separates them. Jesus redefines purity, and when it pertains to people, he heals and cleanses impurity. And, with respect to evil spirits, he never mediates, but *reinforces* the separation.

Spatial symbolism can also be seen in Matthew (especially 8:1–4). Jesus comes down from the mountain (cosmic symbolism) and immediately cleanses a leper; he moves from clean to unclean space and his holiness extends from the center to the periphery. He then travels to Gentile territory (unclean) and heals the centurion's servant. Next, he rebukes a fever, demons, and a storm, and finally goes to a place of ultimate impurity (containing demoniacs, tombs, and swine), which he cleanses. Given the known symbolism of evil, Jesus can be viewed as systematically moving from sacred to profane space, redefining and cleansing this space, and separating evil. The temptation narrative can likewise be viewed in spatial terms. Immediately after his anointing, Jesus goes into the desert where he meets the devil. Spatially, Jesus moves from the center, blessed by God, to the periphery. This narrative has multiple layers of meaning (e.g., Jesus, the new Israel, is tested for forty days, but succeeds where Israel failed).[143]

Devil, 45; Dunn similarly argues that the exorcisms are proof of the defeat of Satan and the arrival of the kingdom; *NT Theology*, 83.

142. Malbon, *Narrative Space*, 11, 130–33, 157. She uses Lévi-Straussian analysis and views "narrative space as a system of relationships" (2–6). There are three types of spatial relations in Mark: geopolitical, topographical, and architectural (8). Topographical terms include "in the boat," "to the other side," "to embark," "to cross over," "to row," "to moor," and "to go before." In the first half of Mark, Jesus sits by the sea and talks about earth; in the second, he sits on a mountain and speaks of heaven (56, 67, 96).The Markan Jesus has an affinity for the space between—the way (between isolated areas and inhabited areas), the mountain (between heaven and earth), the Sea of Galilee (between the Jewish homeland and foreign lands), and the tomb (between outside and inside) (168).

143. In her forty years in the wilderness; Jesus is filled with the Spirit, as opposed

It can also be seen in light of creation theology; Jesus' messianic mission is to establish peace in opposition to chaotic forces (the devil) in creation.[144] Finally, there is an association with *Yom Kippur*. Annually, the Israelites "loaded" sin onto a tote-goat to be sent to Azazel, a desert demon. Jesus in the desert, however, counters Satan's temptations and does not sin. Satan, unlike Azazel, is not "fed." A radical cosmic change occurs that foreshadows Jesus' death and method of atonement. There are hints that *Yom Kippur* is obsolete; Satan is to remain in profane space without any privilege for interaction with sacred space through ritual. It is difficult to see warfare imagery in this story, which depicts Jesus as calmly and quietly quoting sacred texts.

The first exorcism recorded by Mark is the casting out of the unclean spirit in the synagogue (Mark 1:21–27; Luke 4:31–37). There is spatial symbolism in this event because it occurs as Jesus advances into new territory, Capernaum. It is temporally close to the temptation narrative, suggesting a theological link.[145] The spirit(s) recognize Jesus as the Son of God and ask "what have you to do with us," or "what do we have in common," perhaps indicating their awareness of the separation between sacred and profane space.[146] They also ask "have you come to destroy us," recognizing Jesus' authority, and acknowledging their illegitimate location, activity, and even existence.[147] Jesus commands "be silent" and, although the spirit(s) are violent, Jesus is not, and the man is unharmed.[148] The uncleanness of the demonized man is set in binary opposition to the holiness of the synagogue. Jesus, by telling the demon to come out of the man, is both

---

to Israel who grieved the Spirit (Isa 63:10). The forty days correspond with the time of the flood (Gen 7:4, 12, 17), the period Moses was on the mountain (Exod 24:18), and the time Elijah was without food (1 Kgs 19:8). There is also intertextuality with Ps 91 (angels attend Jesus who "tramples serpents"); Garrett, *Temptations*, 55–58.

144. Löning and Zenger, *To Begin with*, 49–50; they think that Mark specifically is shaped by creation theology.

145. Page suggests that this exorcism is a direct consequence of Jesus' victory over Satan; *Powers*, 140.

146. This idiom (echoing 1 Kgs 17:18, 2 Kgs 3:13), also in the story of the Gerasene demoniac, has shades of meaning including the idea of lack of commonality; Marcus, *Mark 1–8*, 188. This phrase was used in antiquity as a defense against evil spirits. Twelftree suggests that it is a pathetic attempt by the demon to avoid expulsion; *Exorcist*, 63–64.

147. In addition, the destruction of evil was expected in the messianic age; Twelftree, *Exorcist*, 66.

148. Marcus suggests that this be understood as a vernacular, "shut up"; *Mark 1–8*, 189; Twelftree notes that "be silent" or "muzzle" also meant to bind; *Exorcist*, 70.

reestablishing boundaries and cleansing sacred space. It is difficult to view this story as warfare.[149]

Arguably, the most significant exorcism story is the Gerasene demoniac (Matt 8:28–34; Mark 5:1–20; Luke 8:26–39; Matthew's version is abbreviated and he names the place Gedara—its exact location has not been determined). Again, there is spatial symbolism as Jesus crosses the sea, moving into new territory. Forsyth points out the series of oppositions in this story: upper/lower worlds, god/demon, clean/unclean, man/animal, Jew/Gentile.[150] The demons recognize Jesus, appearing resigned to their fate; they beg not to be sent out of the area (Mark) or to the abyss (Luke).[151] Although their plea to enter the pigs is granted, they end up in the sea.[152] Spatially, evil spirits are sent out of the human into profane space (sea/abyss/outer-regions) where evil belongs. Dumbrell remarks that Jesus' expulsion of the demons represents an "imposition of normalcy . . . a return to order," especially evident in the man being clothed and in his right mind.[153] Spatial (ordering, setting boundaries) and cleansing imagery are intertwined in this story. Impurity language is abundant: Gentile land, tombs (associated with demons and corpse impurity), and pigs (unclean animals). The unclean demon underscores the abhorrence of this place. Bryan concludes, the "lines between pure/impure are the

149. Curiously, Marcus, who does not otherwise emphasize warfare imagery, describes this event as the "opening battle"; *Mark 1–8*, 186. Klutz sees impurity imagery in this passage (Luke 4:27 is a co-text) and believes the exorcism removes the source of pollution for the entire community; *Exorcism Stories*, 73–79.

150. And one side of lake/other side; Forsyth, *Old Enemy*, 291. Klutz notes that Jesus only undergoes spatial change, from a boat to land, whereas the demoniac undergoes healing. Spatial terms are used eleven times in the story; *Exorcism Stories*, 105–6.

151. A similar idea of sending demons to another region is found in Tob 8:3. "Abyss" (the LXX translation of *tĕhôm*) is common in apocalyptic literature, likely referring to a place of final punishment for evil.

152. Evil spirits plea for leniency in some Second Temple Literature (1 En 12–14; Jub 10). Twelftree also notes some parallels with Babylonian exorcisms in which demons were transferred to animals; *Exorcist*, 75, 153–54. Demons being sent into the sea is similar to the apocalyptic images of the devil and his followers being thrown into the lake of fire (Rev 20:10, 14; 21:8); Forsyth, *Old Enemy*, 293.

153. Dumbrell, *Search for Order*, 190. Twelftree also sees a reference to Isa 65:4, referring to defeat of Gentile "gods" in preparation for Jesus' subsequent ministry; *Miracle Worker*, 72, and notes that in Luke the man was *sōzein* (saved or healed), thus associating salvation and exorcism (156). The dressing of the man relates to the image of Joshua being dressed in clean clothes after Satan is rebuked (Zech 3:1–5).

same as those between good/evil."[154] There is exodus imagery too: the man is delivered from evil beings, and unclean pigs/demons are drowned like "unclean" Egyptians.[155] Hence there is a repeat of the themes in creation and the cult in terms of cleansing and setting boundaries on evil.

The Beelzebul controversy (Matt 12:25–29; Mark 3:23–27; Luke 11:17–23) is significant for understanding evil spirits and is often discussed using battle imagery.[156] However, the primary significance here is eschatological: God redeeming his people from evil through the Spirit.[157] "Tying up" may have some violent connotations, but "bind," or forbid, carries implications of authority and can also be seen as setting limits or boundaries on evil.[158] There is also spatial imagery in this passage in that Beelzebul can be interpreted as "lord of the house."[159] Jesus establishes the reign of God, or the boundaries of the house, by removing Satan. There is further directionality at the end of this passage: one can only be with or against Jesus. The brief story of the restless demon likewise has spatial (but no warfare) imagery (Matt 12:43–45; Luke 11:24–26).[160] The house

154. Bryan, *Israel's Traditions*, 161; see also Page, *Powers*, 149; Dunn, "Jesus and Holiness," 188.

155. Marcus notes linguistic ties between this passage and Exod 14:1—15:22; *Mark 1–8*, 348–49, and Klutz point out the similarities between this story and the crossing of the Red Sea: an army of demons is destroyed in the sea like Pharaoh's army was. One difference however, is that the evil spirits recognize Jesus' authority and superiority; *Exorcism Stories*, 111–14.

156. Boyd equates the "divided" kingdom with the army of Satan and views tying up the strong man as an act of war; *God at War*, 181.

157. There are echoes in this story of the "strong man" prophesied by Isa 49:24–25; Garrett, *Demise of Devil*, 45; Twelftree, *Name of Jesus*, 107–8; Brandon, *Satanic Conflict*, 64. There was also a hope in apocalyptic literature that Satan would be bound (E.g., 1 En 10:4–6; T. Lev 18:12); Marcus, *Mark 1–8*, 274.

158. *Deō* (bind) also meant "forbid" in rabbinic literature; BDAG 221. Cullman describes Satan as being tied with a long rope; *Christ and Time*, 198. Brandon more specifically suggests binding is a metaphor for Satan being defeated but not completed vanquished; *Satanic Conflict*, 64.

159. *DDD* 154–55; BDAG 173; Marcus, *Mark 1–8*, 272; Page, *Powers*, 100–101; Bell, *Deliver Us*, 12, 90. It was translated Beelzebub ("lord of the flies") in the Vulgate probably as a parody. However, *zebul* also has associations with disease, divine dwelling, and the earth. Humphries believes the term defies definitive interpretation; there is no proof that the Jews considered Beelzebul as ruler of demons; *Christian Origins*, 13–22. Twelftree notes the co-text of this passage, the restless demon, in which the house represents a person; thus in the Beelzebul passage, the "house represents Satan's domain from which his property—the person—is taken"; *Name of Jesus*, 114; see also Brandon, *Satanic Conflict*, 61.

160. It has parallels with the ancient world beliefs that demons roam about in the

analogy implies that boundaries need to be maintained to prevent evil spirits from returning; demons are not content to remain in their appropriate zone, but seek to enter people. One's "space" needs to be not only separated from evil but also filled with goodness; i.e., the absence of evil does not imply the presence of good.[161] The demon is also described as unclean and Bryan suggests that this story is associated with Levitical house purification rules.[162] There is a return of uncleanness to its origin, the desert, but it has a propensity to return. Furthermore, because of the co-text regarding the "wicked generation," transgression both signifies impurity and causes it. As in *Yom Kippur*, uncleanness and sin are associated; both need to be removed. In this passage, there is an intertwining of sin, demonization, and impurity, and images of cleansing and setting boundaries on evil.

Boundary metaphors are also evident in the nature miracles. Jesus rebukes a storm in the same manner as a demon (Matt 8:18–27; Mark 4:36–41; Luke 8:22–25).[163] The sea symbolized evil, plus demons were thought to cause storms.[164] This story echoes creation and exodus stories in which God pushes back evil-forces/water. Like Jesus' exorcisms, only a simple command is needed. Hendrickx believes that the stilling of the storm surpasses both healing and exorcism stories, which were not unknown in the ancient world.[165] Interestingly, this event occurs just prior to the Gerasene exorcism, signifying a theological link between storms and demons.[166] Other passages suggest a connection between exorcisms,

---

desert and desire to enter humans; Page, *Powers*, 172; Thomas, *Devil, Disease*, 182.

161. Cf. Matt 12:30; Thomas, *Devil, Disease*, 183–85. Twelftree points out that, in Luke, this passage follows the suggestion that those against Jesus scatter; therefore those who are cleansed need to be gathered as followers of Jesus; *Name of Jesus*, 98.

162. Lev 14:33–53; Bryan, *Israel's Traditions*, 161–63; see also Klutz, *Exorcism Stories*, 131.

163. The only other use of the word, *pephimōso*, is in a command to a demon (Mark 1:25); Twelftree, *Miracle Worker*, 70; *Name of Jesus*, 116; Thomas, *Devil, Disease*, 210–12.

164. E.g., T. Sol 7.5, 22.2, 9–15; Page, *Powers*, 150–55; Bell, *Deliver Us*, 109. Klutz describes Jesus as "master of the storm demon"; *Exorcism Stories*, 148–49. He also notes the association between demons and the Red Sea in Pss 74:13–14; 89:9–10; 104:4–9, 107:23–30; and T. Sol. 23.2; 25:5–7. There is also an association with the story of Jonah; Marcus, *Mark 1–8*, 337–40; Telford, *Mark*, 101; Twelftree, *Miracle Worker*, 71.

165. Indicated by the disciples' comment: "even the wind and the sea obey him"; Hendrickx, *Miracle Stories*, 71–72.

166. Klutz, *Exorcism Stories*, 148–49; Bell, *Deliver Us*, 110. The story of Jesus walking on the water is theologically similar (Matt 14:22–33; Mark 6:45–52; John 6:15–21); Marcus, *Mark 1–8*, 424–29.

cleansing, and limiting evil. The story of the boy with seizures occurs immediately after the transfiguration (Matt 17:14–20; Mark 9:14–29; Luke 9:37–43.). As with Jesus' baptism, there is movement from sacred to profane space.[167] There are also purity associations: the boy looks like a corpse (Mark) and the spirit is "unclean" (Luke). John's description of Jesus as the good shepherd and the gate for the sheep (threatened by wolves, perhaps symbolizing evil forces) can be viewed spatially: the boundaries for sacred space are defined by Jesus, who maintains the separation of good and evil (John 10:1–18). Koester comments, "boundaries play their proper role when they protect the sheep from the wolf, and . . . forces that threaten to take away faith, life and dignity."[168] And Jesus as the gate indicates the boundary is not sealed, allowing the inclusion of newcomers.

The Gospel passages examined in this section illustrate the continuity between sacred space and sacred actions. Jesus goes out from the holy center into all the areas associated with evil—the desert, the darkness, the sea, evil spirits, unclean people, and unclean places. He cleanses the cosmos and sets boundaries on evil; healing, exorcism, and cleansing are intertwined. Sacred space and entrance into it is redefined and made more inclusive; human boundaries are flexible. However, boundaries for the demonic are reinforced (evil is separated). People are healed and cleansed from demonic impurity; demons are relocated. In Israel's cult, impurity could result in the departure of divine presence. Yet, Jesus, the Word of God filled with the Spirit, reasserts his divine presence by going out from sacred space into profane space. He expels demons, thus expanding sacred space. This is further evident in Jesus' death and resurrection.

ATONEMENT

God deals with human sin and cosmic evil through Jesus' teachings and actions as described above. However, arguably more important is how atonement is achieved through Christ's death and resurrection. There are multiple biblical metaphors for this including legal, financial, sacrificial, political, military, and familial.[169] Theologically, four theories are well

167. Page, *Powers*, 160–62. Klutz also comments on the spatio-temporal relation between the two events; *Exorcism Stories*, 179.

168. He believes this story "pictures the community in terms of its center and boundaries"; Koester, *Word of Life*, 199–200.

169. E.g., Marshall, *NT Theology*, 38–51. Ladd notes Messianic, atoning, substitutionary, sacrificial, and eschatological themes; *Theology*, 185–92. This section focuses

known: conflict-victory (*Christus Victor*, associated with Irenaeus and Aulen), satisfaction (associated with Anselm), moral influence (associated with Abelard), and penal substitution (associated with Calvin). Atonement theology is complex, raising questions about the Trinity as well as violence. The last three, or classical theories, focus on humans, thus do not assist in understanding evil spiritual forces. Boyd argues against the anthropocentric emphasis of classic atonement theories, endorsing the *Christus Victor* theory. He claims Jesus's death and resurrection aimed "to defeat once and for all his cosmic archenemy, Satan, along with the other evil powers under his dominion, and thereby to establish Christ as the legitimate ruler of the cosmos."[170] Unlike other models, *Christus Victor* incorporates evil spirits but perhaps attributes excessive power to the devil, and is usually associated with warfare language. Concerns have recently been expressed about violent imagery in many atonement theories. For example, Brad Jersak notes that although the cross involved violence, it was not the violence of God,[171] and Sharon Baker states that, in the crucifixion and resurrection, "God in Christ interrupted the cycle of violence with divine love."[172] Although the crucifixion involved violence, Jesus did not participate in it but surrendered to it, and some nonviolent theories have recently been proposed.[173]

---

on the Gospels' portrayal of atonement, but most theologians discussed here incorporate Pauline theology. Finlan believes the English term "atonement" is problematic because it emphasizes forgiveness and reconciliation whereas it originated in cultic, expulsion rituals; *Cultic Atonement Metaphors*, 1, 2, 51.

170. Boyd, *God at War*, 240, 249. "the work of the cross was about dethroning a cruel, illegitimate ruler and reinstating a loving, legitimate one: Jesus Christ" (246). Interestingly, Boyd uses little warfare language in his discussion of the atonement.

171. Jersak, "Nonviolent Identification," 19. Plus, substitutionary theories imply God to be beholden and retributive (23–24) see also Borg "Executed by Rome," 158. Gunton lists the problems with viewing Jesus as a victim: legal metaphors are isolated, texts are interpreted literally, and a dualism between God and Jesus is created. He defines the actuality of the atonement: "whether the real evil of the real world is faced and healed ontologically in the life, death and resurrection of Jesus"; *Actuality of Atonement*, 165–68.

172. She prefers the term "anti-violent" to nonviolent; Baker, "Repetition of Reconciliation," 223, 227.

173. Jersak endorses identification and solidarity over substitution, the cross being an act of love which overcame violence. He suggests that John's image of the serpent on a pole portrays Christ as "great physician and grand antivenin for what happened in Eden" (John 3:14–17; cf. Num 21:8–9); "Nonviolent Identification," 31, 53; Pinnock believes the legal model should not dominate atonement theology, and emphasizes love and relationship, "union with God"; *Flame of Love*, 108–11, 152–55. See also Sanders, *Atonement and Violence*.

However, there are also ways of viewing the atonement based on spatial and cultic metaphors. As discussed above, Jesus goes out into all areas associated with evil and transforms them. Finally, he enters the realm of death and overcomes it too. Biblical symbolism in the passion narratives is abundant. First, there is exodus symbolism. N. T. Wright insists the last supper was some type of Passover, indicating that a new exodus was happening through Jesus, the people of God being restored.[174] Jesus identified the bread as his body and the wine as his blood (Matt 26:26–28), and his death accomplished what the temple normally would.[175] Second, there is darkness imagery. Judas betrays Jesus at night, and darkness covers the earth at Jesus' death, symbolizing forces of evil that surround Jesus during his last three hours.[176] As before creation, darkness covers the earth for a short while; Barth states that, for a brief moment, Genesis 1:2 becomes real.[177] Hence the overcoming of darkness symbolizes a new creation. Third, the earthquake and the tearing of the curtain represent the destruction of the old creation and the beginning of the new. Beale thinks that the "rending of the veil indicates both a cosmic and cultic reality: the in-breaking destruction of the old creation and inauguration of the new creation . . . introduces access for all believers to God's holy presence in a way that was not available in the old creation."[178] Fourth, the water (cleansing, life-giving) and blood (associated with purification rituals) that flows

174. Wright, *JVG*, 554–62, 594–610. He believes that Satan was the real enemy behind Rome. Coloe also views Jesus' death as a new Passover; *God Dwells*, 194–96.

175. Barker points out that when Jesus broke bread and drank wine, the "action preceded what it represented"; *On Earth*, 604–10.

176. Luke 22:53, 23:44–45 contain echoes of the plague of darkness (Exod 10:21–23); Page, *Powers*, 131.

177. Barth, *CD III.*1.109. Similarities can also be seen in the flood and Red Sea narratives in which (evil) water covers the earth. A parallel can also be made with Jesus descending into the waters (also symbolic of evil) at his baptism, rising out of the water and heading immediately to overcome Satan in the desert. Marcus believes Jesus' baptism anticipates his death: Jesus is sent out by the Spirit/breathes out his spirit; heaven is torn/the curtain is torn; God/the centurion proclaim this is the "Son of God"; *Mark 1–8*, 164.

178. He notes that the veil was embroidered with stars, symbolizing the cosmos; thus its ripping, along with the darkening of the sun and the earthquake, implies the destruction of temple and cosmos. Creation imagery is present in Jesus' promise to the criminal that they would be together in paradise, implying Jesus' death to be a new pathway to Eden; Beale, *Temple*, 189–90. Malbon thinks that the tearing of the curtain indicates a complete breakdown of the sacred/profane distinction; *Narrative Space*, 126, 139. However, it can also be viewed as a loosening of the barriers. Jesus redefines purity, but sacred/profane boundaries still exist.

from Jesus' side symbolizes the gift of life, even before his resurrection is evident (John 19:34). From a cultic standpoint, death is unclean, yet Jesus cleanses.[179] Through his death, he transforms the forces of evil and gives life and light. Kerr notes that Jesus' body "becomes the source of living waters—the Spirit."[180] Finally, there is cultic symbolism in Jesus' death and resurrection with respect to *Yom Kippur*. Substitutionary atonement theories often portray Jesus as the scapegoat, taking our sins upon himself; for instance, Barker suggests that Jesus, like a priest, bore and absorbed the impurities of the people; he transferred sins to himself.[181] However, this is only one aspect of the imagery: Jesus can also be seen as cleansing and separating sin rather than absorbing it; when Jesus touches impure people, he imparts purity to them, not taking impurity upon himself. James Alison argues that Jesus should instead be identified with the high priest who offers himself as a gift to the people. In *Yom Kippur*, the high priest "becomes an angelic emanation of YHWH" who sprinkles the blood of the sacrificed goat to remove the people's impurities. Thus the Lord himself emerges from sacred space to cleanse people and restore creation. It is not about humans trying to satisfy God, but about God taking the initiative in breaking through towards humans, outward from the center.[182] Alison's analysis fits well with a spatial model of atonement.

179. Jesus refers to his death as the "smiting" of the shepherd (Zech 13:7), a passage surrounded by purity imagery: Zech 12:10—the "one whom they have pierced"; Zech 14:8—living waters. Jesus fulfills this OT purification prophecy; Newbigin, *Light has Come*, 258–59; Ladd, *Theology*, 185. Flowing water was also associated with eschatological justice (Amos 5:24); Barker, *On Earth*, 56; Kerr, *Temple*, 239–44.

180. Kerr, *Temple*, 245. Koester similarly notes that living water demonstrates Jesus' death as the source of life; *Word of Life*, 144–46. Barker applies this imagery cosmically: "the water restored the earth, the spirit recreated the earth, the blood/life healed the earth"; *On Earth*, 57. Jesus' death gives further life because dead are resurrected at the moment of his death (Matt 27:52–53).

181. As opposed to giving them to Azazel; cf. Exod 28:38; Isa 53:1–9; Matt 8:17; 2 Cor 5:21; 1 Pet 2:24; Barker, *On Earth*, 55. Dunn agrees, although he emphasizes the metaphorical nature of the sacrifice; *NT Theology*, 79–89. Finlan prefers the term "curse transmission ritual" for *Yom Kippur* because it focuses on the transfer of sin; Paul conflated models of sacrifice, noble death, scapegoat, and redemption price, developing new meaning from mixing metaphors and emphasizing God's generosity, not wrath; *Cultic Atonement Metaphors*, 73, 95, 190–91.

182. Alison, "God's Self-Substitution," 168. He also equates the atonement with the inauguration of creation. This is evident in John 20:1–14: Mary, Peter, and John look for Jesus on the first day of the week, in the garden, and see two angels (like the cherubim of Eden) (171). Gunton somewhat similarly thinks that Jesus, by entering the human sphere of pollution, can bring humanity as an offering to his Father; *Actuality of Atonement*, 161.

Hence the atonement can be viewed in continuity with the OT and Jesus' earthly ministry. Jesus, as light in the darkness, becomes the new creation, putting boundaries on the forces of evil. Jesus, as the new temple, redefines the way in which healing and purity are achieved, and the cosmos cleansed of evil. Jesus, as the locus of divine presence, breaks into earth from heaven and reaches out from the holy of holies to the impure, the demonized, darkness, and death. Through the sacred action of his death, he provides a new way in which the effects of evil can be cleansed, and the power of evil limited. Access to the holy of holies and authority over evil is open to all who believe. This spatial view of the atonement can complement other atonement theories.

Finally, there is an association between Jesus' exorcisms and his death. Twelftree claims that, in John (12:31), the crucifixion can be viewed as "the grand cosmic exorcism," and, for Luke (11:20), the "defeat of Satan was taking place in Jesus' exorcisms."[183] Jesus connected exorcisms and eschatology for the first time. The cross is surely central to understanding the limitation of evil. As Barth asserts, nothingness is the reality that brought Jesus to the cross where, paradoxically, nothingness was defeated. On the cross, its true nature was revealed, and, through Jesus, God had the last word.[184] Bell more deliberately relates exorcism and the atonement. He views the work of Christ as the reversal of the work of the devil, portrayed first in the exorcisms and second on the cross. Exorcisms, using a narrow definition, only apply to a minority of people, yet redemption applies to all. Therefore, Bell suggests considering exorcism in a wider sense as the healing of all disordered humanity. In this perspective, all require deliverance, if not exorcism in a narrower sense.[185]

183. Twelftree, *Name of Jesus*, 134–35, 196. Twelftree argues for a two-stage defeat of Satan: the first occurring in the exorcisms (a preliminary binding), the second at the eschaton. The exorcisms do not represent a final defeat of evil, suggested by the demons' questioning, "before our time." Yet Satan's defeat is also futuristic evidenced in the parable of the weeds. Twelftree admits some ambiguity regarding the time of the final defeat, and tension between defeat in the exorcisms and at the eschaton. He also points out the difference between the Synoptics, in which exorcisms were tied to the defeat of Satan, and John, in which the defeat of Satan occurs primarily on the cross; *Exorcist*, 114–15, 220–24; *Name of Jesus*, 135, 169, 196. Twelftree is unclear where the crucifixion fits into these stages, and does not incorporate other imagery regarding the defeat of Satan. As discussed previously, the "angelic fall" is complex, and cannot be easily consigned to separate "stages."

184. Barth, *CD III*.3.305, 312, 363–64.

185. Bell, *Deliver Us*, 64, 319–31. He believes the link between exorcism and the cross is especially prominent in Mark. Like Twelftree, he views Jesus' death as the

It is helpful to view exorcisms and the cross in continuity with each other and with the rest of the Bible. Bell's suggestion of a broad conception of exorcism fits better with a nonlinear view of the defeat of evil. Perhaps the defeat of evil is a progressive and continual process. This concurs with the view of the kingdom of heaven as dynamic and nonlinear. In spatial terms, Jesus' actions in both the exorcisms and the crucifixion involve going out from sacred space into profane space to reestablish boundaries on evil, and cleanse people from its effects. On the cross, Jesus subversively overcomes evil forces. He provides the way, the truth, and the life to those who are in darkness, or under the influence of evil. The atonement can be viewed as both putting boundaries on evil and cleansing the cosmos. However, there is no evidence that evil spirits can be atoned for. This is further evident in Jesus' teaching regarding evil and eschatology.

Eschatological Separation of Evil

Jesus often teaches about the fate of those who oppose God and the final separation of good and evil. This language fits well with the theme of setting boundaries on evil. Hades ("hell," the LXX translation of Sheol) is spatially opposed to heaven, and a place where sinners are sent (Matt 5:22; 11:23; Mark 9:43–47; Luke 10:15; there is a great chasm between heaven and hell [Luke 16:26]; like Sheol, it has metaphorical gates [Matt 16:18]). Wicked people, those who refuse the invitation of the kingdom, will be separated from the righteous, and doomed to death or outer darkness (Matt 24:48–51; "outer darkness" is unique to Matthew [8:12, 22:13, 25:26–30] and is clearly spatial). The parable of the weeds teaches that evil will ultimately be permanently separated from the children of God (Matt 13:24–30, 36–43).[186] Getty-Sullivan states that, despite the implication that nothing can be done about evil, hearers likely understood that "weeds need to be controlled," "but they cannot be eliminated."[187] Although Boyd interprets this parable within a warfare framework, the language is

---

"great" exorcism. The Holy Spirit demonstrates the defeat of the devil in both exorcisms and the cross, which are both historical and meta-historical, or existential (326–28).

186. Page, *Powers*, 117. Marcus points out the parallels with 4 Ezra 4:26–29: both suggest an intermediate period of perplexity prior to the harvest; *Mark 1–8*, 296. There are similar separations described in the parables of the dragnet and the goats and sheep (Matt 13:47–50, 25:31–46); Page, *Powers*, 117–18; Getty-Sullivan, *Parables* 110–11.

187. Getty-Sullivan *Parables*, 60–64. Wenham similarly notes that the co-existence of evil with good does not necessitate the acceptance of evil; *Parables*, 58–65.

of separation, not battle.[188] John's depiction of Jesus as the true vine also contains spatial imagery; those who do not abide in him are cut off and thrown into the fire (John 15:1–10; also Matt 7:19; 13:40–42, 50; 25:41). Thus, at the eschaton, sacred and profane space will be completely separated. Until then, the separation and cleansing of evil continues, but powers of evil have the ability to infiltrate sacred space; life in this "already-but-not-yet" age is experienced as grey, shadows sometimes obscure the light. Consequently, humans have much responsibility in this complex world.

Human Responsibility

This section briefly summarizes the gospel teaching regarding human responsibility, framing it in spatial terms. Humans can be described as accountable for belief, obedience, following Jesus, and setting boundaries on evil.

BELIEF AND DISCIPLESHIP

In Israel's cult, ritual made possible the forgiveness of sin and participation in the divine presence. With Jesus, ritual becomes obsolete. He provides access to the divine presence and forgiveness of sins. Many of Jesus' teachings are directional: "follow me" (Matt 4:19; 19:21; Mark 1:17; 10:21; Luke 5:27; 9:23; John 1:43; 21:19), "enter" the kingdom or the narrow gate (Matt 5:20; 18:3, 8, 9; Mark 10:15, 23–25; Luke 13:24; 18:17; John 3:5), and choose the "way" (Mark 10:52; John 14:4–6). Like exorcism language, the language is flexible and there are no formulae. Spatial concepts suggest that faith, like the kingdom, is dynamic (e.g., the man who believes but asks for help with his "unbelief" [Mark 9:24], the disciples who do not have "enough" faith [Matt 17:20]). Green defines the goals of discipleship using semi-spatial terms: "To align oneself with Jesus, who aligns himself . . . absolutely with God," and Newbigin uses dark/light metaphors to highlight the choice humans have: "either come to the light or turn away into the darkness"; the only way to move from the "realm of darkness and death into the realm of light and life" is through Jesus.[189]

188. Boyd, *God at War*, 222.

189. Green, *Luke*, 49; Newbigin, *Light has Come*, 104–6. The Synoptics also contain the admonition to be "filled with light" (Matt 6:22–23; Luke 11:33–36). Löning and Zenger note that in human experience, darkness is the refusal of light; *To Begin with*, 60. Koester similarly notes that the transition between spheres of evil and God is depicted as "coming to the light" (John 3:20); *Word of Life*, 137.

Entry into this new sacred space is no longer determined on ethnic grounds but requires one to have faith, believing in Jesus, the Christ, the Son of God.[190] People need to hear and see, and respond to the signs with faith. There is a call to choose a direction—life or destruction.[191] Interestingly, disciples are given *exousia* ("authority") to believe (John 1:12).[192] There are also indications that the new community of followers becomes the new temple (Mark 14:58; John 2:19).[193] Entry into sacred space is made possible through the Holy Spirit who evokes faith. John (3:3–8; 14:16; 15:26—16:15) teaches that one needs to be born of the Spirit, and the Spirit is promised to indwell believers, conveying the divine presence and leading into truth.[194] Boundary markers for the community of faith are less legalistic but more rigid, internal rather than external (Matt 5:17–48; 15:10–20; Mark 7:15–23). Following Jesus is associated with repentance of sin, especially in Jesus' pronouncement of the kingdom (Matt 4:17; Mark 1:15). In spatial terms, turning to Christ involves turning from evil. Sin is at times personified—it defiles (John 8:34), requires purification (Matt 15:18, 19; Mark 7:20–22), and can perhaps cause disease (Luke 5:24), since forgiveness and healing are sometimes associated. As in the OT, there is a complex relationship between sin and the demonic. At times, Jesus conquers sin in the same manner he conquers evil (John 1:29). In the parable of the sower (Matt 13:18–23; Mark 4:13–20; Luke 8:11–15), the boundaries between evil influences and human-will are blurred.[195] Interestingly, faith is not required for exorcism, although those who demonstrate faith are commended.[196] Faith is diverse and dynamic.

190. *Pisteue* (believe, have faith) occurs thirty-six times in John (cf. Matt 17:20; Mark 11:22); Ladd, *Theology*, 306–7. Healing, a blessing associated with sacred space, is often, though not always, related to faith (e.g., Matt 15:28; Luke 5:20; 8:48; 17:19); Gaiser, *Healing in the Bible*, 177.

191. Koester, *Word of Life*, 163–64. Wenham notes the OT echoes in the background of Matt 7:13–14, e.g., Jer 21:8; *Parables*, 193–96.

192. Brown, *John 1–12*, 11; Koester, *Word of Life*, 137.

193. Dunn, *NT Theology*, 107–8, 117. Dunn summarizes: Jesus pushed back the boundaries around Israel, and challenged the boundaries within Israel; it is now acceptance by God that determines membership of God's people; "Jesus and Holiness," 110–11.

194. Witherington and Ice, *Shadow of the Almighty*, 128; Koester, *Word of Life*, 137, 147.

195. Marcus, *Mark 1–8*, 312.

196. The Canaanite woman's daughter is freed from her demon and praised for her faith (Matt 15:21–28; Mark 7:24–30). Bell notes that exorcisms are performed on the unbelieving community; *Deliver Us*, 332.

An interesting question is whether cultic grades of holiness are evident or relevant with the advent of Christ. Bryan suggests that, since Jesus refused to grant meaning to ritual purity, the eschaton must be already here, therefore, grades of holiness are obsolete.[197] Yes, Jesus radically redefines and expands purity, but sin and evil persist in the world, and faith is complex (implying graded holiness). Ladd, with reference to the "restless demon" story, points out that healing is only preliminary to God taking "possession"; a person may be clean but empty. Exorcism can be seen as a negative side to salvation, the indwelling of the Spirit of God the positive side.[198] Ladd implies that grades of holiness/wickedness persist. Sorensen more extensively argues that exorcism is preliminary to reception of the Holy Spirit; the NT language of indwelling spiritual possession is used to describe people's relation to both divine and demonic.[199] Since physiological possession causes impurity, exorcism restores demoniacs to a clean but profane condition. The invocation of the Holy Spirit elevates the person further from a clean to a sanctified condition. Sorensen implies that grades of holiness persist. This idea accords with the nature of faith as dynamic, and the complex interplay between divine grace, human responsibility, and demonic influence.

Humans who choose to turn away from Christ and towards evil experience consequences. The results of sin are the same as in Genesis: expulsion from sacred space and separation from God. As Marshall states, "to disobey God and rebel against him is to break the personal relationship with God, and thus in a sense to cut oneself off from him. Thus it is appropriate for God to respond to those who cut themselves off from him by excluding them from his kingdom."[200] Entry into sacred space is made possible through the Holy Spirit, therefore those who reject the Spirit (the "unforgivable" sin) do not have access to the realm of God. Humans are aided by the Holy Spirit, but nevertheless have responsibility in the direction they choose: outward towards the evil periphery, or inward, following Jesus, the way, the truth, and the life—the new sacred space.

---

197. Bryan, *Israel's Traditions*, 187.

198. Ladd, *Theology*, 75.

199. Sorensen, *Possession*, 153–67.

200. Marshall, *NT Theology*, 33.

Those who respond to Christ with faith are given further responsibility—to assist in cleansing and setting boundaries on evil. This aspect of discipleship is often phrased in warfare language (e.g., Köstenberger and Swain describe the mission of Jesus' followers as "spiritual warfare").[201] However, it can be also phrased in the language of authority and boundary-setting. Disciples are given authority over demons and disease, and instructed to proclaim the gospel (Matt 10:1; Mark 3:14, 15, 6:7; Luke 9:1, 2; 10:19). As in Jesus' ministry, the expansion of the kingdom correlates with removing evil from sacred space. Disciples are advised to pray for protection from the evil one, and their success has cosmic consequences, evident in Jesus' vision of Satan "falling" (Matt 6:13; Luke 10:18; see discussion in chapter 4). They are advised not to delight in their authority over demons, but that they belong to the kingdom; their success is attributed to the Holy Spirit. Sorensen contrasts "divine possession" with its antithesis, demonic possession: The Holy Spirit enables one to heal, demons cause illness; the Spirit counters weakness, evil spirits debilitate; the Spirit restores life, demons try to kill; the Spirit establishes community, evil spirits cause separation.[202] The Holy Spirit and evil spirits are in binary opposition, the center contrasted with the periphery. Jesus' disciples are commissioned to discern the difference; to be filled with and spread the light of Christ.

Counteracting Evil

To summarize, God, in Jesus, deals with evil not primarily through warfare, but through cleansing and setting boundaries on evil. Sacred space correlates with sacred action: Jesus embodies sacred space plus extends it. He operates through the authority of the Holy Spirit, calmly instructing demons to move back to profane space where they belong. He also enters into death, in order to overcome the effects of evil. At the eschaton, there will be a final and complete separation between God and evil. Until then, however, humans have responsibility to follow Christ and continue to set boundaries on evil through divinely appointed authority.

201. Although they do not elsewhere use military imagery; Köstenberger and Swain, *Father, Son,* 158. Similarly, N. G. Wright refers to the "army" of disciples; *Dark Side,* 169.

202. Sorensen, *Possession,* 146. Welker also contrasts the Spirit, who causes gathering and strengthening of individuals and community, with evil spirits that cause isolation and disintegration; *God the Spirit,* 201.

Using spatial conceptions, humans live in grey zones between the central light of Christ and the darkness of the evil periphery. Previously evil could only be limited through the rituals of Israel's cult. Now, through the work of Christ, evil can be limited by humans through proclaiming the kingdom of heaven, spreading the light, and exercising authority over demons.

A spatial view of the Gospels informs our understanding of evil. Boundary metaphors affirm that evil has potential to infiltrate intermediary space and cause harm, but do not consider evil a force that is equal to God. Cleansing metaphors, in continuity with cultic metaphors, imply that evil is like dirt, matter out of place that needs to be relocated. Healing metaphors suggest that evil is infectious, like a virus or parasite that afflict humans; it is secondary and has little reality apart from its dependence on a host. Cultic metaphors allow for a conception of Christ not as involved in warfare, but as voluntarily coming down from heaven to provide a new method for dealing with sin and evil. Recognizing the interrelation of these metaphors, as well as the association between exorcisms and the cross, provides a broader view of evil.

A Model for Conceptualizing Evil

The question now is whether the cultic model developed in the previous chapter is applicable to the depiction of evil in the Gospels. Here I summarize the preceding discussion, then refine and evaluate the model.

Summary

The work of Christ can be viewed in cosmic and spatial terms. The semantic domain of evil in the Gospels includes darkness, impurity, death, hell, sin, and demons. These metaphors are in continuity with the OT, and perhaps best understood as chaotic, disorganized forces with reduced ontology (compatible with ideas developed in previous chapters). This can be explained by divine absence: without the Holy Spirit who provides life, order, and reality, they have little substance, existing only at the periphery of godly reality, "encircling the world." Unfortunately, they can violate their boundaries and attain reality; consequently, they are experienced as very real to those afflicted. They are exposed for what they are by Jesus Christ.

The semantic domain of holiness includes ultimate reality, light, life, truth, holiness, purity, heaven, and of course, Jesus. In the OT, God could not look upon evil, and severe sin led to the withdrawal of his presence.

However, through Christ, God enters into evil zones to offer forgiveness and healing, and an exit for those trapped in such space. The Son of God bursts into the world as the new sacred space: he replaces the temple, becoming the locus of divine presence. He is the light that shines in the darkness, showing the way and bringing life. In his ministry and death, he goes out from the center of holiness to cleanse and reestablish boundaries on evil; he will finalize the separation of evil at the eschaton. He operates with authority, not violence. Purity is redefined, and ritual is replaced by belief in Christ. In the cult, ritual functioned to separate clean and unclean; now Jesus separates only demonic evil, and welcomes all humanity to his kingdom. All those previously "outside the camp" are invited in, and demons that have violated their boundaries are relocated to the periphery. Jesus' holiness and purity is a power that cleanses; his kingdom a palpable force. He sifts and sorts, separating demons and humans, and then heals humans; he renews creation and restores order. Cleansing, healing, and exorcisms are interrelated, and the atonement can be understood through metaphors of cleansing and boundaries. The Gospels teach that humans are responsible for belief and following Jesus, as well as participating in setting boundaries on evil, through the authority of the Spirit. Sacred space is maintained through sacred actions, which are dynamic and continual.

Recall that spatial metaphors are universal, and that metaphors depict reality. Jesus and his disciples, through an authoritative word, effect a real change: demons are relocated to the periphery of reality, and humans are healed. However, intermediate zones remain. There are humans who refuse to follow Jesus, and some who are healed but do not necessarily follow Jesus; there is evidence that evil spirits are able to violate their boundaries. The relationship between sin, impurity, and the demonic is complex, which is why the world is best described as grey. Intermediate space still receives the light emanating from the sacred center, but is also influenced by the black periphery.

Model

The cultic model is applicable to the gospel portrayal of evil with a few modifications. The zones are similar, but boundaries are redefined, using internal, not external, criteria. Sacred space is dynamic and flexible, and boundaries are flexible, therefore it is perhaps more accurate to blend this model with Figure 6.2, as well as imagining it in three dimensions, with heaven at the top. However, for ease of conception, the following will be used to illustrate the further development of the model:

Figure 6.3: A Model for Conceptualizing Evil

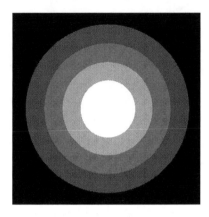

In this model, five zones can still be discerned. The center, formerly the holy of holies, is extended in meaning to include the person of Jesus and the Holy Spirit. All other space is dependent on it, and its holiness radiates outward. With the tearing of the veil, access to sacred space is not restricted to the priest but open for all who believe. The periphery is still inhabited by the devil and demons, those who reject divine grace. Without the light of Christ, it is qualitatively less real. Intermediate zones are dynamic, comprising varying degrees of faith and gradations of holiness. Those who reject divine invitation perhaps live close to the periphery; they may choose evil, but the invitation to join the kingdom is open. Disciples of Jesus possible live close to the center. Given the tendency of humans to sin, we only have glimpses of heaven, brief experiences of the center. All grey areas can be understood as neutral (or perhaps good in a general manner since they receive divine grace) but influenced by both light and dark (the light of course able to overcome the darkness).

Unfortunately, it is difficult to distinguish between zones, and humans may move between zones, choosing to turn towards God or evil. This accounts for the degrees of grey in the world at any one time. Disciples of Christ are responsible for extending the kingdom, as well as maintaining boundaries on evil, through direct commands to demons, or indirectly, through healing, cleansing, and proclaiming the gospel. Obedience perhaps strengthens boundaries on evil; disobedience may cause loosening. Thus confession and repentance can reverse the process, cleansing the cosmos and returning evil to its place. As in the cultic model, Christ's light and life flow out into all reality; but evil spirits sometimes violate their boundaries, usually influenced by human choice, and spread darkness and death.

Evaluation

This model provides a framework for understanding reality that is applicable to the realm of evil spirits. Its multiple metaphors offer more information than simple literalistic language. This model is inclusive yet uncomplicated and fits with the Gospels' portrayal of evil. It has the same advantages over a warfare model discussed previously, and is more comprehensive, not being limited to exorcism passages but able to incorporate other texts, being compatible with OT depictions of evil, and including both spatial and action metaphors. This model allows for a conceptualization of reality that can guide our actions within it. God/Jesus/the Spirit is at the center of the cosmos, the source of all life, and the means by which the world is preserved and order maintained. Evil forces are relegated to the outer realms and, although they have some power for destruction, it is minimal compared with the power of God. Thus God's sovereignty is affirmed. He does not battle demons, but merely assigns limits. He does not condemn but simply rejects that which rejects him. This model is less dualistic than a warfare model; shades of grey allow for nuances in the biblical texts and experience. It fits the biblical portrayal of evil as a complex interplay between human sin and diabolic evil. This model emphasizes human responsibility, incorporating ethics while affirming the potential reality of evil forces. It emphasizes the role of the Holy Spirit, and provides some insights into the nature of evil spirits. Finally, this model is potentially more accessible than a warfare model since spatial/boundary metaphors are readily comprehensible.

This model offers an improvement over the cultic model mostly because of its blurred, flexible boundaries, which better represent textual ambiguities and life experience. In addition, it reflects the inclusion of all peoples. But there are some challenges: Conceiving of Christ and his ministry in spatial terms may mitigate the significance of his work and his gracious gift to creation, and the exact nature of the boundaries is difficult to ascertain, being multifaceted and elastic. Like all models though, this one is not meant to be perfect but to provide a framework for conceptualizing evil and an alternative model to "spiritual warfare."

7

CHURCH: A COMMUNITY
AMIDST CHAOS

The Holy Spirit looks upon you and discovers its very own dwelling place.[1]

THE FINAL BIBLICAL THEME to be discussed, the church, is especially relevant to Christianity today. The daily news is filled with stories of crime, disasters, and suffering; consequently followers of Christ need to know how to understand, discern, and counteract evil. Yet ecclesiology is seldom examined with a focus on the church's role in setting boundaries on evil spiritual forces. "Spiritual warfare" literature has relied heavily on certain texts in the epistles, making this theme important. Teaching regarding the church, or community of Christ-followers, is primarily found in the epistles, with contributions from the Gospels, Acts, and Revelation. This chapter explores the theme of the church, particularly with respect to conceptualizing and counteracting evil. As in previous chapters, continuity with creation, Israel's cult, and Christ is emphasized, and a broad, diachronic approach employed.[2] First, I examine NT metaphors for evil, with a focus on sin and the powers, and then discuss sacred space in terms of the indwelling Spirit and the church. I explore sacred

---

1. Hildegarde of Bingen, Hymn "O Felix Anima."

2. Following Dunn; *NT Theology*, viii–ix and Marshall; *NT Theology*, 711–26. Marshall points to the context of the church's mission (the story of God the Father, and humans), the center of the mission (Jesus Christ as the saving event) and the community of mission (the renewed Israel). He suggests that the diverse passages in the NT testify to the same complex reality.

actions with respect to divine initiative and human responsibility, including non-warfare metaphors for dealing with the demonic. Human roles include walking in the Spirit, discerning evil, and setting boundaries on evil through preaching, healing, and exorcism. Finally, I evaluate the relevance of the model developed in previous chapters.

Profane Space

Evil forces in opposition to the church are described with terms similar to those used in the OT and the Gospels; there is overlap of the multiple metaphors within the semantic domain of evil and, again, no cohesive demonology. Influences from ANE religions, ancient Judaism, and Greco-Roman culture are apparent.[3] The light/dark dualism of the Second Temple Period (and John's Gospel) persists.[4] Sin is understood broadly and overlaps with the world and the flesh, all in binary opposition to divine reality. Some terms unique to Paul appear, usually described as "the powers." These will be discussed and evaluated in turn.

Satan and Evil Spirits

As in the Gospels, Satan is called the "evil one" (Eph 6:16; 1 John 2:13, 14; 3:12; 5:18, 19), and is associated with a serpent (2 Cor 11:3;[5] Rev 12:9),

---

3. Baal is not to be worshiped (Rom 11:4); Beliar is named (2 Cor 6:15; the LXX translates Belial as *anomos*, "lawless," 2 Thess 2:9); death is personified (Rom 5:14; 1 Cor 15:26, 54–55; Rev 20:13, 14), the sea has sinister connotations (the devil thrown into the lake of fire, Rev 20:10; Forsyth, *Old Enemy*, 294–96); Greek gods were worshipped (Apollo, 1 Cor 1:12; 3:4–6, Artemis, Acts 19:24–35, Zeus and Hermes, Acts 14:11–13); Athens was full of idols (Acts 17:16); magic was practiced (Acts 8:9, 19:19); magicians were equated with the devil (Acts 13:6–10); and Hades and Tartarus are mentioned (Rev 1:18; 6:8; 20:13, 14; 2 Pet 2:4; Hades being both a place and a god of the underworld in Greek mythology; Tartarus being the place the Titans were imprisoned; Russell, *Devil*, 135–36, 143).

4. It is antithetical to light and Christ (Rom 13:12; Eph 5:8; 1 Pet 2:9; 1 Thess 5:5; 1 John 1:5, 2:8); associated with sin (2 Cor 6:14; 1 John 2:9, 11), evil spirits (Eph 6:12), powers (Col 1:13), and hell (2 Pet 2:4, 17); it is the destination of evil spirits and sinners (Jude 6, 13). Darkness appears to have power (Col 1:13; Eph 6:12) and Christians are encouraged to "lay aside the works of darkness" (Rom 13:12); Forsyth, *Old Enemy*, 248; Klawans, *Impurity and Sin*, 153. With respect to the Johannine Epistles, J. C. Thomas comments that this darkness is not neutral, but a "sinister force that is active in its malevolence"; 1 *John*, 107.

5. A possible reference to Apoc Mos; Forsyth, *Old Enemy*, 268.

a dragon (Rev 12:9), a wild animal (1 Pet 5:8, echoing Ps 22:13), a beast (Rev 13:1–18; 16:14), death (Heb 2:14), and darkness (Acts 26:18; 2 Cor 6:14, 15). He is described as a liar (2 Thess 2:9), deceiver (Rev 12:9), adversary (1 Tim 5:14–15; 1 Pet 5:8), and accuser (Rev 12:10). His activity is primarily towards followers of Christ: he tempts (1 Cor 7:5; 1 Thess 3:5), incites sin (Rev 12:10; Acts 5:3), oppresses people (Acts 10:38), blocks the way (1 Thess 2:18), has the power of death (Heb 2:14), and can hold people captive (1 Tim 3:7; 2 Tim 2:26; Rev 2:10). Uniquely, he can disguise himself as an angel of light (2 Cor 11:14). He blinds the minds of unbelievers preventing them from seeing Christ.[6] As in John's Gospel, Satan is described as the god of this world (2 Cor 4:4) and ruler of the "power of the air" (Eph 2:2), and the world is under his power (1 John 5:19); again there is no evidence this rule is legitimate.[7] Although on occasion God uses Satan as an instrument of grace (Paul's "thorn in the flesh," 2 Cor 12:7), usually Satan works in opposition to God. At the eschaton, the devil will be destroyed; his defeat attributed to Christ (Rev 20:10; Heb 2:14; 1 John 3:8).

Terms unique to the non-Pauline epistles include false prophets and antichrists. Peter and Jude claim false teachers deny Christ, malign the truth, cause division, lack divine authority, and are devoid of the Spirit (2 Pet 2:1–3; Jude 19).[8] John describes many antichrists who deny Jesus is the Christ (1 John 2:18–22).[9] The abundance of terms for evil in Revelation is unsurprising given the apocalyptic genre of this book. In addition to the devil, there are blasphemous beasts, a false prophet who spews evil spirits, and a leader named destroyer (Rev 9:1–3, 11; 11:7; 13:1–18; 16:13; *Abaddon* and *Apollyon* are the Hebrew and Greek terms for destroyer). They mostly arise from the abyss.[10] A Satanic "trinity" of the dragon, the

6. Another image of darkness (2 Cor 4:4); Page, *Powers*, 184; Bell, *Deliver Us*, 239. The "god of this age" who has "blinded eyes" is a possible reference to Sammael; Forsyth, *Old Enemy*, 208–9.

7. The "powers of the air" could be a collective term for spiritual forces over which Satan rules; an abstract noun referring to realm; a spiritual climate; or the actual air, reflecting the widespread ancient belief that demons dwell in the air; Page, *Powers*, 184–86.

8. Skaggs points out these false teachers have violated boundaries, like the lawless one; *1 Peter*, 114, 154, 168.

9. Thomas notes that the "spirit of the antichrist" should not be viewed as equal and opposite to the Spirit of Christ; *1 John*, 125, 205.

10. 1 En 88 describes it as a bottomless cavern for the imprisonment of evil spirits; Skaggs and Benham say the abyss is fathomless; *Revelation*, 98.

beast, and the false prophet is sometimes described.[11] Yet, as is typical, the terms overlap, especially evident in Revelation 12:9 where the dragon is also called the ancient serpent, the devil, Satan, and the deceiver of the world. Skaggs and Benham suggest that these terms are a "graphic description of the supernatural demonic powers released to torment humanity."[12] Collins argues that Revelation is best understood in the framework of the combat myth, pointing out the universal and systematic nature of rebellion.[13] Certainly, the imagery (not necessarily the framework) of the combat myth is present in Revelation, which affirms previous arguments about the importance of viewing these terms as a cluster of metaphors for evil in binary opposition to God.

Multiple metaphors are used in the epistles to refer to demons. The terms used in the Gospels reappear: evil spirit (Acts 19:15), demon (1 Tim 4:1; Jas 2:19), and unclean spirit (Rev 18:2). Demons are again associated with wild animals (snakes and scorpions, Rev 9:3; locusts, Rev 9:3–10; foul birds and hateful beasts, Rev 18:2), act violently (Acts 19:16), and recognize Jesus for who he is (Jas 2:19).[14] Like Satan, they deceive people and inspire false teaching (1 Tim 4:1; Jas 3:15; 1 John 4:1–3).[15] Demons are seen to underlie idolatry especially in Paul's teaching. Although he argues that idols are "not real" and are worthless besides Christ, the one true God, they have reality as the habitation of demons (1 Cor 8:4–6; 10:14–21; 1 Thess 1:9; cf. Acts 14:15; Rev 9:20).[16] Since pagans sacrifice to demons, eating such food meant the Corinthians were participating in idolatry and aligning themselves with demons; drinking the cup of demons is incompatible with drinking the cup of the Lord.

11. E.g., Unger, *Biblical Demonology*, 173.

12. Skaggs and Benham, *Revelation*, 101.

13. Collins, *Combat Myth*, 76, 83, 166, 232. The LXX translates Leviathan as dragon. Specifically the "dragon" connotes the chaos monster, the abyss is like the deep, and Satan's rebellion against God relates to the battles between Marduk and Tiamat, Zeus and the titans, and Baal and Mot (discussed in chapter 4).

14. James' statement that demons shudder in their belief in God echoes the Greco-Roman magical belief that demons tremble in the presence of a phylactery (PGM IV: 3014–18).

15. Fee, *Empowering Presence*, 761–71.

16. Schlier, *Principalities and Powers*, 26; Marshall, *NT Theology*, 259; Ladd, *Theology*, 440. Fee also notes that in antiquity the eating of cultic meals was common, and gods were thought to be present since the meals were in their honor. Such feasts were likely also associated with sexual immorality. He believes Paul is following the OT teaching that pagan "gods" were actually demons (Deut 32:17); *Corinthians*, 360–474.

Like the OT, the NT affirms the reality of evil spirits but places them in proper perspective. In the epistles, the power of ANE and Greek "gods" is greatly reduced compared with other ancient cultures. It is not clear that demons have individual personality and names, and there is no conclusive evidence of a unified demonic kingdom headed by Satan. In fact, there is a story of demons fighting other demons (the seven sons of Sceva, Acts 19:15–16), which suggests disunity rather than unity. And the variety of terms used indicates disorder; disorganization rather than organization (Satan and demons are not always clearly distinguished; recall that Jesus is described as healing those afflicted by both the devil and demons). The description of demonic forces as locusts fits particularly well with the suggestion made in chapter 3 that such beings are best modeled by chaos-complexity theory. Again, it seems more helpful to consider these terms as a cluster of metaphors within the semantic domain of evil, inhabiting profane space and existing in opposition to God, holiness, and sacred space.

The Powers

The much debated Pauline "powers" also belong in the semantic domain of evil. These include *archai* (principalities or rulers, 1 Cor 15:24; Eph 1:21; 3:10; 6:12; Col 1:16; 2:10, 15),[17] *exousias* (authorities, 1 Cor 15:24; Eph 1:21; 2:2; 3:10; 6:12; Col 1:16; 2:10, 15),[18] *dunameis* (powers, Eph 1:21),[19] *kosmokratores* (world rulers, Eph 6:12),[20] *pneumatika* (spiritual forces, Eph 6:12),[21] and *stoicheia* ("basic principles," NIV; "elemental spirits," NRSV, Gal 4:3, 8; Col 2:8, 20);[22] the first two being the most common. These terms frequently cluster (Rom 8:38; Eph 1:21; 6:12; Col 1:16). At times the

17. These are generally considered spiritual beings, *DDD* 77–80.

18. Probably a cultic epithet denoting celestial forces; *DDD* 124; BDAG 352–53; *exousia* can also refer to the sphere in which power is exercised.

19. *DDD* 267–70; BDAG 262–63.

20. *DDD* 908–9; BDAG 561. This term is unique to Paul; in pagan literature it usually referred to gods, thus is most likely a reference to the demonic world.

21. BDAG 837.

22. Ladd suggests these be interpreted as similar to one of Paul's views of *kosmos*—the whole complex of human relationships; *Theology*, 442 (see discussion below). H. D. Betz claims the "elements" represent demonic forces, consistent with the Greco-Roman-Jewish syncretic worldview of demonic entities of cosmic proportions; *Galatians*, 204. Arnold claims the *stoicheia* are always malevolent and should be viewed as similar to the principalities and powers used elsewhere by Paul; "Domain of the Powers," 1, 55–76.

powers refer to human institutions (Rom 13:1), other times they depict spiritual forces in opposition to God (1 Cor 15:24; Col 1:16; Eph 6:12), and sometimes they are ambiguous, or neutral (Rom 8:38; Eph 3:10). The meaning is usually discernible from context. The powers are created and implicated as rulers of the world, although they have limited knowledge (Col 1:16; 1 Cor 2:6, 8). They are associated with Satan, darkness, and deceit, and can hold people captive, even though they are weak (Gal 4:3, 8, 9; Eph 6:12; Col 2:8). Like Satan, the powers are doomed to destruction (1 Cor 2:6; 15:24; Col 2:15). However, as Wink puts it, Paul's language is "imprecise, liquid, interchangeable, and unsystematic."[23] Ladd suggests that Paul deliberately used "vague and varied terminology" as a polemic against other religions, which elaborated precise angelic hierarchies.[24] In general, the NT demonstrates little theoretical or speculative interest in the powers and there is no effort to differentiate or "arrange the various names or appearances systematically" (unlike popular "spiritual warfare" literature, and in keeping with conclusions in previous chapters regarding the chaotic nature of evil).[25]

Despite the flexible language, there is consensus that the powers represent evil celestial forces. Thomas Yoder Neufeld, for example, describes them as "diverse manifestations of a seamless web of reality hostile to God."[26] Bell helpfully points out that the powers demonstrate that evil spirits can be disembodied and personal, especially given the similarities between "power of the air" (Eph 2:2) and "heavenly powers" (Eph 6:12).[27]

---

23. Wink, *Naming*, 9. Most of these terms have a wide semantic range; there are no biblical antecedents, and few extra-biblical references (e.g., 1 En 61:10). Arnold suggests Paul drew from a reservoir of terms and "lumped all manner of spirits together"; *Powers of Darkness*, 54, also 38–39, 218. Twelftree similarly argues that Paul widened the scope of demonic language to include the powers (explicit in Acts 13:9–12, 16:16–18); *Name of Jesus*, 57–77; see also Dumbrell, *Search for Order*, 298–99; Fee, *Empowering Presence*, 725.

24. Ladd, *Theology*, 441–42. Cullman suggests that the powers are not explained by Paul since he assumed their identity would be known; *Christ and Time*, 191.

25. Schlier, *Principalities and Powers*, 13.

26. Yoder Neufeld, *Armour of God*. Boyd in particular believes that Paul views the powers as personal transcendent beings which, because they operate at the societal level, are more sinister than individual demons. Boyd claims these beings exert influence over general aspects of creation; *God at War*, 271–76. Interestingly Barth affirms the reality of the powers as "lordless forces"; *CD IV*, 214–17.

27. Bell, *Deliver us*, 237, 345–47; he concurs the powers are hostile with underlying demonic activity.

Some scholars associate the powers and demons.[28] Many "spiritual war-fare" advocates not only insist the powers are demons, but also claim that they represent a hierarchy of evil spirits. For instance, Boyd believes the powers are organized hierarchically;[29] and Clinton Arnold thinks the terms may refer to a hierarchy of beings, but admits we cannot know how they are ranked.[30] Attempts to speculate about hierarchies pay insufficient attention to the semantic flexibility and ambiguity of biblical language; I do not believe there is enough evidence to make conclusions regarding demonic hierarchies. These authors perhaps attempt to "fill the gaps" with speculation. However, at the other end of the spectrum, some deny that the powers represent evil forces.

Likely influenced by the demythologizing program of Rudolph Bult-mann (discussed in chapter 1), many scholars argue that the powers are not evil beings. Hendrik Berkhof was one of the first to claim that Paul viewed the powers as "structures of earthly existence."[31] Wesley Carr goes even further in his assertion that the powers are not evil, but represent the neutral host of God; and at the time of Paul, there was "no demand from the world for release from powers."[32] Wink also advocates a demy-thologizing approach to the powers, although he is more nuanced. He thinks the ancients only personified evil forces because they had no other way of describing them and that it is "impossible" for moderns to "be-

28. Schlier believes they are a "collective spirit of evil" that do not just have power, but "exist as power"; *Principalities and Powers,* 19; Fee suggests Paul has taken over and pluralized the language of powers and made it equivalent with evil spirits; *Empowering Presence,* 725; Page claims the devil and powers form a "united front"; *Powers,* 188.

29. Boyd, *God at War,* 274–76. He supports this by noting that *archai* referred to high-level angelic beings, 1 and 2 Enoch describe angelic hierarchies and the culture of the time viewed the air as the dwelling place of evil spirits.

30. Arnold, *Powers,* 98–99. The powers are part of Satan's kingdom and Satan rules over them (80, 92, 3). Arnold is more conservative in his later work; *3 Crucial Questions,* 39. He claims there is biblical evidence for the existence of territorial spirits (Deut 32:8, 17; Ps 96:5; 106:37–38; Dan 10:13, 20; Rev 2:12; 12:7–9), but advises caution in how they are dealt with, suggesting through prayer only (150–60, 185–98).

31. Berkhof, *Christ and the Powers,* 23. G. B. Caird similarly defines the powers as "demonic forces of legalism"; *Principalities and Powers,* 51.

32. Carr, *Angels and Principalities,* 111, 175. He supports these conclusions by asserting that in Jewish literature evil was focused on one being and there is no evidence of demonic powers. He apparently ignores the prolific literature of Second Temple Judaism and, curiously, names this "one" being Satan, Belial, Mastema, and the dragon (37, 122, 128). Carr's work has been criticized as unsound by Arnold; "Exorcism of Ephesians 6:12," 71–87; Wink, *Naming,* 23–24, and Fee, *Empowering Presence,* 725.

lieve in the real existence of demonic or angelic powers." Wink suggests using "power" in its broadest meaning as referring to both heavenly and earthly, human and divine, spiritual and political, invisible and structural aspects.[33] The powers are a "generic category referring to the determining forces of physical, psychic, and social existence"; they consist of an outer, visible manifestation (e.g., political institutions), and an inner spirituality; they "must become incarnate, institutionalized or systemic in order to be effective."[34] Wink believes the powers are good; idolizing them is the issue. Although good, the powers are fallen, and therefore must be redeemed; he insists all three aspects must be held together.[35] Yong follows Wink to a degree in arguing that evil spirits (including the powers) are nothing if not incarnate. As discussed earlier, he also suggests that the demonic and the powers are only emergent, not independent realities.[36]

Some scholars attempt to find a middle ground in viewing the powers as both human and spiritual, or human instruments of spiritual forces.[37] Noll is unconvinced that the powers are synonymous with demons, suggesting they can be viewed as "angels on the way to ruination." In Paul's theology, "principalities and powers stands for a worldwide web of human affairs grounded in a spiritual hierarchy."[38] N. G. Wright argues that the form of the powers is not that of "free floating or abstract entities that maraud in the heavenlies and attack individuals" but that they manifest through social structures. He thinks Paul was likely referring to

---

33. Wink, *Naming*, 4, 7, 10–11, 39, 100. He follows the depth psychology of Carl Jung. For a recent engagement with his work see Gingerich and Grimsrud, *Transforming the Powers*.

34. Wink, *Unmasking*, 4. Wink advocates social justice and nonviolent resistance to overcome the effects of the powers in social institutions; *Engaging*, 175–275. Interestingly, in a later work, Wink relates the powers to contemporary science, especially field theory and the interconnectedness of all things; "New Worldview," 17–28.

35. Wink, *Naming*, 77; *Engaging*, 10. R. Webber agrees that Satan works through societal structures to pervert the good and the powers will be redeemed since they were initially good, and are only influenced by the demonic; *Church in the World*, 27, 29, 39, 286–90. I believe they are both being somewhat speculative as there is no clear biblical evidence for the redemption of evil powers.

36. Yong, *Beyond the Impasse*, 129, 138; *Spirit of Creation*, 173–225.

37. E.g., Cullman, *Christ and Time*, 191. Page notes a difference though in that believers are to fight against powers but submit to human rulers (Eph 6:12; Titus 3:1); *Powers*, 263.

38. Noll, *Angels of Light*, 138, 147. Wa Gatumu has a similar definition: the supernatural powers are "a heuristic reference to the personal or impersonal invisible forces outside or within human beings"; *Pauline Concept*, 128.

both spiritual entities and social structures, but the concept of powers is helpful in putting the demonic on a broader canvas; relating individual to political, and heeding the social nature of evil, while recognizing its individual aspects.[39] These observations accord with my argument regarding the large semantic domain of evil, which also includes human sin and the world (discussed further below). Thus multiple biblical metaphors, including the powers, are used to depict evil in binary opposition to holiness. Although scholars do not usually interact with metaphor theory, most recognize the diversity of terms known as "the powers." Heinrich Schlier believes the various names refer to a phenomenon that is similar to the demons, and cannot be described with only one term.[40] Wink does not use metaphor theory but recognizes the importance of mythic language in describing "the powers"—without myth, "we have no other form of access to this realm." He points out that the category of power in the ancient world was mythic and there was not a sharp distinction between material and spiritual, earth and heaven. So NT authors could substitute terms such as "sin," "flesh," and "death" for "Satan," "Azazel," and "demons" common in Jewish apocalyptic literature. [41]

Wink is correct to acknowledge the fluidity of the Pauline language, correct in viewing the powers in opposition to God, and is to be commended for emphasizing human responsibility. However, I believe he goes too far in his demythologization and psychologization of the powers, minimizing or even dismissing experiential accounts of horrific evil, and minimizing the biblical idea of evil as opposition.[42] Recall that metaphors can depict supersensible reality. Recognizing, as Schlier and others seem to, that the rulers, authorities, principalities, and powers are a cluster of metaphors used to describe evil forces in opposition to God allows for improved conceptual clarity and consistency. Given the

39. N. G. Wright, *Dark Side*, 133, 138, 139, 143; see also Yong, *Discerning*, 103.

40. "We are dealing with a single phenomenon which is diffused, and which concerns us in various manifestations"; Schlier, *Principalities and Powers*, 16, 17.

41. Wink, *Naming*, 4, 100, 102, 142, 145.

42. He also does not account for pre-humanoid evil or experiential reports of disembodied spirits, and claims demons are a "late arrival," ignoring the OT and Second Temple Literature (the second point also noted by M. Dawn, *Powers, Weakness*, 16). Arnold criticizes Wink for ignoring the context of the powers, especially Hellenistic magic, imposing post-Enlightenment thought onto the biblical text, and making linguistic errors by generalizing rather than considering the context of each text; *Ephesians*, 50; *Powers*, 200; Noll also faults Wink for not distinguishing between God and Satan, or angels and powers; *Angels of Light*, 25; Bell criticizes Wink for failing to recognize that evil spirits can be disembodied; *Deliver Us*, 345–46.

overlap, interchangeability, and semantic range of the terms, this approach is consistent with biblical evidence and with other biblical metaphors for evil that are similarly vague, such as "chaos." I agree with Wink that the powers should be conceived of broadly, but would add that, as powerful metaphors, they depict the reality of the evil spiritual realm. Finally, the multitude of terms suggests that the powers are characterized by disorganization, consistent with previous conclusions. They are analogous to uncleanness as a miasmic force. Perhaps, drawing on chaos-complexity theory, the powers can be viewed as self-organized demons.

Sin

A prominent concept in the epistles, which fits in the semantic domain of evil, is sin. The most commonly used term is *hamartia* (to miss the mark or depart from a standard).[43] As Mark Biddle remarks though, one English word fails to do justice to the wide range of meaning implied in the multiple biblical words.[44] Sin is associated with deceitfulness (Heb 3:13), lawlessness (1 John 3:4; 2 Thess 2:7–10), iniquity (Rom 4:7; 6:19; 1 John 3:19), darkness (Rom 13:12), and death (Rom 5:12–21; Col 3:5; Jas 1:15; 5:20; 1 John 5:16). It is compared with a weight (Heb 9:28, 12:1; 1 Pet 2:24; cf. Ps 38:4; Isa 1:4; 5:18), can enslave people (Rom 3:9; 7:14, 25), and is at times depicted as a superhuman power (Rom 6:12–23; 7:8; Heb 3:13; Jas 1:15). Sin is a ubiquitous reality, affecting Jews, Christians, and pagans alike (Rom 3:9; 5:12; Rev 2:9, 13; 3:9). Those who claim to be without sin are described as liars and without God (1 John 1:8–10; 3:4–6).[45] The concept of sin overlaps with impurity, the flesh, the law, the world, and the demonic.

As in cultic theology, sin defiles and requires purification (Acts 22:16; Rom 6:19; 1 Cor 6:11; Heb 1:3; 2 Pet 1:9; 1 John 1:7, 9).[46] In fact,

43. BDAG 50–51. Other terms include *parabasis* (transgression of a boundary), *parakoe* (disobedience), *paraptoma* (violation of moral standard), and *agnoema* (sin committed in ignorance); BDAG 766–67, 770, 13 respectively; Smith, *Willful Intent*, 284. Thomas notes that *hamartia* occurs seventeen times in the Johannine Epistles, and its verb form ten times; demonstrating its importance to that community; *1 John*, 78.

44. Biddle, *Missing the Mark*, xiv.

45. Smith; *Willful Intent*, 289–310; Biddle, *Missing the Mark*, 35, 64; Thomas, *1 John*, 85, 154.

46. Sin as defiling points to the need for both baptism and the cleansing work of Christ; Marshall, *NT Theology*, 676; Smith, *Willful Intent*, 307; Biddle, *Missing the Mark*, 127.

Christ's purpose is described as cleansing (Heb 1:3). Impurity is in binary opposition to holiness (1 Thess 4:7). Paul particularly relates impurity to sexual sin and idolatry (Rom 1:21–25; 6:19).[47] As impurity is associated with the demonic, so is sin. Gordon Fee points out that since idolatry was associated with demons, there is a need for cleansing from this spiritual pollution.[48] Like the priestly conception of impurity as a dynamic, potent force, sin can be described as a "vicious and destructive power."[49] Sin in the NT is not limited to specific acts but, like impurity, is broader, a nebulous force in opposition to God. Paul associates sin with "flesh" and juxtaposes it with new life in Christ and the Spirit (Rom 8:5–10; 1 Cor 3:3; Gal 5:19–21; 6:8; Eph 2:3). Indeed flesh and Spirit are incompatible.[50] Flesh is related to the law, the world, and death.[51] It is usually considered to represent the whole fallen nature of humanity, or creaturely, unregenerate life.[52] Fee believes it to be an eschatological, not anthropological, concept, referring to the old age, or those outside of Christ.[53] He thinks that the flesh is a prime target for Satan. Thus flesh relates to sin and the demonic, and exists in spatial opposition to God.

In the epistles, sin is often described as a violation of the law, or disobedience (Rom 2:1–19; Eph 5:6; 2 Thess 2:1–12; Heb 4:11; 10:28; Jas 2:8–13). The association between sin and lawlessness is complex.[54] Although knowing the law gives knowledge about sin, even Gentiles are without excuse (Rom 1:18–32; 3:1–31).[55] As in the OT, idolatry is a particularly bad sin; it is associated with sexual immorality and idolaters

47. Klawans, *Impurity and Sin,* 150.

48. Fee, *Empowering Presence,* 338.

49. Smith, *Willful Intent,* 313; recall similar descriptions of sin in chapter 5.

50. *Sarx* versus *pneuma.* Fee argues that the Spirit and the flesh are not in a constant state of warfare, but belong to two different ages; those in the flesh are apart from Christ; *Empowering Presence,* 434, 817–20.

51. Esp. evident in Rom 8:1–17; Fee, *Empowering Presence,* 438, 504, 541, 555.

52. Smith, *Willful Intent,* 299; Ladd, *Theology,* 509–14.

53. Fee, *Empowering Presence,* 95, 817–20. It is likely a multivalent metaphor representing both those outside of Christ and the "sinful" part of Christians, who also struggle with the flesh.

54. Specifically in 1 John 3:4. However, Paul is clear the law does not equal sin (e.g., Rom 7:7). Thomas believes there is a progression from sin to lawlessness; *1 John,* 154–55; see also Smith, *Willful Intent,* 300.

55. Biddle suggests that Paul expands the concept of the law to include the human conscience. Disobedience refers not so much to breaking the Mosaic law, but violating the relationship with God, as manifest through Christ. Furthermore, wisdom, which allows one to live in obedience, is freely available; *Missing the Mark,* 38–44, 56–57.

will not inherit the kingdom. Idolatry not only violates the law (repeating the recurrent sin of the Israelites) but seeks to replace God with "no thing," or demon worship (Acts 15:20, 29; Rom 1:18–27; 1 Cor 8:1–22; Gal 5:20; 1 Pet 4:3; Rev 9:20).[56] This connection between idolatry, lawlessness, and demons is evident in the "man of lawlessness" (1 Thess 2:9) and the turning over of sinners to Satan (1 Cor 5:1–5; 1 Tim 1:20). In the future temple, the antichrist acts like a god and disobeys biblical laws (2 Thess 2). In addition, the law can be misinterpreted (likely due to the influence of Satan) and idolized (Rom 7:8; 1 Tim 1:8). When this occurs, it functions like the devil, destroying, deceiving, tempting, accusing, acting as a stumbling block, and holding people captive (Rom 4:15; 7:6, 11, 23; 2 Cor 3:6).[57] The law is often personified and associated with the flesh and death (Rom 7:4–6; 8:3, 7; 1 Cor 15:56; Gal 5:15–21).[58] Lawlessness is in binary opposition to God and righteousness (2 Cor 6:14; 2 Thess 2:1–12). Death is another metaphor associated with sin (Rom 5:12–21; 7:13; 1 Cor 15:56; Col 3:5, Jas 1:15; 5:20).[59] Death, like sin, is personified and can be considered an "invading sovereign power" (Rom 5:12–14; 2 Cor 4:12; Rev 6:8).[60] It is described as an enemy (1 Cor 15:26), is opposed to life and love (1 John 3:14) and thus can be conceived in binary opposition to God. Similar to the "unpardonable sin" in the Synoptics, there are hints in the epistles of a sin that is unforgivable and leads to death (Heb 10:36–21; 1 John 5:16).[61] Death, like sin and the devil, has been and will be destroyed (1 Cor 15:26; 2 Tim 1:10; Heb 9:26, 27).

56. Marcus. "Idolatry," 152–64; Fee, *First Corinthians*, 370–468; Smith, *Willful Intent*, 319. With respect to Revelation 9, Skaggs and Benham remark that idolatry and its associated demon worship was prevalent at the time; originating in the refusal to worship God (Rom 1:18–32); rebellion against God leads to a distortion of the truth; *Revelation*, 103.

57. Smith, *Willful Intent*, 297; Bell, *Deliver Us*, 239–40; Fee, *Empowering Presence*, 761–71.

58. Caird suggests that sin, death and the law operate as a team and cannot be separated, and that the law is like one of the powers; *Principalities and Powers*, 41–45; see also Fee, *Empowering Presence*, 504.

59. Death is likely used by Paul metaphorically. Smith describes death as spiritual separation from God; *Willful Intent*, 291, 305; Caird points out that sin separates people from God; death involves a final separation; *Principalities and Powers*, 91; recall discussions on death in chapters 4 and 5.

60. Smith, *Willful Intent*, 290.

61. The first passage refers to continued willful sin; Ladd, *Theology*, 632. The second is unexplained, but proposals include intentional sin, blasphemy against the Holy Spirit, unrepentant sin, sexual immorality (Corinthians), and apostasy (Hebrews); it is likely a metaphorical, spiritual death; Thomas, *1 John*, 169–71.

The *kosmos* ("world") is also often associated with sin. Although at times the world is God's good creation (Col 1:16; Heb 1:2; Acts 17:24), it is usually described as sinful, in need of judgment and salvation (Acts 17:31; Rom 5:12, 13, 8:19–22; 1 Cor 6:2; 2 Pet 1:4; 2:20; 1 John 2:2, 16; 4:14).[62] The world is similar to the OT "nations" and is set in opposition to the kingdom of God.[63] It is commonly associated with the flesh and the devil, and can be conceived of as under the domain of evil powers, including sin, impurity, and death (Rom 5:12–14; Gal 4:3; Eph 2:2; Jas 1:27; 2 Pet 1:4; 1 John 4:1–6).[64] Followers of Christ are not to follow the ways of the world (Rom 12:2), the spirit of the world is contrasted with the Spirit of God (1 Cor 2:12), and those who love the world are enemies of God (Jas 1:27; 4:4, 5; 1 John 2:15, 16, 4:1–6). Thomas describes *kosmos* as the portion of humanity hostile to Jesus, and the place where false prophets and antichrists are active;[65] Clinton Arnold believes *kosmos* represents structural evil;[66] and Smith suggests it refers to a collective concept of sin, demonic in nature.[67] Hence it appears that *kosmos* approximates chaos, both in the biblical and scientific sense. Recall that scientific chaos is semi-structured, supporting Arnold's view. *Kosmos* and chaos have a broad semantic range, and overlap with other metaphors for evil. In the Bible, both exist in opposition to sacred space.

The relationship between sin and the demonic is definite but complex. As mentioned, Satan is associated with lawlessness and misconceptions of the law, as well as the world and the flesh; demons are connected with idolatry and impurity. Smith notes that *hamartia* ("sin") is close

---

62. Paul intertwines cosmology and anthropology; the creation "groans" while it awaits redemption; Jackson, *New Creation*, 155–69. Ladd notes five meanings of *kosmos*: the universe, the inhabited earth, humanity, humanity in hostility to God, and the whole complex of human relations; *Theology*, 437–38.

63. Webber, *Church in the World*, 279–82.

64. Arnold, *Powers*, 124; *3 Crucial Questions*, 32–37; Bell, *Deliver Us*, 233. This accords with John's description of the devil as ruler of the world (John 12:31). With respect to James, D. Lockett believes purity language functions figuratively to delineate the worldview of Christ-followers in opposition to the profane world; *Purity and Worldview*, 116–20, 130–40.

65. Thomas, *1 John*, 209. He further notes, with respect to 1 John 5:4, that the world's "opposition to God and association with the evil one is very clear" (245).

66. Arnold, *Powers*, 203; like the views of E. Lewis (discussed in chapter 3) and Burnett (discussed in chapter 4).

67. Although this does not preclude individual responsibility; Smith, *Willful Intent*, 328.

in meaning to *ponēros* ("evil one").[68] Sin as collective, or a superhuman power akin to an impure force, is close to the idea of evil spiritual forces; thus Bell describes it as a "diabolical power."[69] Sin on an individual level is also connected to the devil. The story of Ananias is explicit: his sin is described as originating both from Satan and from within his heart (Acts 5:3, 4).[70] Those who commit sin are called children of the devil (1 John 3:8) and accused of dwelling in a "synagogue of Satan" (Rev 2:9, 13; 3:9).[71] Babylon, whose sins are heaped high, is a dwelling place of demons (Rev 18:2, 5). Like demons, sinners are to be rebuked (1 Tim 5:20). The devil is a source of temptation, which may lead to sin (1 Cor 7:5; 1 Thess 3:5).[72] Sin, such as conceit or anger, allows one to fall under the condemnation of the devil, or gives the devil a foothold (Eph 4:26, 27; 1 Tim 3:6).[73] Sin as an entry point for the demonic is a common idea in popular "spiritual warfare" literature, as discussed previously. N. G. Wright comments that deliverance "will not avail if we do not deal with the supply lines of sin that enable the power of darkness to replenish itself parasitically from the human race."[74] This idea of sin as a doorway to the demonic is intuitive and supported by many texts, but it is wise to remember that not all sin has demonic origin, and that evil spirits can afflict those who are without sin. Sin also originates with evil desires (Jas 1:13, 14), and Satan can afflict people without sin (e.g., Job, and children in the Gospels, presumably with no or little sin, who were demonized). This is similar to the relationship

68. Smith, *Willful Intent*, 284. *Hamartia/hamartolos* always refers to sin against God, therefore is evil.

69. Although he notes it may not be at the same level of demonic forces; Bell, *Deliver Us*, 233–35. This idea is relatively common: O. Pfleiderer thinks sin in Paul is a demonic spirit; *Primitive Christianity*, 1.280 (quoted in Ladd, *Theology*, 512); Dumbrell believes there is a nexus between sin and the powers; *Search for Order*, 298–99.

70. His sin is primarily lying to the Spirit which fits with the Johannine description of Satan as the father of lies (John 8:44). Smith describes sin as "slavery to falsehoods fostered by Satan"; *Willful Intent*, 301.

71. Smith notes, with reference to 1 John, that those who sin have the same nature as the devil; *Willful Intent*, 305. Thomas similarly observes that "those who sin reject the Son and identify with the Devil"; *1 John*, 273. Skaggs and Benham think the synagogue of Satan refers to Jewish people engaged in evil activities; *Revelation*, 36, 49.

72. Although a person's own desires may also lead to sin; 1 Tim 6:9; Jas 1:14, 15. Smith thinks Satan is the original source of temptation and seduces people into sin, either by putting evil within hearts or drawing out evil desires that are already there; *Willful Intent*, 332, 383.

73. Fee, *Empowering Presence*, 712–13.

74. In his critique of Wink; Wright, *Dark Side*, 57.

between illnesses and the demonic discussed previously; some sin/illness, but not all, is caused by evil spirits.

The above observations indicate the large semantic domain of sin: impurity, the flesh, lawlessness, death, the world, and the demonic. Sin exists in binary opposition to purity, the Spirit, obedience, life, the kingdom of heaven, and holiness. This antithesis is explicit in the Pauline (righteousness/lawlessness, believer/unbeliever, Christ/Beliar, light/dark, and God/idols; 2 Cor 6:14–16) and Johannine (light/dark, Christ/antichrist, God/world, children of God/children of the devil, truth/lies, and love/hate; 1 John 1:5–10; 2:8–11, 15–23; 3:7–10; 4:1–6; 5:18, 19) literature. With respect to Paul's writings, Fee claims that sin, the law, and the flesh are intertwined; death is a result of sin, or following the flesh; all are hostile to life, God, and the Holy Spirit.[75] In terms of John's Epistles, Thomas points out that fellowship with God is impossible for those who walk in darkness, do not keep God's commands, or, most heinously, accuse God of being a liar; those who lie are of the devil: "connections between evil works, darkness, lies, and deception converge."[76] Arnold, drawing on both Pauline and Johannine images, suggests that the world, the flesh, and the devil represent three strands, or three equal overlapping circles that influence people away from God.[77] Clearly, there is overlap between these concepts, but I am not convinced they can even be separated in three strands. As discussed, the flesh and the world are both influenced by the devil. It is perhaps more helpful to consider these as a cluster of metaphors for sin, and the evil forces associated with it. Sin, like the demonic, is best considered a nonlinear system, not amenable to simple classification. Using the model of chaos-complexity, demons could be viewed as clustering around basins of sin; conversely, they are repulsed by holiness, obedience, and purity.

There have been attempts to summarize sin. Smith concludes that sin transcends selfishness and idolatry, and has at its root the rejection of God as God, which includes rejection of Christ.[78] Biddle views sin as mistrust of God. He is more nuanced in that he incorporates sin as rebel-

75. Rom 7:4–6; 8:5–8, 12, 13; cf. Gal 5:13–24; Fee, *Empowering Presence*, 438, 504, 541, 555, 558.

76. 1 John 1:6, 10—2.4; cf. John 8:44; Thomas, *1 John*, 76, 85, 96. Thomas claims that those who ignore the seriousness and reality of sin do so at their own peril (91); see also Smith, *Willful Intent*, 303.

77. Arnold, *3 Crucial Questions*, 32–37.

78. E.g., 1 Cor 8:12. He believes idolatry is a form of rejection of God, which seeks to replace him with an object of one's own choosing; Smith, *Willful Intent*, 301–26.

lion or arrogance as well as underachievement, or despondent passivity. Underlying both is an unwillingness to place one's ultimate trust in God as revealed in Christ. Biddle emphasizes the systemic and dynamic nature of sin: "sin's afterlife vibrates throughout the system and . . . will continue to twist existence and limit freedom" until the eschaton. He defines sin as a "system of organically related phenomena, a nexus of cause-effect-cause."[79] Understanding sin not simply as individual "wrongs" but as systemic, dynamic, and organic helps frame the multiple metaphors for sin, and also elucidates its association with evil forces. Furthermore, sin can be viewed spatially, in terms of boundary violation (one of the terms for sin, *parabasis,* in fact means transgression of a boundary, and sinners will not enter the kingdom of God, a spatial concept).[80] Frank Tupper suggests that sin is both common to human experience and an intruder into life.[81] This conceptualization illuminates the relationship between sin and the demonic; moving outside of sacred space puts one under the influence of evil forces. Few academic treatments of sin incorporate its demonic dimension, or its complex-chaotic nature. Sin, and, by association, impurity, flesh, law, world, death, and the demonic, is complex both in a semantic sense and in a scientific (chaos-complexity) sense. Viewing sin spatially, in binary opposition to sacred space, can perhaps shed light on this ubiquitous phenomenon.

Summary: The Threat to Divine Reality

The semantic domain of evil in opposition to the church (individually and corporately) includes Satan, the enemy, the adversary, the beast, the serpent, the dragon, the deceiver, demons, evil spirits, idols, lies, false prophets, antichrists, rulers, authorities, principalities, powers, darkness, the abyss, impurity, lawlessness, the world, the flesh, sin, and death. These terms intertwine and overlap, particularly the "powers," as discussed above. With respect to the Johannine Epistles, Thomas thinks it is "unlikely readers would see a rigid division between the spirit of antichrist and the spirit of deception, on the one hand, and the Devil, on the other hand." These metaphors provide multiple snapshots of the evil reality that exists in antithesis to godly reality: friendship with the world means

---

79. Biddle, *Missing the Mark,* 76, 136, 130, 136; arrogance is typically a "masculine" sin; passivity a "feminine" one.

80. BDAG 766–67; 1 Cor 6:9; Gal 5:21.

81. Tupper, *Scandalous Providence,* 137.

enmity with God (Jas 4:4); the realm of darkness is "diametrically opposed both to the realm of God and to walking with Jesus"; "lies and the truth are as irreconcilable as light and darkness, as love and hate."[82]

As in creation, the cult, and Christ, these evil forces can be considered qualitatively less real than divine reality, since profane space connotes "unreal": idols are "not real" besides God, demons are disorganized, the powers are disorderly, sin is a perversion. The depiction of evil forces in opposition to the church is compatible with previous assertions regarding their existence in profane space in binary opposition to holiness, their unreality, disorderliness, and nothingness. As before, evil spirits can be viewed as parasitic, seeking to attain full reality by violating their boundaries and intruding upon divine reality. They can be understood as chaotic, nonlinear, and dynamic, comprising multiple components, which interact with each other, lacking individuality and intelligence but with potential to self-organize into powerful forces. These evil forces continue to threaten sacred space, the church. It is into this *kosmos*, this chaos of sin, the powers, and Satan, that followers of Christ are called to minister.

Sacred Space

As in creation, the cult, and Christ, sacred space in the church is characterized by divine presence, holiness, truth, light, and life. However, it is redefined: followers of Christ are now indwelt by the Holy Spirit, described as the new temple, and are thus the locus of divine-human interaction. They are also given responsibility as the church, or body of believers. These aspects of sacred space are discussed in turn.

The Indwelling Spirit

In the Gospels, disciples of Christ are given authority to continue his ministry; John (20:22) specifically notes that they are given the Holy Spirit (in fulfillment of OT prophecy, Ezek 11:19; 36:26, 27; 37:1–14). Jesus assures his followers that the divine will be present in their midst (Matt 18:20; 28:16–20). Acts and the epistles greatly expand on the concept of believers as bearers of the Spirit, the dwelling place of God, the new temple, the new creation, and hence the new sacred space. Following the ascension of Christ, there is a spectacular outpouring of the Spirit on the day

---

82. Thomas, *1 John*, 105, 131, 208.

of Pentecost (Acts 2:1–13). This event can be seen as the establishment of a new temple: It likely occurred in the temple, tongues of fire echo OT theophanies, and it fulfills prophecy regarding the destruction and rec-reation of the temple (Acts 2:2–36; Joel 2:28–32).[83] As these Spirit-filled followers of Christ spread the gospel, others receive the Spirit and sacred space expands; in fact, a Samarian (Acts 8:12–17), Ephesian (Acts 10:34–48), and Gentile (Acts 19:1–7) Pentecost can be described in addition to the Jewish one. The gift of the Spirit is continual (Rom 5:5; 2 Cor 1:22; Gal 3:2, 14; 4:6).[84]

Later in Acts, Paul speaks about human-made structures being in-adequate (Acts 17:24). James tells how Gentiles are included in this new "temple" if they receive the Spirit by faith (Acts 15:16).[85] The Pauline epistles more explicitly claim a new temple has been inaugurated; the Spirit dwells in the community of Christ, or the new temple, as well as in individual believers (Rom 8:9; 1 Cor 3:16, 17; 2 Cor 6:16; Eph 2:19–22). The metaphor of indwelling is threefold: individual, corporate fellowship, and the universal church; those who identify with Christ become the true temple.[86] The presence of the Spirit, not the law or circumcision, is their new identity marker.[87] As the new temple, believers are to be holy, set apart for divine use. They are holy as a result of the blood of Christ and the gift of the Spirit (1 Pet 1:15–22; 2:5, 9).[88] Because their body is a temple, believers must remain pure and avoid all immorality (1 Cor 6:19;

---

83. Beale points out that in the OT God is described as filling the temple with fire and smoke (Isa 30:27–30; Exod 40:34; 1 Kgs 8:6–13); the shaking of the earth and darkening of the heavens is common "cosmic dissolution language" (e.g., Isa 13:10–13; 24:1–6; Hab 3:6–11) that indicates the arrival of a new order. He also sees a relation-ship between Pentecost and Babel; at Babel people were trying to reach heaven, at Pen-tecost the Spirit of God freely comes down from heaven and the language confusion is due to blessing, not punishment; 201–15; see also Dumbrell, *Search for Order*, 223.

84. Ladd, *Theology*, 383; Marshall, *NT Theology*, 451.

85. Beale, *Temple* 230–33; Humans are needed to fulfill the Adamic commission.

86. Beale, *Temple* 254, Ladd, *Theology*, 585; Fee, *First Corinthians*, 146–49; *Em-powering Presence*, 541, 689, 843–45. Beale notes the garden imagery in 1 Corinthians 3, which suggests an association between Eden and the temple (1 Kgs 7) and the OT background in 2 Corinthians 6, with respect to purity and divine indwelling (e.g., Lev 26:11, Isa 52:11, Ezek 11:17, 20–34, 40).

87. Although cultic language is applied to the community of believers (1 Cor 3:16; Gal 3:1–5); Fee, *Empowering Presence*, 114, 383; Barton. "Dislocating," 201.

88. They are often called saints (Rom 1:1–7; 12:1; 1 Cor 1:2; 3:17; Eph 1:4; 2:21; Col 1:22; 3:12; 1 Thess 4:7; 1 Pet 1:15); Fee, *Empowering Presence*, 116, 338; Ladd, *Theology*, 589; Barton, "Dislocating," 201; Marshall, *NT Theology*, 650.

1 Thess 4:1–7).[89] Similarly, idolatry is incompatible with existence as the temple of God (2 Cor 6:16). The holiness and purity previously associated with cultic rituals is now attained through the Spirit: "Holiness as purity is displaced and relativized by holiness as charismatic endowment."[90] Furthermore, Paul describes those in Christ as a new creation; God, who said "let light shine" at creation, now shines in hearts to give knowledge of Christ (2 Cor 4:6; 5:17; Gal 6:15; Eph 2:10).[91] It is the Spirit who gives life (2 Cor 3:6).[92] Beale asserts, "the Spirit himself is the beginning evidence of the new creation, wherein is resurrection existence and the abode of the cosmic temple."[93] The divine presence, formerly limited to the temple, now extends throughout creation. Followers of Christ are "re-created" into the divine image through the Holy Spirit (2 Cor 3:18). They now live for Christ, not themselves.[94]

John also writes about the indwelling Spirit, but uses the language of mutual indwelling, or remaining; God abides in believers through the Spirit (John 15:1–27; 1 John 3:17–24).[95] The language of indwelling (in Paul particularly) is fluid and trinitarian in that believers are described as indwelt by Christ or the Spirit of Christ as well as the Holy Spirit (Rom 8:9; Gal 2:20, 21). God, through Christ, puts a seal on his followers, giving them the Spirit as a deposit or first installment (2 Cor 1:21, 22; 5:5;

89. Beale, *Temple*, 252. Fee points out that if one's body belongs to God, uniting with a prostitute is not possible; *Corinthians*, 260.

90. Barton, "Dislocating," 199.

91. Bell comments that faith develops through the creative power of God; *Deliver Us*, 239. Fee notes the individual and corporate nature of this imagery; *Empowering Presence*, 331; Barton suggests this new creation allows for a unity that was not possible with cultic rituals in which continual separation occurred; "Dislocating," 208–10; and Jackson argues that Paul's concept of new creation is soteriological and eschatological, including individuals, the community, and the cosmos (which accords with the earlier discussion regarding the relationship between the world and sin); Isa 40–55, esp. 43:18, is likely informing Paul's theology; *New Creation*, 83–149.

92. Fee notes the echoes of Ezek 37:1–13 here; *Empowering Presence*, 304.

93. Beale, *Temple*, 258. Paul's teaching is remarkable given that the Jerusalem Temple was likely still standing at the time of his writings. Sweeney suggests that Paul was drawing on Jesus' temple action in his teaching about our earthly tent being destroyed (2 Cor 5:1, 621); similarly Paul refers to Christ as the cornerstone (Eph 2:20), which Christ himself did (Mark 12:10, 622); "Jesus, Paul, Temple," 608.

94. Fee, *Pauline Christology*, 485–87; Marshall, *NT Theology*, 294.

95. Coloe believes John's "abiding in the vine" metaphor implies "reciprocal immanence and a profound divine/human intimacy"; *Household of God*, 159; see also Thomas, *1 John*, 143, 194.

Eph 1:13, 4:30).[96] Fee claims "the believer's spirit is the place where, by means of God's own Spirit, the human and the divine interface in the believer's life."[97] Clearly the imagery has shifted and is complex. Believers both dwell in sacred space and embody that space. However, this is conditional on being steadfast in faith and filled with the Spirit (Col 1:23).[98] Unlike Christ, humans sin; the boundaries of sacred space are therefore fluid. The other complexity relates to temporal issues: the "already-but-not-yet" of the kingdom, the first installment of the Spirit. "Our citizenship is in heaven," but, as Fee notes, "empowered by the Spirit, we now live the life of the future in the present age."[99] The language of heaven is also more symbolic than cosmological. Marshall believes it includes the idea of "an invisible spiritual sphere in which the presence and power of God are experienced by people living in the world."[100]

The Temple of Israel, built and indwelt by God the Spirit, is metaphorically replaced by the community of believers (this is not a simple substitution however; God has not rejected Israel, Rom 11:1, 2). Thus, the Spirit sustains the kingdom of God. Beale explains the progression from the cultic model to the church, particularly with respect to omnipresence: The divine presence was more immanent in the holy of holies, although there was special revelatory presence; then the divine presence was in Christ, then God's tabernacling presence occurred in the Holy Spirit; those identified with Christ are now part of the temple; the center (holy of holies) is still in the heavenly realm, the holy place is the spiritual dimension that extends to earth, God's people are a kingdom of priests, the outer court is the church's physical presence in the world; thus graded holiness continues.[101] I agree with him regarding degrees of holiness, but am not

96. Fee notes that seal refers to a stamped imprint in wax, denoting ownership and authenticity; *Empowering Presence,* 807. The complex relationships within the Trinity have been much discussed. Fee suggests the fluidity of Paul's language is because his concerns were primarily soteriological, not ontological; *Empowering Presence,* 374, 590, 838. Ladd believes the indwelling of Christ and the Spirit are two aspects of the same reality; *Theology,* 530–31.

97. Fee, *Empowering Presence,* 25, 338; *First Corinthians,* 264. Furthermore, "believers are those who are not in the flesh but in *the Spirit,* inasmuch as *the Spirit of God dwells in them*"; *Empowering Presence,* 374.

98. Pinnock uses the phrase "union with the Spirit" and points to the two-way nature of this relationship; "Spirit may draw, but people must consent"; *Flame of Love,* 158.

99. Phil 3:20; Tit 3:4–7. Fee, *Empowering Presence,* 804.

100. In his discussion on Colossians; Marshall, *NT Theology,* 463.

101. Beale, *Temple,* 388–89.

convinced it can be so neatly categorized. It is perhaps better viewed with shaded, overlapping meaning. Fee provides a fitting conclusion: "Here is the ultimate fulfillment of the imagery of God's presence, begun but lost in the Garden, restored in the tabernacle in Exodus 40 and in the temple in 1 Kings 8. It is God's own presence among us that marks us off as the people of God . . . not only do we have access to the presence of God . . . but God himself by the Spirit has chosen to be present in our world in the gathered church."[102]

The Church

Matthew (16:13–18) reports Jesus' promise to build his church against which the gates of Hades will not prevail.[103] Hence the church can be seen in spatial opposition to profane space. It can also be considered the new locus of divine presence and the new temple. There is overlap with temple imagery, but other images are present. Paul uses three images for the church: family (Rom 8:29; 1 Cor 8:12; Gal 1:2; 6:10), temple (discussed above), and body of Christ (Rom 7:4; 1 Cor 12:12–31; Eph 4:4–16; Col 1:18, 24).[104] Like other sacred space, the church is characterized by purity, light, love, and truth. John describes followers of Christ as the household of God, refers to God as their Father, calls them children of God, and uses homely imagery such as foot-washing (John 8:35; 12:1–8; 13:1–20; 20:17; 1 John 3:1–10; 5:19). He describes his Father's house with many rooms, suggesting a mutual immanence between Father/Son and Jesus/believers, made possible through the Spirit (John 2:16; 14:2).[105] There is intertwining of household and temple imagery. Other writings use household language; Paul even claims believers are adopted by the Spirit as children (Rom 8:14–17).[106] Spatial metaphors, like house and temple, demonstrate good

102. Commenting on Ephesians 2:19–22; Fee, *Empowering Presence*, 689–90.

103. Sweeney believes Pss 9:13, 107:18 and Isa 38:10–20 are in the background here; "Jesus, Paul, Temple" 615–18. Curiously, Boyd thinks this is a metaphorical expression for "the fortified walls of the satanic fortress"; *God at War*, 216. He does not explain exactly how or where this fortress exists.

104. Body imagery is unique to Paul with unknown antecedents; Fee, *First Corinthians*, 18, 19; *Empowering Presence*, 873; Ladd, *Theology*, 590–92; Marshall, *NT Theology*, 275.

105. Jesus promises that if his followers are obedient, he and his Father will "make our home with them" (John 14:23); Coloe, *Household of God*, 145–48.

106. Also 1 Tim 3:15, Heb 3:6; 1 Pet 4:17; Marshall, *NT Theology*, 416, 467, 654; Skaggs, *1 Peter*, 66.

continuity with previous metaphors of sacred space in creation, the cult, and Christ. Furthermore, the church is sometimes depicted with container metaphors, believers being described as "in Christ" also fitting a spatial model (Rom 12:5; 1 Cor 4:15; Gal 1:22; Eph 3:21; Col 1:2).

Membership in the church is not dependent on heritage or ritual, but attained through faith (Eph 2:8; 3:17; Gal 5:6; Heb 11:1—12:2).[107] The church is dependent on obedience to Christ as head (Eph 1:22, 23). Consistent with creation imagery, followers of Christ are brought out of darkness and called "children of the light" (Acts 26:18; Col 1:13; Eph 5:8; 1 Thess 5:5). Furthermore, the church is not static, but growing; it is an organism rather than an organization, an "expanding, living temple of witness to God's saving presence."[108] Marshall notes that there is "nothing static about the understanding of the church . . . [it is] a body that grows, a temple that is in process of building, a company of believers who are progressing toward maturity."[109] The church can thus be described with the same metaphors for sacred space used elsewhere, a new temple, a new creation, as well as the household of God. It too is dependent on the indwelling Spirit: "the church rides the wind of God's Spirit."[110] Its dynamic nature fits well with the image of the kingdom as dynamic, and helps with conceptualizing the intrusion of evil into the church.

Conceptualizing Evil

The community of Christ, or the church, is indwelt by the Holy Spirit and is now the locus of divine presence. This sacred space is dynamic, separated from profane space, and characterized by the presence of the Spirit. There is sufficient continuity between the church and images of sacred space in creation, the cult, and Christ for the previous models for conceptualizing sacred space in binary opposition to profane space to be valid. If sacred space is defined by the presence of the Spirit, it stands to reason that profane space be defined by the absence of the Spirit (akin to the false

---

107. Thus it is more inclusive than the OT temple; Dunn, *NT Theology*, 107–17.

108. 1 Pet 2:4; Beale, *Temple*, 395. Beale sees the church as the initial phase of the end-time temple; there is on-going construction; the temple "not made with human hands" (2 Cor 5:1) refers to the eschatological temple; *Temple*, 257–63.

109. He continues with unfortunate warfare metaphors: "a company of soldiers who are engaged in defensive battle against the powers of evil"; Marshall, *NT Theology*, 466.

110. Pinnock, *Flame of Love*, 114.

prophets of Jude 19 who lacked the Spirit). This absence contributes to the unreality of profane space. Given the nonlinear nature of both sacred and profane space, one can conceive of the profane intruding upon the sacred, opposing the extension of sacred space and seeking to parasitically attain reality. Recognizing the necessity of the Spirit in defining the church also informs the role of the community of Christ in discerning and dealing with evil. However, unlike cultic sacred space and Christ, there is no suggestion that the community of Christ is sinless and perfectly holy.[111] The church is indwelt by the Spirit, yet the relationship between the two is mutual and dynamic. Conceiving of shades of grey can be helpful; the church can vary from being filled with light to being mostly dark. Although not explicit in the epistles, grades of holiness can still be conceptualized, as Beale suggests above.

Sacred Actions

Previous chapters have examined how God establishes sacred space, maintains it, and expands it through cleansing and setting boundaries on evil. This occurs first through creation, then Israel's cult, and then through Christ, all enabled by the Holy Spirit. In the church, human responsibility is the primary focus, with less emphasis on divine initiative, although humans are enabled by the Spirit. Human responsibility includes cleansing, discerning, and setting boundaries on evil.

Divine Initiative

God, through Christ and the Spirit, graciously offers salvation from sin and evil to those who believe; he enlightens, strengthens, and protects believers, and initiates defeat of evil spiritual forces. The Gospels and epistles proclaim that salvation is effected by Christ who conquers sin, cleanses, and sanctifies, making access to sacred space possible for all who believe (Rom 6:1—8:39; Gal 3:22; Heb 10:1–39; 1 Pet 2:22–24; 1 John 2:2; 4:10).[112] However, the Holy Spirit is essential in appropriating this salvation: John promises that the Spirit will lead disciples in truth (John 14:16, 17; 16:13);

---

111. This is evident in the difficult Johannine passage, which implies that is impossible for a child of God to sin (1 John 3:7–10). Thomas notes that *hamartia* is always in present tense, therefore it is better interpreted as an impossibility of habitual sin, although this does not explain the force of the statement; *1 John*, 166–67.

112. Marshall, *NT Theology*, 273, 624; Fee, *Empowering Presence*, 501.

Paul is clear that the Spirit is superior to the law and is God's provision for Torah fulfillment; he encourages believers to ask the Holy Spirit for help in understanding God's truths (Rom 8:1–11; 2 Cor 3:6; Gal 5:18; Eph 1:17–19); and Peter assures his readers that the Spirit strengthens and restores them (1 Pet 5:10).[113] The Spirit illumines understanding (1 Cor 2:10, 11; Eph 1:17–18), intercedes on behalf of believers (Rom 26–27), warns about the need to guard their faith (1 Tim 4:1), and in fact helps guard faith (2 Tim 1:14).[114] Followers of Christ are also protected from the evil one (2 Thess 3:1). In addition to atoning for sin, Christ's death destroyed the devil and his work (Heb 2:14, 17; 1 John 3:8). Caird describes divine love as absorbing and neutralizing evil (cleansing imagery).[115] This victory extends to evil spirits (implied in the difficult text about Christ preaching to the spirits in prison; 1 Pet 3:19, 20), and the powers (Col 2:15).[116] The Holy Spirit works in opposition to the devil (the "spirit" who leads people into falsehood, anger, slander, and other sin, Eph 4:17—5:20). Hence the Spirit sustains sacred space, and enables believers to participate in its expansion and maintenance. Graeme Goldsworthy notes that "all 'A.D.' history is in crisis because the Holy Spirit constantly reapplies the decisive victory of Calvary and the empty tomb through the preached word of the gospel."[117] It is perhaps more correct to say that history is in crisis because of the persistence of evil; the Spirit works against evil through the victory of Christ and the ministry of the church. Direct divine initiative is promised at the eschaton when Christ will return and finalize the separation of evil (presented in the complex apocalyptic texts found primarily in Revelation 5–20; also 1 Thess 4:16, 17, 5:1–6; 2 Thess 2:1–12; 2 Pet 3:8–13). Until then, humans have an important role to play in setting limits on evil.

---

113. Fee, *First Corinthians*, 110–12; *Empowering Presence*, 544. Skaggs points out "restores" could also mean "puts in order"; *1 Peter*, 73. This fits with ordering metaphors developed in chapter 5

114. Marshall, *NT Theology*, 273; Fee, *Empowering Presence*, 579–81; Cole, *He who Gives Life*, 263–66; Pinnock, *Flame of Love*, 218–22, 227–31.

115. Caird, *Principalities and Powers*, 101; Smith, *Willful Intent*, 307. Given the above discussion on the relationship between sin and Satan, this twofold purpose is unsurprising. Page suggests that "destroy the devil" is better interpreted as "render ineffective," which fits better with John's description of Christ destroying the works of the devil; *Powers*, 204.

116. The Peter text probably represents a proclamation of victory to evil spirits who most likely are fallen angels; Ladd, *Theology*, 648; Skaggs, *1 Peter*, 51–52. Caird believes the powers lost control because death, the weapon of the powers, has been removed by Christ (Rom 6:7); *Principalities and Powers*, 91–92; Page, *Powers*, 254.

117. Goldsworthy, *Gospel in Revelation*, 125.

Human Responsibility

Although the Holy Spirit is bestowed as a gift, humans are responsible for reception of that gift. In biblical stories, when believers are filled with the Spirit, an action often follows (Acts 13:9, 10).[118] The church can be seen to have a threefold task: to walk by the Spirit, including belief and obedience; to maintain the boundaries of sacred space through ordering and cleansing; and to expand the boundaries of sacred space. This is accomplished only through the Spirit and can be described without using warfare language.

WALKING BY THE SPIRIT

In the Gospels and epistles, the human response to the work of Christ is primarily faith, which includes commitment to God and confession of Jesus as Lord (Acts 3:16; Eph 1:13; 2 Thess 2:13; Heb 13:15; 1 John 4:15).[119] This is described as a continual process, akin to "abiding" in the Spirit, discussed above (Rom 13:11–14; Phil 2:12; 1 John 2:24–28; 4:13–16).[120] Human response to divine initiative can be described in spatial terms using directional metaphors and binary oppositions. Believers turn from darkness, or the power of Satan, to the light of God (Acts 26:18); from wicked to righteous ways (Acts 3:26); and from idols to the true God (1 Thess 1:9). Some turn away to follow Satan, or a false spirit, and thus grieve the Holy Spirit (1 Tim 5:15; Eph 2:2; 4:30).[121] The metaphor of "two-ways" is evident in Peter's and Paul's preaching in Acts (3:19; 15:19; 26:20), as well as the epistles (Gal 3:8, 9; 2 Tim 4:3, 4; 1 Pet 3:11; 2 Pet 2:21).[122] This spatial metaphor is explicit in James (4:7, 8): resisting the devil is juxtaposed with drawing near to God, and First John (3:1–10): people are either children of God or children of the devil.[123] Fee points out that

118. Cole, *He who Gives Life*, 218.

119. This faith is contrasted with obedience to the law; Marshall, *NT Theology*, 444; Ladd, *Theology*, 632.

120. Caird, *Principalities and Powers*, 94; Ladd, *Theology*, 646.

121. Fee thinks sins that divide come from Satan; *Empowering Presence*, 680, 713.

122. Skaggs, *1 Peter*, 115. This metaphor is also common in Ancient Jewish and early Christian literature, as discussed in previous chapters.

123. With respect to John, Page points out there is no middle ground; *Powers*, 206; Thomas notes that those who walk in darkness are far from God, whereas those who walk in the light have their path illumined; *1 John*, 106, 7. Recall the universality of direction and journey metaphors.

life in Christ and life apart from Christ are the only two alternatives, and Caird remarks that there is a choice between the dominion of elemental spirits and the dominion of Christ: "those who voluntarily re-enter one are thereby severing their connection with the other."[124] Although neither employs spatial imagery, both point to the incompatibility of the realms of light and darkness and the importance of the choice between the two.

Those who choose Christ are encouraged to walk and live in the Spirit (Gal 5:16), including sowing to the Spirit (Gal 6:8).[125] As Fee notes, for Paul "conversion by the Spirit involved a life of commitment to a life of walking in the Spirit, being led by the Spirit, and sowing to the Spirit." Walking in the Spirit involves avoiding sin, or repenting of it (2 Cor 7:10; Jas 5:16; 1 John 1:9), and living a life of prayer and virtuous behavior.[126] The sacraments and church fellowship can also be seen as ways of walking in the Spirit. Followers of Christ are to be light in the darkness and "shine like stars" in a wicked world (Phil 2:15; incorporating the binary images of church/world and light/dark). Walking by the Spirit involves love first for God then for the community, which may include social justice activities (1 Cor 13:1–13; Eph 5:2; 1 Thess 3:6; Heb 10:24; 1 Pet 4:8; 1 John 4:7–21; 2 John 1–6). Hence believers are to simultaneously turn towards Christ, and minister outwards in the world.

WARFARE?

As discussed in chapter 1, overcoming evil is described in popular literature using warfare language, usually with reference to Ephesians 6:10–17.

---

124. Fee, *Empowering Presence*, 547; Caird, *Principalities and Powers*, 95. Many theologians comment on human choice, e.g., Pinnock: humans have been "placed at the right epistemic distance from God to make it a real decision"; *Flame of Love*, 75.

125. Ladd believes this involves moment by moment direction from the Holy Spirit; *Theology*, 517; Fee points out that walking in Paul's writing referred to ethical behavior, and one could only walk in the sphere of the Spirit through the empowering of the Spirit; *Empowering Presence*, 429, 467. Christians are also advised not to "quench the Spirit" (1 Thess 5:19).

126. With the help of the Spirit (1 Cor 14:13–15; Eph 3:14–21; 1 Thess 5:17; 1 Tim 2:8; Jas 5:13–16); Fee, *Empowering Presence*, 467, 864; Smith, *Willful Intent*, 305–9. Virtue lists in include humility, goodness, godliness, self-control, endurance, love, patience, kindness, faithfulness, gentleness (1 Cor 13:4–7; Eph 4:2; Col 3:12; 2 Pet 1:5–7); and are also called fruit of the Spirit (Gal 5:22, 23). The Holy Spirit has commonly been described as a sanctifier, nurturing holiness in God's people (2 Thess 2:13); Cole, *He who Gives Life*, 228–29; Pinnock, *Flame of Love*, 175–77.

Most academic discussions of this passage employ warfare language,[127] Boyd's work being perhaps the most emphatic. He refers to Satan's war against the church, describes Christian life as warfare and "spiritual military service," believes we are to throw "all we have into *guerrilla warfare* against the occupying army", and claims "the whole of the Christian life is an *act of warring* against the enemy."[128] The military metaphors in Ephesians 6 likely originated from a combination of OT imagery, Jewish literature, and Roman military culture.[129] It is usually this last that is emphasized; however, the armor described correlates inexactly with soldier's armor, and the term *palē* ("struggle," NRSV; "contending," NIV) is closer in meaning to "wrestle" (athletic imagery).[130] Furthermore, this passage talks more about "standing strong" than waging war. *Antistēte* ("resist," "withstand") is used elsewhere to refer to standing firm in faith and resisting the devil (1 Pet 5:8, 9; Jas 4:7), and can also connote confidence and a stance of victory.[131] Standing firm is also used with respect to temptation (1 Cor 10:12, 13). Paul describes Christian life as a struggle (Col 1:29), but struggle is not synonymous with warfare. He encourages believers to be alert and courageous, and to stand firm in faith; similar terms to those used in Ephesians, but lacking warfare imagery (1 Cor 16:13; cf. 1 Pet 5:9). Yoder Neufeld suggests that the emphasis in Ephesians 6 is on Christian virtues (truth, justice, peace) rather than battle.[132]

Paul uses military imagery to a lesser extent elsewhere (Rom 6:13, 23; 13:12; 2 Cor 6:7; 10:4; 1 Thess 5:8), but he employs other metaphors

127. E.g., Page describes believers as equipping themselves as the Divine Warrior; *Powers*, 187; Arnold presumes "spiritual warfare" in Ephesians 6; *Powers*, 149–57; *3 Crucial Questions*, 37–44.

128. Boyd, *God at War*, 217, 278–82, 281; italics mine. Boyd also describes the heart of a believer as a battlefield (2 Cor 2:10–11; Eph 4:26–27; 279).

129. Esp. Isa 11:5; 59:17 (11:4, 5 to a lesser extent) and 1QM—the war between the sons of light and darkness; Page, *Powers*, 187. R. Martin believes the Roman soldier is the closest background in this passage; *Ephesians*, 75, but Lincoln (*Ephesians*, 436–38) and Yoder Neufeld (*Armour of God*, 131) argue the OT background is the most important. In terms of context, Ephesus had a history of interest in magic and Artemis worship (and its consequent demonic associations), and likely required strong teaching regarding evil spiritual forces (Acts 19:1–41); Arnold, *Powers*, 149.

130. BDAG 752; Lincoln, *Ephesians*, 444. No bow or lance is mentioned; Lincoln, *Ephesians*, 436; Marshall, *NT Theology*, 389; Yoder Neufeld, *Armour of God*, 150.

131. Yoder Neufeld, *Armour of God*, 128–31; BDAG 90; Lincoln, *Ephesians*, 445; Ladd, *Theology*, 638; Skaggs, *1 Peter*, 72.

132. Yoder Neufeld, *Armour of God*, 134–51. Dawn follows him in suggesting an ecclesiology based on weakness; *Powers*, 130.

as well and there is no reason to privilege warfare metaphors. One could also question whether an ancient Roman metaphor is appropriate for contemporary culture. Marshall insists this passage is a "vivid teaching aid and nothing more."[133] In his analysis, Guelich concludes that there is no basis for positing in Paul the thought of a cosmic struggle between God and Satan that works itself out in human history as a great "spiritual war" waged between God's and Satan's forces. Paul views Satan as an adversary only. He notes that the Ephesians 6 passage portrays defense more than offence; "prayer" and "alertness" are hardly armor.[134] Elsewhere Paul uses clothing metaphors: "putting on" Christ (Rom 13:12, 14; Gal 3:27, Eph 4:42), being clothed with the temple and clothing oneself with virtues such as love, compassion, kindness, and patience (2 Cor 5:1–4; Col 3:10–14). Armor can perhaps be viewed as clothing, without military overtones. It can be seen as a boundary between holiness and evil. Metaphors of standing firm accord with the concept of setting boundaries on evil. Followers of Christ can use their authority in Christ to "resist" the devil and "stand firm" against evil spirits (1 Pet 5:9; Eph 6:13). The Word of God may be the source, not the weapon, of authority. Moreover, there are many images of weakness and peace in the epistles: disciples are "crucified with Christ" (Gal 2:19), Paul has an infirmity (Gal 4:14), and God chooses the weak and the foolish (1 Cor 1:18–2:5).[135] In sum, although there is warfare imagery in Ephesians 6, there are non-warfare metaphors as well; it is unnecessary to use military metaphors to the exclusion of other imagery.

Setting Boundaries on Evil

The response of the church to evil can be understood in terms of cultic metaphors of cleansing, ordering, and boundary-setting. First, consistent with OT practices, followers of Christ are to be holy and pure, symbolically cleansing themselves from evil (1 Cor 6:9–11; 2 Cor 7:1; Jas 4:8) and

---

133. Marshall, *NT Theology*, 389. Fee, perhaps in reaction to its overuse in contemporary Charismatic Christianity, suggests the critical point of this passage is "not some ad hoc word directed at Satan," but taking the enemy on by Spirit empowered proclamation and Spirit empowered prayer. With reference to the Spirit and the flesh in Gal 5:16–18, he believes there is no hint of "warfare" in the human heart. The Spirit is opposed to flesh but is also the enabling power over flesh; *Empowering Presence*, 435, 728–31.

134. Guelich, "Jesus, Paul, Peretti," 45, 46, 50.

135. Many scholars have emphasized weakness over power, e.g., Dawn, *Powers*, 41–56; Gingerich and Grimsrud, *Transforming the Powers*.

living holy lives (Rom 12:1, 2; Phil 1:10; 1 Tim 5:22; 2 Pet 3:11; Jas 1:27), so as to be acceptable "sacred space" individually and collectively.[136] Specifically, by practicing godliness they maintain boundaries on evil, evident in the admonitions to "be angry, but sin not" to prevent giving the devil a foothold (Eph 4:26, 27) and to resist the devil in order to maintain purity (Eph 6:11; 1 Pet 5:9). James (4:7, 8) particularly uses spatial and cleansing imagery in his juxtaposition of resisting the devil, drawing near to God, cleansing hands, and purifying hearts.[137] As discussed above, there is a close relationship between sin and the demonic; one of the ways to set boundaries on evil is through godly behavior.

Second, believers are encouraged to be aware of evil forces that threaten sacred space, and are enabled by the Spirit to do so (1 Cor 2:10–16; 2 Cor 2:11; Heb 5:14; 1 Pet 5:8).[138] Discernment of evil spirits is critical to the task of setting boundaries on evil, yet there are few biblical guidelines and little academic discussion on the topic. John provides perhaps the clearest guideline in stating that spirits that deny Jesus are not from God (1 John 4:1–3). In theology, most discussions on discernment (prominent in the Roman Catholic tradition) focus only on hearing the voice of God; yet the NT teaches about awareness of Satan's activities (2 Cor 2:11; 1 Pet 5:8) and discerning good from evil (Heb 5:14). In a critical evaluation of "discerning of spirits" in 1 Corinthians 12:10, Peter Cavanna notes it to be "the most indefinable of all the charismata." He concludes it functions more as a control for the gift of prophecy, rather than as a "demon detector."[139] The *EPCC* gives a broad definition of discernment: "the charismatic gift and cognitive ability to recognize, judge, and distinguish the correlation of the inner spirit to its concrete physical manifestation."[140]

---

136. Purity and obedience are specifically associated in 1 Pet 1:22; cleansing and virtuous lives are associated in 2 Pet 1:3–9; both echo OT purity texts; Skaggs, *1 Peter,* 28, 94–103, 132–38. Skaggs points out that godly life is a collaborative effort: the Holy Spirit gives the grace that enables believers to develop virtues (112).

137. J. Lockett notes that "hands" and "heart" refer to "both external behavior and internal attitude," and relate to both actions and a right relationship with God (cf. Ps 24:3, 4; 51:10); since the world is defiled by the devil, followers of Christ need to symbolically purify themselves; *Purity and Worldview,* 130–37. Recall the relationship between sin and the demonic: resisting the devil and resisting temptation are thus similar (Jas 1:13–15).

138. Fee puts it well: "those whose lives are invaded by the Spirit of God can discern all things, including those without the Sprit; but the inverse is not possible"; *First Corinthians,* 118.

139. Cavanna, *Discerning the Spirits,* 3–5, 12–13; recall discussion in chapter 1.

140. Bryant, "Discernment," 134.

This definition appears to follow Yong's view; he interprets discernment broadly claiming it is "both a divine gift and a human activity aimed at reading correctly the inner processes of all things." He also believes the two work together; the Spirit operates through human faculties, and intuition can characterize discernment. Yong suggests the development of criteria and a strategy prior to discernment, but rightly notes the complexity of discernment: it is always "inherently ambiguous"; "norms and criteria are never exhaustive."[141] I agree regarding the complexity of discernment, but Yong and the *EPCC* seem to preclude discerning evil spirits that do not have concrete manifestations. "Inner process" is a broad, ambiguous term; perhaps discernment could be considered as both reading the "inner spirit" and the presence of evil spirits. Interestingly, elsewhere the *EPCC* lists symptoms of demonization: "persistent evil or destructive behaviors or emotions; extreme mood fluctuations; superstitions, idolatry or 'unnatural asceticism'; resorting to charms, divinations or sorcery; enslaving habits; and an antipathy to the power of the Holy Spirit."[142] "Checklists" to determine the presence of demons are better viewed as guidelines only. We need humble reliance on God. However, discernment of evil is not an option for those who align themselves with the Spirit of God. Given the complexities of humans and their interactions with each other and the spirit world, viewing discernment as both natural and divinely inspired is a logical approach. Following metaphors used in this study, the closer one is to the light (which illuminates darkness), the easier one can discern the darkness. Godly characteristics enable one not only to set boundaries on evil, but to discern it as well.[143]

Third, as discussed in chapter 6, followers of Christ are authorized, filled, enabled, and gifted by the Spirit to continue the ministry of Christ in maintaining the boundaries of sacred space. Paul equates Jesus' "fullness" of the Spirit, which gives him power and authority over evil, with the "fullness" the believer now has (Col 2:10; Eph 3:19).[144] The Spirit equips the community of believers by gifting them as appropriate; these gifts enable the ministry of Christ to continue (1 Cor 12:1–11; Heb 2:4). Disciples are given authority to teach, as well as to heal. Filled with the Spirit, they

141. Yong, "Spiritual Discernment," 84, 93; *Beyond Impasse*, 153–67. Yong is in turn influenced by Wink and his discussion of the Pauline powers as the interiority of human structures; *Discerning*, esp. 127–31.

142. Henderson, "Deliverance," 125.

143. As recommended by contemplatives, as discussed in chapter 1; Shuster, *Power, Pathology*, 239, 262.

144. Arnold, *Powers*, 116–17.

preach the gospel, encourage and reprove the community of believers, and heal the ill (Acts 2:38–42; 3:1–10; 4:7–12; 19:8; 2 Cor 10:8; 13:10; Titus 2:15; Jas 5:16.); thus cleansing and maintaining sacred space.

Finally, the community of Christ cleanses and maintains sacred space by expelling evil spirits. Summary statements of healing and deliverance are similar to those written about Jesus' ministry (Acts 5:16). Although overt exorcism stories are not common in the epistles, they are explicit in Acts, are indirectly referred to in miracle stories, and were likely part of the early church (Acts 13:9–12; 16:16–18; 2 Cor 12:12; Heb 2:4; Jas 2:19).[145] The church itself is also to be kept holy, evidenced in the story of the sexually immoral man being expelled and "handed over to Satan" (1 Cor 5:5; 1 Tim 1:20; also reminiscent of the deaths of Ananias and Sapphira, Acts 5:1–10; the specific sin, incest, is prohibited in the Levitical code, Lev 18:8). This story has interpretive challenges; Fee believes it is best understood as exhorting the church to a deep sense of holiness and hatred of sin; developing an awareness of how sin, like leaven, infiltrates and defiles the church; and turning the immoral man "back out into Satan's sphere."[146] George Shillington interestingly suggests that *Yom Kippur* is the context for this passage. He points out its communal emphasis and thinks "the spirit" to be redeemed refers not to that of the man, but to that of the Spirit of Christ resident in the church. Paul's concern is that the church is contaminated by the one sin that remains unatoned for, particularly given Paul's earlier reference to the holiness of the temple (1 Cor 3:16, 17; 6:10).[147] His approach explains the otherwise puzzling implication that Satan has a role in salvation but does not adequately explain individual redemption, a prominent theme elsewhere in Paul's writings. It is likely that Paul had both individual and community in mind. The purpose of both the Azazel ritual and the handing of the sinner over to Satan is to cleanse the community, since the dwelling place of God is incompatible

145. Twelftree argues that Paul's writing is not that dissimilar to the Synoptics, and that Paul also likely practiced exorcism, especially given the stories in Acts; *Name of Jesus*, 57–77, 177, 289–91.

146. Fee, *First Corinthians*, 200–216; *Empowering Presence*, 126–27. He further notes that the purpose of this is redemption; separation from the community would likely lead to repentance of sin. See also Smith, *Willful Intent*, 300.

147. Shillington, "Atonement Texture," 34–35, 41–44. Both Azazel and Satan are in opposition to the Lord. Paul would have been familiar with the Azazel tradition both from his knowledge of the Torah, and familiarity with Second Temple texts. Shillington notes that Tertullian first suggested the spiritual life of the community was Paul's primary concern, not the individual, but this was surpassed by Origen's focus on the individual (30–31).

with evil. This story accords with spatial imagery in that realms of holiness and evil are kept separate; sacred space is maintained through cleansing, ordering, and setting boundaries on evil. Beale provides an apt summary of the task of the church: "To keep the order and peace of the spiritual sanctuary by learning and teaching God's word, by praying always, and by being vigilant in keeping out unclean moral and spiritual things."[148]

EXTENDING SACRED SPACE

Humans are also responsible for extending sacred space. Once filled with the Spirit, followers of Christ immediately set out to proclaim the gospel and expand the kingdom, continually guided by the Spirit. As seen in Jesus' ministry, there is an association between advancing into new territory and encounters with the demonic; the light dispels the darkness. Acts (8:7) describes multiple evil spirits leaving when Christ is proclaimed.[149] Even a sorcerer (whose practice of magic likely had demonic underpinnings) is converted and baptized; people turn from following him to following Christ (Acts 8: 9–13). Those who seek to hinder this proclamation are stopped (e.g., the false prophet Bar-Jesus, called a son of the devil, is struck blind, Acts 13:6–11).[150] Exorcism is also a means of salvation, as in the story of the Philippian slave girl with the spirit of divination (Acts 16:16–18).[151] And, like the Gospel stories, it has an eschatological dimension in Acts; the good news spreads and the kingdom is made manifest through the expulsion of demons.[152] Thus the cosmos is cleansed and ordered—Christ triumphs again over chaos.

---

148. Beale, *Temple,* 398; he points out that this is similar to Adam's task.

149. Twelftree notes that exorcisms occur symbiotically with the message; *Name of Jesus,* 145. Garrett believes the message of the kingdom was also a message about release from Satan's authority; *Demise of Devil,* 65–67.

150. In keeping with his allegiance to the darkness; Garrett, *Demise of Devil,* 81–83.

151. This exorcism resulted in Paul's imprisonment and consequent conversion of the jailer and his family; Klutz, *Exorcism Stories,* 207–29. Twelftree notes the parallels with the Gerasene demoniac in the recognition of "God Most High"; *Name of Jesus,* 145–47.

152. Acts 16:16–18, as above, and the story of the seven sons of Sceva (Acts 19:13–20). This last story has ties to the Gerasene demoniac (Matt 8:28–34, Mark 5:1–20; Luke 8:26–39): both include extraordinary strength, nakedness and leaving homes, suggesting the exorcisms of Paul are contiguous with those of Jesus; Page, *Powers,* 176–9; Klutz, *Exorcism Stories,* 232–39.

As in Jesus' ministry, there are no exorcism formulae and authority, not technique, is emphasized. This is evident in the healing (from disease and demons) of those who touched Paul's clothing (Acts 19:12), the failure of itinerant exorcists who were using the "name of Jesus" (with an implied prohibition against using Jesus' name as a magical formula, Acts 19:13), and the expulsion of demons with merely a word (Acts 16:18).[153] The demons acknowledge the authority of both Jesus and Paul, and Paul expels demons with the authority given by Jesus and the Spirit.[154] Twelftree emphasizes, "it is the presence of the Spirit, rather than anything that is said or done by Christians that defeats the demonic in a powerful and effortless fashion"; he further describes the exorcisms in Acts using spatial imagery: the "combating of evil on the unclear borders on the edge of Christianity."[155] Although the disciples are obedient to their mission, it is ultimately the indwelling Spirit who expands sacred space; as Dumbrell observes, the Spirit is bestowed at critical stages of missionary expansion.[156] Beale again summarizes the task of the church well (unfortunately omitting the church's role in limiting evil): to "be God's temple, so filled with his glorious presence that we expand and fill the earth with that presence."[157]

Counteracting Evil

The chiastic structure of 1 John provides a summary of sacred space and its concomitant actions: love at the center, antichrists on the periphery.[158] Followers of Christ have a threefold task: to walk by the Spirit, focusing on the center, the light, and the truth; to maintain sacred space by confessing sin, cleansing, and healing those afflicted by evil, and relocating evil back to the periphery; and to move out to the dark periphery, spread the light,

---

153. Page, *Powers*, 177; Twelftree, *Name of Jesus*, 149; Klutz, *Exorcism Stories*, 221, 240; Garrett, *Demise of Devil*, 93. The caution about not using the name of Jesus as a magical formula is particularly applicable to contemporary deliverance ministry.

154. The demons in the sons of Sceva acknowledge Jesus and Paul (Acts 19:15); Paul is filled with the Spirit when confronting Bar Jesus (Acts 13:8–11). With respect to the latter, Garrett notes this implies "Paul must himself be invested with authority that is greater than Satan's own"; *Demise of Devil*, 84.

155. Twelftree, *Name of Jesus*, 148, 54.

156. Dumbrell, *Search for Order*, 223; e.g., the Spirit appoints and sends Barnabas and Paul to preach to the Gentiles (Acts 13:2, 4); see also Cole, *He who Gives Life*, 213.

157. Beale, *Temple*, 401.

158. Thomas, *1 John*, 56.

and expand sacred space. This is only possible because they are indwelt by the Holy Spirit, gifted with discernment, and given authority over evil. The church's dealing with evil spirits does not have to be conceived of in terms of warfare; rather it can be viewed as cleansing, ordering, and boundary-setting, performed calmly and with authority. Cultic language provides alternative language. As the new creation, followers of Christ are to participate in pushing back the darkness, locking the doors of the sea, and keeping the circle of creation clean. As the new tabernacle, the church is to maintain order and purity. Through the indwelling Spirit, Christians are called to be holy, to keep sacred space holy, and to relocate evil to the periphery of godly reality. Recalling the cultic conception of evil as dirt, the Johannine metaphor of the "household of God," and the notion of evil as a lesser reality, followers of Christ could be considered to engage in "holy housekeeping," dispelling dirt and irritating pests. (Perhaps the Spirit who "hovers" over creation also "hoovers.") A spatial model can reframe the church's ministry endeavors.

A Model for Conceptualizing Evil

Based on above explorations of the nature of sacred space in the church and its accompanying sacred actions with respect to evil, as well as the model developed in previous chapters, it is helpful to summarize and develop the framework for understanding evil without using warfare metaphors.

Summary

Acts and the epistles make frequent references to demonic beings, albeit renaming them at times. The darkness, the deep, and the chaos that threatened creation, plus the impurity and disorder that threatened the cult continue to threaten the church. Because sin is emphasized as an evil force in opposition to holiness, human responsibility becomes paramount. However, as a result of Christ's defeat of evil on the cross, sacred space is redefined, and followers of Christ are enabled through the Spirit to continue setting boundaries on evil and restoring order.

The semantic domain of evil in opposition to the church includes many of the same metaphors for evil forces (Satan, demons, darkness, impurity) that threaten creation, the cult, and Christ. There is also an emphasis on sin and the powers; both can be understood as unclean demonic forces. Although sin is complex, it can be viewed spatially as a boundary violation: deliberately turning away from God puts one under the influence of evil forces (like the "first" sin in Eden). The powers are multivalent but can perhaps be viewed as a cluster of demons. In continuity with creation, the cult, and Christ, evil spirits are best understood as chaotic and disorganized with a reduced ontology; unsurprising given that they lack the Holy Spirit. Profane space, devoid of the light and life of the divine, is naturally less real. However, beings in this space continually seek to attain reality parasitically by intruding upon sacred space.

The church, as the revised definition of sacred space, is indwelt by the Holy Spirit, characterized by holiness and purity, and can be viewed as a new creation and a new temple. These aspects apply both individually and communally. Through the enabling and authority of the Spirit, the church is responsible for maintaining the purity and order of sacred space as well as expanding its boundaries. Followers of Christ are to walk in the Spirit, discern, and separate evil from holy. With respect to the expulsion of evil spirits, metaphors of ordering, cleansing, and healing are viable alternatives to warfare metaphors. The church as sacred space is not a new concept; however, viewing this space in binary opposition to profane space is a new way of conceptualizing the mission and ministry of the church.

Model

The church can be understood in spatial and cosmic terms, compatible with sacred space in creation, the cult, and Christ. This space can be perceived at the center of reality, indeed defining reality, as the locus of divine-human interaction. It is characterized by holiness, purity, light, life, and the presence of the Holy Spirit. It exists in binary opposition to evil, including Satan, demons, the powers, sin, the world, impurity, darkness, and death. However, in between these two opposing zones is much grey: the blessings of the Spirit extend out from the center, sin can be redeemed, people cleansed and healed; simultaneously, evil forces intrude upon divine reality, sometimes invited by sin, other times without apparent invitation. This intermediate area is dynamic and complex. The model (figure 7.1) developed in previous chapters is still applicable for conceptualizing the church, at least in theory. In reality, the situation probably fluctuates within shades of grey (figure 7.2).

Figure 7.1: A Model for Conceptualizing Evil

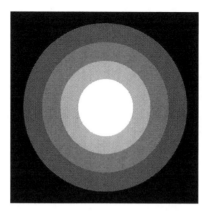

Figure 7.2: An Alternate Model for Conceptualizing Evil

The sacred center is dependent on the Holy Spirit, but even those who do not acknowledge the Spirit benefit from the blessings that extend into the grey zones. Those who follow Christ are responsible for embodying sacred space, keeping it clean and ordered, and expanding its boundaries. The church functions to renew creation, restore order, assign limits to evil, and cleanse the cosmos. This is a continual process because evil forces continually threaten the church. The boundaries between zones are fluid; unlike the cultic model, the criteria are internal, not external. Perhaps people who choose evil can be conceptualized as dwelling close to the periphery; those who reject Christ but otherwise choose good could be seen to dwell in middle zones. The exact nature of these boundaries is difficult to discern, but may be possible through an on-going relationship with the Spirit of God, who gifts his followers with discernment.

Continuing with the cultic conception of graded holiness allows for a less dualistic and more nuanced, realistic view of reality than that of a warfare model. The different zones can incorporate the complex relationship between sin and the demonic for example: if sin violates a boundary, it opens a door for evil spirits to enter. A spatial model with zones of grey emphasizes human responsibility. People have choice with respect to which zone of metaphorical space they dwell in; they can draw near to God and resist the devil. Being "called out of darkness" involves not warfare, but an invitation to move from profane space to holy space. A model of graded holiness can also incorporate ideas of sanctification, or the work of the Spirit in gradually drawing humans closer towards the center. It can guide the church with respect to mission and ministry; as in Acts, when followers of Christ move outward to spread the light, they can expect to encounter darkness, and can employ the authority of the Spirit in expelling evil spirits, returning them to the periphery.

Evaluation

This model is comprehensive, intelligible, and consonant with biblical texts, tradition, and anecdotal experience; yet it is uncomplicated and can provide a perception of reality, which can guide the church's actions with respect to evil. As before, multiple metaphors provide multiple snapshots of a multi-layered reality and offer an alternative to warfare imagery in understanding evil. This model incorporates shades of grey and blurred boundaries. Locating evil at the periphery affirms its reality while minimizing its ontology. This model, it should be stressed, is only a model; it is not a claim that this is *the* way reality is structured, but offers a new framework, a way of conceptualizing reality that may assist the church in understanding and dealing with evil. Specific limitations include the unclear and complex nature of sacred space (e.g., the church is sinful yet divinely appointed) and the unclear and complex boundaries between zones. However, I believe it provides a viable, more comprehensive option to warfare imagery, is applicable to the church's mission and ministry, and is compatible with theological views of evil. These issues are addressed next.

8

CONCLUSION: CLEANSING THE COSMOS

> Holy Spirit, making life alive,
> Moving in all things, root of all creative being,
> Cleansing the cosmos of every impurity.[1]

W E LIVE IN AN impure cosmos: a world in which terrorism is a reality, a world in which children are subjected to heinous abuse, a world in which the demonic manifests in multiple ways—in short, a world filled with evil. Although followers of Christ are called to a kingdom not of this world, they are also called to engage the world and to participate in at least decreasing the horrors of the world. Ignoring evil is not an option. The aim of this study was to develop a new model for conceptualizing evil. Evil is an important topic for Christian theology and has been addressed mostly from philosophical or historical perspectives. When demonology is considered, "spiritual warfare" is the predominant model, used mostly without awareness of its metaphorical status. Furthermore, there is often a divide between Old and New Testament studies; between biblical and theological approaches to evil, especially with respect to the ontology of evil; and between theological and practical approaches. The role of the Holy Spirit with respect to counteracting evil is not usually emphasized. Therefore, further aims of this research were to increase our understanding of the nature of evil, work towards bridging the gaps between biblical and theological studies, and to explore pneumatology with respect to evil.

1. Hildegarde of Bingen, "Hymn to the Holy Spirit."

251

This study used a linguistic, thematic approach to the biblical text in order to find alternative metaphors to "spiritual warfare." The Bible is replete with figurative language; myth, symbol, and metaphor are all intertwined as reflections of divine truth. Such language is complex, cognitive, and conceptual. Metaphors can provide new information regarding an unknown reality and act as a vehicle for discovery, thus offer an indispensable tool for understanding supersensible reality. Notably, spatial metaphors are universal. Models, or extended metaphors, offer an imaginative perspective on reality, an organizing network of images. Like metaphors, they move from the familiar to the unfamiliar and offer semantically rich representations of reality. Models can be used to bridge the gap between biblical studies and theology, and religious models are only effective if they have explanatory power. This study also affirmed critical realism: there is a reality (likely multi-leveled) that is separate and distinct from language, but it is only known through our interaction with it. Figurative language affords the best way to understand, or at least provide a framework for understanding, that reality. If new metaphors are found, new conceptions of reality are possible; metaphor does not create reality, but can add new dimensions to our understanding of it. Thus conceptual metaphors can open theological space, and ideas of metaphorical space can open conceptual space for understanding evil.

To assist the search for alternative metaphors, a review of metaphors from diverse disciplines was undertaken. From anthropology, the binary oppositions of structuralist theory and Eliade's observations regarding the universality of the sacred/profane polarity were found to be useful. From theology, Barth's idea of nothingness was deemed helpful. And from science, theories on chaos-complexity theory and dark matter/energy were considered potential models for evil. Thus, rather than limiting the study to the semantic domain of evil in the Bible, theological, anthropological, and scientific metaphors were used to supplement biblical metaphors. In this final chapter, I summarize the findings of this study, initially from the perspective of the new creation, then with respect to the model developed. Specific contributions of this model to pneumatology and demonology are discussed, and then potential applications of this study's findings with respect to ministry (missions and counseling) are examined. Finally, I evaluate the model proposed in this study and suggest further research.

Cleansing and Creation

Although the previous four chapters focused on different aspects of the biblical view of evil in binary opposition to good, they have all emphasized creation as a continual process. Because evil recurrently intrudes upon godly reality, the cosmos requires on-going cleansing and reestablishment of boundaries on evil. The situation changes in the promised new creation. In fact, the previous discussion can be summarized and further illuminated from the perspective of the new heaven and earth promised at the end of Revelation. This section first examines the new creation, then reviews the previous biblical "creations" that were discussed under the themes creation, cult, Christ, and church, and summarizes the model that was developed as a result of this research.

New Creation

There are marked differences between the new creation and previous one(s). This is the creation longed for by Israel (Isa 25:8, 9; 60:19, 20; 65:17–25), promised by Christ (John 14:2, 3), and anticipated by the church (Phil 2:10, 11; 2 Thess 1:10). Here there is no sea, darkness, suffering, uncleanness, death, or evil; the river of life flows freely, gates are open, the city is composed of sparkling gems, and God dwells with his people, filling creation with light and life (Rev 21:1—22:5).[2] This temple city is unimaginably large, like a cosmos. Heaven comes down to earth; the two concepts merge into the New Jerusalem. This is ultimate sacred space, the epitome of holiness. Unlike Eden, there is now a city, not a garden; nothing is forbidden; there are no cherubic guards; and God does not just visit but dwells permanently in creation.[3] Whereas creation in the OT only contains a temple, in Revelation it *becomes* the temple.[4] Unlike the tabernacle/

2. The images of new creation, temple, and Jerusalem are indistinguishable. Goldsworthy notes that Revelation 21 weaves together images from "Eden, Canaan, Jerusalem and Jesus Christ"; *Gospel in Revelation*, 134. There is debate whether this is a totally new creation or a renewed creation. Skaggs and Benham suggest that "new" suggests fresh, rising from the decay of the old world; *Revelation*, 227. However, from a metaphorical perspective the distinction is not critical.

3. Dow, *Images of Zion*, 194–97, 200–205. Skaggs and Benham also believe the river of life is symbolic of the presence of the Holy Spirit; *Revelation*, 227. The fact that God dwells with his people fulfills the promises of Ezek 37:27; Zech 2:11; 8:8; and Isa 43:19; 44:6; 55:1; Koester, *Revelation*, 193.

4. Beale believes the perimeters of the temple encompass the entire new creation, and points out similarities between the temples in Revelation 11:1–5 and 21:10–27:

temple, there are no gradations of holiness in the new creation: *everything is holy.*[5] Because there is no evil, Christ has no need to exorcise demons and the church has no need to minister to those afflicted by evil. The threat to divine reality is eliminated; the separation between good and evil finalized and complete. The "barriers of sin and mortality are removed by the grace of God."[6] Not just God's people but the whole creation is restored.

There are also similarities between the new creation and previous descriptions of sacred space. Revelation is almost completely figurative in its language and lends itself well to comparisons with previous creation imagery. Like Eden, the new creation is lush with life. Like the temple, holiness and purity permeate the place. Old Testament prophecies regarding a future temple are fulfilled.[7] The heavenly scenes earlier in Revelation (3:1–6; 7:9–17) also anticipate the new creation, depicting a multitude of multinational worshipers, robed in white, who are promised elimination of suffering.[8] Revelation capitalizes on preceding biblical symbolism. The New Jerusalem, as the dwelling place of God, is identical to the kingdom of God; it is a renewed world/paradise/cosmic mountain and fulfills eschatological expectations of Zion.[9] It is first and foremost the place of divine presence; holy because God dwells there; the place where intimacy is experienced.[10] Beale summarizes aptly: "The various forms of the temple in the Old Testament were intended to point to the final eschatological goal of God's presence filling the entire creation in the way it had formerly filled only the holy of holies"; "this heavenly temple comes down completely to envelop the entire cosmos at the end of the age."[11]

---

both have Ezek 40–48 in the background (and Zech 4 and 7), the tree of life and the lampstand are symbolic of God's presence *Temple*, 314–27, 366.

5. Fee, *Empowering Presence*, 391.

6. Koester, *Revelation*, 200.

7. Esp. Ezekiel's visionary temple (40–48); also Isa 60–66; Ezek 37; and Zech 14; Beale, *Temple*, 367; Dow, *Images of Zion*, 194.

8. White robes, like that of Zechariah's vision, symbolize purification and holiness; Dow, *Images of Zion*, 188; Skaggs and Benham, *Revelation*, 46, 88.

9. Dumbrell, *Search for Order*, 11, 344.

10. Dow believes the particular name in the Revelation account affirms the uniqueness of God's revelation in Jerusalem. The new creation fulfills the expectations of the Zion tradition, such as the longing for intimacy; *Images of Zion*, 213–16. Beale points out that the divine presence, formerly limited to the temple, is now throughout creation. God's throne was in heaven, with a footstool in the holy of holies, now his throne includes the whole cosmos; *Temple*, 368–70.

11. Beale, *Temple*, 313, 331. Furthermore, "eschatology not only recapitulates the protology of Eden but escalates it" (368).

However, like the chaos before creation and the flood before the Noahic covenant, there is a time of great evil before the new creation. This is characterized by judgment and destruction, as well as the final defeat of evil (described in most of Revelation 12–20 and foretold in the OT "day of the Lord" passages [see chapter 5] and NT apocalyptic passages [Matt 24:15–28; Mark 13:14–27; Luke 21:20–28; 1 Thess 5:3]). Military imagery is evident in these passages, which Dumbrell summarizes as a "cosmic conflict in which the empires of the world embody the demonic threat of chaos against order."[12] However, imagery of standing firm is also apparent, as Beale says: "God's spiritual temple on earth is to draw its power from the Spirit, the divine presence, before God's throne in its drive to stand against the resistance of the world."[13] As argued in chapter 4, *Chaoskampf* can be described using boundary imagery. Although it may be that events at the eschaton are best described with warfare language, this does not mean that such language is the *only* way to describe Christian life in the world today. And, given the poetic nature of Revelation, warfare language should be interpreted with caution.

Imagery in Revelation, consistent with descriptions of evil elsewhere in the Bible, gives insight into the nature of evil. Babylon is described as the antithesis of the new creation: it is full of demons, darkness, sin (especially idolatry), and impurity (Rev 14:8–11; 17:1–6; 18:2–24).[14] In the new creation, nothing unclean will enter (Rev 21:27).[15] There is no sea, darkness, or opposition to God and his church; cosmic evil is eliminated.[16]

---

12. Dumbrell, *Search for Order*, 332. A. Y. Collins believes Revelation should be understood in terms of the combat myth, relating the dragon to Leviathan, Behemoth, and Daniel's "beast"; and the abyss to the deep; *Combat Myth*, 76, 161–66; recall discussion in chapter 4.

13. With reference to Revelation 11; Beale, *Temple*, 321; akin to "standing firm" against the powers, discussed in chapter 7.

14. Darkness arises from light being extinguished and smoke rising; Dow, *Images of Zion*, 210–11; Koester, *Revelation*, 196.

15. It is not clear whether this is because the unclean are eliminated, or merely outside the gates of the new creation. Beale believes the unclean are outside the bounds of the new creation, however, he does not elaborate; *Temple*, 366. Skaggs and Benham point out further inconsistencies as the nations have been destroyed in Revelation 19; they suggests it refers to their activities, and probably means they are never allowed in at end time; *Revelation*, 225–56. Dow notes that the river of life is only for those who thirst, which is why some are outside city; *Images of Zion*, 216–18. The passage is perhaps simply emphasizing the purity of the new creation.

16. This most likely refers to the elimination of cosmic evil, given the OT imagery of the sea; however, it could also mean that there is no need for cleansing as all have been washed in the blood of the lamb, or that there is no longer any separation

The disappearance of chaos challenges theories (discussed in chapter 4) that chaos/evil is neutral or can give rise to creativity: if chaos has positive elements, why would it be eliminated? The picture of the new creation is one in which nothing exists in binary opposition to God or his good creation. Darkness and shades of grey are eliminated—only pure light remains. God's work through Christ and the Spirit in establishing boundaries on evil, separating it from sacred space, begun at creation, and continued through the cult, Christ, and the church is complete. The hints about hell as a place of separation from God have come to fruition. Hell is obviously a complex issue from biblical, philosophical, and ethical perspectives, beyond the scope of this study. One problem is whether evil is annihilated or only separated. Two general options are that there is no hell (evil is annihilated; 1 Sam 2:9; Obad 16; Matt 25:41; 2 Thess 1:9; 2 Pet 2:4; Rev 16–18), or that hell involves eternal punishment in a separate reality (Isa 66:22–24; Dan 12:1–2; Matt 18:6–9; 25:31–46; Mark 9:42–48; 2 Thess 1:5–10; Jude 7, 13; Rev 14:9–11, 20:11–13).[17] Both are compatible with this model. (Figure 8.1 depicts the separate reality view.)

Figure 8.1: The New Creation

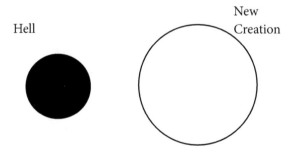

Hell

New Creation

---

between heaven and earth, or in the philosophical view of evil as "soul-making" it serves no purpose anymore (as discussed in chapter 3). Dow notes "multiple meanings with all meaning intended are a feature of the Johannine corpus"; *Images of Zion,* 211–12; see also Koester, *Revelation,* 192; Skaggs and Benham, *Revelation,* 213–14.

17. E.g., Fudge and Peterson, *Two Views of Hell.* As discussed with respect to original creation, God rejects those who reject him. Boyd reconciles the "eternal suffering" texts with the "annihilation" texts by noting it depends on perspective: eternal suffering (i.e. separation from God) to those in hell; annihilation from the view of the new creation; *Satan,* 319–57.

Retrospect

The new creation contains no evil, but, until the eschaton, evil is present and needs to be understood. In this study, evil was investigated in four biblical themes: creation, cult, Christ, and church. In the beginning (as discussed in chapter 4), uncreated darkness, the deep, and chaos exist as sinister forces that envelop the earth; there are echoes of ANE demons in the terms. The origins of evil are not explicit, but the concept of a primordial angelic fall offers a logical explanation. Forces of evil are no match for the good Creator God whose Spirit imposes order. God, through merely his word, separates the darkness from the light, and draws a circle on the face of the deep. Evil is *limited*, not eliminated; chaos is *confined*; God rejects that which rejects him. Eden, the first sacred space, is filled with life and is the place of divine-human interaction. This sacred space, however, is not perfect: a malevolent snake leads the first humans to mistrust God. Their disobedience results in expulsion from the garden into the liminal space between light and dark, although they continue to benefit from divine blessing. Their sin is a boundary violation, which in turn allows evil forces to violate their God-given boundaries. Microcosms of creation can be seen in the narratives of the flood, the crossing of the Red Sea, and the tabernacle/temple.

The chapter on Israel's cult examined the functions of sacred space and ritual in dealing with evil. New sacred space (tabernacle/temple) is constructed and includes symbolism of a sacred center and cosmic mountain, which mediate the earth-heaven connection and provide a microcosm of the universe. Sacred space is central, holy, and pure; the dwelling place of God. Binary oppositions of holy/profane, clean/unclean, life/death, and order/chaos are prevalent in cultic texts. The tabernacle/temple contains gradations of holiness; the five-zone model was deemed the most helpful for conceptualizing grey zones and incorporating the periphery, associated with the wilderness, demons, death, and chaos. Sacred space is threatened by sin and defilement, and there is a close relationship between sin, impurity, and the demonic. When categories of holiness are violated, there is a collapse of order and chaos ensues. Purity/order is maintained and restored through covenantal obedience and ritual; for example, *Yom Kippur* involves sending sin to the realm of disorder/impurity, thus cleansing the cosmos. Yet Israel continues to sin, to turn away from the sacred center to the evil periphery. Prophets warn of retribution and offer hope of redemption, but evil persists.

Consequently, prior to the advent of Christ, the world is filled with evil; some people are even demonized. Christ bursts into the world as the light in the darkness, the new sacred space, the new creation, the new temple—the locus of divine-human relationship. He is authorized by the Holy Spirit and announces the arrival of the kingdom of heaven, which is holy, pure, and dynamic. Jesus embodies sacred space, extends it, and redefines it, emphasizing moral over ritual impurity. In his ministry and death, Jesus goes out from the center to cleanse and reestablish boundaries on evil. He expels demons with a word, not with weapons of war. He sifts and sorts, separating demons and humans, and then healing humans, restoring them to health; Christ thus renews creation. Healing, cleansing, and exorcisms are intertwined and can be seen as manifestations of creation. Finally, Jesus enters the realm of death and overcomes it too in the "grand cosmic exorcism." Humans are responsible for believing in Jesus; they are also given authority over demons and disease. There is a complex relationship between divine grace, human responsibility, and demonic influence. Followers of Christ are often symbolized by the church. They are indwelt individually and corporately by the Holy Spirit and can be viewed as the new creation, the new temple, and the new locus of divine-human interaction. The church has a threefold task: to walk by the Spirit, to maintain the boundaries of sacred space through ordering and cleansing, and to expand the boundaries of sacred space through mission. All of this is accomplished only through the Spirit, and can be described in terms of the cultic metaphors of cleansing, ordering, and setting boundaries. Their work is hindered by Satan, sin (which is systemic, dynamic, and organic), and the powers, all existing in binary opposition to the church. The church functions to renew creation, restore order, assign limits to evil, and cleanse the cosmos.

A model for conceptualizing evil was inspired by the sacred space approach to creation, the cult, Christ, and the church, as well as a broad metaphorical conception of evil. This model was initiated by the sacred space of Eden and the grey zone between it and the surrounding darkness/sea/evil/chaos, and was further refined by the cultic conception of graded holiness. It was found to apply to Christ and the church as the new sacred space, although some boundaries were redefined (figure 8.2 illustrates the model's progression).

Figure 8.2. Development of a Model for Conceptualizing Evil

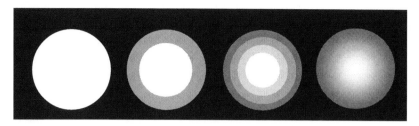

This model incorporates cosmic dualism, but is not limited to it. The center is symbolized by light, life, purity, holiness, Christ, and the church, and is filled with divine presence. All other space is dependent on it. The periphery is symbolized by death, darkness, uncleanness, sin, and the demonic, and is characterized by divine absence. However, there are buffer zones between the extremes of holy and evil. Importantly, all space is dynamic, holiness is graded, and it is difficult to distinguish between "zones." The middle zones allow for the extension of God's grace. Experiential evil can be understood as a consequence of boundary violation; the evil periphery intruding into the grey zones.

Space also involves actions. Whereas actions at Zone 1 (e.g., blessing) and Zone 5 (e.g., demonic affliction) are unidirectional, actions in middle zones are bidirectional. Humans can choose to turn towards God or towards evil. Those who choose evil likely dwell close to the periphery of reality, subject to demonic influence, although the invitation to join the kingdom remains open. Those who worship the one true God are responsible for distinguishing between good and evil, continually reapplying the limits on evil, returning it to the outer regions of chaos, and consequently cleansing the cosmos. Obedience leads to the strengthening of boundaries on evil; disobedience results in these boundaries being loosened. Unlike a warfare model, which emphasizes battle imagery, this model uses metaphorical systems of boundaries, ordering, and cleansing to describe the maintenance and extension of sacred space. God, through his Spirit, primarily maintains order in the world and purifies it from sin and uncleanness; his light and life flow out into all reality, and he operates with authority not warfare. However, humans have much responsibility. Building on the cultic conception of dirt and disorder, and the imagery of the church as the household of God, one could conceive of evil as household dust and dirt. It tends to accumulate and requires regular cleaning, or "holy housekeeping." Similarly, sacred actions can be viewed as the expansion and maintenance of the household or sacred space, spreading the light of Christ and sending demons back to their peripheral dwelling. This model not only provides alternate language for discussing evil, but also furthers our understanding of evil.

Cleansing and Theology

The results of this study interface with various aspects of theology, many of which have been alluded to. Creation theology fits well with a model of sacred space and sacred actions, especially with respect to creation involving separation, order, and boundary-setting. Creation is often viewed as a continual process (recall discussion in chapter 4), which correlates with the dynamic nature of this model. Soteriology can be understood in spatial terms as Christ redefining sacred space, and humans having the choice of either turning towards the sacred center or the evil periphery. Eschatology can be viewed as the final spatial separation of evil. Theology of religions can be informed by the model of light spreading out from the center and blessing all. This study particularly informs pneumatology, especially as it applies to evil, and demonology.

Pneumatology

Studies of evil have typically focused on God as the divine warrior and/ or Christ as battling demons. This is perhaps due to a concomitant focus on warfare imagery, but potentially results in a minimization of the third person of the Trinity.[18] The activity of the Spirit is evident in all the themes examined in this book. Note that pneumatology is emphasized here because it is an area that has been somewhat neglected in the study of evil; this is not meant to elevate the Spirit above other members of the Trinity. An emphasis on the Spirit may also provide a way to integrate biblical and theological views, plus Western and non-Western views. Furthermore, Charismatic Christianity has emphasized both the Holy Spirit and demonology, although not always relating the two. In this section, I discuss the ontology and activity of the Spirit, plus the conundrum of omnipresence and divine absence.

---

18. The relationship of the Spirit to the Trinity has been much discussed; briefly, I follow the traditional doctrine of *perichoresis*, the interrelatedness of the trinity; Cole, *He Who Gives*, 59–91; Pinnock, *Flame*, 21–48.

ONTOLOGY AND ACTIVITY

There are multiple biblical metaphors for the Spirit: life-breath, wind, fire, water, cloud, and dove. Numerous theological metaphors have also been suggested: midwife, companion, gardener, and waiter.[19] Notably, the Spirit is never described with warfare imagery.[20] Historically he has been associated with peace, comfort, consolation, humility, and quietude, none of which is battle-like.[21] Wind imagery, prominent in OT texts, may provide alternative language to warfare. The Spirit blows away the waters of chaos and breathes life into humans. Through the Spirit/breath of God, demons are expelled. Wind and breath imagery imply awe and mystery, not violence.[22] Interestingly, there is no wind imagery in the new creation (suggesting that the action of the Spirit with respect to evil is no longer required). Viewing the Spirit as wind may provide insight into both the ontology and activity of the Spirit, and offer ways to conceptualize counteracting evil. Some contemporary theologians use wind imagery; for example, Welker: "The wind sent by God is a power that defines and changes history and representative identities."[23] Pannenberg has extended this imagery and related it to science by envisioning the Spirit as a force field.[24] A force field is dynamic and powerful, but not warring. This view

---

19. Kärkkäinen, *Pneumatology*, 23–25; Edwards, *Breath of Life*, 110–16. E. Dreyer believes metaphors are often more helpful than the abstractions with which the Spirit has commonly been described; *Holy Presence*.

20. As Welker states, the Spirit is "anything but a Spirit of war" or "military enthusiasm;" he is "not a spirit of war, but delivers out of distress and helplessness as a Spirit of righteousness and mercy"; *God the Spirit,* 54–57.

21. Especially in the medieval period; Burgess, *The Holy Spirit: Medieval.*

22. E.g., Cole, *He Who Gives,* 41; Pinnock, *Flame,* 9, 144. Wind imagery was emphasized by Basil of Caesarea, who insisted that the Word of God and the Breath of God are inextricably associated; *On the Holy Spirit,* 9.23, 16.38–39, 18.46–47, 19.49. It should be noted that perceiving the Spirit as a force does not preclude or diminish his status as a person; Oberdorfer, "The Holy Spirit—A Person?" 27–46.

23. And leads people out of "danger, out of demonic possession, and . . . self-destruction"; Welker, *God the Spirit,* 28, 99; see also Packer, *Keep in Step,* 57–59; Ferguson, *Holy Spirit,* 18.

24. Pannenberg, *ST 1,* 79–101, 370–84, 2.20–34, 76–77, 198–99, 451–52. His followers include Pinnock, *Flame,* 25; Welker, *God,* 22; "The Holy Spirit," 236–48, and Yong, *Discerning,* 226–33. From a scientific perspective, Toolan notes that all matter is characterized by fields or waves; the universe is radically interconnected; "God is no idler but the great Energy Field in whom all creation lives and moves and has its being"; *Home in the Cosmos,* 181, 200; recall discussion on Chaos and Science in chapter 3.

emphasizes the role of the Spirit in creation; as a field, it is the way in which all creation participates in the divine life. As discussed previously, the Holy Spirit plays a pivotal role in establishing God's kingdom, from original creation to temple, from Christ to church. The Spirit hovers over creation and breathes life into all things. He provides Israel with divine care, divine governance, and divine communication (through the prophets). There are many promises of renewal, restoration, and re-creation provided by the Spirit,[25] as well as multiple pneumatological moments in the earthly ministry of Christ (discussed in chapter 6). The Spirit fills believers and births the church. He is involved in regeneration and continual creation (Tit 3:5). Various scholars throughout Christian history have noted the Spirit's role in creation, which relates to wind imagery (discussed in chapter 4). Sometimes the Holy Spirit is described as preserving creation rather than re-creating. However, both require activity, the difference is one of degree.[26] This activity can also be viewed as ordering and cleansing, in keeping with cultic imagery, although this theme is not prominent in theology. John Calvin particularly associates the activity of the Spirit with order. He views the fall as a violation of divine order; creation is now dependent on the Creator for the maintenance of order, the reordering of the world, and the prevention of the intrusion of disorder. In fact, the entire cosmic structure would collapse if God's Spirit were withdrawn. The Spirit exercises "chaos management."[27] There is a complex interplay between order and disorder/chaos and ordering is a dynamic notion, fitting with wind imagery. Denis Edwards notes that "the Spirit goes 'out' to what is not divine and enables it to exist by participating in the divine being." He

---

25. E.g., Ezekiel's prophecies about a new heart and cleansing (36:22–26; 37:1–14); see also Isa 32:9–18; 44:1–4; Cole, *He Who Gives*, 136–37, 140–41; Welker, *God*, 142–44.

26. This difference is not often emphasized; Pinnock, *Flame*, 52–61. Edwards emphasizes continual creation, which is similar to preservation; *Breath of Life*, 47. Cole believes most evidence suggests that the Spirit is not actually creative but life-giving; *He Who Gives*, 104; but I am not sure such a distinction can or should be made. Assuming a high pneumatology, all three members of the Trinity are equally active in creation, therefore giving life can be seen as equivalent to creating.

27. Calvin, *Institutes*, I.xvi.2–4; 1.13.22; *Commentary on Ezekiel*, 20:12; *Commentary on Isaiah*, 44.4; *Comment on Genesis* 1:2. Divine ordering of creation has also been discussed with reference to science, although without an emphasis on the Spirit. Torrance emphasizes the contingency of creation: left to itself, contingent reality retreats from order into chaos and nonbeing; *Divine and Contingent Order*, 91. He notes that both science and theology operate under a constraint of the ultimate ground of order; *Christian Frame of Mind*, 20–21.

relates the dynamic and relational nature of the Spirit with the nature of the universe.[28] All creation benefits from the activity of the Spirit; this idea is known as common grace.[29] The dynamic Spirit thus organizes chaos and extends the boundaries of divine reality. Through the breath/Spirit of God, evil spirits are dispelled. Demons are dealt with in the same manner as chaos.

Water or cleansing imagery can also be used to describe the activity of the Spirit, which accords with this study's finding that cleansing and ordering are intertwined. The Spirit's role in cleansing is associated with his role as sanctifier.[30] And, as discussed in chapter 5, holiness relates to separation and ordering. Sanctification can be considered both individualistically and corporately. Followers of Christ need to turn to the sacred center before ministering to the periphery. Finally, the Spirit is involved in the maintenance and ministry of the church.[31] He is responsible for revelation, inspiration, and illumination. The role of the Spirit in enabling Christians to discern evil spirits has been discussed, and will be further addressed in the section on counseling.

RECONCILING DIVINE PRESENCE AND ABSENCE

Many contemporary theologians assert that the Spirit is universal and ubiquitous. Thus Moltmann: "God's Spirit is life's vibrating, vitalizing field of energy: we are in God, and God is in us";[32] and Clark Pinnock: The Spirit is "an ocean containing the world"; everything "from spiders to galaxies, manifests the power of the Spirit"; "God's breath is everywhere."[33] This relates to the classic theological doctrine of omnipresence.[34] Omni-

---

28. The universe being also dynamic and relational; Edwards, *Breath of Life*, 120, 127, 130–39.

29. Cole, *He Who Gives*, 110–11.

30. Ibid., 228–29; see also Moltmann, *Source of Life*, 48–53.

31. Pinnock, *Flame*, 113–47.

32. Moltmann, *Spirit of Life*, 161; *Source of Life*, 55, 117. Moltmann's views are panentheistic but perhaps border on pantheism; see also Edwards, *Breath of Life*, 139–42; Jantzen, *God's World*.

33. Pinnock, *Flame*, 36–41, 62, 70, 186–90; "the Spirit hovers over the world, beyond the church, providing universal access to God and ubiquitous inspiration" (192–205). Part of his motive for emphasizing the universal Spirit is to argue for the wideness of God's mercy in the possibility for salvation outside of the Christian Church; see also Edwards; *Breath of Life*, 50, 139–42.

34. Omnipresence has been relatively neglected in classic Western Theology,

presence is seldom discussed with respect to the philosophical problem of evil or evil spirits, yet if God indwells everything, the problem is obvious: divine presence within evil is logically and ontologically absurd. From the perspective of philosophy, this implicates God as the perpetrator of evil;[35] from the perspective of demonology, it is difficult to imagine evil spirits and God's Spirit cohabiting. However, the few scholars who do discuss omnipresence and evil sometimes appear contradictory. Yong proclaims the universal presence of the Spirit, yet believes evil is characterized by divine absence.[36] He compares pneumatological categories of divine presence (truth, goodness, beauty) and divine absence (destruction, lies, evil, profane), and is correct in his assertion that discussions of divine presence necessitate discussions of divine absence.[37] Curiously, he describes the demonic as "force fields that neutralize the presence of the Holy Spirit and counter his activity even while they originate and perpetuate destruction and evil in the world." Surely no force is stronger than the Holy Spirit. Yong elsewhere claims that the demonic is nothing if not personally manifest, which appears to contradict his assertion of the demonic as a force field.[38] Moltmann is also confusing in emphasizing the kenosis of the Spirit and "God-forsaken space," which he does not reconcile with omnipresence.[39] Pinnock is similarly confusing in his assertions of omnipresence and his

compared with its partners omnipotence and omniscience, and is often assumed unreflectively. Definitions range from a "weak" form, "the world is present to God"; Aquinas, *Summa Contra Gentiles*, III.68.3, to a strong form, "God indwells and contains all things"; Highfield, *Great is the Lord*, 283. The "strong" view has historical precedent: Augustine described God as "wholly everywhere," "filling heaven and earth with omnipresent power"; *City of God*, VII.30; Aquinas claimed God exists "everywhere in everything," sustaining existence; *Summa Theologica*, I.8.1–3.

35. Philosophies that demythologize or psychologize evil spirits and monistic views that attribute evil to God do not challenge the doctrine of omnipresence. However, semi-dualistic theologies, which affirm the reality of demons and seek to dissociate God from evil, need to wrestle with the concept of omnipresence.

36. Compare Yong, *Beyond the Impasse*, 43–46 with Yong, *Discerning*, 127. He believes the pneumatological imagination is well equipped to consider diverse forms of the Spirit's presence and absence and suggests that "the experience of divine *absence* . . . is properly termed 'demonic'"; *Discerning*, 127, 178–9, 233–49.

37. Yong, *Beyond the Impasse*, 165; *Discerning*, 243. He states there are no pure categories of divine and demonic; *Beyond the Impasse* 167; I agree regarding the complexity of evil, but this statement does not accord with experiential accounts of "pure evil" (e.g., Peck, *People of the Lie*).

38. Yong, *Discerning*, 240; *Beyond the Impasse*, 129, 138.

39. Wind, light, and fire represent kenosis of personhood; Moltmann, *Spirit of Life*, 12, 51, 61–64.

statement that the Spirit is up against those who negate God, "locked in mortal combat" with powers of resistance.[40] These apparent contradictions can be informed by the results of this study.

Defenders of omnipresence often quote Psalm 139:7, "Where can I flee from your presence?" (this however, is not primarily a metaphysical statement about omnipresence but a cry from an ardent follower who gives the impression he does not *want* to flee God's presence);[41] Acts 2:17, the Spirit poured out on all flesh ("flesh" confirms the absence of the divine in evil spirits, and contra Pinnock, disqualifies divine presence in galaxies and, in my opinion, spiders); and Wisdom 12:1, God's "immortal Spirit is in all things" (like Ps 139, the intent of this verse is praise, not philosophy). However, as shown in chapters 4 through 7, divine presence is complex: it is dynamic, can indwell people and places, and varies in intensity. There are general assurances that God's majesty and provision is present in nature (Ps 8:3; Isa 40:12; Jer 23:24; Matt 5:45), that he is nearby (Jer 23:23) and "not far from each one of us" (Acts 17:27), and that Christ is present wherever two or three are gathered in his name (Matt 18:20, 28:16–20). (This last statement is potentially ambiguous: if divine presence accompanies "two or three" gathered in Jesus' name, is he not present with only one, or those not gathered in his name?) However, this presence is not guaranteed (David's petition is well known: "Do not cast me away from your presence," Ps 51:11; Jonah "flees from the presence of the Lord," Jonah 1.3). People are given a choice whom they follow and which direction they turn (e.g., "choose life," Deut 30:19; "whoever is not with me is against me," Matt 12:30; "You cannot drink the cup of the Lord and the cup of demons," 1 Cor 10:21). They can blaspheme and grieve the Spirit (Isa 63:10; Matt 12:32; Mark 3:29); some are "alienated from the life of God because of their ignorance and hardness of heart" (Eph 4:18); and believers are encouraged to discern between good and evil (1 John 4:1–3); although if the divine is omnipresent, is there need for discernment? Furthermore, there is evidence that God does not reconcile evil but separates it from his good creation: He blows away waters, departs from the corrupt

40. Pinnock, *Flame*, 62. Andrew Gabriel, who otherwise asserts omnipresence, is contradictory in his claim that discernment is needed because there are evil powers at work distinct from the Holy Spirit (if the Spirit is ubiquitously present, how can there be opposing spiritual entities?), and that Ananias and Sapphira died as a result of the "withdrawal and absence of the power of the Spirit" (is he separating divine presence from activity?); *Lord is the Spirit*, 192, 203.

41. Jantzen points out that this Psalm places more emphasis on God's loving awareness and ability to intervene than on omnipresence; *God's World*, 96.

temple, and sends demons to the abyss. As shown throughout this study, evil or profane space is characterized by darkness, demons, disorder, and divine absence.

There are some possible solutions to this conundrum. First, absence can be considered illusory.[42] This may explain some instances of divine absence but not all, like the separation of evil, and only explains divine absence as it relates to followers of God; there is no indication that divine absence is illusory to those who do not desire divine presence. Second, one could consider God as always present but not always active. This idea seems to be implied by Pinnock and Moltmann, who assert omnipresence but limitation with respect to omnipotence (discussed above and in chapter 4). This is certainly a valid option; it accords with most biblical texts and the idea of varying intensifications of presence (see below). But this idea requires expansion; it does not address the dilemma of divine presence within evil spirits and leads to more questions (e.g., is inactive presence significantly different from absence?). I think it is more difficult to understand a God who is always present but refuses to act, than a God who is not present within perpetrators of evil. Third, and, in my opinion, most viably, one could adopt a general form of omnipresence (the world is present to God; he watches from heaven, intervening when called upon and/or when divinely necessary). This view fits with biblical portrayals of divine absence. This does not mean that God cannot at times gift creation with his presence. However, viewing God as present in every molecule of creation is not required to support the view that God is intimately involved with creation. The primary problem with this view is that the Bible attests that the Spirit gives life—if he is not present within all humans, how is life possible? Two factors offer potential solutions. First, general divine presence, common grace, could be considered sufficient for the sustenance of life. The breath of the Spirit could give life from outside humans, not necessarily from within. As the rain falls on the righteous and unrighteous, even those who reject God can benefit from the air, water, and food provided by creation, without having the indwelling divine presence. As Welker notes, the Spirit is not only given to certain people but "benefits their spatial and

42. Terrien, although he does not focus on evil, argues that God's presence is always hidden, elusive, and fragile; divine absence is an expression of divine mystery; *Elusive Presence*, 321; Pannenberg believes divine absence is a result only of human inability to understand God's ways; *ST* 1, 79–101, 370–84, 410–14. Fretheim, with respect to the departure of God from the temple, claims this does not mean that God is absent but only less intense, and therefore perceived as absent. He claims "actual absence is not a divine possibility in the Old Testament"; *God and World*, 25.

temporal, proximate and distant environments."[43] Second, many biblical texts can be interpreted metaphorically: life means participation in the divine, not necessarily physical life. Just as death was understood as separation from God (discussed in chapters 4, 5, and 7), so life is understood as divine union. Thus physical life can be sustained by common grace, but *true* life requires the indwelling Spirit.

Related to general omnipresence is the idea of varying intensifications of the Spirit. Pinnock, for example, notes that wind imagery varies in intensity from breath to storm; the Spirit is "more present" in humans and "more effectively present" to those who know the risen Christ.[44] Considering divine presence to vary in intensity accords with the biblical evidence and offers some improvement over "strong" views, but can still be inconsistent (does the degree of divine presence ever get so small that it is practically absent?). I believe it is necessary to consider the possibility of divine absence. In this I agree with Welker, who argues against any notion of an abstract ubiquity of the Spirit; it blows "where it wills," is subtle and sensitive, and is not an irresistible force. He also acknowledges the possibility of divine absence.[45] The idea of gradations of divine presence that can fade to absence is supported by the findings of this study. Recall the OT discussion of divine absence as a result of cosmic structure and the boundaries of creation. Recall Barth's idea of evil as nothingness outside that willed by God, existing at the periphery of creation.[46] Recall

43. Welker, *God the Spirit*, 338.

44. Pinnock, *Flame of Love*, 14, 73, 116. Fretheim also believes there are indications of "varying intensifications of the divine presence in the world"; *God and World*, 25. Gabriel argues that although God is omnipresent, the Spirit's presence changes and intensifies in relation to Jesus and the church; *Lord is the Spirit*, 174–78. However, he is somewhat confusing in his insistence that this is not a literal intensification; he "cannot fully articulate why." Welker also endorses varying intensifications of the Spirit, arguing that the "face of God" represents concentrated divine presence; *God the Spirit*, 152; the prophetic endowments and the outpouring of the Spirit at Pentecost demonstrate a "concentrated presence of God in the midst of reality" (155), and Jesus is the concrete bearer of Spirit (183–95).

45. The Spirit does not act and operate in each situation in the same way; Welker, "The Holy Spirit," 243–44. Welker does not explicitly articulate divine absence, but claims that the Spirit is not present "in that which is decaying to dust . . . human beings can grieve and banish God's Spirit"; Welker, *God the Spirit*, 161. Gabriel accuses Welker of failing to recognize that the Spirit is present in different and changing ways; *Lord is the Spirit*, 174–75. However, Welker is otherwise clear regarding varying intensifications of divine presence, and simply takes it a step further in acknowledging divine absence.

46. Interestingly Barth holds a strong view of omnipresence, claiming there is no

that, in Israel's cult, sacred space was defined by the presence of the divine; profane space conversely can be defined by divine absence. True life and absolute reality is experienced by those who choose to be in relationship with the divine, those who are indwelt by the Spirit. (Perhaps texts that suggest "strong" divine presence refer only to divine reality.) Those who oppose God and reject his Spirit are denied divine presence, therefore inhabit a somehow lesser or false reality, although they nevertheless benefit from divine providence. Evil spirits lack divine presence and true reality but seek to attain reality by intruding upon divine reality.

One way to consider omnipresence is to view the divine as going *to* but not *within* all things. The Revelation (3:20) image of Christ standing at the door knocking, but not entering unless invited, can assist conceptualization. When invited, the Spirit indwells believers, but otherwise patiently knocks. Divine limitations have mostly been discussed with respect to power and omnipotence, although with considerable controversy.[47] But there is no reason divine kenosis cannot apply to presence too. The Spirit is *able* to be present in all things, but out of respect for creaturely freedom, he limits his presence. He invites rather than invades. This view is compatible with a general view of omnipresence, divine providence, and graded reality. It accords with biblical images of the divine going to evil and sending it away, not indwelling it: The Spirit "blows away" the sea in creation and the exodus, and Jesus operates through the Spirit in expelling demons. It is perhaps best to understand divine presence metaphorically rather than philosophically.[48] Omnipresence can be understood in a broad manner, divine presence can be conceived of as graded and variable, and divine absence is possible and logically necessary with respect to evil

---

place where God is less present than all other places; *CD* II.1, 470–72; 467–76. It seems that he tries to avoid the issue of divine absence by inventing "nothingness"—because it does not "fully" exist, he can still assert omnipresence. Perhaps what Barth is really saying is that divine omnipresence is limited to godly reality; that to which God says "yes." Evil and demons are separated from God, and therefore associated with divine absence. This comment applies also to Moltmann's idea of God-forsaken space.

47. Explained as the logical necessity of divine restriction in the face of human freedom (e.g., Pinnock et al., *The Openness of God*). Boyd argues that God lovingly chooses to restrict his powers because human and spirit beings have genuine free will; *Satan*, 50–84, 183–85; Edwards states the power of the Spirit is patient and loving; not dominating but freely self-limiting, although he does not discuss evil; *Breath of Life*, 111.

48. As argued in chapter 2 and throughout this book. A. Funkenstein concurs that divine attributes are best understood symbolically rather than philosophically; *Theology and Scientific Imagination*, 49.

spirits. The light shines brightest where the divine is strongly present and its effects radiate throughout the world. However, it fades and eventually disappears; thus there is a dark rim of divine absence. Holiness exudes from the divine presence, yet godly reality can still be threatened by evil human and spiritual forces. We have reason to rejoice that divine presence is available to all who desire it, but we need to be discerning of divine absence and vigilant in working with and through the Spirit to dispel evil.

Demonology

As mentioned earlier, the study of demonology is often polarized between dismissing evil spirits as psychological/mythic projections and ascribing them personhood, power, and organization. There is a gap between anecdotal and theological writings. This study offers further insight into demonology. Unique features of my approach include metaphorical, not propositional or metaphysical, truth; linguistics (metaphors as reality-depicting); critical realism; binary oppositions; and chaos-complexity and dark matter as models for conceptualizing evil. In this section, I summarize and clarify the findings of this study with respect to demonology.

To reiterate, the semantic domain of evil in the Bible includes personal (Satan, Azazel, Beliar), spatial (sea, hell, abyss), abstract (darkness, chaos, powers), and ethical (sin, impurity) metaphors. Multiple terms are used and there is no technical precision with respect to classification; biblical authors are not concerned with distinguishing between abstract evil and concrete evil forces. These multiple metaphors provide several snapshots of the complex reality of evil. There is an evil spiritual reality that is best described metaphorically and can be apprehended, but primarily through the vehicle of metaphor. Thus views of evil as both abstract and personal need not conflict, but can be considered different perspectives on one reality. This may assist in bridging the gap between theological (largely abstract) and biblical (largely personal) perspectives on evil. Further insights from this study include evil as peripheral and quasi-real, and evil as boundary violation.

ONTOLOGY

The two ontological extremes of understanding evil, viewing evil as non-being or psychological projection and ascribing personhood to demons, were deemed unsatisfactory both on theological/logical and practical grounds. I disagree with Wink and Yong who claim evil is not separate from creatures and creation. As shown in this study, evil exists in binary opposition to divine reality, both in terms of space and activity. It is something wholly other that nevertheless can intrude upon creatures and creation. I agree that, on a phenomenological level, the intertwining of sin and evil is not easily distinguished, and I agree that human responsibility should be emphasized. However, if we only consider evil when it intrudes, then we are missing opportunities for prevention; we may also be placing blame where it is not due. Recall that much of the biblical witness depicts evil as separate from creation. I disagree too with Wagner, Kraft, Boyd, and others who suggest that demons have intelligence and great autonomy, and are engaged in warfare with God and humanity.

This study suggests a moderate position, arguing that evil can be considered as peripheral to godly reality, disordered, and semi-real. First, the sheer number, diversity, and frequent ambiguity of biblical terms imply disorganization and disorder, not order. Second, many biblical metaphors point to evil as chaotic and quasi-real: darkness and chaos imply disorder, waste and void imply unreality, some biblical passages suggest the semi-real nature of demons (discussed in chapters 4 through 6), and others refer to evil as disrupting the order of creation (e.g., the angelic "fall," discussed in chapter 4). Third, when evil is understood in binary opposition to God/holiness/sacred-space, further insight is obtained: sacred space is characterized by order, ultimate reality, truth, divine presence, and centrality, therefore evil can be conceived of as disorder, lesser reality, untruth, divine absence, and peripheral to divine reality. Evil can attain reality when it violates God-given boundaries. In philosophical terms one could consider that evil spirits have ontology but not personhood, or perhaps that they gain some degree of personhood when they enter people. They can be considered both impersonal (illustrated by the biblical metaphors, darkness and chaos) and personal (when they enter a person and in the biblical metaphors, Satan and demons). Biblical metaphors reflect the reality of evil spiritual forces as having reduced ontology and existing outside the structure of divine reality. This idea, obtained through metaphor theory, is compatible with, and maybe clarifies, a metaphysic of evil as outside the boundaries of reality and being quasi-real, which has been alluded to throughout this book.

Conceiving of evil as semi-real is preferable to the alternatives of unreal, which does not explain biblical or experiential demonization, and "excessively" real, which includes only a few of the biblical descriptors and tends to be dualistic. Viewing it as less real may reconcile the various biblical metaphors, some of which imply unreality (darkness) and some of which imply reality (demons). It accords with anecdotal descriptions of evil spirits as "shadowy" (e.g., Wagner, discussed in chapter 1). This view may provide a way to reconcile philosophical/abstract approaches to evil (nothingness) with demonological/concrete ones (Satan, demonization). It concurs well with Eliade's observations about the dichotomy of the sacred real and the profane unreal, and also informs some theological assertions. Barth's idea of nothingness is compatible with and perhaps improved by findings of this research. Nothingness, an awkward term, is easier to conceive of as a lesser reality; that which rejects God and which he in turn rejects; a reality that has potential to become real. In using the term "quasi-real," in some ways I am agreeing with Barth. I am also approving of N. G. Wright (the "devil possesses a much-reduced . . . way of being"[49]) and perhaps elaborate on his view using a biblically-based model. On the "real-unreal" spectrum however, my view is likely closer to "real" than these two scholars.

Other theologians have described evil in terms of quasi-reality, although without elaboration; for example, Robert Jenson: Evil is a "black hole that sucks in everything that approaches it."[50] From a psychological perspective, Shuster describes evil spirits as lacking "humanness," being empty, barren, and boring, with a deadening sameness.[51] The semi-real nature of evil is modeled well by scientific observations of quantum mechanics, chaos-complexity theory, and dark matter. Physics points out that empty space is composed of quasi-real particles and energy fields. Many systems in nature are dynamic and, although lacking intelligence, can self-organize into groups with destructive potential, the abstract becoming concrete. These models fit well with biblical depictions of evil as both abstract and concrete, and can explain the seemingly organized activity of

49. N. G. Wright, *Dark Side,* 76–82; and is "subpersonal or antipersonal" (40). He draws on Cook, who associates "Black Noise" and evil spirits suggesting that evil itself is impersonal but appears to the human consciousness as personal; "Devils," 181–82, and Noble, who suggests evil spirits are "damaged persons" or "anti-persons"; "Spirit World," 217. Interestingly, the subtitle of Wright's book, *Putting the Power of Evil in its Place,* is similar to my notion of putting evil in its place, returning it to outer regions. However, Wright is using the phrase in a philosophical sense, how we think about evil, whereas I am using it in a spatial-metaphorical manner.

50. Jenson, "Introduction," 6; see also N. G. Wright, *Dark Side,* 72–74, 79–81; Schwarz, *Evil,* 74, discussed previously.

51. Shuster, *Power, Pathology,* 187. Interestingly, primordial chaos is also described as empty (discussed in chapter 4).

demons. Perhaps abstract evil is partly composed of concrete evil spirits; the miasma of impurity in cultic theology can be seen as abstract evil; the Pauline powers could be viewed as self-organized demons. Evil spirits are best understood as a complex-chaotic system; nonlinear, and dynamic, comprising multiple components that interact with each other, lacking individuality and intelligence but with potential to self-organize into powerful forces. In short, *semi-real*.

Evil is frequently described as infectious, viral, or parasitic; usually without elaboration.[52] There is also sometimes inconsistency in the use of the metaphor; for example, Boyd, who otherwise argues for the autonomy of evil spirits, compares demons with "viruses that cannot survive long on their own; they need to infect someone or something."[53] Daniel Day Williams, who argues against any independent ontological status of demons, labels Satan a parasite with no independent existence.[54] However, as microbiologists would argue, parasites do have ontology, but not personhood. Medically we need to know about them in order to prevent disease and diagnose conditions caused by parasites. Perhaps parasites can be viewed, like subatomic particles, as quasi-real. This analogy concurs with this study's proposal for the ontology of evil as semi-real but able to attain reality when it violates a boundary.

According to the biblically-based model developed in this study, evil space is peripheral to sacred space and consequently characterized by divine absence and quasi-reality. It is inhabited by the devil and demons, those who have and always will reject divine grace. Without the light of Christ, it is qualitatively less real. It is hell that has not yet been completely separated, but is still an option for those who reject divine reality and choose life (really lack of life) apart from the Spirit. This idea of evil as semi-real is illustrated nicely in some fictional works. C. S. Lewis describes the devil as having such unstable reality that he inadvertently becomes a centipede when angry; and heaven as being more solid, more real than hell.[55] The demonic goblins in George MacDonald's children's classic had once lived above ground like humans, but "seeing they lived away from the sun, in cold and wet and dark places . . . were now . . . absolutely hideous or

---

52. E.g. Mallow, *The Demonic*, 158–61; N. G. Wright; *Dark Side*, 51–52, 57; Noble "The Spirit World," 215, 217; Russell, *Cosmology*, 233; all discussed previously, plus Yong, *Spirit of Creation*, 219–20; *Discerning*, 235; C. S. Lewis, *Mere Christianity*, 45.

53. Boyd, *God at War*, 195.

54. Williams, *Demonic and Divine*, 36.

55. Lewis, *Screwtape Letters*, 89; *Great Divorce*.

ludicrously grotesque."[56] Deprived of the Light, their existence is less real than that of humans. J. R. R. Tolkien's satanic figure, Sauron, exists only as a malevolent force until human wickedness gives him more substance, and Tolkien's Ringwraiths are similar quasi-real evil beings.[57]

ACTIVITY

This study examined demonology using spatial metaphors. Understanding the dynamics of sacred and profane space enables us to conceive of the activity of evil spirits as boundary violation. Sacred space and the Spirit who emanates from it are described as dynamic. Furthermore, since biblical sacred space is described as dynamic, evil spiritual forces can also be considered dynamic, nonlinear, complex systems. Consequently, they are able to violate their God-appointed boundaries and inflict evil on people in God's good creation. Creation texts suggest that God sets a boundary on chaos, but it continually seeks to cross its boundaries—and evil is experienced in the world. With respect to the angelic "fall," many texts point to this resulting from angels violating their God-given boundaries. The serpent/devil in Genesis also illustrates boundary violation. The notion of evil being due to boundary violation is particularly prominent in cultic theology. Defilement occurs when boundaries are crossed; this results in disorder (a characteristic of profane space). Sin, related to the demonic, can also be seen as transgressing a limit with consequent chaos. In the Gospel stories, it was noted that people are demonized because evil spirits have violated their boundaries, infiltrated godly reality (even appearing in a Synagogue), intruded upon humans (even children), and caused disruptions in the weather. The church, too, is affected by evil; sin especially being viewed as violating boundaries and thus allowing evil to intrude upon sacred space. The biblical descriptions of Satan's activity as deceiver and adversary, who oppresses people, blocks the way, and can hold people captive are compatible with boundary violation. The idea of evil occurring as a result of boundary violation has been implied, although not fully developed by some theologians, thus Origen: Evil occurs when human or supernatural beings "violate the divinely ordered administration of the universe and intentionally inflict harm";[58] Augustine: "Evil enters in when some member of the universal kingdom . . . renounces its proper

56. MacDonald, *Princess and the Goblin*, 13, 14.
57. Tolkien, *Lord of the Rings*.
58. Summarized by Pagels, *Origin*, 141.

role in the divine scheme and ceases to be what it is meant to be";[59] Barth: Nothingness/evil attains reality when it crosses its boundaries;[60] Tupper: "Whenever we violate creaturely boundaries of human existence . . . we unleash the destructive violence of chaos into human life";[61] and David Bentley Hart: The sea (evil), does not always stay "within its appointed bounds."[62]

However, the nature of the boundaries is complex, the relationship between sin and the demonic is complex, and the degree of autonomy that evil has is complex. A difficult question not fully addressed in this study is the issue of agency: Do evil spirits have complete autonomy, able to violate their boundaries at will; do they have limited autonomy; or are they completely under divine control? The biblical evidence is ambiguous; for example, the Satan of Job's prologue appears to be merely a servant of God but the Satan in the Gospels is clearly labeled an enemy who thwarts God's purposes. At times God appears to directly make use of evil; he punishes disobedience by letting evil forces out of their bounds, opening the gates and allowing them to reap destruction (e.g., the flood and the exodus, discussed previously). At other times evil forces appear to defy their God-ordained boundaries and encroach upon neutral zones.[63] There is also evidence that evil is contingent on sin, neither ordained by God, nor completely autonomous. It is clear that demons are compelled to obey Christ and those whom he authorizes, but this does not mean that all evil is under divine control.

This model supports a view of evil as semi-autonomous. This is compatible with an ontology of evil as semi-real, but attaining full reality through sin. It is perhaps the best way to make sense of the various biblical depictions of evil; a middle ground between no autonomy and full autonomy. Viewing evil as peripheral, albeit able to violate its boundaries, allows the recognition of the paradox between evil as real but limited. It also

59. Summarized by Hick, *Evil*, 53.

60. Barth, *CD III*.3.300, 307–8, 310, 350; Yong uses similar language in describing evil as intrusion; *Beyond the Impasse*, 55.

61. Tupper, *Scandalous Providence*, 141.

62. Hart, *Doors of the Sea*, 2.

63. Recall previous mention of the serpent, the *bĕnê ĕlōhîm*, psalmists' pleas for deliverance, Job, demonized children, and a storm being rebuked. This observation is supported by Cullman's rope analogy (*Christ and Time*, 198) which he furthers by suggesting that "the devil is bound to a line which can be lengthened, even to the point where for a while Satan can make himself independent and has to be fought against by God"; *Prayer in the NT*, 141.

emphasizes human responsibility. When people turn away from holiness, they automatically turn towards evil, in a sense inviting it in. Rejection of God, obvious in idolatry, results in implicit acceptance of the demonic and its associated evil. Furthermore, the Lord's blessing is required to maintain sacred space. With blatant disobedience, he withdraws his presence with a natural consequence of evil forces being let loose. However, because God is sovereign, he can dip into the darkness, using evil to accomplish his purposes (e.g., sending an evil spirit), or merely loosen the boundaries (e.g., the flood), or take advantage of times when evil has already violated its boundaries (perhaps Judas). But just because God does this sometimes, does not mean that *all* evil should be explained as divinely ordained.[64] Rather, some (I suspect little) evil is a result of God's will, some is a consequence of human free will and sin (one's own or others), and some is due to the action of evil spirits (operating out of limited freewill, violating their boundaries, and inflicting evil on people or other complex systems such as the weather). The agency of evil spirits relates to chaos-complexity theory. All natural systems are open and dynamic, involve multiple interactions with their environment, and are inherently unstable. Demons can be considered as having a large effect by influencing small factors. I suspect most experiential evil is a consequence of some combination of many different factors.

A related issue is that of sin as boundary violation and its relationship to the demonic. The sin of the first humans can be viewed thus: their sin opened the doors to evil. In cultic theology, sin, impurity, and the demonic were found to be intertwined. Sin is dynamic and systemic, sometimes depicted as a miasmic force or a superhuman power. It is described as originating both from Satan and from the heart. On occasion people are afflicted with demons as a consequence of sin, and Christians are warned not to sin and give the devil a foothold. Sin perhaps can be better understood within a spatial framework. Both sin and the demonic are in binary opposition to God and holiness. If people sin, they violate a boundary and open a door for evil spirits to enter, affirming the idea that demons are parasitic on sin. Sin as an entry point for the demonic was discussed previously, but recall that not all sin has demonic origin, and evil spirits

---

64. I agree with Boyd on this aspect (e.g., *God at War*, 81, 154). However, Boyd appears to assign complete autonomy to evil spirits. He labels people casualties of war, which suggests they are innocent bystanders. He also goes too far in stating that Jesus "understood all the evil in the world . . . as being ultimately . . . due to the work of the all-pervasive Satanic kingdom" (235). Somewhat inconsistently, he includes an appendix on the "theology of chance" in *Satan*.

can afflict those who are without sin. It should be noted that boundary violation can be bidirectional: evil beings may transgress their boundaries to tempt or incite humans to sin; if humans do sin (turning away from God and thus transgressing their boundaries), then evil spirits can further violate their boundaries, and inflict humans further. Thus there is an intertwining spiral of sin and demonic affliction.[65]

Viewing evil as boundary violation allows for a less dualistic conception of evil than a warfare model, and a greater emphasis on human responsibility. Given the nonlinear nature of both sacred and profane space, one can conceive of the profane intruding upon the sacred and opposing the extension of sacred space. Evil spirits can be viewed as dynamic and parasitic, seeking to attain full reality by violating their boundaries (which are also dynamic and fluid) and intruding upon divine reality. They are perhaps best understood as having autonomy that is limited by God and the church, but expanded by human sin. The dynamic nature of space implies that boundaries are not fixed but fluid. They continually need to be maintained and sometimes redefined. We need to be aware of evil violating its boundaries both at the individual level (demonization) and the communal level (structural evil). Humans move freely in the grey zones between sacred and profane space; demons move, not quite as freely, from the black zone of profane space into the grey zones of reality.

Cleansing and Ministry

The findings of this study interface with many aspects of Christian ministry, and the model suggested has multiple potential applications. Even those areas that are not particularly concerned with evil can benefit from the increased awareness of the evil periphery that this model provides. The idea of focusing on sacred space/center/light/holiness is similar to teachings in Christian mysticism and spiritual formation. This model's emphasis on human response, both individual and corporate, can confirm evangelistic efforts, which invite people to turn from dark to light, from

65. This is contrary to Powlison's contention that sin and the demonic are separate phenomena; sin is never a cause of demonization; *Power Encounters*, 66–74. He is critiquing the "spiritual warfare" literature but goes too far in my opinion. By contrast, Cook suggests that the demonic can be viewed as simultaneously internal (Jungian sin) and external (as in traditional African religion), although he does not develop this idea; "Devils and Manticores," 177; and Noble posits a symbiotic relationship between sin and the demonic; "Spirit World," 215. I think symbiotic is too strong a term, implying equality of sin and the demonic; parasitic is better.

the periphery to the center. Some aspects of ecclesiology include maintaining the boundaries of the church, healing those within and inviting those without. Worship functions to reinforce boundaries on evil by proclaiming and exalting Christ. The sacrament of Baptism can be conceived of as cleansing, and in fact was associated with exorcism in ancient and orthodox churches.[66] Soaking in the center and receiving the Spirit dispels evil spirits. The Eucharist can be a reminder of the defeat of evil at Christ's death and resurrection, thus reinforcing boundaries on evil.[67] However, Christians are called out from the center to minister to the periphery. This section focuses on two aspects of ministry: missiology and counseling/deliverance.

Missiology

In the past, much mission theology was based on a few "proof-texts," but there is a recent move to integrate theology with missions and develop an overall framework for understanding mission.[68] It is also increasingly recognized that mission is not just geographic, but holistic.[69] There are multiple metaphors for mission in the Bible.[70] Demonology is an important aspect of missiology, but missionary dealings with the demonic are usually described in terms of "power encounters" (as discussed in chapter 1). Although this may be the preferred model in some situations, the model developed in this book offers an alternative framework for a theology of mission. Missiology and Anthropology have much in common;

66. Hippolytus, *Apostolic Tradition*, 20:3, 21.7–10; Russell, *Satan*, 101; Twelftree, *Name of Jesus*, 218–19; 259–62; Daunton-Fear, *Healing*, 83–100; Pinnock, *Flame*, 123–26.

67. Pinnock, *Flame of Love*, 126–28.

68. D. Bosch claims it is impossible to infer mission principles from isolated texts and there is no uniform theology; "Biblical Models of Mission," 175–92; *Transforming Mission*, 16. Some recent attempts at an integrated missiology include the above plus Tippet, *Introduction to Missiology*; Bauckham, *Bible and Mission*; Ott et al., *Theology of Mission*. There is also increasing recognition of what can be learned from other religions; Yong, *Beyond the Impasse*, 35–41; Ferdinando, "Spiritual Realm," 21–41; Anderson, "Demons and Deliverance," 42–62.

69. J. Scherer states mission is not geographical but involves "crossing the frontier between faith in Christ as Lord and unbelief"; "Mission Theology," 197; Pinnock believes mission is holistic because sin affects world structures; *Flame*, 145–46.

70. E.g., agriculture, military, architectural, athletic, and market; Muck and Adeney, *Christianity Encountering Religions*, 10, 311–16, 20–28, 353–77. They suggest the metaphor of gift.

therefore, the anthropological foundations of this model make it pertinent to missiology. Recall the observations of Eliade that sacred/profane dichotomies are universal, and of Douglas that order/disorder metaphors are common to most religions. Rather than using warfare imagery, evil spirits could be discussed and counteracted using the language of cleansing and setting boundaries. The universal images of space, centrality, and light are likely applicable cross-culturally. It may be helpful to use multiple metaphors, some of which may provide common ground between differing religions, thus enhancing communication. Imagery can cross language barriers. In cultures in which belief in spirit beings is prominent, using alternate images may provide a way to affirm the reality of demons while putting them in proper perspective.

The ideas of space and direction have been suggested by some missiologists, with some points of interaction with the model developed in this study. Richard Bauckham notes the biblical movement from the center to the periphery, Jerusalem to the ends of earth: "mission is a movement toward ever-new horizons." Directions include centripetal (inwards) and centrifugal (outwards), but the dominant image is centrifugal (God sending prophets, his Son, and his disciples). A centripetal model is used to show God as the author of mission.[71] Ott et al. suggest that mission in the NT changes to centrifugal (the sending of disciples to the nations) from an OT centripetal movement (nations turning towards Israel), although they admit it is complex. The church today continues to live in the "movement from Pentecost to Christ's return, from creation to new creation, from Jerusalem to the ends of the earth, to the new Jerusalem."[72] David Forney expounds a spatial model for mission. In the Hebrew tradition, the tent of meeting and the unclean were outside the camp; Jesus was also crucified outside the city; the "city and the trash heap are connected; Jerusalem and Golgotha are inextricably linked."[73] He suggests that Christians are to live liminally by living in the city and journeying outside the gate; when we journey to Jesus outside the gate, the encounter sends us back to the city to serve. Forney's model has some similarities to my model but differs greatly in terms of directionality. I believe the predominant imagery is that the "city" is central. As discussed in chapter 6, Jesus went out of holy space

---

71. Bauckham, *Bible and Mission*, 14, 26, 72–79; the new center is "everywhere and nowhere."

72. Ott et al., *Theology of Mission*, 21–41, 52.

73. Forney, "Living in the City," 60; but he misses the point that Jesus went out into unclean spaces in order to cleanse them.

in order to cleanse profane space, which explains why he was crucified outside the gate. We are to encounter Jesus in the metaphorical space of the city, then go outside to serve.

The model suggested by this study can be thus applied to mission: We first meet Jesus in sacred space (worship, prayer, church fellowship); when fortified and filled with the Spirit, we can journey outwards to serve and spread the good news of what Christ has accomplished; as we encounter evil spirits, we can command them, as authorized by Christ, to leave afflicted people, thus resetting boundaries on evil and healing/cleansing the cosmos.

Christian Counseling and Deliverance

Many of the findings of this study have implications for counseling and deliverance ministries. Although these are not necessarily new, their association with a cohesive and comprehensive model is. This section does not constitute an attempt to offer a new counseling technique or a comprehensive integration of psychology and theology.[74] Rather, it looks for applications of the findings of this study to counseling and deliverance, as well as points of interaction with existing literature. Recall that warfare language, often associated with violence, is poorly applicable to counseling and in fact may constrain therapeutic progress due to the limitations of warfare metaphors. The emphasis on power encounters in a warfare model makes it a hardly ideal model for counseling those who have been wounded by the abuse of power. Interestingly, "spiritual warfare" literature is often inconsistent: those doing therapy do not necessarily use warfare language, although they conceive of demonization in those terms.[75] In fact, metaphors of space and boundaries are used intuitively, without

---

74. There have been attempts at integrating theology and psychology: L. Crabb describes various approaches, including viewing the Bible and psychology as separate but equal or arbitrarily using different aspects of both; he advocates an approach that uses psychology cautiously, ensuring it is compatible with the Bible; *Effective Biblical Counselling*, 26–47; Anderson et al. categorize the different models for integrative counseling as Bible-only, closet (being Christian privately), closed (integrated but not open), and conjoint (the most balanced in their opinion); types of therapists include Christian professional (emphasis on psychology) and lay (emphasis on the Bible); *Christ-Centered Therapy*, 62–71.

75. E.g., Bufford in his section titled "spiritual warfare" suggests submitting to God, resisting temptation and confessing sin as counseling techniques—these actually fit better within a spatial framework; *Counseling and the Demonic*, 150–51; see also Scanlan and Cirner; *Deliverance from Evil Spirits*, 85–90.

overt awareness of the inconsistency between the model used ("spiritual warfare") and the counseling metaphors used. It is advantageous to have a model that is consistent in theory and praxis. One point of interaction of this study and counseling is the use of figurative language. Since counseling is predominantly "talk-therapy," psychologists have pointed out the importance of language.[76] Imagery and metaphor in counseling have been discussed, with suggestions for using guided imagery and being attuned to the spontaneous emergence of metaphor.[77]

The spatial model suggested in this study offers a way of conceptualizing reality that may assist counselors in understanding and dealing with evil. People come for counseling because their lives are disordered and chaotic: they are experiencing the infiltration of evil forces from the periphery of reality. Part of the therapist's responsibility according to this model is to help reestablish order. Almost all the source of the disorder is rooted in sin (their own or their suffering due to someone else's sin) and/or demonic affliction. Interestingly, models of human anthropology often use concentric circles similar to the spatial model developed in this study. The spirit is at the center, followed by the heart/mind/emotions/will and body.[78] The spirit is perhaps most able to connect to the Spirit of God; the body at the periphery perhaps most vulnerable to demonic influence. Some have suggested viewing spirit, soul, and body as separate,[79] but biblical thought (especially Hebrew) usually views humans holistically.[80] A concentric model of human anthropology accords with suggestions from cultic theology that human structure is a microcosm of cosmic structure (e.g., Eliade, Simkins, and Douglas, discussed previously).

76. More prominent in the last few decades with the emergence of Cognitive Behavioral Therapy (CBT) and Narrative Therapy, e.g., Barden and Williams, *Words and Symbols*.

77. Hall et al., *Guided Imagery*; Singer, *Imagery in Psychotherapy*; CBT works in some ways by shifting metaphors, which can then shift thought and represent the fuller context of a situation. Using the journey metaphor in particular has been suggested; Lines, *Spirituality in Counseling*, 123–37; see also Jäkel, discussed in chapter 5. In terms of deliverance, Payne relates an occasion in which she saw an evil "eel-like thing slithering away"; she knew it was a demonic, stubborn spirit but did not conclude that "stubborn spirits are eel-like"—that would have meant mistaking the "symbolic form for the thing itself"; *Healing Presence*, 175.

78. Anderson et al., *Christ-Centered Therapy*, 86.

79. E.g., John and Paula Sandford, *Healing the Wounded Spirit*, 7–14.

80. E.g., Seamands, *Redeeming the Past*, 13.

The model suggested by this study has potential specific applications for counseling. First, a focus on the center equips the counselor.[81] With respect to deliverance, Leanne Payne encourages "practicing the presence" within, without, and all around, like carrying the cross. If we "do not practice the Presence of God, we will practice the presence of another."[82] She encourages knowing one's identity in Christ, seeking the truth of the Spirit and forgiving others as a way to overcome evil. Payne insists we are to be Christ-centered, not demon-centered.[83] Some counselors suggest qualifications for those dealing with the demonic, such as belief, humility, compassion, wisdom, boldness, and dependence on other Christians.[84]

Second, this model can guide discernment. This study suggested evil as having multifactorial causation; exorcism, healing, and cleansing are intertwined; sin and demonization are related; illness and demonization are sometimes associated. Because evil is a result of a complex interaction of multiple factors, including diabolical persuasion, demonic affliction, and human choice (sin), discernment involves not simply a "black and white" decision about whether demons are the cause of a problem or not, but a consideration that demons may be one of many possible factors which affect the complex systems characteristic of most of the world. Diagnoses of mental illness and demonization are not competing explanations for the same phenomenon but often coexist.[85] As Shuster notes, all pathology has a spiritual component. She has an interesting explanation for demonization, believing the "emptiness" that many people feel may give a "structural opening (although not a necessary and sufficient cause)

---

81. E.g., M. McMinn stresses the importance of the therapist working on their own spirituality, such as incorporating spiritual disciplines; *Psychology, Theology*, 242. He believes the ability to perform redemptive counseling is related more closely to the counselor's theological and spiritual insight, than to any specific technique.

82. Payne, *Healing Presence*, 13, 73, 197–229. She draws from classic contemplatives such as Brother Lawrence and recognizes the importance of symbolic language and the "true imagination."

83. Payne, *Christian Soul*, 25–54, 80–90, 207–10; see also Anderson, *The Bondage Breaker*, 102. Arnold similarly notes the importance of prayer, knowing one's identity in Christ, and being part of a Christian community; *3 Crucial Questions*, 115, 121.

84. E.g., Anderson, *Bondage Breaker*, 68–71; Kelsey, *Discernment*, 100–105; Friesen, *Mystery of MPD*, 243; MacNutt, *Deliverance*, 133–43.

85. E.g., Bufford, *Counseling and the Demonic*, 133; Scanlan and Cirner, *Deliverance from Evil Spirits*, 97; Anderson et al. suggest an assessment should include worldly, fleshly, and satanic influences; although I see these as intertwined; *Christ-Centered Therapy*, 177–79.

for possession."[86] Psychopathology often results in compensatory power-seeking, which makes the sufferer vulnerable to demonic attack. Spiritual forces work through and upon the will.[87] Demonization is associated with the sin of turning away from the greater good, self-centeredness, and refusal to change one's views. Shuster does not develop a biblical model, but her observations (if somewhat abstract) concur with the findings in this model, especially regarding the complexities of sin and demonization, and the role of human choice. This study also suggested that discernment is a complex interaction of divine initiative and human responsibility (discussed in chapters 1 and 7). Godly characteristics enable one to discern and set boundaries on evil. The idea that evil is characterized by divine absence, and that demons are devoid of the Spirit, may also inform discernment of evil. In sum, Christian counselors need to be able to discern evil while recognizing its complex manifestations and intertwining with human choice.

Third, a spatial model emphasizes human responsibility. Humans can choose which zone of metaphorical space they dwell in—they can draw near to God and resist the devil. This resonates with both psychology and theology. As McMinn and Campbell point out, when people make choices towards change, they improve from a psychological perspective (behavior change) and a theological perspective (exercising God-given responsibility).[88] G. May insists that we can choose between willingness and willfulness (how he defines sin). He recognizes, however, that evil spiritual forces energize our willfulness. "Both sin and evil involve a destructive separation of oneself from God and from other people. In sin, this separation is a mistake. In evil, it is intended."[89] May is partially

---

86. Shuster, *Power, Pathology*, 179–81; demonic bondage and psychopathology cannot be neatly differentiated; the two are "intertwined in a complex manner" (183–84). Interestingly her views of psychological structure concur with the idea presented in this study of evil as existing outside the structure of creation, but able to violate its boundaries.

87. Shuster, *Power, Pathology*, 11, 12, 67–91, 105, 132. Power is a union of structure ("any set of ordered relationships") and will ("an ordering and choosing consciousness") (95–96); trauma may result in extreme fear or despair and also provide an opening for the demonic. Demonization is most correlated with activities that combine psychic passivity (such as induced by drugs or occult involvement) and a turning of the will away from God. However, the will is not always conscious; it is possible that other sources of energy can will evil. Evil, which can be internal (sin) or external (demonic), occurs when there is a disruption of either structure or will.

88. McMinn and Campbell, *Integrative Psychotherapy*, 124.

89. May, *Will and Spirit*, 233, 244–45, 267, 278–82.

correct. I think the situation is more complex; sometimes sin is deliberate, and sometimes human evil, if demonically inspired, is mistaken. Shuster, as above, puts human responsibility on an equal footing with demonization, in accord with a spatial model.[90] Her views on sin concur with the view suggested in this study. Rather than viewing sin as a "do not" list, it can be understood spatially as turning away from God, thus allowing for the nuances and complexities of sin.

Fourth, this study suggests some metaphors that can be used in counseling practice. Clients can be encouraged to choose to follow the truth of God rather than the lies of the enemy, to draw near to God and resist the devil, and to stay in the light and avoid the darkness. The language of boundaries is already commonly used in terms of interpersonal boundaries and is easy to extend to boundaries on evil spirits (both sin and demonization can be seen as boundary violation). Once people understand this concept, they can work towards strengthening boundaries. Any counselor can benefit from using multiple metaphors (responsibly) as therapeutic tools.[91] I believe it is also helpful to have, and be conscious of, an underlying biblical framework from which to counsel.

Fifth, the model developed in this study can provide insights regarding techniques of deliverance. Much of the "spiritual warfare" literature elevates the ontology of demons; many suggest engaging in dialogue with demons during deliverance in order to know their name, personality, or rank (discussed in chapter 1). By contrast, Jesus primarily sent demons away with a simple command, and only once asked a demon its name. This study emphasized authority (such as a parent-child relationship) over power. Wind imagery can inform deliverance ministries: demons can be expelled not through warfare, but merely a word (used with the authority and breath of the Spirit). This study suggested that holiness dissolves impurity; the counselor can offer cleansing to demonized people. Rather than using power, humble dependence on God can be encouraged as a way for demons to be expelled. As Shuster points out, power only magnifies the potential for wickedness and if demons are defeated through force then their mode of being is justified. She uses the themes of word (the

---

90. Shuster, *Power, Pathology,* 95–96.

91. I use the metaphors of "giving" sin and pain to Jesus (rather than to the demonic as in the Azazel ritual); holy housekeeping—not "making a nice home" for the demonic; and light/dark metaphors such as encouraging people to "stay in the light." Shuster uses this metaphor too: a person walking in the light "knows less and less of evil;" "the more the light puts out the darkness," and "the better we know God the less we can know of evil"; *Power, Pathology,* 239, 262.

divine word creates and orders) and weakness (in our weakness God can manifest his power), "fellowship and forgiveness" (we should bear one another's burdens), and "prayer and praise" (evil perishes when we refuse it and embrace God's way not the world's way; we should take evil seriously, but never so seriously that it extinguished the light of praise).[92] May has a somewhat similar approach encouraging awareness of evil forces without paying them undue attention. They should be confronted in a matter-of-fact way and not be allowed to side track one from the therapeutic goal. "There is no battle, but neither is there avoidance."[93] Rather than categorizing demons as some suggest, they can be dealt with on a case-by-case basis. Instead of waging war with the demonic, we can treat them as irritating pests or dirt that needs to be swept away. As this study proposed a reduced ontology of evil, I concur with May and encourage maximal awareness of the demonic, but with minimal attention given to it.

Finally, this model, being less dualistic than a warfare one, allows for the complexities and grey areas experienced frequently in the practice of counseling. Sometimes deliverance may precede counseling, sometimes this may be reversed, but mostly the two are intertwined. As God, through his Spirit, dispelled evil forces at creation, established purity rituals to separate evil in the cult, and sent Christ to cast out demons and relocate evil, so we are to continue the work of reestablishing order, relocating evil, and establishing boundaries on disorder. A spatial model, which views the demonic as peripheral, allows for focus on the center while being aware of potential demonic influence. Using a spatial rather than a warfare model for counseling and deliverance may keep demonization in perspective. Righteous living, following biblical truth, prayer, church fellowship, and maintaining an awareness of evil spirits can all help prevent and counteract demonization.

Conclusions, Questions, Suggestions

This study developed a model for conceptualizing evil based on biblical spatial metaphors as an alternative to a warfare model, demonstrating that the language of cleansing, ordering, and setting boundaries on evil is a viable option for Christian theology. To summarize: boundary metaphors affirm that evil has potential to invade intermediary space and cause

92. Shuster, *Power, Pathology,* 199–253; like Dawn's focus on weakness in ecclesiology, discussed above.

93. May, *Will and Spirit,* 281.

harm, but do not consider evil as a force that is equal and opposite to God; cleansing metaphors, in continuity with cultic metaphors, imply that evil is like dirt, matter out of place that needs to be relocated; healing metaphors suggest that evil is infectious, like a virus or parasite, that has overrun humans; it is secondary and has little reality apart from its dependence on a host. This model also has several advantages over a warfare model: it is less dualistic (incorporating grey space and the complexities of evil with its multi-factorial causation), more comprehensive (incorporating OT and NT texts, space and actions, the Trinity), allows for views of a decreased ontology of evil and an increased sovereignty of God, emphasizes human responsibility (in terms of discerning evil and choosing which direction to turn), and provides language not associated with violence (making it more broadly applicable). Cultic metaphors allow for a conception of Christ, not as involved in warfare, but as voluntarily coming down from heaven to provide a new method for dealing with sin and evil. Furthermore, emphasizing the metaphorical nature of evil as depicted in the Bible opens theological space, may help bridge the gap between theology and biblical studies with respect to evil, and may inform philosophical views of evil (perhaps structure can be emphasized over agency). Recall that models are representation of reality and can foster the imagination, and that new metaphors can provide new insight—all of which I believe are applicable to my model. Although a warfare model may be applicable in certain situations, at the very least this model provides an alternative.

This model offers a fresh framework for conceptualizing evil and, I believe, contributes to our overall understanding of evil; however, there are some unresolved issues. A primary question is whether it is feasible to "lump all manner of metaphors together" in the semantic domain of evil.[94] One obvious weakness of this approach is that it does not elucidate the relationship between Satan and the demons or other terms (e.g., the powers and demons) or the relationship between OT and NT terms. However, I believe the advantages of this approach outweigh its weaknesses. As noted in chapters 2 and 3, multiple metaphors usually increase information about a concept; there is complex coherence across metaphors. Considering metaphorical clusters and semantic domains not only furthers understanding of evil, but also can help interpret multivalent metaphors. Biblical metaphors are fluid and flexible, therefore perhaps our conception of evil needs to be too. There may be occasions in which one metaphor proves superior or at least preferable to others; emphasizing the continuity

94. As Arnold notes that Paul did; *Powers of Darkness,* 54.

between metaphors does not obliterate their discontinuity. The concern is if one is used to the exclusion of others (such as what I believe has happened with warfare metaphors). Those with a Newtonian mind-set may be dissatisfied with envisioning the sea and the demons in the same semantic domain; there are differences, but the advantage to this approach is that one metaphor is not privileged over another and the multiple metaphors can inform each other. Furthermore, biblical metaphors for evil relate to theological metaphors for the nature of evil (nothingness, unreality), furthering our understanding of evil and improving conceptualization. Interestingly, relationships between metaphors in the semantic domain of holiness are also not well explained (e.g., the overlap between creation/tabernacle/temple, the relationships within the Trinity).

A second concern with this model is possible idolization and misapplication, which is a potential problem with all models; for example, "cleansing" could evoke images of the "ethnic cleansing" associated with Nazi Germany, therefore, clarification and contextualization are imperative. Third, this study has not offered significant contributions to the philosophical issue of how the demonic interacts with the world, the ideas of spirit-matter dualism, energy transmission, and noumenal/phenomological distinctions.[95] On a practical, related level, this study has only minimally addressed demonic possession of places and objects. Spatial metaphors could also be misinterpreted as endorsing the idea of territorial spirits and "mapping"; a concept I think has insufficient biblical support. Biblical metaphors for evil suggest that evil forces are both personal and impersonal. However, the impersonal have reduced ontology, so perhaps can influence but not indwell space and objects. These topics are worthy of further study. Fourth, a danger of suggesting a reduced ontology for evil is that the demonic may not be taken seriously enough. However, I think this risk is justified as a balance to the "excessive" ontology suggested by most "spiritual warfare" literature. Fifth, the metaphor "spiritual warfare" (which admittedly provides a better "catch-phrase" than "cleansing the cosmos") may be so entrenched in Christian theology that alternate metaphors may be difficult to assimilate. Finally, it could be argued that this model is not significantly different from a warfare one; for example, "defending" the boundaries of godly reality could be considered warfare language. It might be that boundary and warfare metaphors overlap, or that my model can

95. See Parry, "Introduction," 1–25; Wiebe, "Deliverance and Exorcism," 156–80; Bell, *Deliver Us*, 150–90, 341–60.

incorporate warfare metaphors. Nevertheless, in many ways this model is broader than a warfare model and clearly adds information.

This study suggests future research endeavors such as re-considering the philosophy of evil (reconciling theology and biblical studies) and using this model in practical ministry situations (mission, counseling). Many of the ideas suggested here are worthy of further theological exploration, such as the effect of the demonic on space, the relationship between Satan and the demons, and the idea of evil existing outside the structure of divine reality. There is also room for exploration of how the concepts and framework presented here correlate with anecdotal and experiential evidence of demonization and deliverance. Overall, this study contributes to Christian theology by providing a model for conceptualizing and counteracting evil, real and experienced, as an alternative (possibly an improvement) to a warfare model. It remains to be seen whether this model can interpret new experience.

Until the eschaton, we live in a world in which evil is not only present, but prevalent. We live in a world in which evil does not keep to its appointed limits, but frequently violates its boundaries, intruding upon divine reality. We live in a world in which children are subject to satanic ritual abuse. We live in a world comprised of shades of grey, in which evil manifests in multiple manners. Chaos is a continual threat to creation, darkness sends tendrils into the light, disorder seeks to overcome order, the sea oversteps its bounds, and evil spirits enter God's creatures. It is thus imperative that we understand the nature of the threat to divine reality and have a framework to guide our ministries in counteracting evil. And, as Zechariah informs us,

It's not by might, nor power, but by my Spirit says the Lord.

Bibliography

Aaron, D. H. *Biblical Ambiguities: Metaphor, Semantics, and Divine Imagery.* Leiden: Brill, 2001.

Adams, Jay E. *The War Within: A Biblical Strategy for Spiritual Warfare.* Eugene, OR: Harvest House, 1989.

Alexander, Philip S. "The Demonology of the Dead Sea Scrolls." In *The Dead Sea Scrolls after Fifty Years: A Comprehensive Assessment,* Vol. 2, edited by Peter W. Flint and James C. Vanderkam, 331–53. Leiden: Brill, 1999.

Alison, James. "God's Self-Substitution and Sacrificial Inversion." In *Stricken by God? Nonviolent Identification and the Victory of Christ,* edited by Brad Jersak and Michael Hardin, 166–79. Grand Rapids: Eerdmans, 2007.

Amorth, Gabriel. *An Exorcist Tells His Story.* Translated by Nicoletta V. MacKenzie. San Francisco: Ignatius, 1990.

Anderson, Allen. "Demons and Deliverance in African Pentecostalism." In *Angels and Demons: Perspectives and Practice in Diverse Religious Traditions,* edited by Peter G. and Beverly Smith Riddell, 42–62. Nottingham, UK: Apollos, 2007.

Anderson, Bernhard W. "Biblical Creation Faith." In *Creation in the Old Testament,* edited by Bernhard W. Anderson, 12–15. Philadelphia: Fortress, 1984.

———, editor. *Creation in the Old Testament.* Philadelphia: Fortress, 1984.

———. *Creation versus Chaos.* New York: Association, 1967.

Anderson, Gary A. "The Praise of God as a Cultic Event." In *Priesthood and Cult in Ancient Israel,* edited by Gary A. Anderson and Saul M. Olyan, 15–33. Sheffield, UK: Sheffield Academic Press, 1991.

———. *Sin: A History.* New Haven: Yale University Press, 2009.

Anderson, Neil T. *The Bondage Breaker.* Eugene, OR: Harvest House, 1990.

Anderson, Neil T., et al. *Christ-Centered Therapy: The Practical Integration of Theology and Psychology.* Grand Rapids: Zondervan, 2000.

Anderson, Neil T., and Timothy M. Warner. *A Beginner's Guide to Spiritual Warfare.* Ventura, CA: Regal, 2008.

Arnold, Bill T. *Genesis.* New Cambridge Bible Commentary. Cambridge: Cambridge University Press, 2009.

Arnold, Clinton E. *Ephesians: Power and Magic.* Cambridge: Cambridge University Press, 1989.

———. "The 'Exorcism' of Ephesians 6:12 in Recent Research." *JSNT* 30 (1987) 71–87.

———. *Powers of Darkness.* Downers Grove, IL: InterVarsity, 1992.

———. "Returning to the Domain of the Powers: Stoicheia as Evil Spirits in Galatians 4:3, 9." *Novum Testamentum,* XXXVIII (1996) 55–76.

———. *3 Crucial Questions about Spiritual Warfare.* Grand Rapids: Baker, 1997.

Auffarth, Christopher, and Loren Stuckenbruck. "Introduction." In *The Fall of the Angels,* edited by Christopher Auffarth and Loren Stuckenbruck, 1–10. Leiden: Brill, 2004.

Avis, Paul. *God and the Creative Imagination: Metaphor, Symbol and Myth in Religion and Theology.* New York: Routledge, 1999.

Baker, Sharon. "The Repetition of Reconciliation: Satisfying Justice, Mercy and Forgiveness." In *Stricken by God? Nonviolent Identification and the Victory of Christ,* edited by Brad Jersak and Michael Hardin, 220–41. Grand Rapids: Eerdmans, 2007.

Barbour, Ian G. *Issues in Science and Religion.* Englewood Cliffs, NJ: Prentice-Hall, 1966.

———. *Myths, Models and Paradigms.* London: SCM, 1974.

———. *Religion and Science.* San Francisco: Harper, 1997.

Barden, Nicola, and Tina K. Williams. *Words and Symbols: Language and Communication in Therapy.* Maidenhead, UK: Open University Press, 2007.

Barker, Margaret. *On Earth as It Is In Heaven: Temple Symbolism in the New Testament.* Edinburgh: T. & T. Clark, 1995.

Barth, Christopher. *God with Us: A Theological Introduction to the Old Testament.* Edited by G. W. Bromiley. Grand Rapids: Eerdmans, 1991.

Barth, Karl. *Church Dogmatics.* 4 vols. Translated by G. W. Bromiley and R. J. Ehrlich. Edinburgh: T. & T. Clark, 1956–75.

Barton, John. "The Prophets and the Cult." In *Temple and Worship in Biblical Israel: Proceedings of the Oxford Old Testament Seminar,* edited by John Day, 111–22. London: T. & T. Clark, 2005.

Barton, Stephen C. "Dislocating and Relocating Holiness: A New Testament Study." In *Holiness: Past and Present,* edited by Stephen C. Barton, 193–213. London: T. & T. Clark, 2003.

Batto, Bernard F. "Creation Theology in Genesis." In *Creation in the Biblical Traditions,* edited by Richard J. Clifford and John J. Collins, 16–38. Washington, DC: Catholic Biblical Association of America, 1992.

———. *Slaying the Dragon: Mythmaking in the Biblical Tradition.* Louisville, KY: Westminster/John Knox, 1992.

Bauckham, Richard. *Bible and Mission: Christian Witness in a Postmodern World.* Grand Rapids: Baker, 2003.

Beale, G. K. "The New Testament and New Creation." In *Biblical Theology: Retrospect and Prospect,* edited by Scott J. Hafemann, 159–73. Downers Grove, IL: InterVarsity, 2002.

———. *The Temple and the Church's Mission: A Biblical Theology of the Dwelling Place of God.* NSBT 17. Downers Grove, IL: InterVarsity, 2004.

Becking, Bob, and Marjo C.A. Korpel, "To Create, to Separate or to Construct: An Alternative to the Recent Proposal as to the Interpretation of *bārā* in Genesis 1:1—2:4a." *Journal of Hebrew Scriptures* 10.3 (2010) 2–21.

Bell, Richard H. *Deliver Us from Evil: Interpreting the Redemption from the Power of Satan in New Testament Theology.* Tübingen: Mohr Siebeck, 2007.

Berkhof, Hendrik. *Christ and the Powers.* Translated by John H. Yoder. 1962. Reprint. Scottsdale, PA: Herald, 1977.

Betz, Hans Dieter. *Galatians: A Commentary on Paul's letter to the Churches in Galatia.* Philadelphia: Fortress, 1979.

———, editor. *The Greek Magical Papyri in Translation, including the Demotic Spells.* 2nd ed. Chicago: University of Chicago Press, 1992.

"Biblical Language and Military Metaphors." http://ricklove.net/wp-content/uploads/2010/04/Biblical-Language-and-MilitaryMetaphors-web-copy.pdf.

Biddle, Mark. *Missing the Mark: Sin and its Consequences in Biblical Theology.* Nashville: Abingdon, 2005.

Black, Max. *Models and Metaphors: Studies in Language and Philosophy.* Ithaca, NY: Cornell University Press, 1962.

———. "More about Metaphors." In *Metaphor and Thought,* 2nd ed., edited by Andrew Ortony, 19–43. Cambridge: Cambridge University Press, 1993.

Blocher, Henri. *Evil and the Cross.* 2nd ed. Grand Rapids: Kregel, 2004.

———. *In the Beginning.* Translated by David G. Preston. Downers Grove, IL: InterVarsity, 1984.

Bloesch, Donald G. *The Holy Spirit.* Downers Grove, IL: InterVarsity, 2000.

Boda, Mark J. *A Severe Mercy: Sin and its Remedy in the Old Testament.* Winona Lake, IN: Eisenbrauns, 2009.

Bolt, John. "Satan is Alive and Well in Contemporary Imagination: A Bibliographic Essay with Notes on 'Hell' and 'Spiritual Warfare.'" *Calvin Theological Journal* 29 (1994) 497–506.

Bolt, Peter G. "Jesus, the Daimons and the Dead." In *The Unseen World,* edited by Anthony N. S. Lane, 87–91. Grand Rapids: Baker, 1996.

Bonting, Sjoerd L. *Chaos Theology: A Revised Creation Theology.* Ottawa: Novalis, 2002.

———. *Creation and Double Chaos: Science and Theology in Discussion.* Minneapolis: Fortress, 2005.

Borg, Marcus. "Executed by Rome, Vindicated by God." In *Stricken by God? Nonviolent Identification and the Victory of Christ,* edited by Brad Jersak and Michael Hardin, 150–63. Grand Rapids: Eerdmans, 2007.

Bosch, David J. "Reflections on Biblical Models of Mission." In *Toward the Twenty-First Century in Christian Mission. Essays in Honor of Gerald H. Anderson,* edited by James M. Phillips and Robert T. Coote, 175–92. Grand Rapids: Eerdmans, 1993.

———. *Transforming Mission: Paradigm Shifts in Theology of Mission.* Maryknoll, NY: Orbis, 1991.

Boyd, Gregory A. *God at War: The Bible and Spiritual Conflict.* Downers Grove, IL: InterVarsity, 1997.

———. *God of the Possible.* Grand Rapids: Baker, 2000.

———. *Is God to Blame?* Downers Grove, IL: InterVarsity, 2003.

———. *Oneness Pentecostals and the Trinity.* Grand Rapids: Baker, 1992.

———. *Satan and the Problem of Evil: Constructing a Trinitarian Warfare Theodicy.* Downers Grove, IL: InterVarsity, 2001.

Brandon, Robert Charles. *Satanic Conflict and the Plot of Matthew.* Studies in Biblical Literature 89. New York: Lang, 2006.

Breuninger, Christian. "Where Angels Fear to Tread: Appraising the Current Fascination with Spiritual Warfare." *Covenant Quarterly* 53 (1995) 37–43.

Brewer, David. "Jesus and the Psychiatrists." In *The Unseen World,* edited by Anthony N. S. Lane, 133–48. Grand Rapids: Baker, 1996.

Brinkman, Johan, *The Perception of Space in the Old Testament.* Kampan, Netherlands: Kok Pharos, 1992.

Bromell, David J. "Sallie McFague's 'Metaphorical Theology.'" *Journal of the American Academy of Religion* 61 (1993) 485–503.

Brown, Candy Gunther, editor. *Global Pentecostal and Charismatic Healing.* Oxford: Oxford University Press, 2011.

Brown, Raymond E. *An Introduction to the Gospel of John.* Edited, updated, introduced and concluded by Francis J. Moloney. AB Reference Library. New York: Doubleday, 2003.

———. *John 1–12,* AB. New York: Doubleday, 1966.

Brueggemann, Walter. *Genesis.* IBC, Atlanta: John Knox, 1982.

———. *Old Testament Theology: An Introduction.* Nashville: Abingdon, 2008.

———. *Theology of the Old Testament: Testimony, Dispute, Advocacy.* Minneapolis: Fortress, 1997.

Brümmer, Vincent. *The Model of Love.* Cambridge: Cambridge University Press, 1993.

Bryan, Steven M. *Jesus and Israel's Traditions of Judgment and Restoration.* Cambridge: Cambridge University Press, 2002.

Bryant, Hershel Odell. "Discernment." in *EPCC,* 134–36.

Bubeck, Mark I. *The Adversary.* Chicago: Moody, 1975.

Bufford, Rodger K. *Counseling and the Demonic.* Dallas: Word, 1988.

Bultmann, Rudolph. *Jesus Christ and Mythology.* New York: Scribner's Sons, 1958.

———. *Primitive Christianity in its Contemporary Setting.* Translated by R. H. Fuller. New York, London: Thames & Hudson, 1956.

———. "New Testament and Mythology." In *Kerygma and Myth,* edited by H. W. Bartsch, translated by R.H. Fuller, 1–44. New York: Harper & Row, 1961.

Burgess, Stanley M. *The Holy Spirit: Ancient Christian Traditions.* Peabody, MA: Hendrickson, 1984.

———. *The Holy Spirit: Medieval, Roman Catholic and Reformation Traditions.* Peabody, MA: Hendrickson, 1997.

Burke, Trevor J. *Adopted into God's Family: Exploring a Pauline Metaphor.* Nottingham, UK: InterVarsity, 2006.

Burkholder, Lawrence. "The Theological Foundations of Deliverance Healing." *Conrad Grebel Review* 19 (2001) 38–68.

Burnett, Joel S. *Where is God? Divine Absence in the Hebrew Bible.* Minneapolis: Fortress, 2010.

Caird, G. B. *The Language and Imagery of the Bible.* London: Duckworth, 1980.

———. *Principalities and Powers: A Study in Pauline Theology.* Oxford: Clarendon, 1956.

Carr, Wesley. *Angels and Principalities: The Background, Meaning and Development of the Pauline Phrase hai archai kai hai exousia.* Cambridge: Cambridge University Press, 1981.

Carson, D. A. "God, the Bible, and Spiritual Warfare: A Review Article." *JETS* 42 (1999) 251–69.

Cavanna, Peter. *Discerning the Spirits: Evaluating the Prophetic Voice.* Cambridge: Grove, 2006.

Cencini, Massimo, et al. *Chaos: From Simple Models to Complex Systems.* Series on Advances in Statistical Mechanics, vol. 17. London: World Scientific, 2010.

Charlesworth, James H. *The Good and Evil Serpent: How a Universal Symbol Became Christianized.* New Haven, CT: Yale University Press, 2010.

Childs, Brevard S. *Myth and Reality in the Old Testament.* Naperville, IL: Allenson, 1960.

———. *Old Testament Theology in a Canonical Context.* Philadelphia: Fortress, 1985.

Chilton, Bruce. *Pure Kingdom: Jesus' Vision of God.* Grand Rapids: Eerdmans, 1996.

Clark, Stuart "Protestant Demonology." In *New Perspectives on Witchcraft, Magic and Demonology,* edited by Brian P. Levack, 179–215. New York: Routledge, 2001.

Clifford, Richard J. *The Cosmic Mountain in Canaan and the Old Testament.* Cambridge, MA, Harvard University Press, 1972.

———. "Introduction: The Theology of Creation Traditions." In *Creation in the Biblical Traditions,* edited by Richard J. Clifford and John J. Collins, 1–15. Washington, DC: Catholic Biblical Association of America, 1992.

Cohen, Jack, and Ian Stewart. *The Collapse of Chaos: Discovering Simplicity in a Complex World.* London: Penguin, 1994.

Cohen, Robert L. *The Shape of Sacred Space: Four Biblical Studies.* Chico, CA: Scholars, 1981.

Cole, Graham H. *He Who Gives Life: The Doctrine of the Holy Spirit.* Wheaton, IL: Crossway, 2007.

Cole, Susan Guettel. "Greek Religion." In *A Handbook of Ancient Religions,* edited by John R. Hinnells, 266–317. Cambridge: Cambridge University Press, 2007.

Coles, Peter. *From Cosmos to Chaos: The Science of Unpredictability.* Oxford: Oxford University Press, 2006.

Collins, Adela Yarbro. *The Combat Myth in the Book of Revelation.* Missoula, MA: Scholars, 1976.

Collins, James M. *Exorcism and Deliverance Ministry in the Twentieth Century: An Analysis of the Practice and Theology of Exorcism in Modern Western Christianity.* Milton Keynes, UK: Paternoster, 2009.

Coloe, Mary L. *Dwelling in the Household of God: Johannine Ecclesiology and Spirituality.* Collegeville, MN: Liturgical, 2007.

———. *God Dwells with Us: Temple Symbolism in the Fourth Gospel.* Collegeville, MN: Liturgical, 2001.

Cook, Robert. "Devils and Manticores: Plundering Jung for a Plausible Demonology." In *The Unseen World,* edited by Anthony N. S. Lane, 165–84. Grand Rapids: Baker, 1996.

Copan, Paul, and William Lane Craig. *Creation out of Nothing: A Biblical, Philosophical, and Scientific Exploration.* Grand Rapids: Baker Academic, 2004.

Cotterell, Peter, and Max Turner. *Linguistics and Biblical Interpretation.* London: SPCK, 1989.

Crabb, Lawrence J. *Effective Biblical Counselling: How to Become a Capable Counsellor.* London: Marshal Pickering, 1977.

Crabtree, Harriet. *The Christian Life: Traditional Metaphors and Contemporary Theologies.* Harvard Dissertations in Religion 29. Minneapolis: Fortress, 1991.

Cullman, Oscar. *Christ and Time: The Primitive Christian Conception of Time and History.* Translated by Floyd V. Filson. Philadelphia: Westminster, 1964.

———. *Prayer in the New Testament.* Translated by John Bowden. Minneapolis: Fortress, 1995.

Cuneo, Michael W. *American Exorcism: Expelling Demons in the Land of Plenty.* New York: Doubleday, 2001.

Bibliography

Cunningham, Lawrence S. "Satan: A Theological Meditation." *Theology Today* 51 (1994) 359–66.

Daunton-Fear, Andrew. *Healing in the Early Church.* Studies in Christian History and Thought. Milton Keynes, UK: Paternoster, 2009.

Davenport, Gene L. *Into the Darkness: Discipleship in the Sermon on the Mount.* Nashville: Abingdon, 1988.

Davies, D. "An Interpretation of Sacrifice in Leviticus." *ZAW* 89 (1977) 387–99.

Davies, Paul. *The Mind of God.* New York: Simon & Schuster, 1992.

Dawn, Marva J. *Powers, Weakness, and the Tabernacling of God.* Grand Rapids: Eerdmans, 2001.

Dawson, John. *Taking our Cities for God: How to Break Spiritual Strongholds.* Lake Mary, FA: Creation House, 1989.

Day, John. *God's Conflict with the Dragon and the Sea.* Cambridge: Cambridge University Press, 1985.

———. *Yahweh and the Gods and Goddesses of Canaan.* JSOTSup 265. Sheffield, UK: Sheffield Academic Press, 2000.

Day, Peggy L. *An Adversary in Heaven: Satan in the Hebrew Bible.* Harvard Semitic Monographs 43. Atlanta: Scholars, 1988.

Del Colle, Ralph. *Christ and the Spirit: Spirit Christology in Trinitarian Perspective.* Oxford: Oxford University Press, 1994.

Dempsey, Carol J. "Creation, Evolution, Revelation and Redemption: Connections and Intersections." In *Earth, Wind and Fire,* edited by Carol Dempsey and Mary Margaret Pazdan, 1–23. Collegeville, MN: Liturgical, 2004.

Dille, Sarah J. *Mixing Metaphors: God as Mother and Father in Deutero-Isaiah.* Edinburgh: T. & T. Clark, 2004.

Douglas, Mary. *In the Wilderness: The Doctrine of Defilement in the Book of Numbers.* Sheffield, UK: Sheffield Academic Press, 1993.

———. *Jacob's Tears: The Priestly Work of Reconciliation.* Oxford: Oxford University Press, 2002.

———. *Leviticus as Literature.* Oxford: Oxford University Press, 1999.

———. *Natural Symbols: Explorations in Cosmology.* New York: Pantheon, 1970.

———. *Purity and Danger.* London: Routledge & Kegan Paul, 1966.

Dow, Lois K. Fuller. *Images of Zion: Biblical Antecedents for the New Jerusalem.* Sheffield, UK: Sheffield Phoenix, 2010.

Downame, John. *The Christian Warfare.* 1604. Reprint. Norwood, NJ: Johnson, 1974.

Dozeman, Thomas B. "Biblical Geography and Critical Spatial Studies." In *Constructions of Space 1: Theory, Geography and Narrative.* Library of Hebrew Bible/OT studies, edited by John L. Berquist and Claudia V. Camp, 87–108. London: T. & T. Clark, 2007.

Dryer, Elizabeth A. *Holy Presence, Holy Power: Rediscovering Medieval Metaphors for the Holy Spirit.* New York: Paulist, 2007.

Dudley, Guilford III, *Religion on Trial: Mircea Eliade and his Critics.* Philadelphia: Templeton University Press, 1977.

Dumbrell, William H. *The End of the Beginning: Revelation 21–22 and the Old Testament.* Homebush West, NSW: Lancer, 1985.

———. *The Search for Order: Biblical Eschatology in Focus.* Grand Rapids: Baker, 1994.

Dunn, James D. G. "Jesus and Holiness: The Challenge of Purity." In *Holiness: Past and Present,* edited by Stephen C. Barton, 168–92. London: T. & T. Clark, 2003.

————. *New Testament Theology: An Introduction.* Nashville: Abingdon, 2009.

Ediger, Gerry. "Strategic-level Spiritual Warfare in Historical Retrospect." *Direction* 29 (2000) 125–41.

Edwards, Denis. *Breath of Life: A Theology of the Creator Spirit.* New York: Orbis, 2004.

Eliade, Mircea. *Myth and Reality.* Translated by Willard R. Trask. New York: Harper & Row, 1963.

————. *The Myth of the Eternal Return, or Cosmos and History.* Translated by Willard R. Trask. 1954. Reprint. Princeton: Princeton University Press, 1974.

————. *Patterns in Comparative Religion.* Translated by Rosemary Sheed. London: Sheed & Ward, 1958.

————. *The Sacred and the Profane.* Translated by Willard R. Trask. 1957. Reprint. New York: Harcourt, Brace & World, 1959.

Ellis, Bill. *Raising the Devil: Satanism, New Religions, and the Media.* Lexington, KY: University Press of Kentucky, 2000.

Engelsviken, Tormod. "Spiritual Conflict: A Challenge for the Church in the West with a View to the Future." In *Paradigm Shifts in Christian Witness: Insights from Anthropology, Communication and Spiritual Power: Essays in Honor of Charles Kraft,* edited by Van Engen et al., 116–25. Maryknoll, NY: Orbis, 2008.

Erickson, Millard J. *Christian Theology, Vol. 1.* Grand Rapids: Baker, 1983.

Fauconnier, Gilles, and Mark Turner. *The Way We Think.* New York: Basics, 2002.

Fee, Gordon D. *The First Epistle to the Corinthians.* NIC. Grand Rapids: Eerdmans, 1987.

————. *God's Empowering Presence: The Holy Spirit in the Letters of Paul.* Peabody, MA: Hendrickson, 1994.

Ferdinando, Keith. "The Spiritual Realm in Traditional African Religion." In *Angels and Demons: Perspectives and Practice in Diverse Religious Traditions,* edited by Peter G. and Beverly Smith Riddell, 21–41. Nottingham, UK: Apollos, 2007.

Ferguson, Sinclair B. *The Holy Spirit.* Downers Grove, IL: InterVarsity, 1996.

Finlan, Stephen. *The Background and Content of Paul's Cultic Atonement Metaphors.* Atlanta: SBL, 2004.

Fisher, Len. *The Perfect Swarm: The Science of Complexity in Everyday Life.* New York: Basic, 2009.

Fitzmyer, J. A. *The Gospel According to Luke.* AB. New York: Doubleday, 1981.

Forney, David G. "Living in the City—Journeying outside the Gate: A Missional Approach to Polity." In *The Missional Church and Denominations: Helping Congregations Develop a Missional Identity,* edited by Craig Van Gelder, 46–74. Grand Rapids: Eerdmans, 2008.

Forsyth, Neil. *The Old Enemy: Satan and the Combat Myth.* Princeton: Princeton University Press, 1987.

Foster, Benjamin R. "Mesopotamia." In *A Handbook of Ancient Religions,* edited by John R. Hinnells, 105–60. Cambridge: Cambridge University Press, 2007.

Fretheim, Terence E. *Creation Untamed: The Bible, God and Natural Disasters.* Grand Rapids: Baker Academic, 2010.

————. *Exodus.* IBC. Louisville: John Knox, 1991.

————. *God and World in the Old Testament.* Nashville: Abingdon, 2005.

Freud, Sigmund. *Totem and Taboo: Resemblances between the Psychic Lives of Savages and Neurotics.* Translated by A. A. Brill. 1918. Reprint. New York: Random House, 1947.

Bibliography

Frey, Helmut. *Geschichte des Altertums,* 2nd ed. Stuttgart: Cotta Nachf, 1909.

Friesen, James. *Uncovering the Mystery of MPD.* Nashville: Nelson, 1991.

Friesen, Randy. "Equipping Principles for Spiritual Warfare." *Direction* 29 (2000) 142–52.

Fudge, Edward William, and Robert A. Peterson. *Two Views of Hell: A Biblical and Theological Dialogue.* Downers Grove, IL: InterVarsity, 2000.

Funkenstein, Amos. *Theology and the Scientific Imagination from the Middle Ages to the Seventeenth Century.* Princeton: Princeton University Press, 1986.

Gabriel, Andrew K. *The Lord is the Spirit: The Holy Spirit and Divine Attributes.* Eugene, OR: Pickwick, 2011.

Gage, Warren Austin. *The Gospel of Genesis: Studies in Protology and Eschatology.* Winona Lake, IN: Carpenter, 1984.

Gaiser, Frederick J. *Healing in the Bible: Theological insight for Christian Ministry.* Grand Rapids: Baker Academic, 2010.

Gan, Jonathan. *The Metaphor of Shepherd in the Hebrew Bible.* Lanham, MD: University Press of America, 2007.

Gane, Roy. *Cult and Character: Purification Offerings, Day of Atonement and Theodicy.* Winona Lake, IN: Eisenbrauns, 2005.

Garrett, Susan. *The Demise of the Devil: Magic and the Demonic in Luke's Writings.* Minneapolis: Fortress, 1989.

———. *The Temptations of Jesus in Mark's Gospel.* Grand Rapids: Eerdmans, 1998.

Genz, Henning. *Nothingness: The Science of Empty Space.* Translated by Karin Heusch. Reading, UK: Perseus, 1999.

Getty-Sullivan, Mary Ann. *Parables of the Kingdom: Jesus and the Use of Parables in the Synoptic Tradition.* Collegeville, MN: Liturgical, 2007.

Gibson, J. C. L. *Language and Imagery in the Old Testament.* London: SPCK, 1998.

Gingerich, Ray, and Ted Grimsrud, editors. *Transforming the Powers: Peace, Justice and the Domination System.* Minneapolis: Fortress, 2006.

Girardot, Norman J. "Introduction." In *Imagination and Meaning: The Scholarly and Literary Worlds of Mircea Eliade,* edited by Norman J. Girardot and Mac Linscott Ricketts, 1–16. New York: Seabury, 1982.

Goldingay, John. *Models for Scripture.* Grand Rapids: Eerdmans, 1994.

Goldsworthy, Graeme. *The Gospel in Revelation.* Carlisle, UK: Paternoster, 1994.

Gordon, Cyrus H., and Gary A. Rendsburg. *The Bible and the Ancient Near East.* New York: Norton, 1997.

Gorman, Frank H. *The Ideology of Ritual: Space, Time and Status in the Priestly Theology.* JSOTSup. 91. Sheffield, UK: Sheffield Academic Press, 1990.

Grant, Robert M., with David Tracy. *A Short History of the Interpretation of the Bible.* 1963. Reprint. London: SCM, 1984.

Green, Joel B. "Scripture and Theology: Uniting the Two So Long Divided." In *Between Two Horizons: Spanning New Testament Studies and Systematic Theology,* edited by Joel B. Green and Max Turner, 23–43. Grand Rapids: Eerdmans, 2000.

———. *The Theology of the Gospel of Luke.* Cambridge: Cambridge University Press, 1995.

Green, Michael. *I Believe in Satan's Downfall.* 1981. Reprint. London: Hodder & Stoughton, 1999.

Greenwood, David C. *Structuralism and the Biblical Text.* New York: Mouton, 1985.

Gregersen, Niels Henrick. "Critical Realism and Other Realisms." In *Fifty Years in Science and Religion: Ian G. Barbour and his Legacy,* edited by Robert John Russell, 77–95. Burlington, VT: Ashgate, 2004.

Grelot, Pierre. *The Language of Symbolism: Biblical Theology, Semantics and Exegesis.* Translated by Christopher R. Smith. Peabody, MA: Hendrickson, 2006.

Grenz, Stanley J. *Theology for the Community of God.* Grand Rapids: Eerdmans, 1994, 2000.

Gribbin, John. *Deep Simplicity.* New York: Random House, 2004.

Guelich, Robert A. "Spiritual Warfare: Jesus, Paul and Peretti." *Pneuma* 13 (1991) 33–64.

Gunkel, Herman. *Schöpfung und Chaos in Urzeit und Endziet.* Goettingen: Vandenhoeck und Ruprecht, 1895.

Gunton, Colin E. *The Actuality of the Atonement.* Edinburgh: T. & T. Clark, 1988.

———. *Christ and Creation.* Grand Rapids: Eerdmans, 1992.

Haber, Susan. *They Shall Purify Themselves: Essays on Purity in Early Judaism.* Edited by Adele Reinhartz. Atlanta: SBL, 2008.

Hall, Eric, et al. *Guided Imagery: Creative Interventions in Counseling and Psychotherapy.* London: Sage, 2006.

Hallo, William W., editor. *The Context of Scripture: Canonical Compositions from the Biblical World, Vols. I–III.* Leiden: Brill, 1997.

Hammond, Frank, and Ida Mae. *Pigs in the Parlour.* Kirkwood, MN: Impact, 1973.

Hanson, Paul D. "Rebellion in Heaven, Azazel and Euhemeristic Heroes in 1 Enoch 6–11." *JBL* 96 (1977) 195–233.

Haran, Menahem. *Temples and Temple-Service in Ancient Israel: An Inquiry into the Character of Cult Phenomena and the Historical Setting of the Priestly School.* Oxford: Clarendon, 1978.

Harper, Michael. *Spiritual Warfare.* London: Hodder & Stoughton, 1970.

Harrington, Hannah K. *Holiness: Rabbinic Judaism and the Greco-Roman World.* New York: Routledge, 2001.

———. "Purity and the Dead Sea Scrolls—Current Issues." *Currents in Biblical Research* 4 (2006) 397–428.

———. *The Purity Texts.* London: T. & T. Clark, 2004.

Harrison, R. K. *Leviticus.* Leicester, UK: InterVarsity, 1980.

Hart, David Bentley. *The Doors of the Sea.* Grand Rapids: Eerdmans, 2005.

Hart, Trevor. "Tradition, Authority, and a Christian Approach to the Bible as Scripture." In *Between Two Horizons: Spanning New Testament Studies and Systematic Theology,* edited by Joel B. Green and Max Turner, 183–204. Grand Rapids: Eerdmans, 2000.

Hayles, N. Katherine, editor. *Chaos and Order: Complex Dynamics in Literature and Science.* Chicago: University of Chicago Press, 1991.

Hénaff, Marcel. *Claude Lévi-Strauss and the Making of Structural Anthropology.* Translated by Mary Baker. 1991. Reprint. Minneapolis: University of Minnesota Press, 1998.

Henderson, James M. "Deliverance." In *EPCC,* 123–26.

Hendrickx, Herman. *The Miracle Stories.* San Francisco: Harper & Row, 1987.

Hick, John. *Evil and the God of Love.* London: McMillan, 1966.

Hiebert, Paul G. "Anthropology, Missions and Epistemological Shifts." In *Paradigm Shifts in Christian Witness: Insights from Anthropology, Communication and*

Spiritual Power: Essays in Honor of Charles Kraft, edited by Van Engen et al., 13–23. Maryknoll, NY: Orbis, 2008.

———. "The Flaw of the Excluded Middle." *Missiology* 10 (1982) 35–47.

———. "Spiritual Warfare and Worldviews." *Direction,* 29 (2000) 114–24.

———. *Transforming Worldviews: An Anthropological Understanding of How People Change.* Grand Rapids: Baker Academic, 2008.

Highfield, Ron. "The Problem with "The Problem with Evil": A Response to Gregory Boyd's Open Theist Solution." *Restoration Quarterly* 45.3 (2003) 165–80.

———. *Great is the Lord: Theology for the Praise of God.* Grand Rapids: Eerdmans, 2008.

Holloway, Steven W. "What Ship Goes There: The Flood Narratives in the Gilgamesh Epic and Genesis Considered in Light of Ancient Near Eastern Temple Ideology." *ZAW* 103 (1991) 328–55.

Holvast, René. *Spiritual Mapping in the United States and Argentina, 1989–2005: A Geography of Fear.* Leiden: Brill, 2008.

Homan, Michael M. *To Your Tents, O Israel!: The Terminology, Function, Form, and Symbolism of Tents in the Hebrew Bible and the Ancient Near East.* Leiden: Brill, 2005.

Hooper, Dan. *Dark Cosmos: In Search of our Universe's Missing Mass and Energy.* New York: HarperCollins, 2007.

Hoskins, Paul M. *Jesus as the Fulfillment of the Temple in the Gospel of John.* Paternoster Biblical Monographs. Milton Keynes, UK: Paternoster, 2006.

Humphries, Michael L. *Christian Origins and the Language of the Kingdom of God.* Edwardsville, IL: Southern Illinois University Press, 1999.

Jabbour, Nabeel T. *The Unseen Reality: A Panoramic View of Spiritual Warfare.* Singapore: Navigators Singapore, 1995.

Jacobs, Cindy. *Possessing the Gates of the Enemy.* Tarrytown, NY: Chosen, 1991.

Jackson, T. Ryan. *New Creation in Paul's Letters.* Tübingen: Mohr Siebeck, 2010.

Jäkel, Olaf. "How Can Mortal Man Understand the Road He Travels? Prospects and Problems of the Cognitive Approach to Metaphor." In *The Bible through Metaphor and Translation,* edited by Kurt Feyaerts, 55–86. Oxford: Lang, 2003.

Jantzen, Grace. *God's World, God's Body.* London: Darton, Longman & Todd, 1984.

Jenson, Philip Peter. *Graded Holiness: A Key to the Priestly Conception of the World.* JSOTSup 106, Sheffield, UK: Sheffield Academic Press, 1992.

———. "Holiness in the Priestly Writings." In *Holiness: Past and Present,* edited by Stephen C. Barton, 93–121. London: T. & T. Clark, 2003.

Jenson, Robert. "Much Ado about Nothingness." In *Sin, Death and the Devil,* edited by Carl E. Braaten and Robert W. Jenson, 1–6. Grand Rapids: Eerdmans, 2000.

Jeremias, Joachim. *New Testament Theology: The Proclamation of Jesus.* New York: Scribner's Sons, 1971.

Jersak, Brad. "Nonviolent Identification and the Victory of Christ." In *Stricken by God? Nonviolent Identification and the Victory of Christ,* edited by Brad Jersak and Michael Hardin, 18–53. Grand Rapids: Eerdmans, 2007.

Jewett, Paul K. *God, Creation and Revelation.* Grand Rapids: Eerdmans, 1991.

Johnson, Mark. *Spiritual Warfare for the Wounded.* Ann Arbor, MI: Vine, 1992.

Kärkkäinen, Veli-Matti. *Pneumatology: The Holy Spirit in Ecumenical, International and Contextual Perspective.* Grand Rapids: Baker Academic, 2002.

Kaufmann, Y. *The Religion of Israel.* Translated and abridged by M. Greenberg. Chicago: University of Chicago Press, 1960.

Kay, William, and Robin A. Parry, editors. *Exorcism and Deliverance: Multidisciplinary Perspectives.* Milton Keynes, UK: Paternoster, 2011.

Keck, David. *Angels and Angelology in the Middle Ages.* Oxford: Oxford University Press, 1998.

Kee, H. C. "The Terminology of Mark's Exorcism Stories." *NT Studies* 14 (1968) 232–46.

Keller, Catherine. *Face of the Deep: A Theology of Becoming.* New York: Routledge, 2003.

Kelly, Henry Ansgar. *Satan: A Biography.* Cambridge: Cambridge University Press, 2006.

Kelsey, Morton. *Discernment: A Study in Ecstasy and Evil.* New York: Paulist, 1978.

Kerr, Alan R. *The Temple of Jesus' Body: The Temple Theme in the Gospel of John.* JSNTSup. Sheffield, UK: Sheffield Academic Press, 2002.

Kittay, Eva F., and Adrienne Lehrer. "Semantic Fields and the Structure of Metaphor." *Studies in Language* 5.1 (1981) 31–63.

Kittay, Eva F. *Metaphor: Its Cognitive Force and Linguistic Structure.* Oxford: Clarendon, 1987.

Klawans, Jonathan. *Impurity and Sin in Ancient Judaism.* Oxford: Oxford University Press, 2000.

———. *Purity, Sacrifice and the Temple.* Oxford: Oxford University Press, 2006.

Klingbeil, Gerald A. *Bridging the Gap: Ritual and Ritual Texts in the Bible.* Bulletin for Research Sup. 1. Winona Lake, IN: Eisenbrauns, 2007.

Klutz, Todd. *The Exorcism Stories in Luke-Acts: A Sociostylistic Reading.* Cambridge: Cambridge University Press, 2004.

Knowles, Murray, and Rosamund Moon. *Introducing Metaphor.* London: Routledge, 2006.

Koester, Craig R. *The Dwelling of God: The Tabernacle in the Old Testament, Intertestamental Jewish Literature, and the New Testament.* CBQ Monograph 22. Washington, DC: Catholic Biblical Association of America, 1989.

———. *Revelation and the End of All Things.* Grand Rapids: Eerdmans, 2001.

———. *Symbolism in the Fourth Gospel: Meaning, Mystery, Community.* Minneapolis: Fortress, 2003.

———. *The Word of Life: A Theology of John's Gospel.* Grand Rapids: Eerdmans, 2008.

Köstenberger, Andreas J., and Scott R. Swain. *Father, Son and Spirit: The Trinity and John's Gospel.* NSBT 24. Downers Grove, IL: InterVarsity, 2008.

Kraft, Charles H. *Christianity with Power.* Ann Arbour, MI: Servant, 1989.

———. *Confronting Powerless Christianity: Evangelicals and the Missing Dimension.* Grand Rapids: Chosen, Baker, 2002.

———. "Contemporary Trends in the Treatment of Spiritual Conflict." In *Deliver us from Evil: An Uneasy Frontier in Christian Mission,* edited by A. Scott Moreau et al., 177–202. Monravia, CA: World Vision International, 2002.

———. *Defeating Dark Angels.* Ann Arbor, MI: Servant, 1992.

Kraft, Marguerite G. *Understanding Spiritual Power: A Forgotten Dimension of Cross-Cultural Ministry.* Maryknoll, NY: Orbis, 1995.

Krotke, Wolf. *Sin and Nothingness in the Theology of Karl Barth.* 2nd ed. Translated by Philip G. Ziegler and Christina-Maria Bammel. Studies in Reformed Theology and History. Princeton: Princeton Theological Seminary. 2005

Kuhn, Thomas. *The Structure of Scientific Revolutions.* 1967. Reprint. Chicago: Chicago University Press, 1970.

Kunin, Seth D. *God's Place in the World: Sacred Space and Sacred Place in Judaism.* London: Cassen, 1998.

Kyle, Richard, "The Occult Roars Back." *Direction* 29 (2000) 91–97.

Ladd, George Eldon. *A Theology of the New Testament.* Rev ed. by Donald A. Hagner. 1974. Reprint. Grand Rapids: Eerdmans, 1993.

Lakoff, George, and Mark Johnson. *Metaphors We Live by.* 1980. Reprint with Afterword. Chicago: University of Chicago Press, 2003.

Lakoff, George. *Women, Fire and Dangerous Things. What Categories Reveal about the Mind.* Chicago: University of Chicago Press, 1987.

Lakoff, George, and Mark Turner. *More than Cool Reason. A Field Guide to Poetic Metaphor.* Chicago: University of Chicago Press, 1989.

Lane, Anthony N. S., editor. *The Unseen World.* Grand Rapids: Baker, 1996.

Lausanne Committee for World Evangelism. http://www.lausanne.org.issue-inter cession/spiritual-warfare-1993.html.

Levenson, Jon D. *Creation and the Persistence of Evil: The Jewish Drama of Divine Omnipotence.* San Francisco: Harper, 1988.

———. *Sinai and Zion: An Entry into the Jewish Bible.* Minneapolis, MN: Winston, 1985.

Levine, Baruch A. *In the Presence of the Lord: A Study of Cult and Some Cultic Themes in Ancient Israel.* SJLA 5, Leiden: Brill, 1974.

Lévi-Strauss, Claude. *From Honey to Ashes.* Vol. 2 of *Mythologies.* Translated by John and Doreen Wightman. 1966. Reprint. New York: Harper & Row, 1973.

———. *Myth and Meaning: Five Talks for Radio.* Toronto: University of Toronto Press, 1978.

———. *The Naked Man.* Vol. 4 of *Mythologies.* Translated by John and Doreen Wightman. New York: Harper & Row, 1971, 1981.

———. *The Origin of Table Manners.* Vol. 3 of *Mythologies.* Translated by John and Doreen Wightman. 1968. Reprint. New York: Harper & Row, 1978.

———. *The Raw and the Cooked.* Vol. 1 of *Mythologies.* Translated by John and Doreen Wightman. 1964. Reprint. New York: Harper & Row, 1969.

———. *Structural Anthropology.* Vol. 1. Translated by Claire Jacobson and Brooke Grundfest Schoepf. New York: Basic, 1963.

Lewis, C. S. *The Great Divorce.* San Francisco: HarperCollins, 1946.

———. *Mere Christianity.* San Francisco: Harper, 1952.

———. *The Screwtape Letters.* New York: Mentor, 1942.

Lewis, Edwin. *The Creator and the Adversary.* New York: Abingdon-Cokesbury, 1948.

Lichtenberger, Hermann. "The Down-Throw of the Dragon in Revelation 12 and the Down-Fall of God's Enemy." In *The Fall of the Angels,* edited by Christopher Auffarth and Loren Stuckenbruck, 119–47. Leiden: Brill, 2004.

Lincoln, Andrew T. *Ephesians.* Word Biblical Commentary. Dallas: Word, 1990.

Lines, Dennis. *Spirituality in Counseling and Psychotherapy.* London: Sage, 2006.

Lockett, Darian. *Purity and Worldview in the Epistle of James.* London: T. & T. Clark, 2008.

Lodahl, Michael E. *Shekinah Spirit: Divine Presence in Jewish and Christian Religion.* New York: Paulist, 1992.

Lohfink, Norbert. *Theology of the Pentateuch: Themes of the Priestly Narrative and Deuteronomy.* Translated by Linda M. Maloney. Minneapolis: Fortress, 1994.

Longman, Tremper III, and Daniel Reid. *God is a Warrior.* Grand Rapids: Zondervan, 1995.

Löning, Karl, and Erich Zenger. *To Begin with, God Created . . . : Biblical Theologies of Creation.* Translated by Omar Katz. Collegeville, MN: Liturgical, 2000.

Lowe, Chuck. *Territorial Spirits and World Evangelism?* Fearn, UK: Mentor, 1998.

Ma, Wonsuk. "The Presence of Evil and Exorcism in the Old Testament." In *Exorcism and Deliverance: Multidisciplinary Perspectives,* edited by William Kay and Robin A. Parry, 27–44. Milton Keynes, UK: Paternoster, 2011.

Maccoby, Hyam. *Ritual and Morality.* Cambridge: Cambridge University Press, 1999.

MacDonald, George, *The Princess and the Goblin.* Reprinted. London: Puffin, 1979.

Macky, Peter W. *The Centrality of Metaphors to Biblical Thought.* Lewiston, NY: Mellen, 1990.

MacNutt, Francis. *Deliverance from Evil Spirits.* Grand Rapids: Chosen, 1995.

———. *Healing.* Notre Dame, IN: Ava Maria, 1974.

Madigan, Kevin J., and Jon D. Levenson. *Resurrection: The Power of God for Christians and Jews.* New Haven: Yale University Press, 2008.

Malbon, Elizabeth Struthers. *Narrative Space and Mythic Meaning in Mark.* San Francisco: Harper & Row, 1986.

Mallone, George. *Arming for Spiritual Warfare.* Downers Grove, IL: InterVarsity, 1991.

Mallow, Vernon R. *The Demonic: A Selected Theological Study.* Lanham, MD: University Press of America, 1983.

Marcus, Joel. "Idolatry in the New Testament." *Interpretation* 60 (2006) 152–64.

———. *Mark 1–8: A New Translation with Introduction and Commentary.* AB. New York: Doubleday, 1999.

Marino, Adrian "Mircea Eliade's Hermeneutics." In *Imagination and Meaning: The Scholarly and Literary Worlds of Mircea Eliade,* edited by Norman J. Girardot and Mac Linscott Ricketts, 37–45. New York: Seabury, 1982.

Marshall, I. Howard. *Aspects of the Atonement.* Milton Keynes, UK: Paternoster, 2007.

———. *New Testament Theology.* Downers Grove, IL: InterVarsity, 2004.

Martin, Ralph T. *Ephesians, Colossians,* and *Philemon.* IBC, Atlanta: John Knox, 1991.

May, Gerald G. *Addiction and Grace.* San Francisco: HarperCollins, 1988.

———. *Will and Spirit: A Contemplative Psychology.* San Francisco: Harper Collins, 1982.

May, Gerhard. *Creation Ex Nihilo: The Doctrine of "Creation out of Nothing" in Early Christian Thought.* Translated by A. S. Worrall. Edinburgh: T. & T. Clark, 1994.

Mays, James L. "'Maker of Heaven and Earth': Creation in the Psalms." In *God who Creates: Essays in Honor of W. Sibley Towner,* edited by William P. Brown and S. Dean McBride, 75–86. Grand Rapids: Eerdmans, 2000.

McBride, Dean. "Divine Protocol: Genesis 1:1—2:3 as Prologue to the Pentateuch." In *God who Creates: Essays in Honor of W. Sibley Towner,* edited by William P. Brown and S. Dean McBride, 3–41. Grand Rapids: Eerdmans, 2000.

McCarthy, Dennis J. "Creation Motifs in Ancient Hebrew Poetry." *CBQ* 29 (1967) 87–100.

McConville, Gordon, "Jerusalem in the Old Testament." In *Jerusalem Past and Present in the Purposes of God.* 2nd ed., edited by Peter W. L. Walker, 21–51. Grand Rapids: Baker, 1994.

McFague, Sallie. *Metaphorical Theology: Models of God in Religious Language.* Philadelphia: Fortress, 1982.

McGrath, Alister. *The Science of God.* Grand Rapids: Eerdmans, 2004.

———. *Scientific Theology: Vol. 1, Nature.* Grand Rapids: Eerdmans, 2001.

McKay, J. W. "Helel and the Dawn-Goddess: a Re-Examination of the Myth in Isaiah 14:12–15." *Vestus Testamentum* 20 (1970) 451–64.

McMinn, Mark R. *Psychology, Theology and Spirituality.* Wheaton, IL: Tyndale, 1996.

McMinn, Mark R., and Clark D. Campbell. *Integrative Psychotherapy.* Downers Grove, IL: InterVarsity, 2007.

Middleton, J. Richard. "Created in the Image of a Violent God?" *Interpretation* 58 (2004) 341–55.

———. *The Liberating Image: The Imago Dei in Genesis 1.* Grand Rapids: Brazos, 2005.

Milgrom, Jacob. "Concerning Jeremiah's Repudiation of Sacrifice." *ZAW* 89 (1977) 274–75.

———. *Cult and Conscience: The Asham and the Priestly Doctrine of Repentance.* Leiden: Brill, 1976.

———. "Israel's Sanctuary: The Priestly Picture of Dorian Gray." *RB* 83 (1976) 390–99. Reprinted in Milgrom, *Studies in Cultic Theology*, 75–84.

———. *Leviticus 1–16: A New Translation with Introduction and Commentary.* AB 3. New York: Doubleday, 1991.

———. *Leviticus: A Book of Ritual and Ethics.* Continental Commentary. Minneapolis: Fortress, 2004.

———. *Studies in Cultic Theology and Terminology.* SJLA 36. Leiden: Brill, 1983.

Miller, Patrick D. Jr. *The Divine Warrior in Early Israel.* Cambridge: Harvard University Press, 1973.

———. "The Poetry of Creation: Psalm 104." In *God who Creates: Essays in Honor of W. Sibley Towner,* edited by William P. Brown and S. Dean McBride, 87–103. Grand Rapids: Eerdmans, 2000.

Moltmann, Jürgen. *The Crucified God: The Cross of Christ as the Foundation and Criticism of Christian Theology.* Translated by R. A. Wilson and John Bowden. London: SCM, 1974.

———. *God in Creation.* 2nd ed. Translated by Margaret Kohl. Minneapolis: Fortress, 1993.

———. *Science and Wisdom.* 2nd ed. Translated by Margaret Kohl. Minneapolis: Fortress, 2003.

———. *The Source of Life: The Holy Spirit and the Theology of Life.* Translated by Margaret Kohl. Minneapolis: Fortress, 1997.

———. *The Spirit of Life: A Universal Affirmation.* Translated by Margaret Kohl. Minneapolis: Fortress, 1992.

Montgomery, John Warwick, *Demon Possession: A Medical, Historical, Anthropological and Theological Symposium.* Minneapolis: Bethany Fellowship, 1976.

Moreau, A. Scott. *The Essentials of Spiritual Warfare.* Wheaton, IL: Shaw, 1997.

———. *Gaining Perspective on Territorial Spirits.* In Lausanne Movement Documents online, LCWEhttp://www.lausanne.org/nairobi-2000/documents.html

———. "A Survey of North American Spiritual Warfare Thinking." In *Deliver Us from Evil: An Uneasy Frontier in Christian Mission,* edited by A. Scott Moreau et al., 117–26. Monravia, CA: World Vision International, 2002.

Moreau, A. Scott, et al., editors. *Deliver Us from Evil: An Uneasy Frontier in Christian Mission.* Monravia, CA: World Vision International, 2002.

Mosko, Mark S. "Introduction: A (Re)turn to Chaos." In *On the Order of Chaos: Social Anthropology and the Science of Chaos,* edited by Mark S. Mosko and Frederick H. Damon, 1–46. New York, Oxford: Berghahn, 2005.

Motyer, J. Alec. *The Prophecy of Isaiah: An Introduction and Commentary.* Leicester, UK: InterVarsity, 1993

Muck, Terry, and Frances S. Adeney. *Christianity Encountering World Religions: The Practice of Mission in the Twenty-First Century.* Grand Rapids: Baker Academic, 2009.

Mullen, E. Theodore Jr. *The Divine Council in Canaanite and Early Hebrew Literature.* Harvard Semitic Monographs, Chico, CA: Scholars, 1980.

Murphy, Ed. *The Handbook for Spiritual Warfare.* Rev. ed. Nashville: Thomas Nelson, 2003.

Naugle, David K. *Worldview: History of a Concept.* Grand Rapids: Eerdmans, 2002.

Neusner, Jacob. *The Idea of Purity in Ancient Judaism.* Leiden: Brill, 1973.

Neville, Robert Cummings. *On the Scope of Truth and Theology: Theology as Symbolic Engagement.* London: T. & T. Clark, 2006.

Newbigin, Lesslie. *The Light Has Come: An Exposition of the Fourth Gospel.* Grand Rapids: Eerdmans, 1982.

Nickelsburg, George W. E. *Jewish Literature between the Bible and the Mishnah.* Minneapolis: Fortress, 2005.

Nigosian, Solomon. *Magic and Divination in the Old Testament.* Brighton, UK: Sussex Academic, 2008.

Noble, Thomas A. "The Spirit World: A Theological Approach." In *The Unseen World,* edited by Anthony N. S. Lane, 185–223. Grand Rapids: Baker, 1996.

Noll, Stephen F. *Angels of Light, Powers of Darkness.* Downers Grove, IL: InterVarsity, 1998.

Noort, Ed. "The Creation of Light in Genesis 1:1–5: Remarks on the Function of Light and Darkness in the Opening Verses of the Hebrew Bible." In *Creation of Heaven and Earth: Re-Interpretation of Genesis 1 in the Context of Judaism, Ancient Philosophy, Christianity and Modern Physics,* edited by George H. Van Kooten, 3–20. Leiden: Brill, 2005.

Noppen, J. P. van. *Metaphor: A Bibliography of Post-1970 Publications.* Philadelphia: Benjamin, 1985.

Noppen, J. P. van, and Edith Holls. *Metaphor II: A Classified Bibliography of Publications 1985–1990.* Philadelphia: Benjamin, 1990.

North. J. A "Religions in the Roman Empire." In *A Handbook of Ancient Religions,* edited by John R. Hinnells, 318–63. Cambridge: Cambridge University Press, 2007.

Oberdorfer, Bernd. "The Holy Spirit—A Person? Reflection on the Spirit's Trinitarian Identity." In *The Work of the Spirit: Pneumatology and Pentecostalism,* edited by Michael Welker, 27–46. Grand Rapids: Eerdmans, 2006.

O'Grady, Joan. *The Prince of Darkness.* Dorset, UK: Element, 1989.

Olyan, Saul M. *Rites and Rank.* Princeton: Princeton University Press, 2000.

Otis, George Jr. *The Twilight Labyrinth: Why Does Spiritual Darkness Linger Where it Does?* Grand Rapids: Chosen, 1997.

Ott, Craig, et al. *Encountering Theology of Mission: Biblical Foundations, Historical Developments and Contemporary Issues.* Grand Rapids: Baker, 2010.

Otto, Rudolph. *The Idea of the Holy: An Inquiry into the Non-rational Factor in the Idea of the Divine and its Relation to the Rational.* 3rd ed. Translated by John W. Harvey. 1917. Reprint. London: Oxford University Press, 1925.

Packer, J. I. *Keep in Step with the Spirit.* Leicester, UK: InterVarsity, 1984.

Page, Hugh Rowland, Jr. *The Myth of Cosmic Rebellion: A Study of its Reflexes in Ugaritic and Biblical Literature.* Vestus Testamentum Sup. 65. Leiden: Brill, 1996.

Page, Sydney H. T. *Powers of Evil: A Biblical Study of Satan and Demons.* Grand Rapids: Baker, 1995.

Pagels, Elaine. *The Origin of Satan.* New York: Random House, 1995.

Pannenberg, Wolfhart. *Systematic Theology. Vol. 1, 2.* Translated by Geoffrey W. Bromley. Grand Rapids: Eerdmans, 1994.

Parry, Robin A. "Introduction." In *Exorcism and Deliverance: Multidisciplinary Perspectives,* edited by William Kay and Robin A. Parry, 1–25. Milton Keynes, UK: Paternoster, 2011.

Parsons, Martin, "Binding the Strong Man: The Flaw of the Excluded Middle." In *Angels and Demons: Perspectives and Practice in Diverse Religious Traditions,* edited by Peter G. and Beverly Smith Riddell, 106–25. Nottingham, UK: Apollos, 2007.

Payne, Leanne. *The Healing Presence: Curing the Soul through Union with Christ.* 1989. *Reprint.* Grand Rapids: Baker, 1995.

———. *Restoring the Christian Soul through Healing Prayer.* Wheaton, IL: Crossway Books, 1991.

Peck, M. Scott. *Glimpses of the Devil.* New York: Free, 2005.

———. *People of the Lie.* New York: Simon and Schuster, 1983.

Penn-Lewis, Jessie, with Evan Roberts. *War on the Saints.* Fort Washington, PA: The Christian Literature Crusade, 1973.

Peretti, Frank. *This Present Darkness.* Westchester, IL: Crossway, 1986.

Pfleiderer, Otto. *Primitive Christianity.* New York: Putnam's Sons, 1906.

Pinnock, Clark H., et al. *The Openness of God: A Biblical Challenge to the Traditional Understanding of God.* Downers Grove, IL: InterVarsity, 1994.

Pinnock, Clark H. *Flame of Love: A Theology of the Holy Spirit.* Downers Grove, IL: InterVarsity, 1996.

Polkinghorne, John. *Exploring Reality.* New Haven: Yale University, 2005.

———. "Kenotic Creation and Divine Action." In *The Work of Love: Creation as Kenosis,* edited by John Polkinghorne, 90–106. Grand Rapids: Eerdmans, 2001.

———. *Quarks, Chaos and Christianity.* 2nd ed. New York: Crossroad, 2005.

———. *Science and Providence: God's Interaction with the World.* 2nd ed. Philadelphia: Templeton Foundation, 2005.

Powlison, David. *Power Encounters: Reclaiming Spiritual Warfare.* 1995. Reprint. Grand Rapids: Baker, 2000.

Priest, Robert J. et al. "Missiological Syncretism: The New Animistic Paradigm." In *Spiritual Power and Missions: Raising the Issues,* edited by Edward Rommen, 9–77. Pasadena, CA: William Carey Library, 1995.

Prinsloo, W. S. "Isaiah 14:12–15—Humiliation, Hubris, Humiliation." *ZAW* 93 (1981) 435–36.

Rad, Gerhard von. *Genesis: A Commentary.* London: SCM, 1963.

Radin, Dean. *The Conscious Universe: The Scientific Truth of Psychic Phenomena.* New York: HarperOne, 1997.

Reed, Anette Yoshiko. *Fallen Angels and the History of Judaism and Christianity: The Reception of the Enochic Literature.* Cambridge: Cambridge University Press, 2005.

Richards, I. A. *The Philosophy of Rhetoric.* Oxford: Oxford University Press, 1936.

Ricoeur, Paul. *Figuring the Sacred.* Translated by David Pellauer, Edited by Mark I. Wallace. Fortress, 1995.

———. *Interpretation Theory: Discourse and the Surplus of Meaning.* Fort Worth, TX: Texas Christian University Press, 1976.

———. *The Rule of Metaphor.* Translated by Robert Czerny. Toronto: University of Toronto Press, 1977.

———. *The Symbolism of Evil.* Translated by Emerson Buchanan. Boston: Beacon, 1967.

Riddell, Peter G., and Beverly Smith. *Angels and Demons: Perspectives and Practice in Diverse Religious Traditions.* Nottingham, UK: Apollos, 2007.

Robertson Smith, William. *Lectures on the Religions of the Semites: The Fundamental Institutions.* 3rd ed. 1889. Reprint. KTAV, 1961.

Rodin, R. Scott. *Evil and Theodicy in the Theology of Karl Barth.* New York: Lang, 1997.

Rogerson, John. "What is Holiness?" In *Holiness: Past and Present,* edited by Stephen C. Barton, 3–21. London: T. & T. Clark, 2003.

Routledge, Robin. *Old Testament Theology: A Thematic Approach.* Nottingham, UK: InterVarsity, 2008.

Russell, Jeffrey Burton. *The Devil: Perceptions of Evil from Antiquity to Primitive Christianity.* Ithaca, NY: Cornell University Press, 1977.

———. *History of Heaven.* Princeton: Princeton University Press, 1997.

———. *Lucifer: The Devil in the Middle Ages.* Ithaca, NY: Cornell University Press, 1984.

———. *Mephistopheles: The Devil in the Modern World.* Ithaca, NY: Cornell University Press, 1986.

———. *The Prince of Darkness.* Ithaca, NY: Cornell University Press, 1988.

———. *Satan: The Early Christian Tradition.* Ithaca, NY: Cornell University Press, 1981.

Russell, Robert John. *Cosmology: From Alpha to Omega.* Minneapolis: Fortress, 2008.

———. "Ian Barbour's Methodological Breakthrough: Creating the 'Bridge' between Science and Theology." In *Fifty Years in Science and Religion: Ian G. Barbour and his Legacy,* edited by Robert John Russell, 45–59. Burlington, VT: Ashgate, 2004.

Ryken, Leland, et al., editors. *Dictionary of Biblical Imagery.* Downers Grove, IL: InterVarsity, 1998.

Sanders, John. *Atonement and Violence: A Theological Conversation.* Nashville: Abingdon, 2006.

Sandford, John and Paula. *Healing the Wounded Spirit.* Tulsa, OK: Victory House, 1985.

Sandford, John and Mark. *Deliverance and Inner Healing.* Grand Rapids: Chosen, 1992.

Saussure, Ferdinand de. *Course in General Linguistics.* Translated by Wade Baskin. New York: McGraw Hill, 1966.

Scanlan, Michael, and Randall J. Cirner. *Deliverance from Evil Spirits.* Ann Arbor, MI: Servant, 1980.

Scherer, James A. "Mission Theology." In *Toward the Twenty-first Century in Christian Mission. Essays in Honor of Gerald H. Anderson,* edited by James M. Phillips and Robert T. Coote, 193–202. Grand Rapids: Eerdmans, 1993.

Schlier, Heinrich. *Principalities and Powers in the New Testament.* Freiburg: Herder, 1961.

Schwarz, Hans. *Evil: A Historical and Theological Perspective*. Minneapolis: Fortress, 1995.

Scobie, Charles H. H. "History of Biblical Theology." In *New Dictionary of Biblical Theology*, edited by T. D. Alexander and B. S. Rosner, 11–20. Leicester, UK: InterVarsity, 2000.

Scotland, Nigel. "The Charismatic Devil." In *Angels and Demons: Perspectives and Practice in Diverse Religious Traditions*, edited by Peter G. and Beverly Smith Riddell, 84–105. Nottingham, UK: Apollos, 2007.

Seamands, David. *Redeeming the Past*. 1981. Reprint. Colorado Springs: Cook, 2002.

Segal, Robert A., editor. *The Myth and Ritual Theory: An Anthology*. Oxford: Blackwell, 1998.

———. *Myth: A Very Short Introduction*. Oxford: Oxford University Press, 2004.

Sheriff, John K. *The Fate of Meaning: Charles Peirce, Structuralism, and Literature*. Princeton: Princeton University Press, 1989.

Sherrer, Quin, and Ruthanne Galrock. *A Woman's Guide to Spiritual Warfare: A Woman's Guide for Battle*. Ann Arbor, MI: Servant, 1991

Shillington, V. George. "Atonement Texture in 1 Corinthians 5:5." *JSNT* 71 (1998) 29–50.

Shuster, Marguerite. *Power, Pathology, Paradox: The Dynamics of Evil and Good*. Grand Rapids: Zondervan, 1987.

Simkins, Ronald. *Creator and Creation*. Peabody, MA: Hendrickson, 1994.

Singer, Jerome L. *Imagery in Psychotherapy*. Washington, DC: American Psychological Association, 2006.

Skaggs, Rebecca. *1 Peter, 2 Peter, Jude*. PC. Cleveland, OH: Pilgrim, 2004.

Skaggs, Rebecca, and Priscilla C. Benham. *Revelation*. PC. Blandford, UK: Deo, 2009.

Sklar, Jay. "Sin and Impurity: Atoned or Purified? Yes!" In *Perspectives on Purity and Purification in the Bible*, edited by Baruch J. Schwartz et al., 18–31. London: T. & T. Clark, 2008.

Sluhovsky, Moshe. *Believe Not Every Spirit: Possession, Mysticism and Discernment in Early Modern Catholicism*. Chicago: University of Chicago Press, 2007.

Smith, David. *With Willful Intent: A Theology of Sin*. Wheaton, IL: Bridgepoint, 1994.

Smith, Leonard. *Chaos: A Very Short Introduction*. Oxford: Oxford University Press, 2007.

Smith, Mark S. *The Early History of God: Yahweh and the Other Deities in Ancient Israel*. 2nd ed. Grand Rapids: Eerdmans, 2002.

———. "Like Deities, Like Temples (Like People)." In *Temple and Worship in Biblical Israel: Proceedings of the Oxford Old Testament Seminar*, edited by John Day, 3–27. London: T. & T. Clark, 2005.

———. *The Priestly Vision of Genesis 1*. Minneapolis: Fortress, 2010.

———. *The Ugaritic Baal Cycle. Vol. I: Introduction with Text, Translation and Commentary of KTU 1.1–1.2*. Leiden: Brill, 1994.

Sorensen, Eric. *Possession and Exorcism in the New Testament and Early Christianity*. Tübingen: Mohr Siebeck, 2002.

Soskice, Janet Martin. *Metaphor and Religious Language*. Oxford: Oxford University Press, 1985.

Stanford, Peter. *The Devil: A Biography*. New York: Holt, 1996.

Stewart, Ian. *Does God Play Dice? The New Mathematics of Chaos*. 2nd ed. New York: Penguin, 1997.

Stienstra, Nelly. *YHWH is the Husband of His People: Analysis of a Biblical Metaphor with Special Reference to Translation.* Kampen, The Netherlands: Kok Pharos, 1993.

Stiver, Dan R. *The Philosophy of Religious Language.* Cambridge, MA: Blackwell, 1996.

Sweeney, James. "Jesus, Paul and the Temple: Some Patterns of Continuity." *JETS* 46 (2003) 605–31.

Telford, W. R. *The Theology of the Gospel of Mark.* NT Theology. Cambridge: Cambridge University Press, 1999.

Terrien, Samuel L. *The Elusive Presence: Toward a New Biblical Theology.* San Francisco: Harper & Row, 1978.

Theron, Jacques. "A Critical Overview of the Church's Ministry of Deliverance from Evil Spirits." *Pneuma* 18 (1996) 79–92.

Thiselton, Anthony C. *New Horizons in Hermeneutics.* London: HarperCollins, 1992.

———. *The Two Horizons.* Grand Rapids: Eerdmans, 1980.

Thomas, John Christopher. *The Devil, Disease and Deliverance: Origins of Illness in New Testament Thought.* Journal of Pentecostal Theology Sup. Sheffield, UK: Sheffield Academic Press, 1998, 2005.

———. *1 John, 2 John, 3 John.* PC. Cleveland, OH: Pilgrim, 2004.

Tippet, Alan R. *Introduction to Missiology.* Pasadena, CA: William Carey Library, 1987.

Tolkien, J. R. R. *The Lord of the Rings.* London: Allen & Unwin, 1954–55.

Toolan, David. *At Home in the Cosmos.* New York: Orbis, 2001.

Torrance, Thomas F. *The Christian Frame of Mind.* Edinburgh: Handsel, 1985.

———. *Divine and Contingent Order.* Oxford: Oxford University Press, 1981.

———. *Theological Science.* London: Oxford University Press, 1969.

Tshishiku, Tshibangu. "Eschatology and Cosmology." In *Cosmology and Theology,* edited by David Tracy and Nicholas Lash, 27–34. Edinburgh: T. & T. Clark, 1983.

Tsumara, David. *Creation and Destruction.* Winona Lake, IN: Eisenbrauns, 2005.

Tupper, E. Frank. *A Scandalous Providence: The Jesus Story of the Compassion of God.* Macon, GA: Mercer University Press, 1995.

Turner, Victor. *The Ritual Process: Structure and Anti-structure.* Ithaca, NY: Cornell University Press, 1969.

Twelftree, Graham H. *Christ Triumphant: Exorcism Then and Now.* London: Hodder & Stroughton, 1985.

———. *In the Name of Jesus: Exorcism among Early Christians.* Grand Rapids: Baker, 2007.

———. *Jesus the Exorcist: A Contribution to the Study of the Historical Jesus.* Tübingen: Mohr Siebeck, 1993.

———. *Jesus the Miracle Worker.* Downers Grove, IL: InterVarsity, 1999.

Unger, Merrill F. *Biblical Demonology.* Wheaton, IL: Van Kampen, 1952.

VanGemeren, Willem. *Interpreting the Prophetic Word.* Grand Rapids: Zondervan, 1990.

———. "The Sons of God in Genesis 6:1–4." *Westminster Theological Journal* 43 (1981) 320–48.

Van Hecke, P., editor. *Metaphor in the Hebrew Bible.* Leuven: Leuven University Press, 2005.

Vanhoozer, Kevin. *The Drama of Doctrine.* Louisville, KY: Westminster John Knox, 2005.

Bibliography

Van Wolde, Ellen. *Stories of the Beginning: Genesis 1-11 and other Creation Stories.* Translated by John Bowden, London: SCM, 1996.

———. "Why the Verb *bārā* Does Not Mean 'To Create' in Genesis 1:1—2:4a." *JSOT* 34 (2009) 3–23.

Wa Gatumu, Kabiro. "Deliverance and Exorcism in Theological Perspective 2: New Testament Evidence for a Theology of Christ's Supremacy." In *Exorcism and Deliverance: Multidisciplinary Perspectives,* edited by William Kay and Robin A. Parry, 222–42. Milton Keynes, UK: Paternoster, 2011.

———. *The Pauline Concept of Supernatural Powers.* Milton Keynes, UK: Paternoster, 2008.

Wagner, C. Peter. *Confronting the Powers: How the New Testament Church Experienced the Power of Strategic-Level Spiritual Warfare.* Ventura, CA: Regal, 1996.

———. *Engaging the Enemy: How to Fight and Defeat Territorial Spirits.* Ventura, CA: Regal, 1991.

———. *Warfare Prayer.* Ventura, CA: Regal, 1992.

Wakeman, Mary K. *God's Battle with the Monster.* Leiden: Brill, 1973.

Walker, Andrew G. "The Devil You Think You Know: Demonology and the Charismatic Movement." In *Charismatic Renewal: The Search for a Theology,* edited by Tom Smail et al., 86–105. London: SPCK, 1993.

———. *Enemy Territory: The Struggles for the Modern World.* London: Hodder & Stoughton, 1987.

Walsh, Brian J., and J. Richard Middleton. *The Transforming Vision.* Downers Grove, IL: InterVarsity, 1984.

Waltke, Bruce K. "The Creation Account in Genesis 1:1–3. Part II: The Restitution Theory." *Bibliotheca Sacra* 132 (1975) 136–42.

———. "The Creation Account in Genesis 1:1–3. Part III: The Initial Chaos Theory and the Precreation Chaos Theory." *Bibliotheca Sacra* 132 (1975) 216–28.

———. "The Creation Account in Genesis 1:1–3. Part IV: The Theology of Genesis I." *Bibliotheca Sacra* 132 (1975) 327–42.

———. *An Old Testament Theology: an Exegetical, Canonical and Thematic Approach.* Grand Rapids: Zondervan, 2007.

Walton, John H. *Ancient Near Eastern Thought and the Old Testament: Introducing the Conceptual World of the Hebrew Bible.* Grand Rapids: Baker Academic, 2006.

———. "Creation in Genesis 1:1—2:3 and the Ancient Near East: Order out of Disorder after *Chaoskampf.*" *Calvin Theological Journal* 43 (2008) 48–63.

Wardlaw, Terence R. *Conceptualizing Words for God Within the Pentateuch: A Cognitive Semantic Investigation in Literary Context.* London: T. & T. Clark, 2008.

Warner, Timothy. *Spiritual Warfare.* Wheaton, IL: Crossway, 1991.

Watson, Francis. *Text and Truth: Redefining Biblical Theology.* Grand Rapids: Eerdmans, 1997.

Webber, Robert. *The Church in the World: Opposition, Tension, or Transformation.* Grand Rapids: Zondervan, 1986.

Weiss, Johannes. *Jesus' Proclamation of the Kingdom of God.* [1892]. Translated, edited, and introduced by Richard Hyde Hiers and David Larrimore Holland. Philadelphia: Fortress Press, 1971.

Welker, Michael. *Creation and Reality.* Minneapolis: Fortress, 1999.

———. *God the Spirit.* Minneapolis: Fortress, 1994.

———. "The Holy Spirit." In *The Oxford Handbook of Systematic Theology*, edited by John Webster et al., 236–48. Oxford: Oxford University Press, 2007.

Wellhausen, Julius. *Prolegomena to the History of Israel*. [1885]. Atlanta: Scholars, 1994.

Wenell, Karen J. *Jesus and Land: Sacred and Social Space in Second Temple Judaism*. London: T. & T. Clark, 2007.

Wenham, David. *The Parables of Jesus: Pictures of Revolution*. London: Hodder & Stoughton, 1989.

Werrett, Ian. *Ritual Purity and the Dead Sea Scrolls*. Leiden: Brill, 2007.

Westermann, Claus. *Creation*. Translated by John J. Scullion. Minneapolis: Fortress, 1974.

Wiebe, Phillip H. "Deliverance and Exorcism in Philosophical Perspective." In *Exorcism and Deliverance: Multidisciplinary Perspectives*, edited by William Kay and Robin A. Parry, 156–80. Milton Keynes, UK: Paternoster, 2011.

Wiles, Maurice. "Myth in Theology." In *The Myth of God Incarnate*, edited by John Hick, 148–66. Philadelphia: Westminster, 1977.

Williams, Daniel Day. *The Demonic and the Divine*. Edited by Stacy A. Evans. Minneapolis: Fortress, 1990.

Wimber, John with Kevin Springer. *Power Evangelism*. San Francisco: Harper & Row, 1986.

Wink, Walter. *Engaging the Powers: Discernment and Resistance in a World of Domination*. Minneapolis: Fortress, 1992.

———. *Naming the Powers: The Language of Power in the New Testament*. Philadelphia: Fortress, 1984.

———. "The New Worldview: Spirit at the Core of Everything." In *Transforming the Powers: Peace, Justice and the Domination System*, edited by Ray Gingerich and Ted Grimsrud, 17–28. Minneapolis: Fortress, 2006.

———. *Unmasking the Powers: The Invisible Forces that Determine Human Existence*. Philadelphia: Fortress, 1986.

Wise, Michael O., et al. *The Dead Sea Scrolls: A New Translation*. 1996. Reprint. San Francisco: HarperSanFrancisco, 2005.

Witherington, Ben III, and Laura M. Ice. *The Shadow of the Almighty: Father, Son and Spirit in Biblical Perspective*. Grand Rapids: Eerdmans, 2002.

Womack, Mari. *Symbols and Meaning: A Concise Introduction*. New York: Altamira, 2005.

Woodberry, J. Dudley. "Introduction." In *Paradigm Shifts in Christian Witness: Insights from Anthropology, Communication and Spiritual Power: Essays in Honor of Charles Kraft*, edited by Van Engen et al., 87–89. Maryknoll, NY: Orbis, 2008.

Worthing, Mark William. *God, Creation and Contemporary Physics*. Minneapolis: Fortress, 1994.

Wright, Archie T. *The Origin of Evil Spirits*. Tübingen: Mohr Siebeck, 2005.

Wright, David P. *The Disposal of Impurity: Elimination Rites in the Bible and in Hittite and Mesopotamian Literature*. Atlanta: Scholars, 1987.

———. "The Spectrum of Priestly Impurity." In *Priesthood and Cult in Ancient Israel*, edited by Gary A. Anderson and Saul M. Olyan, 150–82. Sheffield, UK: Sheffield Academic Press, 1991.

Wright, N. T. *Evil and the Justice of God*. Downers Grove, IL: InterVarsity, 2006.

———. "Jerusalem in the New Testament." In *Jerusalem Past and Present in the Purposes of God*. 2nd ed., edited by Peter W. L. Walker, 53–77. Grand Rapids: Baker, 1994.

Bibliography

————. *Jesus and the Victory of God*. London: SPCK, 1996.

————. *The New Testament and the People of God*. London: SPCK, 1992.

Wright, Nigel G. "Charismatic Interpretations of the Demonic." In *The Unseen World*, edited by Anthony N. S. Lane, 149–63. Grand Rapids: Baker, 1996.

————. "Deliverance and Exorcism in Theological Perspective 1: Is There Any Substance to Evil?" In *Exorcism and Deliverance: Multidisciplinary Perspectives*, edited by William Kay and Robin A. Parry, 203–21. Milton Keynes, UK: Paternoster, 2011.

————. *A Theology of the Dark Side: Putting the Power of Evil in its Place*. Downers Grove, IL: InterVarsity, 2003.

Wyatt, Nick. *The Mythic Mind: Essays on Cosmology and Religion in Ugaritic and Old Testament Literature*. London: Equinox, 2005.

————. "Religion in Ancient Ugarit." In *A Handbook of Ancient Religions*, edited by John R. Hinnells, 105–60. Cambridge: Cambridge University Press, 2007.

Yoder Neufeld, Thomas R. *"Put on the Armour of God": The Divine Warrior from Isaiah to Ephesians*. JSNTSup. 140. Sheffield, UK: Sheffield Academic Press, 1997.

Yong, Amos. *Beyond the Impasse: Toward a Pneumatological Theology of Religions*. Grand Rapids: Baker Academic, 2003.

————. *Discerning the Spirit(s)*. Sheffield, UK: Sheffield Academic, 2000.

————. *The Spirit of Creation: Modern Science and Divine Action in the Pentecostal-Charismatic Imagination*. Grand Rapids: Eerdmans, 2011.

————. "Spiritual Discernment: A Biblical-Theological Reconsideration." In *The Spirit and Spirituality: Essays in Honor of Russell P. Spittler*, edited by Wonsuk Ma and Robert P. Menzies, 83–107. London: T. & T. Clark, 2004.

Yung, Hwa. "A Systematic Theology that Recognises the Demonic." In *Deliver Us from Evil: An Uneasy Frontier in Christian Mission*, edited by A. Scott Moreau et al., 3–282. Monravia, CA: World Vision International, 2002.

Author Index

311

Subject Index

Made in the USA
Columbia, SC
11 January 2020